W9-ANM-348

LIBRARY OF
DAS

Planning and Developing Innovative Community Colleges

N. DEAN EVANS

President, Burlington County College

ROSS L. NEAGLEY

Professor, Department of Educational Administration
College of Education, Temple University

Prentice-Hall, Inc., Englewood Cliffs, New Jersey

Library of Congress Cataloging in Publication Data

Evans, Norman Dean.
   Planning and developing innovative community colleges.

   Includes bibliographies.
     1. Municipal junior colleges—Planning—United States.
2. Educational innovations. I. Neagley, Ross Linn,
joint author. II. Title.
LB2328.E9   378.1'07   72-5735
ISBN 0-13-679456-4

© **1973 by Prentice-Hall, Inc., Englewood Cliffs, New Jersey**

All rights reserved. No part of this book
may be reproduced, by mimeograph or any other means,
without permission in writing from the publisher.

Printed in the United States of America

10 9 8 7 6 5 4 3 2 1

Prentice-Hall International, Inc., *London*
Prentice-Hall of Australia Pty. Ltd., *Sydney*
Prentice-Hall of Canada, Ltd., *Toronto*
Prentice-Hall of India Private Limited, *New Delhi*
Prentice-Hall of Japan, Inc., *Tokyo*

*To our colleagues in education
from whom we have learned much.*

Contents

v

Appendixes   267

Index   365

Preface

Hundreds of new two-year community colleges, most of them public institutions, will be planned and built in the United States during the next decade. Many others will open in countries around the world, extending educational opportunity to millions of students. The leaders of established community colleges are seeking ways to keep abreast of the latest educational frontiers. In a fast-changing world we are building and expanding colleges to provide excellence in learning experiences well into the twenty-first century. As the most dynamic and exciting institutions in higher education today, community colleges can be the leaders in creative, flexible, individualized approaches to the learning process.

It is the major purpose of this handbook, therefore, to present a vigorous, comprehensive, and daring approach to the planning, design, and development of modern community colleges—institutions that will offer the best in student learning opportunities and instructional strategies, and that will pioneer in human development as a major goal.

In general, college administrators, trustees, and faculty members have barely begun to use the significant research evidence on instructional methodology and the learning process that points clearly to more creative and varied educational and architectural solutions. It is increasingly impossible to design a "traditional" community college that will meet the societal and educational demands of the future.

What Is a Community College? The fundamental concept of the community college, as it has evolved during the twentieth century in America, is the extension of opportunities for higher education to all citizens who can profit from the experience. This usually means an "open door" admissions policy for all high school graduates and older adults, and a comprehensive educational program to meet the variety of learning needs presented by this population.

Although each community college defines its own philosophy, goals, and institutional objectives based on its perceived mission in the local community, there are certain common characteristics of most community colleges. The range of educational offerings will usually include developmental or remedial courses below collegiate grade; one- and two-year programs in technical and semi-professional fields leading to careers after graduation; and transfer programs that qualify the graduate to enter the third year of a four-year college or university. Most two-year curricula lead to an associate degree. In addition, a wide variety of courses, seminars, and short programs, both credit and noncredit, are generally offered for the part-time student during day or evening hours. The word "community" implies services to the greater community beyond the educational offerings, and the public two-year college often becomes one of the cultural and intellectual centers of the area it serves.

To all of its students the modern community college offers a variety of services, including counseling, placement opportunities, student activities, cultural programming, and participation in the governance of the institution. This, then, is the community college—flexibly designed and programmed to meet the higher educational needs of its community.

This handbook should be useful to the following persons: college trustees, members of citizens' higher education committees, administrators and planners of new and developing community colleges, and students of college administration and instructional supervision.

The authors express their appreciation to Mrs. Joan Phillips for typing the manuscript.

N. Dean Evans
Ross L. Neagley

1

The
State and the Community
College

State Planning and Regulation

Community college planners must be familiar with the various laws, rules, and regulations that govern the planning of a community college in their states. They, likewise, should be knowledgeable about their state's master plan for higher education if one exists. Students of community college administration also need to have an understanding of the great variation that exists among the different states in respect to these laws, regulations, and master plans.

The purpose of this chapter, then, is to impress upon the local community college planner the fact that he must be state oriented. He must be constantly aware that understanding the overall state plans and regulations and laws enabling establishment of community colleges is the first step in the planning process. Local boards of trustees or councils for higher education (see Chapter 2) must read and study all available material on the community college movement in their states. It would be wise for them to meet with state officials and to obtain from them as much information as possible concerning state plans and procedures.

A second purpose is to acquaint community college planners and students of the administration of higher education with background material that will enable them to understand and appreciate the role played by the states in the community college movement. They also will gain an understanding of procedures that have been utilized in the establishment of community colleges.

State Patterns of Community College
Development and Planning

The procedures utilized in the establishment of community colleges in the fifty states have been truly illustrative of the diversity and originality so characteristic of our nation. However, although no two states have followed identical procedures in establishing the various types of two-year institutions of higher learning, it has been possible to examine the sequential steps followed in the different states. A general description of the procedures states have followed in establishing community colleges will be given. However, no attempt will be made here to identify individual states. Other publications[1] have made a state-by-state analysis of these procedures; they have been used as sources for this resumé.

State Patterns of Community College Development

In general there are three categories of public two-year colleges found in the United States, namely, (1) local community colleges, (2) state two-year colleges, and (3) branch campuses and extension centers. Technical institutes sometimes are considered as a fourth category.

Initiation of movement. In the first category—local community colleges—the responsibility for initiation usually rests with the proposed local districts, which may vary in size from several square miles to a number of counties. The petitioning agencies include groups of qualified voters, county committees on school district organization, governing boards of high school districts, local school boards, state boards of junior or community colleges, boards of free-holders, trustees of existing institutions, citizens' committees, state councils on higher education, and community college advisory committees. In a number of states a referendum must be held in order to make the petition effective.

In the second category—state two-year colleges—initiation takes place as a result of special legislation, petitioning by city, county, county school systems, independent school districts, and other political subdivisions with taxing power. Others originate as a result of actions taken by authorities such as state boards of community colleges, state junior-college boards, and state councils on higher education.

In the third category—branch campuses and extension centers—branch campuses of community colleges are usually established as a result of need as expressed by citizens and groups in the areas to be served and by decisions of state higher education authorities. In the instance of extension centers of four-year institutions, they have been established as a natural outgrowth of off-campus centers, special legislations, and as a result of requests of alumni and other interested individuals.

---

[1]D. G. Morrison and Clinette F. Witherspoon, *Procedures for the Establishment of Public Two-Year Colleges* (Washington, D.C.: Department of Health, Education, and Welfare, OE-57006, Bulletin 1966, No. 14); and Roger Yarrington, ed., *Junior Colleges: 50 States/50 Years* (Washington, D.C.: American Association of Junior Colleges, 1969).

State Patterns of Community College Planning

The oldest functioning publicly supported junior college in the United States was founded in Joliet, Illinois, in 1901. With the establishment of a two-year college in Fresno in 1910, California initiated what has now become our nation's most extensive system of community colleges. However, in spite of these early beginnings, it was not until 1960 that California adopted the first state master plan for higher education in our country. As a result of this master plan, community colleges for the first time received official sanction as a segment of a state system of higher education. This historic first master plan of higher education was extensively studied throughout the nation, and an ample number of states have since adopted similar plans.

Extent of State Planning

The most authoritative survey on the status of state master plans was made in 1968 by the ERIC Clearinghouse for Junior Colleges. At that time thirty states reported that their public junior colleges were not being operated under a state master plan, although a number of them had master plans in some stage of formulation. Five states indicated that they did not operate a state system of public community colleges at all, five failed to reply, and two sent only copies of their laws governing community colleges. The author of the report cautions that it would be erroneous to assume that the extent of state planning can be gauged by the number of states with officially adopted master plans. Much additional evidence of statewide planning was obtained from letters, feasibility studies, consultants' reports, proposed plans, and reports of other groups. Examination of state laws, proposed laws and regulations, and state standards and guidelines likewise supported the thesis that statewide planning was taking place. The report concludes that on the basis of evidence gathered at least half of the states had shown an active concern for it.[2]

Master Plans and State Planning

On the basis of information received from nineteen states Hurlburt concludes that:

> "Master plan" is by no means a generic term. In one state, it connotes a priority system for establishing colleges; in another, it describes a detailed plan of operating a system of two-year colleges; and in a third, it is a plan for all higher education.
> Many plans contain a mix of statutory or other provisions with force of law and recommendations of a governing board or other group. Some deal with citizens' needs and provisions for meeting them in sweeping generali-

[2] Allan S. Hurlburt, *State Master Plans for Community Colleges,* Monograph Series, No. 8 (Washington, D.C.: American Association of Junior Colleges, 1969), pp. 2-3.

ties. Others give detailed formulas for budgetary or other operational procedures.

Comprehensive state plans for all of higher education tend to present community college information with less detail and identity than do plans devoted to community colleges exclusively.[3]

According to the above quotation, considerable variation exists among the states in respect to master plans.

Purposes and Uses of State Master Plans

Fortunate indeed are the community college planners who find themselves in states that have well-developed master plans. If the community college movement is to fulfill its mission, state master plans must be developed, amended from time to time, and implemented.

An understanding of the rationale for developing state master plans should assist community college planners and potential administrators to obtain a better grasp of the value of these state plans to the community college movement in particular and to the entire higher education field in general. This knowledge should also encourage supporters of community colleges to work for the development of master plans in states where they are in their early stages of development or nonexistent. The following major purposes, or uses of state master plans have been suggested:

1. The state master plan is a way for the state to express its concern for the educational welfare of its adolescent and adult citizens.
2. The state master plan describes an organized system of higher education, not just a group of institutions.
3. A state master plan provides a way of meeting both universal needs and diverse needs.
4. A state plan is an effective way to describe a minimum foundation program.
5. A state plan assists communities to assess their own capabilities and readiness to develop a college.
6. A master plan provides a means of removing community college establishment and development from purely political considerations and local pressures.
7. The state master plan is an effective vehicle for systematic planning and for establishing priorities.
8. A state plan serves to insure coordination of higher education effort.
9. An adequate master plan provides a basis for further planning.
10. The development of a state plan opens areas of needed research.
11. The development of a master plan encourages and facilitates systematizing routine state services.

[3]Ibid., p. 35.

12. Cooperative state planning, including both public and private institutions, improves both state and local planning.

13. The development of a master plan reveals inadequacies in legal provisions for community colleges, hence it is a basis for preparing new laws.

14. A master plan is an effective public relations instrument.[4]

Examination of the above major purposes and uses of state master plans should convince both state and local planners of the importance of having a well-defined master plan. Those states that have formulated workable master plans can be of great assistance to other states that are still in the early stages of planning, and particularly to states that have not as yet begun to plan. States should be encouraged to share master plans with each other. This could be accomplished, for example, through the Compact of States Organization.

As previously suggested, local planners should be familiar with state rules and regulations including the state master plan if one exists. Students of the administration of higher education will be interested in the following excerpts taken from different master plans.

The goals of a master plan for higher education in Maryland are three: (1) quality education, (2) higher educational opportunity for all citizens, and (3) the variety and size of programs sufficient to satisfy the professional and skilled manpower needs of the economy. *Quality* is the key to the first goal; the essence of the second is *opportunity for all,* and *satisfying the manpower needs* is central to the third.[5]

In the same document the following eleven objectives are found:

1. The Master Plan must make clear the value of *committing funds to higher education consistent with Maryland's ability to pay.* The Master Plan should exhibit the benefits, both personal and societal, to be derived from higher education and to consider the relative and absolute amounts of money it will take to finance such an investment in people.

2. The Master Plan should encourage all those concerned with higher education to unite in a *cooperative effort aimed at satisfying the educational needs of the State.* Through carefully defined and shared responsibilities, the various segments of higher education, the public and the private colleges, and the state agencies can replace today's competitive and independent practices with coordinated application of their talents and resources to the solutions of the problems that face society and its institutions.

3. *Provisions for programs to suit diverse interests and needs* should be included in the Master Plan. Traditional programs in the arts and

---

[4]Ibid., pp. 3-7.

[5]*Master Plan for Higher Education in Maryland—Phase One* (Baltimore: Maryland Council for Higher Education, 1968), p. 1.

sciences, contemporary programs in the natural and social sciences, programs and continuing education for all aspects of our intricate commercial and social complex, and opportunities for theoretical and applied studies in the fine arts and continuing and reeducation in the professions and technologies must be available to Maryland citizens.

4. *Requirements of the state for professional manpower*—law, medicine, dentistry, education, and engineering, to mention only a few—*must be met*. Maryland must plan to educate its share of these professionals for the state, the region, and the country.

5. The Master Plan should assist the institutions in setting up post-secondary, but prebaccalaureate, *programs necessary to prepare and retrain individuals for the many semiprofessional, technical, and skilled jobs* that modern civilization requires. Without the support of trained people at this level the task of the professional would probably become an impossible one. (In recent years, we have begun to realize how many supportive jobs are part of any profession, and as our population increases, the semiprofessional performing these tasks will enable the professional to serve a much larger clientele.)

6. *Financial handicaps* to obtaining postsecondary school education *should be removed*. No citizen should be denied the advantages of higher education on financial grounds alone. Various loan, scholarship, and work programs as means of financial assistance need to be explored.

7. In order to maintain the quality education that is a goal of this Master Plan, the Master Plan must speak to *insuring quality faculty for Maryland's public institutions*. Two specific factors in attracting quality faculty are institutional salaries and the recognition of the faculty's role in developing institutional policy.

8. The Master Plan must establish *realistic criteria for the size and location of public institutions* of higher education within the state. To complement the planned growth of existing institutions, the Master Plan should provide educational and regional planners with guidelines for the establishment of new institutions and the enlarging of operating ones. Academic quality, accessibility, proximity to other colleges, both public and private, and financing will be components of such criteria.

9. The Master Plan should *assist the continued presence and development of private collegiate institutions* in Maryland. These institutions have long educated large numbers of Marylanders, and today they offer students educational opportunities not available in the public institutions. Such choices should remain available to Maryland citizens and the institutions should be aided in meeting the demands that are made upon them.

10. Provision for *continuing and reeducation must be an integral part* of the Master Plan. Because of the rapid changes in established occupations and the multiplicity of new technologies, specialized skills must be repeatedly updated and new ones taught if the manpower resources are to be fully and effectively utilized.

11. Last, but not least, the Master Plan must provide this *quality educa-*

tion at a reasonable cost to all the citizens. This involves not only the student who attends classes and pays a nominal tuition, but also the taxpayer who contributes to higher education through his tax bill and is entitled to know that he is purchasing a quality product.[6]

To obtain an idea of the comprehensiveness of the Maryland master plan the reader is referred to its table of contents, a copy of which appears in Appendix 1, p. 269.

Gannon points out one of the dilemmas of local versus state control of community colleges when he writes as follows about Michigan's experiences of the last fifty years:

> Because education in the United States is a function reserved for each state, it is important to record how Michigan community colleges have gone through the process of change. Some states have taken a position that central control and financing should remain at the state level with varying degrees of citizen participation. Michigan's tradition has been that local control, delegated by the state, and citizen involvement at all levels of decision making, is a meaningful and lasting way to develop an educational system.
>
> Consequently, over the years Michigan public community colleges have progressed by using a coordinated approach that involves the Department of Public Instruction, the legislature, the governor's office and citizen groups. With this kind of commitment, progress has not always been as rapid or as clear-cut concerning overall state planning as may be found in states that centralize most decision making at the state level. However, the benefits from this more flexible position have allowed citizens and educational leaders the opportunity to make decisions and take responsibility for their actions. This commitment appears increasingly difficult to hold in a society that is changing rapidly and becoming more complex. Possibly for this reason, among others, the frequency of studies concerning the needs of the state regarding community colleges have increased along with the request that these groups report more detailed and definite recommendations within a framework which allows for a maximum of local initiative, yet which is sensitive to overall state planning.[7]

By studying the thirty-eight statements quoted below from Michigan's state plan for higher education, the reader can better understand how that state is attempting to resolve the conflict between local initiative and state planning:

1. The role of the State Board of Education as the principal agent for general state planning and coordination of higher education is clear, and in this capacity it is the duty of the State Board of Education to plan for and

[6] Ibid., pp. 6-8.
[7] Philip J. Gannon, "Fifty Years of Community Involvement in Michigan," in Yarrington, *50 States/50 Years*, pp. 104-5.

encourage the orderly development of a comprehensive state system of education beyond the secondary level that will effectively and efficiently serve all the needs of the state.

2. As an initial step in carrying out its constitutional mandate, it is the responsibility of the State Board of Education to assemble information concerning the existing educational pattern of each baccalaureate institution and community college and analyze such information in terms of its recognized educational responsibilities and the scope of its services and offerings.

3. The State Board of Education will establish advisory committees of college and university administrators and faculty members. In addition, the State Board, from time to time, will create other advisory committees as may be appropriate.

4. The State Board of Education expects to seek additional methods by which the private institutions can be properly assisted. Therefore, the State Board reaffirms its support for private higher education, and will seek to foster its welfare and development by appropriate measures, consistent with con- stitutional and statutory provisions and sound public policy.

5. Because of the increasing demands for greater numbers of technically trained people and the rapidly increasing number of vocational-technical programs in community colleges, it is the intent of the State Board of Education, in cooperation with the four other state agencies responsible for the supervision of proprietary schools, to develop administrative rela- tionships to coordinate the program developments of proprietary schools as part of the overall system of higher education.

6. Since revisions of long-range enrollment projections are necessary in determining the need for educational programs, space, and faculty, and because of the important variables affecting the college-going rate, it is the responsibility of the State Board of Education to maintain updated long- range projections of potential and probable student enrollments.

7. The State Board of Education will continue to take the initiative and encourage the community colleges, public and private colleges and univer- sities, and others involved with education and welfare of our youth to seek out and assist those who have the ability to do the required academic work but who, because of inadequate academic preparation or other reasons, are unable to meet the prescribed admission standards of the institutions.

8. Therefore the State Board of Education will continue to support and promote the liberal arts programs in the colleges and universities, and encourage all studies which aim at producing responsible members of modern society—citizens who are knowledgeable of our western heritage, appreciative of other cultures, concerned with social problems, and respectful of common human values.

9. The State Board of Education needs to be informed concerning changes in demands for persons trained for the professions, sciences, and technical fields of various kinds. Therefore, the State Board of Education will encourage and initiate studies of the needs of people for professional preparation in specific areas and exercise leadership in securing the necessary cooperation among the concerned departments of state, professional associations, and the higher education institutions in carrying out such studies.

10. There is continuous need for studies of society's demands and needs for people with vocational skills. Therefore, the State Board of Education will exercise leadership in promoting and encouraging continuous study of society's demands and needs for people trained in various vocational and technical skills, and to initiate such studies in its own behalf as circumstances dictate.

11. The State Board of Education reaffirms its position that the community colleges should admit any high school graduate or other out-of-school person and counsel with him about the programs or courses for which he is prepared and from which he may benefit.

12. In order that community college transfers to baccalaureate institutions may have the opportunity to achieve their educational goals, the State Board of Education will request baccalaureate institutions to accept the special responsibility to admit academically qualified community college transfers, and to provide them with essential counseling and assistance during the period of transition.

13. Because of the lack of knowledge related to the admission policies and practices of the institutions, the State Board of Education will, in cooperation with the colleges and universities, initiate studies designed to culminate in recommendations concerning admission and retention policies and practices.

14. The State Board of Education will foster the coordination of state, institutional, and federal funds available to students, and will recommend that sufficient state financial assistance be available to every individual who is academically qualified to undertake a higher education program of his choice.

15. The State Board of Education wil seek legislative action to provide sufficient funds for the state guaranteed loan fund and to accomplish greater participation by financial institutions.

16. The establishment of an incentive awards program that would identify high school students from disadvantaged backgrounds who can benefit from further education, is of utmost importance if more young people are to be given an opportunity for higher education. Therefore, the State Board of Education will continue to give high priority to the implementation of such

a program and will urge the legislature to provide sufficient funds to meet the financial needs.

17. For the purpose of enabling the State Board of Education to make annual reassessments of higher education, each baccalaureate institution and community college shall file its updated five-year plan of operations showing its educational roles, its actual and proposed inventory of programs, its required faculties and staff, and its projected operating and capital costs, including self-liquidating facilities.

18. As a result of the growing demands for off-campus programs including educational television and mail order courses at the undergraduate, graduate, and graduate-professional levels, and because there is not now a clear direction as to the overall state planning and coordination of such activities, the State Board of Education will develop, in cooperation with institutional representatives, a statewide plan whereby off-campus education can be encouraged, fostered, and coordinated.

19. As a matter of policy the State Board of Education will, from time to time, recommend that certain community colleges, especially metropolitan community colleges, undertake such of the high-cost vocational-technical programs as they are particularly suited to offer.

20. In order to avoid unnecessary duplication of institutions, facilities, and programs, it shall be the policy of the State Board of Education that, where community colleges exist, the community college shall serve as the post-secondary vocational school for the said area.

21. Due to the great need for pre-vocational technical skills at the secondary level, and in the interest of efficiency and economy in teaching, the State Board of Education will establish appropriate standards for secondary area vocational centers and community colleges to avoid unnecessary duplication of programs and facilities.

22. For the purpose of stimulating cooperative educational, research, and public service programs, the State Board of Education will strive to expedite coordination of regional programs within the state, with neighboring states, and with private organizations.

23. Although it is not clear that there is a unique optimum size for educational institutions, it is believed that an educational institution cannot wisely be expanded indefinitely. Therefore, the State Board of Education will study and recommend a state policy concerning institutional size, and the distribution of students among the institutions.

24. The State Board of Education reaffirms its policy of April 1966, that the existing branches should be provided their autonomy in an expeditious manner.

25. The State Board of Education is responsible for making recommendations

concerning the formation and scope of new public institutions. In recommending the establishment of any new public institution, it will offer guidelines to the new governing board on how the public institution should grow, the level of instruction to be offered, and the variety of professional programs and the timing of their introduction.

26. The State Board of Education believes every resident of the state should have access to community college services. It is therefore the policy of the Board that all areas of the state be included in independent community college districts.

27. The State Board of Education will, based upon appropriate advice, establish guidelines for locating community college sites within the respective districts in such a way as to provide the greatest services to all of the people of the district and surrounding territory.

28. The State Board of Education shall, based upon appropriate advice, establish guidelines for determining the appropriateness of residence halls on community college campuses, and the construction of a residence hall by a community college shall require the prior approval of the State Board of Education.

29. It is the policy of the State Board of Education that no community college should be transformed into a baccalaureate institution. If and when it is determined that an upper division or four-year institution is needed in an area, it should be established in its own right, rather than as an outgrowth of an existing community college.

30. Because of the growing concern over rising tuition and fee charges, the State Board of Education will initiate a study and make recommendations concerning the entire gamut of student charges by the public baccalaureate institutions and community colleges.

31. Baccalaureate institutions shall file financial information upon request consistent with terms of such definitions of accounting and reporting terms as are agreed upon by the institutions and state agencies involved. In addition, the State Board of Education will cooperate with the baccalaureate institutions to bring about a speedy completion of an accounting manual that will be acceptable in meeting the uniform accounting and reporting needs of the state.

32. The present system of counting and reporting students by the public baccalaureate institutions is practical and acceptable to most agencies. The State Board of Education will adopt the system of counting and reporting students as set forth . . . .

33. Because the educational programs of community colleges vary widely and some are penalized by the standard per student appropriation, the State Board of Education, with the advice of the boards of trustees of community

colleges and the State Board for Public Community and Junior Colleges, will recommend a new way of determining appropriations for community college operations consistent with their roles as institutions of higher education.

34. It shall be the policy of the State Board of Education that, when a student attends a community college as a nonresident student because he does not live in a community college district, the excess of the tuition charged over the standard charge to resident students should be paid by the student's local school district. When a student from a community college district attends another community college in order to enroll in a high-cost vocational-technical program or a specialized program not available in his community college, the sending community college should make provisions to pay the difference in tuition charges.

35. As a result, the State Board of Education will assist and encourage the public baccalaureate institutions and the public community colleges to arrive at optimum utilization of their facilities and improved operating efficiency wherever possible; always in light of the need for quality in the education processes.

36. The importance of annual revision of projections for operations cannot be stressed too strongly because conditions constantly change. Therefore, in keeping with its constitutional mandate to advise the legislature, the State Board of Education will carry on a continuous study of the operating needs of both the baccalaureate institutions and community and junior colleges.

37. Due to the emerging role of the community colleges, the State Board of Education will give added study to need for the state to share in the cost of land acquisition. The State Board will review the present procedure and proportion of the state share of capital costs provided community colleges.

38. The projected costs of facilities in terms of future enrollments and programs is an important undertaking if sufficient student spaces are to be available. The State Board of Education will submit updated annual capital outlay projections to the Legislature, consistent with the constitutional mandate to advise concerning the financial requirements of higher education.[8]

State master plans should not result in state control of community colleges in any of the states. The concept of local control is rooted deep in our nature as a result of our experience in the American system of public education. It long has been one of the system's proudest features. It, therefore, would be a grave

[8]*State Plan for Higher Education in Michigan* (Lansing, Mich.: Michigan Department of Education, April, 1969), pp. 8-64.

mistake if state control of community colleges would occur because of lack of flexibility in state master plans.

In a recent report the Carnegie Commission on Higher Education states:

> ... that local community college districts, the states, and the federal government all have responsibilities in relation to the development of community colleges and that these responsibilities should be shared. In general, the federal government's responsibilities should be confined to the provision of limited financial support . . . including the stimulation of planning by the states through planning grants. The states should undertake responsibility for the development of state plans, adequate financial support, and a set of general state criteria and standards for the community colleges. However, within a framework of state planning and guidance, local community college districts should have the responsibility for detailed policy decisions in their districts.
>
> Persons who are thoroughly familiar with their local communities are likely to be far better qualified to make wise decisions about the location and development of community colleges than state officials who are involved in statewide planning. Furthermore, . . . occupational programs need to be geared to local, state, and national labor market trends, and for this reason it is particularly desirable that they be guided by an advisory board composed of persons thoroughly familiar with the local labor market, even though there is also a need for state and national manpower advisory boards . . . .
>
> The preservation of an appropriate relationship among the various levels of government in relation to the governance of community colleges may well be a critical factor in their future development.
>
> . . . The Commission recommends that state legislation should provide for the formation of local community college districts and should prohibit inclusion of community colleges within K-12 local school districts. In every local community college district there should be an elected or appointed board of directors with substantial powers relating to the development and administration of community colleges within the district. The Commission also recommends that local boards delegate substantial responsibility to the administration and faculty and provide for student participation in decisions relating to educational policy and student affairs. When community colleges are part of the state university system, there should be local advisory boards with substantial influence.[9]

According to Clifford G. Erickson, Illinois successfully resolved the state and local control dichotomy. He reported the following observations from the experience:

1. The spring 1967 junior college legislative program developed and supported cooperatively by the State Junior College Board, the local community college

[9]Carnegie Commission on Higher Education, *The Open-Door Colleges—Policies for Community Colleges* (New York: McGraw-Hill Book Company, 1970), pp. 47-48.

boards, and the Illinois Association of Community and Junior Colleges was the most effective in history.

2. The state board and staff have done excellent work in maintaining liaison with local community action groups in formation of community college districts, in annexation hearings, and in other procedures formerly handled through county and state superintendents of instruction.

3. Liaison has been established between the State Junior College Board and the North Central Association to coordinate efforts in the area of state recognition and regional accreditation.

4. A liaison committee is coordinating efforts of the Board of Higher Education, the State Junior College Board, and the Board of Vocational Education (under the state superintendent of public instruction) which continues as the funding agency for the Vocational Education Act of 1963 and for other bills providing grants in occupational fields.

5. The State Junior College Board is maintaining liaison with the certifying and licensing agencies, many of which operate under the state superintendent of public instruction and the Department of Registration and Education.

6. The Board of Higher Education and the State Junior College Board are working effectively with the Illinois Conference on Higher Education (which includes all two- and four-year public and private institutions) in developing improved articulation between two- and four-year colleges. Statewide cooperative research on articulation is being undertaken by a Council on Articulation created by the Illinois Conference on Higher Education.

7. Work is being done to refine and develop the concepts of coordination and planning at the state level and autonomy and control at the local level. We hope that a creative state-local tension will serve as well and keep Illinois in the vanguard of the junior college movement. Interpretation of statutes, guidelines for state recognition and funding, and coordinating procedures such as for cost accounting, enrollment projections, and curriculum planning are being developed with local participation before action is taken by the state board.

8. The State Board has requested all community college presidents to serve on an Advisory Council of Presidents to facilitate communication between local and State Boards and staffs. This council meets at least every two months with the State Board staff and is represented at State Board meetings. The Illinois Association of Community and Junior Colleges is represented at State Board meetings by its executive secretary and, at times, by officers of the coordinating board and of the divisions.[10]

[10]Clifford G. Erickson, "Illinois Balances Statewide Planning and Local Autonomy," *Junior College Journal,* 38, No. 6 (1968), 25.

The respective roles of the federal government, the state, and the local community in public education have long been a debatable issue among educators and laymen in the United States. The debate continues to rage in respect to the community college movement. This chapter has discussed the state's role in planning and regulation of community colleges. Chapters 2 and 3 will be concerned with the role of the local community college district in planning and developing community colleges.

Summary

In order to plan intelligently, community college planners must have an understanding of the laws, rules, and regulations governing the planning and starting of a community college in their state. If the state has a master plan, they must be thoroughly familiar with its contents. To start out, planners should meet with officials from the state department of education to obtain all available information, thus avoiding mistakes.

Community college planners and students of higher education administration alike should understand the procedures utilized in the establishment of community colleges in different states.

Diversity has been the key word. Local junior colleges are usually initiated by the proposed local district. In state two-year colleges initiation takes place as a result of special legislation, petitioning by a political subdivision with taxing power, or actions taken by authorities such as state boards of community colleges, state junior college boards, and state councils on higher education. Branch campuses of community colleges are usually established as a result of need expressed by citizens in the area and by decisions of state higher education authorities. Extension centers of four-year institutions have been established as a natural outgrowth of off-campus centers, by special legislation, and upon requests of individuals or groups.

Many states have been slow in developing a master plan that includes community colleges. However, there is evidence that by now statewide planning actually is taking place. In the states that do have master plans considerable variation of plans exists.

Understanding the purposes of state master plans also is helpful to community college planners. State master plans should not result in state control of community colleges. Local control is an aspect of education of which our nation is proud. There is considerable agreement today that the responsibilities for the development of community colleges should be shared by local community college districts, the state, and the federal government.

Suggested Activities and Problems

1. Obtain a copy of a state master plan for higher education. After studying it, write a commentary on the sections dealing with community colleges.
2. Interview a member of a local council for higher education to ascertain the degree to which the state either assisted in getting the college started or served as a hindrance.
3. Write a paper indicating the roles you believe should be played by the local district, state, and federal government in the planning and building of a community college.
4. Present, in writing, arguments on both sides of the debate that community colleges should be entirely state supported and state controlled.
5. Examine the community college laws in your state and write a paper recommending new legislation. Give the reasons for your action.

Selected Readings

Blake, Larry J., "A New Start in Montana," *Junior College Journal,* 38, No. 7 (1968), 22.

Christian, Floyd T. and James L. Wattenbarger, "Ten Years—A Plan Evolves in Florida," *Junior College Journal,* 38, No. 1 (1967), 44.

Erickson, Clifford G., "Illinois Balances Statewide Planning and Local Autonomy," *Junior College Journal,* 38, No. 6 (1968), 22.

Hurlburt, Allan S., *State Master Plans for Community Colleges,* Monograph Series, No. 8. Washington, D.C.: American Association of Junior Colleges, 1969.

The Open-Door Colleges, Chaps. 2, 3, and 9. A special report and recommendations by the Carnegie Commission on Higher Education. New York: McGraw-Hill Book Company, 1970.

Richardson, Richard C., Jr., Clyde E. Blocker, and Louis W. Bender, *Governance for the Two-Year College.* Englewood Cliffs, N.J.: Prentice-Hall, Inc., 1972, chap. 2.

Yarrington, Roger, ed., *Junior Colleges: 50 States/50 Years.* Washington, D.C.: American Association of Junior Colleges, 1969.

2

Establishing the Need
for a
Community College

The Carnegie Commission on Higher Education has projected a need for 230 to 450 new public community colleges by 1980. It is predicted that forty-seven of the fifty states will have to build new campuses to provide two-year colleges within commuting distance of most potential students.[1] California, long a leader in the field, will probably need to provide 29 to 34 more community colleges in this decade; Minnesota may need 4 or 5; Florida, 11 or 12; and Indiana, 7 or 8. Other national surveys and studies corroborate the conclusions of the Carnegie Commission: most states will be adding to their existing complement of public community colleges.

But where in the various states should the new institutions be built? What is a viable area to support a new community college? As discussed in the preceding chapter, many states either have, or are developing, master plans for higher education that include projected areas for the development of two-year colleges. The state clearly has an important coordinative function in the emerging system of higher education, based in part on the state's increasing financial support of public colleges. However, the focus in this chapter will be on the local effort required to establish the need for a two-year college, since by definition the public community college grows out of the basic community it will ultimately serve. The people in an area must be convinced of the need to develop and

The Carnegie Commission on Higher Education, *The Open-Door Colleges* (New York: Mc Graw-Hill Book Company, 1970), pp. 35-39. Permission granted by The Carnegie Commission on Higher Education. Copyright The Carnegie Foundation for the Advancement of Teaching 1970.

support their own college before it can become a reality. And so a need study must be made as the first step in possibly organizing a new community college.

There are several ways in which the genesis of a local study can emerge. Let's examine a case study.

Dr. Berry, Director of Two-Year Colleges in the state department of higher education, is armed with the latest draft of his state's master plan for higher education. This document pinpoints Suburbia County (located geographically adjacent to the state's largest city, Metropolis) as a viable area for development of a community college. The county's population is presently 225,000 and is projected to increase to 390,000 in seven years. Dr. Berry makes an appointment with Dr. Jones, the superintendent of the new intermediate service unit for public schools in Suburbia County, which has just replaced the venerable county superintendent of schools office. Dr. Berry outines the implications of the state's emerging master plan, especially as it applies to Suburbia County, and asks Dr. Jones if he could designate a professional member of his staff to spearhead the need study for a community college in the county. Dr. Berry promises all of the resources of the state department to assist in the study. Dr. Jones enthusiastically agrees; one of the objectives of his new office is to continually assess educational needs throughout the county.

Or the Suburbia County story could have a reverse twist:

Dr. Jones, recognizing the potential need for a community college in his county, approaches Dr. Berry in the state department to discuss the emerging master plan and its implications for Suburbia County. Dr. Jones then offers to conduct a need study in the county and requests the assistance of state department resource personnel.

In any event, local leadership must be identified to conduct the necessary studies that could ultimately lead to the establishment of a community college in the area. The remainder of this chapter is a step-by-step approach field tested by the writer to establish the need for public two-year colleges at the local level. The suggested plan is specific, yet flexible, and is directed to the local professional educator who will be leading the study project.

Step 1. Identify the Appropriate Agency to Spearhead the Local Study

The regional intermediate unit office serving the area public schools or the county superintendent of schools is a likely agent for organizing the need study. The chief administrator of such a unit usually has no direct ties to the school districts or nearby colleges, and he can well take the initiative. A good first move would be the appointment of a key administrator in this office to give leadership to the entire community college project. Other possible sponsoring agencies for this initial study are the county governing body, a neighboring university, or an existing community college in an adjacent area. From these potential sources, a project study leader should emerge.

Step 2. Organize a Council for Higher Education

It is imperative that a number of outstanding citizens be selected and invited to serve as a highly visible council for higher education. The board of trustees of the organizing agency can appoint the council members, using these guidelines:

1. Identify persons in leadership roles in the community, and aim for diversity of membership. Include business, industrial, and labor leaders; professional persons such as physicians, bankers, attorneys, judges, and educators; the president or other key administrator of a nearby college or university; leaders of service clubs and women's organizations; local government officials; P.T.A. or home and school representatives; the editor of a leading newspaper, and other civic leaders. Go after men and women in the power structure; they will be needed to insure a successful study and follow through.

2. The size of the council for higher education may vary from about fifteen to forty. If more than twenty are appointed, consider organizing an executive or steering committee of about six to eight.

3. Select members from all areas likely to be served by a community college if one should prove feasible. For example, if the geographic area is a county, try to get someone on the council from most, if not all, communities. Include for certain all larger towns in the representation.

An initial meeting of the council should deal with election of officers, and with a statement of the main purpose of the group: to study and report on the need for a two-year public community college. The council should then direct its attention to two main projects: (1) making resources available to the professional leader of the study; and (2) raising sufficient funds to carry out a comprehensive study. If it is possible to obtain a budget of between $15,000 and $50,000, the council can engage one of a number of firms throughout the nation that specialize in demographic studies and educational surveys. In addition to commercial organizations, university service bureaus are also available to perform this type of contract work. Possible sources of funds for this purpose are local businesses and industries, the county planning commission, and service clubs. If sufficient funds are raised, the council will approve their expenditure under the direction of the local professional educator who is leading the study project. Indeed it is his job to guide the operations of the council from its inception. If budget funds are not available, then the study leader will need to use his ingenuity as well as the resources he can command in his own office. The remaining steps can be carried out on a shoestring budget, if necessary.

*Step 3. Study State Legislation, Master Plan, and Regulations
for Community Colleges*

It is important now to assess pertinent legislation providing for establishment of community colleges—to become thoroughly familiar with the provisions for sponsorship, financing, and the relationship of a local community college to the state. The master plan for higher education, if there is one, will give additional information of interest to the local study. And the state department of education or higher education will usually have regulations and/or guidelines to be followed in establishing the feasibility of a two-year college for a local district. By reviewing the legislation, master plan, and guidelines with the chief state official for community colleges, answers to the following questions may be obtained. These are all relevant to the study about to be made under the general direction of the local council for higher education.

1. Who pays for the establishment, building, and operation of community colleges in this state? Most often, there is a percentage split among the state, the local sponsoring agency or district, and the student if tuition is permitted. It is important to know, for example, if the state pays one-third or one-half of capital costs for construction; and what share of the operating cost per student is paid at the state level.

2. Are geographic or population boundaries established for community college districts?

3. How is the governance of a community college provided for in the law and state regulations? For instance, is the board of trustees of the local college appointed by the state board of higher education, elected directly by the people, or appointed by the local governing agency? What authority, if any, does the state board or state department of higher education have over the local board of trustees?

4. Who may sponsor a community college at the local level? County or municipal governments? School districts? Independent college boards with direct taxing powers?

5. Are there state studies and statistics available that will help to determine the need for a community college in the local area?

These questions and many others can be clarified by several direct contacts with state department personnel. A rapport should be established at this time, since numerous other questions will emerge as the study progresses, and the state can be a valuable resource.

Step 4. Organize and Conduct Local Need Studies

The feasibility study at the local level will have at least six components:

1. County or regional population projections for area to be served by potential college.
2. County or regional resources and development survey.
3. Business-industry survey.
4. Professional survey.
5. Student-parent surveys.
6. Enrollment study to predict potential student enrollments in the college.

The population growth of an area is one of the prime predictors in assessing the need for a comprehensive community college, which serves students of all ages in day and evening programs. A minimum population must also be assured to provide stable financing of the operating and capital costs of a new college. The following procedures can be followed to conduct this study.

1. Secure copies of as many other population studies as can be obtained—from the state department of higher education, other community colleges, or a professional consultant.
2. If there is limited money available, consider employing on a per diem basis a professional consultant from a nearby university or state or regional agency. Such an expert will be very helpful in recommending sources for population data, and in guiding the study itself.
3. Establish contacts with all federal, state, regional, and county agencies that have any responsibility for population studies and statistics, from the Bureau of the Census down to the various municipalities in the area.
4. After amassing all available data, analyze them with the best assistance that is available, and develop population projections for the next ten to fifteen years. Pinpointing projected growth patterns by municipality or regional divisions will assist the college board of trustees at some later date in their selection of a site.

The county or regional resources and development survey can be compiled from information that should be available from the county government, the planning commissions, and the chamber of commerce. The character of the area and its major developmental trends should be noted, such as significant changes in land use from farming to residential, business, and industrial applications. The wealth of the region should be summarized in terms of tax ratables and their annual growth; the annual income of residents; and other factors indicative of the economic health of the locality.

The business-industry survey is a key component of the feasibility study. The main purpose is to determine the present and future personnel needs of local business and industries, particularly in occupations that require more than a high school education, but not necessarily a baccalaureate degree. Ideally all businesses and industries should be surveyed, but this is usually not possible in medium- or larger-sized counties. Then a stratified sample of firms of various sizes should be used. In any case, be sure to include all the largest employers in the area to be served by the proposed college. The county chamber of commerce or the United Fund office are two good sources for lists of businesses and industries.

In Appendix 2, p. 273, a business-industry survey form is reproduced. By referring to this survey several points may be clarified. Note that the questionnaire is brief; it was sent to the president or other top executive in each firm, and these are busy men and women. The return rate was 36 percent, which provided a reasonable statistical sample. The 72 responding companies employed 40, 336 regular employees, which was 35 percent of the total work force in the county. Also, the 11 largest companies in the county, employing more than 23,000 persons, all returned the survey form. At the time of this study, the county had a total population of 589,000. This type of questionnaire provides valuable information to be used later in helping to determine initial curricula for the new college. Continuing in Appendix 2, a summary report of the findings of the business-industry survey is presented. Note that *all* of the comments made by executives in this study are recorded, and these provide valuable interpretative data.

After the data have been tabulated in such a survey, the summary report should be presented to the council for higher education for its study and approval.

The professional survey is carried out in much the same manner as the business-industry survey. It is important to sample a good cross section of physicians, lawyers, judges, engineers, educators, clergymen, and other members of professions. The main purpose here is to determine trends and changes in the professions, particularly in the paraprofessional areas. The entire allied health field, for example, is undergoing many changes; and it is important to know if local hospitals and clinics will be looking for medical laboratory technicians, nurses with two-year associate degrees, and medical secretaries. The number of such personnel needed is also critical. The community college makes a major contribution in training persons at the technical and semiprofessional levels.

The council for higher education will of course lend assistance in the conduct of this survey and will study and ultimately approve the findings.

Student-parent surveys provide another key dimension to the need study for a community college. From practical experience, two surveys are recommended—one on the elementary school level and the other for senior high school students and their parents.

To initiate these surveys it is suggested that contacts be made with the guidance counselors in the school districts of the area. These professional educators can assist in planning for and administering the questionnaires in their schools. They are closest to the students and will make many excellent contributions.

A representative high school survey may be found in Appendix 2, p. 273. This questionnaire was developed by a senior high school guidance counselor after considerable research. It was approved by the council for higher education and administered to all eleventh and twelfth graders in the county. (Some high school surveys include the tenth grade also.) The students were asked to take the forms home with a covering letter and a booklet that presented information about community colleges. The letter was addressed to the parents, who were urged to answer the questions jointly with their sons and daughters. Some significant results of this student-parent survey may be noted in Appendix 2 beginning on p. 273. Seventy-eight percent of the 17,400 questionnaires were completed, with a total of 7,864 juniors and seniors responding that they would be likely to attend a two-year community college if one were available. Reasons most often given were low cost, chance to improve scholastic record, opportunity to live at home and to keep a job while going to college. Some random comments from students and parents are included.

At the elementary school level, a survey of fifth- or sixth-grade parents has been found useful to determine the percentage of students likely to attend a community college in six or seven years. A similar questionnaire can be developed for this parent survey, and the inclusion of a fact booklet about two-year community colleges is especially important at this level. Many parents, for example, will not know that a two-year collegiate program leads to the award of an associate degree. In areas where community colleges are a recent development, many people think only in terms of the four-year baccalaureate degree, and do not understand the purposes and programs of two-year institutions. Consequently, surveys such as those proposed here can be educational to citizens as well as useful to the need study.

The reports of the surveys, when tabulated and summarized like the example in Appendix 2, should be presented to the council for higher education for their analysis and approval. These accumulating documents then become important components of the comprehensive study report that will one day emerge.

The enrollment study should now be made to forecast the potential numbers of students likely to enroll in a college if one were established in this area. It would be very useful to secure the services of a consultant for this part of the study. Enrollment projections are a dangerous game at best, and the advice of an experienced hand will pay off at this point if he is deployed over several days at key steps in the process.

Most experts see a close relationship between high school enrollment in the sending area and the ultimate community college enrollment. However, because of substantial enrollment in the part-time and evening programs of a community college, the general population growth is an equally important factor. The first step then is to secure accurate data from all school districts in the area likely to be served by a community college. Most schools make their own enrollment projections for planning purposes and for state reports. These data are often available in the intermediate unit or county superintendent's office. With consultant help, projections for grades nine through twelve and for grade twelve alone can be translated into enrollment projections for the proposed community college. For example, some experts believe that an established community college (four to five years old) may expect a full-time equivalent (FTE) enrollment equal to 20-25 percent of the total pupil enrollment in grades nine through twelve of the sending area. (FTE is computed by adding the number of full-time college students and the number of full-time equivalencies; these are determined by totaling the credit hours of all the part-time students and dividing by fifteen or whatever figure constitutes a full load).

These data should then be related to the population projections for the area derived from the procedures outlined on page 21. With some consultant help, a reasonably accurate enrollment for the proposed new college can be projected. (FTE enrollment may be expected to run from 1 percent to 3 percent of the general population in an established college, depending on variables such as other nearby institutions of higher learning.)

Step 5. Organize a Comprehensive Program of Public Information

As soon as the various need studies are underway (Step 4), begin to set up a public information network. Involve the newspapers, radio and television stations, and other available media. It is imperative that people hear community colleges discussed, and that the citizens be informed about the various current studies to determine the possible need for a two-year college in this area. The members of the council for higher education should be prime movers in the public information effort. Here are some suggestions for specific activities.

1. Begin to get out regular news releases (at least one a week) on: the work of the council; the various need surveys; national and state trends in employment; news about community colleges in other parts of the state; and higher education needs in general.
2. Write and release special reports on various aspects of community college education such as open door concept, associate degrees, changing education needs in technical and semiprofessional fields; and reports of national groups like the Carnegie Commission on Higher Education.
3. Be available to speak at service clubs, civic and church groups, and high schools. Set up a speakers' bureau involving members of the council for higher education to report on the various local studies, and to inform members of organizations about community colleges.
4. Call press conferences to announce the release of each need study report.
5. Arrange coverage on radio and TV interview programs and news spots.

Step 6. Identify and Assess Possible Opposition

As the different components of the feasibility study are completed and released by the council for higher education, watch for the reaction of possible opponents to a community college. These may include: taxpayers' associations, local and county political leaders, several special interest groups, and even persons in a nearby established four-year college or university. A positive public information program, initiated in Step 5, will anticipate much of the opposition. But where it appears, meet all arguments with facts. Be firm but positive in the approach at all times. Insist on a fair hearing for the community college proposal. The issue should be decided on its merits and on the results of the exhaustive studies of the council for higher education. Members of the council will now earn their spurs, as they are called upon to speak out on the community college issue. We recall a particularly agonizing experience involving a banking executive who had agreed to serve on a council for higher education.

> Reports of the various need studies were emerging and a recommendation seemed to be imminent that a community college be organized. The political leadership of the county had taken a stand against the establishment of a two-year college in the area. It so happened that a substantial amount of county funds were invested in the banking executive's institution. The word was passed to him not too subtly that changes might be made in certain investments if he spoke out in favor of a community college. The final report of the council for higher education was clear and unequivocal: a community college should be developed immediately to serve the citizens of the county. The banker voted with his fellow council members in making the unanimous recommendation. He stood on principle when the chips were down, and the investment threat was not carried out.

All such stories, unfortunately, do not have a happy ending. Those who agree to serve on councils of higher education and ultimately on college boards of trustees must be able to withstand the political gaff, sometimes at the risk of real personal sacrifice.

Step 7. Complete and Publish the Feasibility Study

As the component studies are completed, they are written up with appropriate introductory and research material. A final report with recommendations is hammered out. If the establishment of a community college is indicated, further consultations are necessary with state department leaders to insure compliance with state law and regulations. The results of the studies will tend to predict the initial and ultimate size of the new college.

When the council's report is completed and approved, it should be printed in sufficient quantity for wide distribution throughout the area. Every governmental official, school board member, school administrator, and civic leader should have a copy. All possible blanket coverage should be sought through the media, and council members should once again go to the speaker's rostrum to explain the plans for establishment of a local community college. Depending on the enabling legislation, the genesis of the new college can come through: a referendum to establish a local district; a decision to sponsor the college financially by the county governing body; or by action of school districts or municipalities, which may be permitted by law to organize a two-year college. In the next chapter this task of securing a funding base for the proposed college is thoroughly explored. The council for higher education has one more big job ahead—acquiring the necessary state and local support for the establishment of a new community college.

Summary

By 1980 hundreds of new public community colleges will be established in most of the states to provide two-year colleges within commuting distance of potential students. The state has an important coordinative role in the emerging system of higher education. However, the focus in this chapter is on the local effort required to establish the need for a community college.

First, local leadership must be identified to conduct the necessary studies that could lead to the establishment of a community college in the area. The regional intermediate unit office or the county superintendent of schools is a likely agent for organizing the need study.

The next step is the appointment of a highly visible council for higher education, to be appointed by the board of the organizing agency. Membership should be diverse and comprehensive and should include persons in leadership roles in the community. The first meeting of the council should deal with election of officers, and a statement of the main purpose of the group: to study and report on the need for a two-year public community college. If a budget of at least $15,000 can be raised, the council can engage a firm or university service bureau to carry out the need study project, in cooperation with the council. Otherwise, the study can proceed under the direction of a local professional educator from the organizing agency.

It is important to study pertinent state legislation, the master plan for higher education, and the state department regulations or guidelines to be followed in establishing the feasibility of a community college for a local district. Various state studies and statistics may be useful.

A comprehensive feasibility study must be organized and conducted at the local level. It will include: county or regional population projections; a county or regional resources and development survey; a business-industry survey; a professional survey; student-parent surveys; and an enrollment study to predict potential student enrollments at the college.

A public information campaign to include all media is important. Citizens need to hear about community colleges in general, and especially about the current studies being conducted locally. Specific activities should include regular news releases, special reports, speaking engagements, press conferences, and radio and television coverage.

The possible opponents to the idea of a community college should be met with a positive approach, which insists that the proposals for establishment of a new two-year college be given a fair hearing. The issue should be decided on its merits and on the results of the exhaustive studies of the council for higher education.

The final step is the completion and publication of the results of the feasibility study, including all the components. If the establishment of a community college is recommended, then the council's report should be given the widest possible distribution. One big job remains for the council of higher education—acquiring the necessary state and local support for the establishment of a new community college.

Suggested Activities and Problems

1. Select a local county or region that does not have a community college. You are the intermediate unit superintendent. In a short paper, describe the steps you would take to initiate a feasibility study.
2. Interview the president of a recently established community college to seek his evaluation of the need studies leading to the establishment of the new institution. Summarize your findings in writing or in an oral report.
3. Select a county or area that you know best in terms of politics, power structures, influential civic groups, and educational effort. You are asked to recommend citizens to serve on a council for higher education. List your nominations with reasons for naming them.
4. Critically evaluate the business-industry survey reported in this chapter and in Appendix 1. Analyze the form, the procedures followed, and the results.
5. You are the professional educator in charge of a local feasibility study. Describe the procedures you would follow to conduct a population study of your area.
6. In a short paper, explain how you could improve the student-parent surveys discussed in this chapter and in Appendix 2.

Selected Readings

Eastern Iowa Community College Occupational Survey, *A study of the needs for post-high school education in the eastern Iowa community college district.* Bettendorf, Iowa: Eastern Iowa Community College, 1968.

Hale, Morris S., Jr., "A History of Florida Junior Colleges." Unpublished doctoral dissertation, Nashville, Tenn.: George Peabody College for Teachers, 1966.

An Inter-State Study of Educational Needs in the Illinois-Iowa Quad City Area. Bettendorf, Iowa: Black Hawk College and Eastern Iowa Community College, 1968.

The Open-Door Colleges, A special report and recommendations by The Carnegie Commission on Higher Education. New York: McGraw-Hill Book Company, 1970.

Proposed Plan for the Community College of Delaware County. Media, Pa.: Delaware County Board of School Directors, 1966.

Shoemaker, Elwood A. "A Study of the Factors Inhibiting Establishment of Community Colleges in Pennsylvania." Unpublished doctoral dissertation, Temple University, 1970.

3

Securing
Local and State
Support

Funding the College

This is one of the most challenging and critical steps in the establishment of a community college. Adequate funding is essential to the successful development of any college. And many promising community college plans have foundered for the lack of sound, workable financing. The aim of this chapter is to identify various sources of funds and to outline the steps in securing a substantial fiscal base for the new college.

Many developing community colleges in the 1970s have encountered severe funding problems. For example, the Carnegie Commission on Higher Education stated:

> The need for broader financial support for community colleges is critical. They are faced with reductions in federal appropriations, financial stringency in many of the states, and increasing reluctance of voters to approve increased property taxes for the support of community colleges. Furthermore, the development of community colleges has lagged in low-income states and in some of the states with sparse populations. It has also lagged where there has been inadequate provision, or no provision, for state financial support of community colleges.[1]

In Pennsylvania, Shoemaker found that lack of adequate financing was an

[1] The Carnegie Commission on Higher Education, *The Open-Door Colleges* (New York: McGraw-Hill Book Company, 1970), p. 41. Permission granted by the Carnegie Commission on Higher Education. Copyright The Carnegie Foundation for the Advancement of Teaching 1970.

important inhibiting factor in the further establishment of community colleges in that state. The following financial factors were found to be significant in delaying the development of new colleges in many areas of Pennsylvania:

1. Necessity of increasing local taxes to provide for the local sponsor's share of the costs of a community college.
2. Difficulty of obtaining a sponsor for a community college because of the mandated commitments which already absorb the available funds of either school districts or county governments.
3. Inadequate level of state financial support for community colleges.
4. Commitment of local funds, through taxes or voluntary contributions, to local branch campuses.
5. Reluctance to provide, through public funding, opportunities for all youth to attend college.
6. Opposition to the construction of expensive facilities for community colleges.[2]

The members of the local council for higher education will undoubtedly face these and other major challenges as they plan to secure the necessary financial support to launch the new college. There are five usual sources of funding for community colleges: federal, state, local sponsor, student tuition and fees, and private gifts and grants. Both operating and capital funds are required for the initial and succeeding college budgets. Since securing a local sponsor for the proposed college is the real key to all other sources of funding, this important task will be discussed first.

Identifying and Convincing the Local Sponsor

The first step is to list and evaluate all possible local sponsoring agencies that may be permitted by state law.

1. *A directly elected board of trustees for the college, with its own taxing power.* Such an election is usually authorized by a public referendum endorsing the establishment of a community college. This option, if available under state law, has proved itself often superior to the others listed below, since a directly elected board does not have to present budgets to any other public body. It is responsible only to the electorate.

2. *A county or combination of counties* as sponsoring agency. The governing body of the county usually must agree by its own action to support the local share of the community college costs and then appoints a board of trustees to set policy and operate the college. The board presents annual operating and capital construction budgets to the county governing board for its approval.

[2]Elwood A. Shoemaker, "A Study of the Factors Inhibiting Establishment of Community Colleges in Pennsylvania" (Unpublished doctoral dissertation, Temple University, 1970), pp. 202-4.

If more than one county agrees to sponsor a college, formulas are established for the equitable appointment of members of the board of trustees. Each county governing board must then approve the budgets. County sponsorship has the clear advantage of providing a broad tax base.

3. *School board or combination of school boards.* Some states permit school districts to establish community colleges, either alone or in concert with others. In states with county school systems, often the county board of school directors serves as the board for the college or has the power to appoint a college board of trustees. In this latter case the budgets are presented to the elected county school board for their approval.

Some state laws permit local school districts in a county to jointly sponsor a community college. Sponsorship agreements are usually developed, requiring a majority or two-thirds vote of all supporting districts on critical issues such as budgets and building programs. The school directors of all sponsoring districts usually appoint the board of trustees for the college. However, school district sponsorship is unwieldy at best and unworkable at worst because of the number of different boards involved in decision making. Furthermore, K-12 school districts have a comprehensive spectrum already, without adding the whole new dimension of collegiate-level education in the thirteenth and fourteenth years. Significantly, many county and local school boards that operate community colleges have been moving in recent years to divest themselves of direct control of the colleges, and to delegate policy-making authority to the college boards that they appoint, or that are provided for by law. The image of the new community college will be enhanced if it is not tied directly to K-12 school district operation. Two-year colleges are sometimes viewed as "overgrown high schools" and sponsorship by a school district or combination of districts does little to dispel this image. Therefore, this is one of the least desirable options for community college sponsorship.

4. *Municipal sponsorship.* State law sometimes permits municipal governing bodies such as city councils, boards of commissioners, or borough councils to sponsor community colleges, either independently or in concert. In such cases the governing body agrees to support the college, and then appoints the college board of trustees, which operates the college and submits annual and capital budgets to the municipal government for approval. In cities and other populous areas sponsorship by a single municipality is often feasible. However, it should be noted that city and town governments must deal with a multitude of complex problems, most of them with financial implications. A community college becomes another of those problem areas, and may not get the attention that it needs in a city budget. A combination of smaller municipalities as a college sponsor would encounter many of the problems described in joint school district operation above; it is therefore not generally recommended as a viable sponsorship alternative.

5. *State sponsorship.* This option, of course, does not involve local decision

making regarding college sponsorship. Some states do not provide for community college control by local agencies. Instead, a statewide system of community colleges has been authorized by legislation, and a central community college board and department direct the colleges from the state capital. There may be local advisory committees or boards, but they generally do not exercise any significant measure of control, including budget authority. In these states, very little money to support the community colleges is raised locally. The state provides most of the finances, supplemented by tuition. If the need studies described in Chapter 2 call for establishment of a community college in a particular area, then the council for higher education will have to work very closely with state authorities in helping to organize the college.

After listing and evaluating sponsorship alternatives, the next task of the council for higher education is to determine the most viable sponsor for the local community college. This is a key decision, which should be based on a study of many factors. At this point it is usually desirable to employ a consultant for a short period or on a per diem basis to advise the council for higher education. He should be a professional, well experienced in the funding of community colleges—for example, a college president who preferably has worked in several different states, including the one under study. *The basic principles in identifying a local sponsor are: (1) to select the agency that can get the necessary funds most directly, and (2) to establish the broadest possible taxing base.*

Determining needed funds is the next step in convincing the public and a usually reluctant sponsoring agency. In fact, no responsible potential sponsor should be expected to make a commitment until projected operating and capital budgets are available. It is suggested that the council establish at least four task forces to develop preliminary plans for the organization and building of the proposed college. It should be clearly understood that the purpose here is to generate sufficient data to enable fairly accurate cost projections, not to preempt the future authority of the board of trustees and the president of the new college. The proposed task forces, their personnel, and their charges are as follows:

Philosophy and Program

Membership 1. One or two members of the council.
2. A college or university administrator.
3. A school superintendent or high school principal.
4. Several members from business, industry, government, and the professions.

Tasks To state the purposes of the proposed community college and to outline the initial programs and curricula. This task force will use the various surveys from the need studies as a resource.

Basic decision: Is the new institution to be a comprehensive community college, serving a variety of postsecondary needs in the community? For example, will the curricula include transfer, technical, semiprofessional, and developmental or remedial offerings? (For additional information, see Chapters 7 through 10.)

Administrative Organization and Staffing

Membership
1. One or two members of the council.
2. A community college president or dean.
3. A public school administrator.
4. Several members from business, industry, government, and the professions.

Tasks In terms of projected enrollments from the need studies, develop required administrative staffing structure. Based on the programs and curricula identified by the Philosophy and Program Committee, develop the numbers of instructional and noninstructional personnel needed to operate the college initially and at various student full-time equivalent levels. (For additional information, see Chapter 6.)

Facilities Planning

Membership
1. An architect.
2. A county planning official.
3. One or two business-industry executives with building experience.
4. A facilities development administrator from a community college or four-year institution.
5. One or two members of the council.
6. A public school plant administrator.

Tasks Identify possible sites and their cost. (Tentative decisions will have to be made on single or multiple campuses, and optimum size of sites.) Determine initial and ultimate campus building requirements and projected costs. (Note: This task can be accomplished by using predicted enrollments from the need studies; standard formulas on square feet per student; and projected building construction costs for the area.) (For additional information see Chapter 12.)

Finance

Membership
1. A community college business officer.
2. A college president or dean.

3. Several members from business, industry, government, and the professions, preferably with financial backgrounds.

4. A member from the agency that is the leading candidate for local sponsor.

5. Several members of the council.

Tasks Develop proposed operating and capital budgets for initial operation of the college, and project several years ahead to optimum enrollment. Compute potential state, federal, and tuition income. Then determine taxes required by local sponsor to support establishment and maintenance of a community college.

The task force work is coordinated by the professional educator responsible for all the studies and the council work to date. All task forces are given a time limit for their final reports—six weeks is tight but feasible. They are ad hoc groups that will disband after they serve. Stress this when making appointments, and even busy business executives will cooperate.

The council for higher education receives all task force reports, acts upon them, and coordinates them into a comprehensive publication. These important findings and conclusions are then used as follows:

1. Get the final report to key members of the power structure. (Hopefully, some of them are already members of the council.) You cannot sell a community college unless the persons who control and approve expenditures of public funds fully understand the projected plans and costs.

2. Send the final council report to key leaders of business, industry, government, the professions, and the schools.

3. Continue the program of public information initiated earlier. If the steps suggested in Chapter 2 have been implemented, the public is already somewhat aware of the need for a community college in the area. The program of public information must now be expanded in depth so that every citizen hears about the proposed community college and the contributions it will be able to make to individual citizens and the area as a whole. The council must appoint a public information expert, either from its ranks or from the community, to head up the publicity effort. Promising candidates are the editor of an influential newspaper, the executive of a radio or television station, or a public relations expert in public or private service. An effective campaign will include the following thrusts:

    a. Brochures to be mailed to every home, including a summary of the council's final report.

    b. Radio and TV spots and special interview programs.

    c. News releases.

    d. Forums and lectures.

A good public information program will anticipate the negative reactions that often arise from groups such as taxpayers' associations, politicians, special interest groups, and others that will oppose the college for a variety of reasons. The best defense is a positive program to acquaint the public with the facts about the proposed college: why it is needed, how it will be financed, and which benefits will accrue to the community.

By now the potential local sponsoring agency will have all the necessary data on which to make a decision. It is hoped that its members will sense a feeling of community support for the college. The council for higher education should request a meeting with the local sponsor to request formal approval of the community college. This may be facilitated if the sponsoring agency is represented on the council. After thorough consideration of all pertinent factors, the local sponsor may agree to support the establishment of a two-year public community college in the area.

If a referendum is required by law, or if the college is established by the direct election of a board of trustees, then one of the council's final acts will be to help organize the machinery for the necessary public votes.

Securing State Approvals and Assistance

While the process of identifying and securing the local sponsor is underway, further contacts must be made with appropriate state officials who have responsibility for enabling the organization of community colleges. It is necessary to determine the steps required by state law and regulation to effect the establishment of the local college.

The state consultations suggested in Chapter 2 should now be continued. The service area for the college has already been identified from the state master plan or by approval of the state board or department of higher education. The laws and regulations vary from state to state, but it is important to clear the following areas at this time:

1. Filing for state approval of the establishment of a community college.
2. Verifying to the state the local sponsor's ability to support its share of operating and capital costs.
3. Securing approval of start-up costs to be provided by the state.
4. Complying with any other state requirements.

Coordinating state and local actions on establishment of a community college is a delicate business at best. For example, both the local sponsor and the state board of higher education may insist on prior approval of the other group before granting initial funds. We recall an occasion when tentative approval of funding by the county sponsor was arranged at an early morning meeting (subject to state action), approval by the state board at a noon meeting, and final con-

firming action by the county the next day. One learns to be a juggler when faced
with balancing state and local approvals.

Obtaining Federal Funds

The availability of federal money for newly developing community colleges
depends on the action of Congress and the president in any given fiscal year.
Several persons and agencies can offer assistance.

1. Your local congressman is always happy to assist in locating available
   funding.
2. The American Association of Junior Colleges, especially the director of
   Governmental and Urban Affairs.
3. The state department of education or higher education is familiar with
   federal funds such as the vocational education moneys, which are
   administered through state agencies.

Federal funds, as available, do help solve the critical capital and operating
budget problems that most community colleges have been experiencing in the
70s. It is important for a new community college to determine the percentage of
its budget that can be funded from federal sources.

Student Tuition and Fees

If the proposed community college is to be comprehensive in its offerings and
is viewed as an open-door institution, designed to provide a variety of educational fare to all high school graduates and others who can profit from attending,
then the tuition and fees must be kept reasonably low. If the people are to be
served in a community, regardless of their economic status, then the tuition
should not be an inhibiting factor. By its very definition, the community college
is a low-cost institution of public higher education.

The council for higher education should make a study of typical tuition rates
in nearby community colleges and in those of surrounding states. Such data will
assist the council in determining the amount of budget income that will be
available from tuition. Miscellaneous fees, such as a student activity fee, are not
usually computed as part of the budget, but are listed as auxiliary enterprises.

Gifts and Grants

Personal gifts and donations from individuals, and foundation or industry
grants are not a significant part of most community college budgets. However,
some institutions are able to secure occasional funds of this nature. It is
recommended that a developing public two-year college not count on such
moneys as a regular source of income.

Summary

Securing adequate funding is essential to the successful establishment of a community college. There are five usual sources of funds for public two-year colleges: federal, state, local sponsor, student tuition and fees, and private gifts and grants.

Acquiring a local sponsor for the proposed new college is the real key to all other sources of funding. Depending on state law, possible local sponsoring agencies may be one of the following: a directly elected board of trustees with its own taxing power; a county or combination of counties; a school board of combination of school boards; or a municipal governing body. Some states do not provide for local community college control; here a state community college board and department direct the colleges.

From the different alternatives, the most viable sponsor for the local community college must be chosen by the council for higher education. The basic principles in identifying a local sponsor are: (1) to select the agency that can get the necessary funds most directly, and (2) to establish the broadest possible taxing base.

Determining needed funds is the next step in planning. It is suggested that the council establish at least four task forces to develop preliminary plans for the organization and building of the proposed college. The purpose is to generate sufficient data to enable fairly accurate cost projections. The task forces should comprehensively represent the community and should include experts in these specific task areas: philosophy and program; administrative organization and staffing; facilities planning; and finance. The council for higher education receives all task force reports, acts upon them, and coordinates them into a comprehensive publication. The final report is then disseminated to key members of the power structure; business, industrial, government, and professional leaders; and to the public through continuation of the previously established program of public information.

With all of the necessary data on hand, it is hoped that the members of the potential local sponsoring agency will sense a feeling of community support for the college and will agree to sponsor it. If a referendum is required or if the college is established by the direct election of a board of trustees, then the council will help to organize the machinery for the necessary public votes.

Further consultations must be held with appropriate state officials to determine the steps required by state law and regulation to effect the establishment of the local college. Also, the availability of federal funds should be checked out with the area congressman, the American Association of Junior Colleges, and the state department of higher education. It is important to determine the percentage of the new college budget that can be funded from state and federal sources.

The impact of student tuition fees on the budget must be assessed. Tuition should be kept reasonably low in an open door, comprehensive community college. A study of typical tuition rates in nearby community colleges and in those of surrounding states will help the council to determine the amount of budget income that will be available from tuition.

Since gifts and grants are not a significant part of most community college budgets, it is recommended that a new college not count on such moneys as a regular source of income.

Suggested Activities and Problems

1. Defend the hypothesis that a directly elected board of trustees is superior to any other local sponsorship arrangement.

2. Assume that you are chairman of the finance task force described in this chapter. Outline the procedures you would use to determine projected operating and capital budgets for the new community college.

3. Develop an expanded program of public information designed to inform the citizens of a community about the final report of the council for higher education.

4. A local political leader has just announced publicly that he will oppose the establishment of a community college in the county, despite a positive recommendation from the council for higher education. How would you handle this situation as the chairman of the council?

5. Study the community college laws in your state. Write a short paper summarizing the various sources of funds available for establishing and operating a community college. Show the percentages that may be expected from each source.

6. State and defend a philosophy on student tuition at two-year public community colleges.

Selected Readings

Blocker, Clyde E., Robert H. Plummer, and Richard C. Richardson, Jr., *The Two-Year College: A Social Synthesis,* Chap. 4. Englewood Cliffs, N.J.: Prentice-Hall, Inc., 1965.

The Open-Door Colleges, Chap. 8. A special report and recommendations by The Carnegie Commission on Higher Education. New York: McGraw-Hill Book Company, 1970.

Reynolds, James W., *The Junior College,* Chap. 7. New York: The Center for Applied Research in Education, Inc., 1965.

Shoemaker, Elwood A., "A Study of the Factors Inhibiting Establishment of Community Colleges in Pennsylvania." Unpublished doctoral dissertation, Temple University, 1970.

Wattenbarger, James L., Bob N. Cage, and L. H. Arney, *The Community Junior College: Target Population, Program Costs and Cost Differentials.* National Educational Finance Project, Special Study No. 6. Gainesville, Fla.: University of Florida, 1970.

4

Guidelines for
Appointing and Organizing
the Board of Trustees

When the local sponsor and the state have approved the establishment of a community college, attention is focused on the election or appointment of the board of trustees. In accordance with existing state laws and regulations, board members will either be elected by the area voters or appointed by the local sponsoring agency. In state-controlled community college systems, the board may be elected statewide or appointed by the governor.

Regardless of the method of selection, the composition of a board to serve a comprehensive, two-year public college is a vital matter. There are few in-depth studies of the characteristics of community college trustees. In a general survey of college and university trustees, which included a 20 percent sample of public two-year institutions, Hartnett found the following biographical characteristics:

> Data regarding some of the more basic characteristics of college and university trustees conform to previous findings and are not surprising in terms of the nature of the description they provide. In general, trustees are male, in their 50's (though, nationally more than a third are over 60), white (fewer than two percent in our sample are Negro), well-educated, and financially well-off (more than half have annual incomes exceeding $30,000). They occupy prestige occupations, frequently in medicine, law and education, but more often as business executives (in the total sample over 35 percent are executives of manufacturing, merchandising or investment firms and at private universities nearly 50 percent hold such positions). As a group, then, they personify "success" in the usual American sense of that word.
>
> Most are Protestants, with only four percent being Jewish and 17 percent Catholic, the majority of the latter serving on boards of Catholic

institutions. Trustees also tend to identify themselves as Republicans (approximately 58 percent overall) and most often regard themselves as politically moderate (61%) rather than conservative (21%) or liberal (15%).[1]

Characteristics of Florida community junior college trustees were reported by Gilliland and Nunnery from a survey covering 89 percent of the trustee membership.

1. The trustees were overwhelmingly white and male (97.6 per cent white and 89.2 per cent male).
2. They were a well-educated group (70.3 per cent held at least one college degree).
3. Chronologically, the trustees were mature (1.8 per cent were under 35 years of age, 21.8 per cent were in the 35 to 44 category, and 40.6 per cent were 55 years of age or older).
4. They overwhelmingly purported to be Democratic in political affiliation and Protestant in religious preference (86.7 per cent said they were Democrats, and 86.1 per cent indicated a Protestant affiliation).
5. The higher status occupational groups were overrepresented in the trustee group (53.0 per cent were in the professional and technical or the managerial, official, proprietary groups, whereas none were in the skilled, semiskilled, and unskilled groups).
6. Economically, the trustees were relatively affluent (9.7 per cent reported yearly incomes of under $10,000, while 51.5 per cent reported yearly incomes of $20,000 or more).

Opinions of trustees on matters relating to community colleges were reported as follows:

1. 93.3 per cent agreed or tended to agree with the statement that enrollment should be a privilege—not a right.
2. 84.8 per cent agreed or tended to agree that post-high school education should be available to anyone who is able to benefit from it.
3. They strongly favored a comprehensive, balanced program and were quite supportive of the notion that programs should be planned for students with very different ability levels.[2]

Criteria for Selection of Board Members

Although studies such as those quoted above give some clues regarding membership on boards of trustees, there is not necessarily a significant rela-

---

[1] Rodney T. Hartnett, *College and University Trustees: Their Backgrounds, Roles, and Educational Attitudes.* Copyright ©1969 by Educational Testing Service; All Rights Reserved. Reprinted by permission.

[2] J. Richard Gilliland and Michael Y. Nunnery, "Florida Trustees: Characteristics and Opinions," *Junior College Journal,* 40, No. 5 (1970), 26-27.

tionship between background characteristics and potential contributions as a board member. Furthermore, it is far from certain that governors, county commissioners, the mayor, or the electorate will pay any attention to desirable criteria for selection of community college trustees. Nevertheless, members of the council for higher education, the county superintendent of schools, and others with influence should do everything possible to assure appointment or election of qualified board members. Also, every effort should be made to keep partisan politics out of the selection process. Where trustees are elected directly, this should be on a nonpartisan basis.

The following criteria should be discussed with those responsible for appointing or electing members of the community college board.

1. A minimum residence requirement of two to three years in the area is desirable. Local problems and conditions are usually understood better by those who have lived with them awhile.

2. A racial mix should be sought. Minority groups such as Negroes, Puerto Ricans, Mexican-Americans, and American Indians ought to have representation on the board.

3. There should be an age range, from young to mature.

4. It is desirable to have both men and women trustees.

5. All candidates should be civic-minded and committed to service on a community college board. The first few years are especially demanding in time and effort.

6. One or more members of the council for higher education should be encouraged to serve. This provides continuity with the previous work in establishing the college.

7. It is highly desirable to have various religions represented in the total makeup of the board.

8. A good board is cosmopolitan in nature—with persons from government, education, labor, business, industry, and the professions. This will help to assure a range of income levels, as well as a variety of occupations represented.

9. It is important that several members of the new board have demonstrated leadership ability.

10. Political affiliation is not a valid criterion for board membership. Every attempt should be made to resist political appointments to college boards. One enlightened county governing board asked all newly appointed college board members to sign an affidavit that they would not participate in partisan politics while serving as trustees, and for two years thereafter. This policy could well be emulated by all appointing bodies.

If the college board is directly elected, the council for higher education should assume as one of its final tasks the education of the public concerning the criteria for selection discussed above. Upon the appointment or election of a board of trustees for the new college, the council for higher education can treat itself to a farewell dinner, amid self-congratulatory speeches on a job well done.

Organizing the Board of Trustees

As soon as possible after their appointment or election, the members of the new board of trustees will meet to get acquainted and to take the initial organizational steps. A typical board will have from seven to fifteen members, depending on the provisions of state law in this regard. The first meeting will involve the following activities and procedures:

1. Spend considerable time in self-introductions and getting to know one another. The board will be working together for a long time, and the members will need to know each other very well.
2. Discuss ways of organizing the board and developing initial operating procedure. Consider inviting to succeeding meetings such resource persons as the state director of two-year colleges, and possibly a community college president or board chairman from a nearby college in the state to assist with preliminary organizational details.
3. Decide on procedures for electing officers by the next meeting—either from the floor or via a nominating committee. The board will need a chairman, vice-chairman, and secretary-treasurer.
4. Establish a meeting date, and plan on regular monthly meetings, with an additional date identified for supplementary meetings in the early stages.

The remainder of this chapter deals with organizational procedures and guidelines for board members, as they develop working relationships and plan for the tasks ahead. Specific board responsibilities and duties are discussed, and suggestions are offered to facilitate the operation of the board.

The election of officers is necessary to the effective conduct of board business. Members will want to identify promising leaders in the group as chairman and vice-chairman. A secretary-treasurer with some accounting and secretarial skills might be found among the membership. Terms of office are usually prescribed by law. If not, interim terms may be established until the board adopts its bylaws.

The search for a president is one of the most important tasks the board will ever undertake, and the initiation of the process should be one of the first main items of business. The chairman usually appoints an ad hoc presidential committee to organize the search for a chief administrator. Because of the

FIGURE 4-1

critical nature of this process, and the need for special board guidance, Chapter 5 is devoted to the presidential search and selection procedure.

Since the philosophy and thrust of the institution will be largely determined in the initial months by the president working with the trustees, it is strongly recommended that the board make only those decisions that are absolutely necessary before the president is on the job.

Roberts Rules of Order is a sufficient guide for conduct of meetings until the board can develop its own by laws. If there is an attorney among the trustees, he can be delegated the task of drawing up tentative bylaws. Otherwise, they can wait until a solicitor or counsel is appointed.

The solicitor and auditor work closely with the president and other officials of the college, as well as with members of the board of trustees. The solicitor will be called upon for his legal opinion on many decisions as the college develops. The auditor will assist in setting up the permanent accounting system for the college and then will conduct regular audits. The chairman of the board may appoint an ad hoc committee to screen candidates for these two positions, but its final selection should be delayed until the president can take part in the decision.

Concentrated reading and study by the trustees are imperative at this stage in the evolution of the board. All members should read as widely as possible about the role of the board, especially in relationship to the president (see the bibilography for Chapter 4). It has been stated by many that the task of the board is to make policy, and the job of the president is to develop administrative procedures for carrying out the policy and operating the college. However, the relationship is never that clear-cut or simple. The board, for example, will usually look to the president as professional leader to submit proposed policies for the trustees' consideration and possible modification. Most boards are not capable of developing policy without assistance. However, it is true that the board's primary reponsibility is goal setting and policy determination. Toward that end, the trustees may want to supplement their reading about roles by setting up a workshop for themselves. The president and board chairman from a nearby community college (discussed earlier in the organizational steps) could be invited to conduct a Saturday session designed to define the role of the board and the president.

Start-up funds are a necessity; the board should prepare a basic budget anticipating possible expenditures for the next six months. This will include president's salary, secretary's salary, board expenses, legal fees, office furnishings and expenses, printing costs, travel expense, utilities, office rental, insurance, and contingency. The local sponsor should be requested to appropriate the necessary start-up moneys and should also be notified that a revised budget will be submitted after the president is appointed and makes his budget recommendations to the board.

Relationships between the board of trustees and the local sponsoring agency need to develop in a positive way from the start. If the college board does not have its own taxing power, then it usually must present its budgets to the local sponsor for approval. The sponsor may approve, modify, or reject budgets. During the first few years of operation, a "honeymoon" atmosphere exists. The community has just approved, either by direct vote, or through its governing agency, the establishment of a community college. If the board of trustees is realistic and responsible in its budget requests, it may expect to have the cooperation of the taxing board.

It is most important for the college board to act at all times as the independent policy-making body it is. The local sponsor has two main responsibilities: to appoint the trustees, and to approve the college budgets. The trustees must assume the authority of determining college needs, policy, and programs. They must be politically independent in all their actions. The board must establish its autonomy early and learn to be politically aware without becoming politically involved. The relationship between a board of trustees and the local sponsor is critical, and the board must earn and maintain its independence of action for the best interests of the college.

The council for higher education has labored long and hard to establish the new college. The board of trustees might well show its appreciation by inviting the council members to a dinner meeting. At this time, thanks can be adequately expressed, and a progress report presented. (Note: In the future, make sure that the council members are invited to opening convocations, dedications, and commencements. They will appreciate the remembrance.)

The organization of committees is a great American custom. However, aside from the ad hoc groups already suggested, the board should not establish permanent committees. If the size of the board is from five to nine members, it can operate very satisfactorily as a committee-of-the-whole. Advantages are several: (1) All members are totally informed at all times on developing policy and decisions. (2) There is some saving of trustees' time, since committees must meet on their own and then report back to the full board. (3) Committees in such areas as finance, facilities, and curriculum tend to get involved in adminis-trative operations, which should be the clear responsibility of the president. Consideration of any permanent committees should therefore await the arrival of the president and the writing of bylaws.

Study of existing board policy manuals is recommended at this time. An increasing number of community colleges now have well-developed policy and procedures manuals, which provide the basis for the operation of the insti-tutions. When the president arrives, he will be delighted to work with trustees who understand the scope of policies needed to launch a community college.

A statement of philosophy and purpose is one of the first policy documents that should be prepared. In anticipation of the president's leadership in this area, board members might well do some basic reading in the philosophy of com-prehensive public community colleges. They will soon have to decide precisely what kind of two-year college they propose to create. The die may already partially be cast by the preliminary need studies of the council for higher education. The trustees should read all the background studies leading to the establishment of the community college as well as some general books and articles on community colleges.

Pressures to open the college early will develop. There will also be suggestions on possible sites for the campus, and architects will be vying for the job of college designer. Let the board concentrate all possible time and effort on presidential selection and let it delay any decisions on matters such as opening date, site selection, architects, interim and permanent campuses until the president arrives and can study the entire situation. After he has given his recommendations, the board can consider a timetable for master planning and for opening the college to students.

Summary

When the establishment of a community college has been approved, attention is focused on the election or appointment of a board of trustees. Whether board members are elected or appointed depends on state law.

Typical background characteristics of college and university trustees may be found in the literature. With regard to criteria for selection, the members of the council for higher education and others with influence should do everything possible to assure the appointment or election of qualified board members. Also, every effort should be made to keep partisan politics out of the selection process. Among others, the following criteria should be considered: minimum residence; racial mix; age range; dedication to civic enterprise; leadership ability; and experience in government, education, business, industry, and the professions.

As soon as possible after their appointment or election, the members of the new board of trustees will meet to get acquainted and to take the initial organizational steps. The following areas, among others, should receive priority attention by the board: election of officers; determination of initial operating procedures; the search for and selection of a president; concentrated reading and study; securing start-up funds; and establishing positive relationships between the board and the local sponsoring agency. The selection of a president is the most important responsibility of the trustees and should be given top priority. Decisions on matters such as opening date, site selection, architects, and interim and permanent campuses should be delayed until the president arrives and makes his studies and recommendations. Only then will the board be in a position to consider a timetable for master planning and for opening the college.

Suggested Activities and Problems

1. Examine and compare three studies on the characteristics of college board members. Summarize your conclusions.
2. Develop a comprehensive, annotated list of criteria for selection of community college trustees. Defend each criterion.
3. In a paper, attempt to prove or disprove the statement that "Political affiliation is not a valid criterion for board membership."
4. You are the newly elected chairman of a community college board that has just been appointed. Prepare opening remarks to your fellow board members outlining their initial reponsibilities as you see them.
5. Defend or refute the statement that "The search for a president is one of the most important tasks the board will ever undertake."

Selected Readings

Cohen, Arthur M., *Dateline '79: Heretical Concepts for the Community College*, Beverly Hills, Calif.: Glencoe Press, a division of The Macmillan Company, 1969.

Gilliland, J. Richard and Michael Y. Nunnery, "Florida Trustees: Characteristics and Opinions," *Junior College Journal*, 40, No. 5 (1970), 25-29.

Hartnett, Rodney T., *College and University Trustees: Their Backgrounds*,

Roles, and Educational Attitudes. Princeton, N.J.: Educational Testing Service, 1969.

Henderson, Algo D., *The Role of the Governing Board.* Washington, D.C.: Association of Governing Boards of Universities and Colleges, 1967.

Johnson, B. Lamar, ed., *The Junior College Board of Trustees.* Junior College Leadership Program, Occasional Report No. 16. Los Angeles: University of California, Los Angeles 1970.

Parker, Paul W., "Profile of the Kansas Trustees," *Junior College Journal,* 40, No. 7 (1970), 58-70.

Rauh, Morton A., *The Trusteeship of Colleges and Universities.* New York: McGraw-Hill Book Company, 1969.

Richardson, Richard C., Clyde E. Blocker, and Louis W. Bender, *Governance for the Two-Year College.* Englewood Cliffs, N.J.: Prentice-Hall, Inc., 1972, chap. 3.

5

Search
for a President

The Board's First Job

The selection of a community college president is not only the board's first job, but it is likely to be the most important task that it will perform. The president sets the tone for the institution. He, and he alone, is responsible for the organizational climate that can determine whether or not the students, faculty, and community have confidence in the educational enterprise and are happy in their associations with the college.

It is not possible to make an intelligent search for a president until goals for the institution have been formulated and the job he is to perform has been delineated, so that it is clearly understood by all members of the board of trustees.

Herron stressed the importance of these preliminary steps when he wrote:

> Selecting a president is a task of the board and one that should be given its most scrupulous attention. The selection process is tantamount to obtaining the most capable person for the job. The board can follow some guidelines to ensure an orderly process in the selection. Having formulated the goals of the institution, the board must now formulate the job description and expectation of the new president. It must know what type of individual it is seeking before it begins the process of interviews.[1]

Board members serving their first term in office likely will not have the slightest idea of the importance of the key position of the president, and they certainly

---

[1]Orley R. Herron, Jr., *The Role of the Trustees* (Scranton, Pa.: International Textbook Company, 1969), p. 52.

will not be aware of all the tasks he must perform. They must not only be acquainted with the job of the president but also with the personal and professional qualifications required to be successful in the position.

Persons preparing for community college administration, will also benefit from an understanding of the scope of the presidency and of the necessary qualifications.

Therefore, we must discuss the role of the community college president, and the personal attributes, professional training, and experience that are necessary to perform this exacting role.

Importance of the Position

Our nation is committed to the concept that higher education should be within the reach of all individuals who can benefit from it. Necessity dictates that education becomes a lifelong process. Many individuals will need to prepare for at least three different jobs during their lifetime. In addition, old and young alike will require education for avocational pursuits. The institution that most nearly will meet the above needs is the community college. This is the scope of the educational enterprise for which the board of trustees will have to find a president.

As suggested in the introduction to this chapter, the president, to a great extent, makes or breaks the community college. Initially, he plans the educational facilities, selects personnel, shapes the educational policies and academic standards, makes and administers the budget, assumes responsibility for standards of students' conduct, and secures community cooperation and support.

The above activities do not begin to explain the complexity of the job. The position of college president is considered by many to be one of the least enviable in the academic world. There are numerous former college presidents who have gladly returned to teaching, research, and writing after facing an almost impossible situation at the top.

In a recent magazine article Horn quotes William H. Cowley, who gave up the college presidency to become one of America's premier professors of higher education of the last twenty years. Cowley said, "A college president is one of the most harassed, one of the most put-upon people in American life. He is a hewer of wood and a drawer of water, a dray horse, a galley slave, a bellhop, a hack, and a nursemaid, all wrapped up in one."[2] The position is extremely important but also very difficult.

We shall examine the many roles a community college president performs in order to get a better understanding of the qualifications needed.

[2] Francis H. Horn, "The Job of the President," *Liberal Education,* 55, No. 3 (1969), 388.

The President As an Administrator

Administration means different things to different people. Many individuals, including some administrators, believe that the "nuts and bolts" of administration constitute the total job. Too many persons in administrative positions spend their time in shuffling papers and performing other minutiae.

To get agreement among authorities concerning a definition of administration is difficult if not impossible. Throughout history writers have defined it as: (1) management, (2) organization, (3) leadership, (4) process, (5) taxonomy, (6) decision making, (7) human engineering, (8) planning, or (9) a combination of several of the above. No attempt has been made to arrange the above list chronologically, and it is not to be considered as all-inclusive. Neither are the items mutually exclusive.

The present trend to assist the student and practitioner in grasping a better understanding of administration has been the search for a theoretical basis for it. One text on instructional leadership explains this new trend in the following manner:

> After many years of suspicion and misunderstanding, the subject of theory has become a respectable topic for discussion in texts on educational administration. The imaginary chasm between theory and practice is at last being bridged. Writers, professors, and practitioners in the field are beginning to agree that, perhaps, there is nothing as practical as theory after all.[3]

This is not a text on administrative theory. The purpose of mentioning it here is to alert boards of trustees to the trend toward theory. Many books on administration now treat that topic. Several excellent references on administrative theory are listed at the end of this chapter. Board members would be wise to have more than a casual knowledge of the role of theory in administration, so that they can make better judgments in the selection process, and have a more accurate picture of whether or not the new president is fulfilling his role expectations.

The community college president spends a large portion of his workday just planning. He spends long hours in planning with trustees and subordinates. He also plans alone. Moreover he spends time in reviewing and analyzing reports and in authorizing and approving expenditures.

A recent study on how 180 college presidents spent their time revealed that 35.6 percent of their time was utilized in planning and other administrative tasks.[4] The phases of planning and the other administrative tasks mentioned above follow.

---

[3] Ross L. Neagley and N. Dean Evans, *Handbook for Effective Supervision of Instruction,* 2nd ed. (Englewood Cliffs, N.J.: Prentice-Hall, Inc.,© 1970), p. 23.

[4] Herbert J. Walberg, "The Academic President: Colleague, Administrator or

Planning with the Trustees. In the initial stages of designing and building a community college, the president will spend a much larger proportion of his time in administrative planning with the trustees than he will after the college is established. The scope of this initial planning is described by B. Lamar Johnson as follows:

1. Plan, develop, and prepare to offer an educational program designed to achieve the agreed-upon purposes of the college: *Curriculum and Instruction.*
2. Enroll, counsel, and organize students, and provide out-of-class services for them: *Student Personnel.*
3. Employ and organize a staff to administer and to teach the program of the college: *Staff Personnel.*
4. Secure and administer funds to pay the operational and capital outlay costs of the college: *Finance.*
5. Provide adequate plant and facilities in and with which to carry on the educational program: *Plant and Facilities.*
6. Enlist the interest, support, and participation of the community in the college and its program: *Community Service and Relationships.*[5]

The above major tasks are certainly not performed only by planning with trustees. Many other individuals are involved. It is true, however, that in the initial stages of planning and building a community college certain aspects of all these major tasks are considered by the president and the board of trustees. The planning is not only concerned with a wide range of topics but it also includes working with the entire board, possibly committees of the board, and sometimes individual trustees.

In discussing the working relationship of the college president to the board of trustees Praetor explains:

> In working with the board of trustees the president is ever conscious of his responsibility to assist them to understand and appreciate the educational program and the needs of the institution. He is responsible for the two-way communication between the campus communities and the board, and in the process he needs to emphasize the special responsibilities expected of the agencies whose activities he correlates . . . Therefore the president has to be a skillful blender of different points of view which will result in decisions being respected by all agencies affected.[6]

Spokesman," *Educational Record*, 50, No. 2 (1969), 197. (Some of the headings in this chapter were adapted from this same article.)

[5]B. Lamar Johnson, *Starting a Community Junior College* (Washington, D.C.: American Association of Junior Colleges, 1964), p. 5.

[6]Ralph Praetor, *The College President* (Washington, D.C.: The Center for Applied Research in Education, Inc., 1963), pp. 58-59.

Planning with Subordinates. A breakdown of administrative tasks reported in Walberg's survey indicated that the 180 college presidents studied spent 13.5 percent of their time planning with subordinates.[7] Especially in the initial stages of a community college, the president has to spend much additional time to plan with them. The successful college administrator knows that staff members (and students, for that matter) must be involved in planning all phases of the enterprise to the degree that they have something to contribute.

The topics around which the planning and discussion with subordinates revolve are the same ones that constituted the planning areas with the board of trustees. In planning with the trustees, *policy* is being made, whereas in planning with the subordinates, *recommendations* are given for policies, as well as suggestions for the implementation of policies already in effect. In these sessions with subordinates, the introduction of new ideas by faculty, other staff members, and students takes place. Hopefully many of the policies formulated by the president and board of trustees are based on ideas generated in the planning sessions with staff members.

Planning Alone. Walberg found that the college presidents he studied utilized approximately 9.6 percent of their time planning by themselves.[8] It is assumed that this planning took place as part of the regular workday. In addition, the successful college president is continuously planning during all his waking hours and, possibly, even when he is asleep—if we can place any credence in what writers in the field say about our subconscious self.

The college administrator, then, must be a planner. He must be adept at working with trustees, subordinates, and alone. This interpretation of administration is much more sophisticated than a mere execution of policy.

Reviewing and Analyzing Reports. One complaint common to most administrators concerns the mountain of paper work they face each day. Some administrators have jokingly been labeled as "paper shufflers." Reviewing and analyzing reports takes a considerable amount of the college president's time. Whether or not it should is a moot question. The authors take the position that the community college president must know the content of the reports that pass over his desk. They propose that much valuable time of the top administrator may be saved by having other members of the staff (e.g., an administrative assistant) do the reviews and analyses and then brief the president on the contents.

In searching for a president, boards of trustees would be wise to investigate how much time potential candidates spend on paper work in their present positions before they are given serious consideration. Boards should steer clear

[7]Walberg, "The Academic President," p. 197.
[8]Ibid., p. 197.

of applicants who derive their satisfactions from wading through "tons" of paper work.

Authorizing and Approving Expenditures. The administration of the community college budget is a crucial task. This will be dealt with in detail in Chapter 11. It is sufficient to mention here that the community college president must be a wise spender. There are never enough funds. To establish priorities and to see that they are adhered to without offending staff members whose activities are way down on the priority list requires administrative leadership of the highest degree.

Here again, the individual selected for the top administrative position in the community college must be able to work effectively with all members of his administrative team. In this instance, the dean of academic affairs and the dean of administrative services will be the most concerned members of his team, although all staff members will be affected as decisions are being made concerning expenditures.

The President As an Educational Leader

During this century over 600 different investigations have been made of the nature of leadership. In one review of literature on the topic, Bass found more than 130 different definitions of leadership.[9]

Leadership of the community college president, as the authors visualize it, is concerned largely with two aspects, namely, (1) formulating and changing organizational objectives and (2) moving the organization in the direction of these objectives. This is in keeping with the present emphasis on innovation and change in educational administration. The community college president can be the key to educational change and innovation in his institution. In bringing this about, he works with other administrative staff members, faculty, and students.

Cohen and Roueche indicate the importance of educational leadership in community colleges when they state:

> There are compelling reasons why leaders rather than administrators are needed in American two-year colleges. Currently, most of the institutions operate along traditional lines. Their practices, modes of operation, goals, outlooks, and philosophy stem from the university and the public schools. Yet the junior college has been charged with unique tasks—e.g., designing instructional forms suitable to a wide range of students, and being responsible for the entire community's educational needs. It is supposed to be a teaching institution; accordingly, it cannot function well by perpetuating forms developed by and for types of schools in which student learning is a consideration secondary to research or to wholesale sociali-

[9]Bernard H. Bass, *Leadership, Psychology, and Organizational Behavior* (New York: Harper & Row, Publishers, 1960), p. 87.

zation. The fulfillment of a unique mission demands unique forms. Leaders, not administrators, can create them.[10]

According to Walberg's study, college presidents spent 22.7 percent of their time in leadership activities of the type discussed in this section.[11]

Working with Faculty on Curriculum and Instruction. A community college is only as good as its curricular offerings and the opportunities for learning it provides. Although it is expected that the dean of academic affairs will take the leadership in the area of curriculum and instruction, the leadership of the president is also very important. Changes that do not receive his approval have little chance of being adopted, or of surviving, if they are initiated without his blessing.

Designing the various curricula (see Chapter 8) is not a simple task. If they truly are to meet the needs of the wide range of students, continuous planning is necessary.

The same may be said of instruction. The president sees that the necessary funds are available for well-prepared staff members and the new instructional technology.

In the initial phases of planning and building a community college, curriculum and instruction loom as even more important tasks. Unless careful planning has taken place in respect to the purposes and educational offerings of the college, intelligent decisions cannot be reached concerning the personnel needed, the buildings and facilities required, and the finances that must be raised.

Much of this early work on curriculum may be done by the president working with a limited number of staff members employed before the college opens (see Chapter 6).

Counseling Faculty on Personal Problems.[12] There are usually only a few problem instructors in each community college, but all faculty at some time or other have problems. Like all human beings, instructors have financial problems, marital problems, and worries about their offspring. They become ill, lose loved ones, run afoul of the law, and suffer from disasters of various types. Any of the vicissitudes of life are bound in some way to affect the quality of instruction. Some individuals become stronger and better persons as a result of these experiences; others may be defeated by them. Although some community college presidents may be reluctant to become involved in the solution of

---

[10] Arthur M. Cohen and John E. Roueche, *Institutional Administrator or Educational Leader* (Washington, D.C.: American Association of Junior Colleges, 1969), p. 12.

[11] Walberg, "The Academic President," p. 197.

[12] Most of this section on counseling faculty is quoted and adapted from Neagley and Evans, *Handbook for Effective Supervision of Instruction*, pp. 195-96. Reprinted with permission of the publisher.

instructors' personal problems, those who *do* know that the results can be definitely rewarding.

Good personnel leadership requires that administrators show some interest in instructors' personal problems and assist in their solutions whenever it is possible. However, good rapport must exist between the president and the instructor before this type of assistance is welcome or even approved. After rapport has been established, some faculty will come to the president for help with personal problems. If a feeling of mutual respect does not exist, any assistance offered to the instructor may be misconstrued as meddling in affairs that are of no concern to the college president.

Sometimes all that instructors need is the sympathetic ear of someone who is personally interested in them and who can be trusted to keep in confidence what he has heard.

As the college grows larger, the president may become further removed from the personal problems of the faculty. Then, too, deans and division or department chairmen can and should share this role. However, the college president who remains approachable and takes time to listen to the personal problems of staff members irrespective of the size of the organization is a better educational leader than one who has no time.

Formal and Informal Interaction with Faculty. The community college president must be prepared to allocate a segment of his workday for formal and informal interaction with faculty members. This time is in addition to the periods spent in planning with subordinates, working on curriculum, and in counseling faculty on personal matters.

Committee, faculty senate, and regular staff meetings account for a sizable portion of this interaction time with faculty. In some institutions confrontations and collective bargaining are taking additional time of the president, depending upon the role he chooses to play in negotiations.

The president who desires an organization with an open climate will provide numerous opportunities for faculty members, individually and in small groups, to have informal contacts with him. He knows that this time is well spent.

Participating in Instruction. Should the community college president assume any teaching responsibilities? There are those who take the position that if he performs his job adequately, he does not have time to teach. Others contend that if the president assumes the responsibility for teaching at least one course during the academic year, it will help to bridge the widening gap between faculty and administration. It likewise gives the president a better understanding of some of the problems faced by the faculty, and it provides him regular contacts with members of the student body.

If the president is unable to assume a regular teaching assignment because of the pressure of his position, it might be wise for him to serve as guest lecturer and as a substitute instructor on a regular basis. Minicourses taught by the president also could be offered from time to time.

Meeting with Students. As suggested above, the community college president who has dialogue with the students has a better understanding of their viewpoints and they in turn can develop a better appreciation for the problems faced by the administration.

Although most community college campuses have been relatively quiet in recent years compared to the university confrontations, campus unrest may escalate if administrators do not handle legitimate student needs and requests sensitively. The president who meets regularly with students individually and in groups, and who is willing to listen to what they have to say is less likely to have campus demonstrations and other severe forms of protest. Student representation on all college committees and student involvement in making decisions that affect them also can prevent or ameliorate student-administration conflict.

Opportunities should be provided for students to know the community college president as a human being rather than only as an authority figure.

As has been mentioned elsewhere in this chapter, students have many worthwhile suggestions for the improvement of the institution and its program. The wise president provides time in his schedule for frequent dialogues with student groups and with individual students.

The President As a Public Relations Expert

The president represents the college to the public. His actions and the statements he makes in speeches and in writing can affect the reputation of the institution either positively or negatively. He meets with the public concerning college affairs and participates in community activities. He communicates through speeches, news releases, and correspondence, and he raises funds and entertains. Almost a third of his time is spent in these activities.[13]

Meeting with Outsiders on College Affairs. In the planning and development stage of the community college, the president will spend a considerable amount of time meeting with outsiders on college-related activities. For example, he will be meeting with representatives of school systems and community organizations, officials from county, federal, state, and accrediting agencies, and administrators from other higher education institutions in the community college service area. The outcomes of these meetings may determine the progress of the new institution for many years to come. These relationships, once established, must be continuously reviewed and maintained.

[13]Walberg, "The Academic President," p. 197.

As the institution matures, the community college president should set up lines of communication with the alumni. They can become potent forces in furthering the work of the college.

Participating in Community Life. Like so many other public officials, the community college president can rarely shed his professional image. Whatever he does or says will be judged in light of his academic position. His family also may expect to be in the same limelight. This academic aura, however, should not prevent him from participating in community life. He doubtless will become active in the church of his choice and will often join one of the local service organizations. He will participate in community drives, serve on committees that are trying to improve the life of the community, and show concern for the political and economic aspects of life in the community.

Communicating through Speeches, News Releases, and Correspondence. The community college president should be a fluent and interesting speaker. He will be in constant demand as an after-dinner speaker, commencement speaker, and featured orator on programs of various community organizations. Here again, the manner in which he performs will reflect on the institution of which he is president.

News releases from the president's office are read with great interest by faculty, students, and residents of the college service area. Ability to write in a clear concise style, free of clichs and jargon, is an important characteristic to look for in candidates for the community college presidency.

Clarity also is important in correspondence. Ability to include a personal touch in writing that reveals the president as a warm human being rather than an automaton is also a highly desirable trait to look for in applicants for the position.

Although the ability to communicate effectively through the spoken and written word is essential for success in the community college presidency, the willingness to set up and maintain these channels of communication is likewise of great importance. It is safe to hazard a guess that more top administrators possess these communication skills than use them effectively. Unfortunately, the ability to communicate does not insure the desire and willingness to keep the faculty, student body, and public informed. The candidate to look for is the one who *can* and *will* communicate effectively.

Securing Financial Support. The president of the publicly supported community college probably will not spend as much time on this activity as will the head of a private institution. However, it must not be assumed that he will be freed from this responsibility entirely. As head of a publicly supported institution, his budget is subject to the whims of one or more of the following: (1) legislators, (2) local boards of education, and (3) county boards. Federal funds also are available for special programs, and business and industry may become involved in cooperative programs.

The president who sits and calmly waits for the money to come rolling in will not survive long. He must vigorously fight for the approval of his budget and for increased financial support from present sources. Moreover, he must constantly be on the lookout for new sources of revenue to support the educational enterprise.

As the numbers of alumni increase, they may desire to contribute funds to the institution for special projects. The enlightened community college president does not overlook this source of support. As indicated earlier, he encourages a strong alumni association.

It would be hoped that the community college president would be able to spend a large proportion of his time on educational leadership activities, but without financial support, these activities suffer.

Entertaining Officially. On certain occasions throughout the year the community college president is expected to entertain guests. The school year frequently is begun with a social event for trustees and faculty members. Trustees are sometimes invited to dinner and visiting dignitaries usually are entertained by the president. Teas, cocktail parties, and discussions are held in his home from time to time. In considering the fitness of a candidate for this role, his wife and family will bear investigation. More than one college president has failed as an official entertainer because his wife and family were not up to the task.

The President As a Scholar

The old concept of the college and university president was that he was a scholar first and an administrator and educational leader next. However, this is no longer true. The demands of the job are so varied and great that there is little time for the president to conduct research, to write, and to carry on other scholarly pursuits. Also, the community college is a teaching institution and not a research-oriented one. However, this should change.

The real educational leader will be interested in research and writing. He will encourage experimentation and research in the classroom of the action-research type. He will write an article now and then for publication, and he will encourage the members of his staff to do likewise. He will prepare papers to be delivered at national and state meetings and he even may find time to write a monograph or book if he really has something to offer.

Above all, the president must find time for thought and renewal. He must read widely and attend educational meetings in order to keep up to date in a very rapidly changing field. He may even take refresher courses in the administration of higher education from time to time.

Selection Procedures

After becoming acquainted with the job of the community college president and defining the goals of the institution, the board of trustees is ready to begin selection procedures.

Selecting the First President

The remaining sections of this chapter offer specific, practical advice to boards of trustees on the process of selecting a president.

The Selection Committee. It is doubtful that the entire board of trustees will initially want to become involved in the search for the new president. Usually, it is helpful to establish a board committee charged with the responsibility to search for candidates for the position and to do the initial screening. One researcher found that 87 percent of the presidential selections in his study were made by special committees.[14] After careful screening by the committee, a selected number of candidates may be presented to the entire board.

Some boards prefer to engage a consultant or consulting firm to locate candidates, screen applications, and assist in interviewing candidates. Many universities provide these consultant services and reputable private consulting firms are located throughout the nation.

Regardless of whether or not some form of consultant service is provided, the committee of the board must be involved and informed.

It should be understood that this discussion concerns the selection of the first president for a new community college. When a replacement is needed, the selection committee should include staff and student representatives, or a separate staff-student advisory committee might be appointed.

Establishing Qualifications for the Job. Rarely, if ever, do selection committees secure a president who possesses all the qualifications they would like to see in the individual who will serve as their top educational leader. This, however, should not prevent them from setting their sights high. During this process the entire board should be involved at least to the extent that members not on the selection committee have the opportunity to contribute to and review the list of qualifications being established.

Although past and present practices are not necessarily the best, it might be helpful for board members to know the opinions of professors concerning desirable and undesirable characteristics of college presidents. For example, Table 5-1 reveals the opinions of 403 respondents to a survey of 500 professors from ninety-three colleges in twenty-four states made by Tyrus Hillway.

[14]Frederick deWolfe Bolman, *How College Presidents Are Chosen* (Washington, D.C.: American Council on Education, 1965), p. 3.

TABLE 5-1 *Characteristics of College Presidents*

	Percentage Response
Desirable Characteristics of College Presidents	
1. Integrity in personal and professional relations	24%
2. Intellectual ability and scholarship	22
3. Ability to organize and lead	20
4. Democratic attitude and methods	11
5. Warmth of personality	6
6. High moral and intellectual ideals	5
7. Objectivity and fairness	5
8. Interest in education (and ed. philosophy)	2
9. Culture and breeding	1
10. Self-confidence and firmness	1

	Percentage Response
Undesirable Characteristics of College Presidents	
1. Dictatorial, undemocratic attitude	24%
2. Dishonesty and insincerity	15
3. Weakness as educator and scholar	15
4. Vacillation in organizing and leading	15
5. Poor personality	9
6. Bias or favoritism	6

Reprinted with permission from Tyrus Hillway, "What Professors Want in a President," *School and Society,* 87, No. 2156 (1959), 307.

The factors considered by other trustees in judging college presidents might also prove helpful. In another study, Hillway sent 355 questionnaires to trustees in private and public colleges in forty-eight states. Table 5–2 displays the findings from the 148 (42 percent) questionnaires that were returned.

TABLE 5-2 *Factors Considered by Trustees in Judging Presidents and the Most Vital Competencies of a President*

FACTORS CONSIDERED BY TRUSTEES IN JUDGING PRESIDENTS

	Percentage Who Consider
Factor	
1. Leadership in maintaining high academic standards	90%
2. Good judgment in selecting faculty and staff	88
3. Ability to maintain high morale among faculty and staff	86

	Percentage Who Consider
Factor	
4. Facility for making friends in the institution	85
5. General intellectual leadership in the college and community	84
6. Fairness and honesty in treatment of faculty	80
7. Good judgment in promoting faculty and staff	80
8. Ability to maintain a balanced budget	78
9. Respect accorded him by other educators	77
10. Influence of his moral character on students and faculty	76

Percentage Response

MOST VITAL COMPETENCIES OF A PRESIDENT

Competency	
1. Educational leader	52%
2. Management executive	45
3. Public-relations expert	27
4. Money raiser and businessman	16

Reprinted with permission from Tyrus Hillway, "How Trustees Judge a College President," *School and Society,* 89, No. 2168 (1961), 52.

Because of the similarities of the two positions in respect to their leadership functions, it would seem that the community college president should possess some of the same personal characteristics required of a superintendent of schools. A recent text lists the following qualities as essential for that job:

1. High intelligence with a decisive, penetrating, yet flexible mind.
2. A sophisticated analyst and a vigorous actor.
3. The ability to visualize the whole picture and to see each problem in its broader context.
4. Excellent physical and mental health with good emotional stability and self-control.
5. A sensitivity to and understanding of people and skill in human relations that enable him to work successfully with individuals and with groups.
6. A high degree of curiosity and infectious enthusiasm for education and what it can do for individuals and society.
7. A high degree of organizational skill.
8. Creative in his approach, with broad vision, abundant courage, and great integrity.
9. Open-minded and always exercises suspended judgment, but never vacillates in making decisions.
10. Enjoys responsibility and recognizes the magnitude of his job—he is concerned but seldom worries.

11. Personal magnetism that attracts a corps of like-minded assistants who complement each other to form a superior administrative team.[15]

The above list of personal characteristics is formidable indeed and many of them are difficult, if not impossible, to assess in candidates who will be considered for the position. Rauh suggests that:

> Instead of cataloging all the desirable virtues, some boards have found it more profitable to stress the key attributes that would serve identifiable current needs of the institution and to measure candidates in terms of their sympathy with such needs.[16]

Examples similar to the following might be used:

1. An individual who has interest in and talent for planning and building.
2. An individual who has the ability to select a strong staff and quickly weld them into a working team.
3. An individual who is primarily interested in the challenge of the community college and not in being president of a four-year institution.

Gleazer believes that it might be a good idea to measure the candidates' attitudes and abilities against criteria similar to the following:

1. Conviction of the worth and dignity of each individual for what he is and what he can become. Commitment to the idea that society ought to provide the opportunity for each person to continue appropriate education up to the limit of his potential.
2. Appreciation of the social worth of a wide range of aptitudes, talents, interests, and types of intelligence. Respect for translating these into suitable educational programs.
3. Understanding of the interpersonal processes by which the individual comes to be what he is. Appreciation for the interaction of the college and other social institutions and agencies—the community, family, and church organizations—in providing a social milieu for personality development.
4. Knowledge of community structure and processes. Capacity to identify structures of social power and the decision makers involved in various kinds of community issues.
5. Understanding of education in our society and viewpoints about its role. Acquaintance with critical contemporary issues in education. Appreciation of the responsibilities of elementary and secondary education as well as those of higher education. Commitment to community college services as part of a total educational program. Constructive and affirmative views toward the assignment of the comprehensive open-door institution.
6. Some understanding of the elements at work which are changing society

---

[15] Adapted from Neagley and Evans, *Supervision of Instruction*, p. 88.

[16] Morton A. Rauh, *The Trusteeship of Colleges and Universities* (New York: McGraw-Hill Book Company, 1969), p. 13.

throughout the world. Awareness of the significance of population growth, shifts in population, changes in age composition of population, the dynamics of aspirations and ambitions in cultures on all continents, the rapidity of technological development, societal resistance to self-examination and criticism, and other developments foretelling social change.

7. Ability to listen, understand, interpret, and reconcile. Capacity to communicate.[17]

The same authority further suggests that:

Board members will probably have in mind three other questions as they size up a candidate: Has this man enough stature in the field of education so that the leadership of other educational institutions will have respect for him and hence for this new institution we are creating? Or if not now, does he have potential in this regard? Do his attainments suggest to the community that the institution holds marked promise because it can attract a man of this caliber? And most important, what is there about him to persuade outstanding people to join in making this a superior institution?[18]

One very important decision that has to be made before a search for candidates is begun is the kind of education and experience that will be expected of applicants. If the board is going to seek a president who has proven himself on the firing line, a higher salary will have to be offered than if inexperienced candidates are solicited.

It is recommended that the doctorate be required and that candidates have had some course work in the administration of higher education or, at least, some basic work in administration. As was suggested in the beginning of this chapter, educational leadership requires skills, knowledge, and attitudes that must be learned. It is preferable that the president comes to the job with the above qualifications rather than trying to learn too much on the job.

Individuals who have had experience as college deans or as superintendents of schools should be given careful consideration. Persons who have been successful administrators in business and industry are less likely to be able to provide the educational leadership required, but if they have a doctorate, they should not be ruled out. In fact, they may be better candidates than an academician without training and experience in administration.

Search for Candidates. An attractive printed brochure describing the position in terms of the goals and objectives of the college, giving a definition of the job of the president, and containing a description of the community and attendance

---

[17] Edmund J. Gleazer, Jr., *This Is the Community College* (Boston: Houghton Mifflin Company, 1968), pp. 104-5.

[18] Ibid., p. 105.

area that the college will serve should prove to be helpful in attracting desirable candidates. The qualifications required of the candidates—including education and experience—as well as the anticipated salary, terms of employment, and fringe benefits should be included in the brochure.

Sources of candidates include university placement bureaus, private placement agencies, letters to community college presidents soliciting their recommendations of promising individuals they know, and, sometimes, listings in professional magazines.

Universities preparing college administrators maintain placement files at the annual meeting of the American Association of Junior Colleges and can provide the names of promising candidates. There also are agencies that specialize in placing college personnel.[19]

Interviewing the Candidates. If the various sources of supply are contacted and the position is attractive, applications will be received from more candidates than can be interviewed. The usual procedure is to have the selection committee and/or the consultant(s) screen the applications on the basis of the personal, educational, and experiential qualifications that have been predetermined. The individuals who possess most of these qualifications are then given preliminary interviews by the consultants and/or members of the selection committee. Ten or more candidates may be invited for this initial interview. Consultant firms usually prepare brief resumés about each candidate to be interviewed and some system of rating or ranking candidates is decided upon. Initial interviews usually last approximately one hour. It is most desirable to conduct them in a two-day sequence, so that not too much time elapses between the first and last interview.

Since applications may be expected from all sections of the country, it may be desirable to do this initial interviewing at the site of a national meeting. The annual meeting of the American Association of Junior Colleges and the yearly convention of the American Association of School Administrators are two possibilities.

In preparing for these initial interviews, a list of questions based on some of the ideas presented earlier in this chapter must be prepared. If all candidates are asked the same questions, it is easier to make intelligent comparisons.

As a result of the preliminary hearings, the top four or five candidates should be selected as finalists to be interviewed by the entire board of trustees. Although it is not required, it is desirable for the board to pay the expenses incurred by the finalists in the second and eventually subsequent interviews.

The duration of the second interview is usually several hours. Like the first, it must be carefully planned. An expanded list of questions may be used and points cleared up from the initial hearing. One board found it helpful to make a

---

[19] For example, ECS–The Educational Career Services, Inc., One Palmer Square, Princeton, N.J. 08540; also, College and Specialist Bureau, 215 Lincoln American Tower, Memphis, Tenn. 38103.

tape recording of the interviews with the finalists. This enabled board members to better compare the responses the candidates gave to particular questions.

Because of the important role a college president's wife plays in the social life of the college, in the college community, and in supporting her husband professionally and personally, it is an excellent idea to invite wives to the final interview.

If five or six carefully screened candidates are interviewed by the board, it is unlikely that any one candidate will appear as the number one choice to the entire board. This usually means that further investigations should be made of the two or possibly three top men. A visit to their respective communities is next in order, to collect additional information for use in making the final choice.

Now a candidate must be chosen. If the board cannot agree on one individual, additional dialogue should take place. Under no circumstances should a president be selected unless he is the unanimous choice of the board. There are enough problems to be faced at the start of a new community college without adding the likelihood of friction between the new president and one or more board members who preferred another candidate. The confidence and backing of 100 percent of the board is an essential ingredient for the new president to be successful.

If the entire board can agree on a second or even a third choice, it might be a good idea to do so. Many first choice candidates will have changed their minds and will refuse the position for various reasons. A ranking of finalists may save considerable time and energy in the long run. In case the number one choice declines, the position can be offered to the individual agreed upon by the board as second choice.

In spite of the above, any finalist will hopefully be willing to accept the position if it is offered to him. When all conditions of employment, including salary and fringe benefits, are made clear to all candidates in the initial or succeeding interviews, it may be presumed that all finalists will want to accept.

Contract and Salary

A two- or three-year contract should be offered the founding president to provide him time to launch the institution. A top candidate will not accept less than a two-year contract.

Salaries are usually designated in ranges rather than specifics. It deserves consideration to negotiate even the upper *limit* rather than to lose a candidate who after careful selection has become the unanimous choice of the board.

The salary offered the new president should be commensurate with the tremendous task that lies ahead; namely, planning and building a community college from scratch. This is a twenty-four-hour-a-day job, not even comparable to that of the president of an established institution. In terms of dollars to be expended, it is equivalent to a multimillion-dollar operation in the business world.

It should be kept in mind that the initial salary may not be as important to the candidate as the size of guaranteed annual raises and the salary potential.

Fringe Benefits. These can be a deciding factor in persuading the unanimously chosen candidate to accept the position. It is a usual procedure for boards to pay the new president's moving expenses. Some boards of trustees will be in a position to offer the president a residence or a housing allowance.

A college-owned car is a must for the new president. Much of his travel will be for college business and reimbursement for mileage on a personally owned car is never satisfactory.

A liberal expense account with opportunities to travel and attend educational conclaves is another attractive feature that should be included in the agreement. The travel budget during the planning years should be very generous. The new president will need to travel all over the nation, and so will other members of the administrative staff, in order to gather ideas and information helpful in establishing the college.

Each situation is unique and boards of trustees may be able to offer other fringe benefits that will prove attractive to candidates. Anything that can legitimately be done to get the right man for the job is money well spent.

Getting Started on the Job

The remaining chapters of this handbook are concerned with the challenges that face the president and down-to-earth suggestions are made to assist him as he works on these tasks. Only two items will be discussed here, namely, inauguration and the beginning of staff selection.

Inauguration

Since initially the president will have only a limited staff and no student body, the official inauguration—if it is decided to have one—should be postponed until the first year the college is in full operation. To a certain extent, this late inauguration gives the president an advantage over the person who, under the traditional plan, is required to give an inaugural speech before he has been long enough at the college to make any major commitments. A president who has worked hard for one or more years to get things started has a pretty good idea of the commitments he can make for his institution. In discussing inaugurations Herron proposes that:

The inauguration should be a ceremony of great dignity and honor, exhibiting the institution at its best. The facilities in which it is held, the manner of the program, the style of the institution, the method of publicity all contribute to setting the proper stage for his acceptance. The inauguration is a time when the institution can put its best foot forward and have a tremendous opportunity for positive public relations.[20]

The practice of inaugurating the community college president has been adopted from the university and four-year college. Perhaps, because of its uniqueness, a different type of ceremony or no ceremony at all should be planned in a community college, particularly if the president has been in office a year or more before there is a student body. In other words, inaugurations are considered optional in community colleges.

Beginning of Staff Selection

The wise board of trustees will give the president all possible help in the planning stages of the community college. Surveying the needs, planning the curriculum, securing temporary and permanent facilities, equipping the college, meeting with community groups, visiting schools, and a host of other preopening activities cannot be done by the president working alone. As a minimum, deans in academic affairs, student affairs, and administrative services should be employed a year before the community college plans to open (see Chapter 6).

Summary

The selection of a president for the community college is one of the most important functions that a board of trustees performs. Selecting the first president is an even more crucial task. In order to make an intelligent choice, boards must first formulate objectives for the institution.

Board members must also be aware of the importance of the position of community college president and have a good understanding of the roles the president performs as administrator, educational leader, public relations expert, and scholar. They also should know the personal and professional qualifications that are required to effectively fulfill those roles.

Board members should use well-established selection procedures in their search for a president. It is highly desirable to engage a reputable consultant or firm of consultants to assist in this important task.

An attractive brochure containing an accurate description of the position and of the qualifications required should be printed and distributed to all reliable sources of candidates.

[20]Herron, *Role of Trustees*, p. 54.

Screening credentials and interviewing candidates should be done as scientifically as possible by using checklists, interview guides, and tape recordings. In the final interviews the candidates' wives should be invited to attend. It is desirable that all interview expenses of the finalists be paid by the board of trustees.

A candidate should not be offered the job unless he is the unanimous choice of the board. It is usually wise to make a second choice, in case the first choice candidate withdraws.

After the board has unanimously agreed on a candidate, every effort should be made to persuade him to accept the position. He should be offered a two- or three-year contract, a salary commensurate with the job, and a promise of sizeable annual increments. He also should be offered as many fringe benefits as the board is able to provide.

If an inauguration is held, it should be a dignified academic affair. However, depending on various local factors, including the time of the president's appointment, inaugurations in community colleges are optional.

The president should be provided with an adequate staff to assist in the planning and organization of the institution at least a year before the community college plans to open.

Suggested Activities and Problems

1. Read several articles on planning as an administrative function. Write a paper explaining the role of the community college president as a planner.

2. Interview a community college president to determine how he views his role as an educational leader. Write a paper comparing and contrasting what you learn in the interview with the material in the text.

3. Write a paper to support or refute the thesis that the community college president must be a public relations expert.

4. Locate the names of three or more community college presidents in your state. Search through the *Education Index and Reader's Guide* for a ten-year period to determine how many articles each of the presidents wrote during that period. Write a critique of one or more of the articles.

5. Prepare a list of twenty-five or more questions that you believe should be posed to prospective community college presidents during their interview. Give reasons for including each question on your list.

6. Using examples where possible, relate each of the eleven personal characteristics found on page 62 of the text to the actual job of the community college president.

Selected Readings

Bolman, Frederick deWolfe, *How College Presidents Are Chosen.* Washington, D.C.: American Council on Education, 1965.

Carmichael, John, "Origin and Mobility of Presidents," *Junior College Journal,* 39, No. 8 (1969), 30.

Cohen, Arthur M., and John E. Roueche, *Institutional Administrator or Educational Leader.* Washington, D.C.: American Association of Junior Colleges, 1969.

Getzels, Jacob W., James M. Lipham, and Roald F. Campbell, *Educational Administration As a Social Process: Theory, Research, Practice,* chaps. 1, 2, 3, and 4. New York: Harper & Row, Publishers, 1968.

Halpin, Andrew W., *Theory and Research in Administration.* New York: The Macmillan Company, 1966.

Herron, Orley R. Jr., *The Role of the Trustees,* chap. 3. Scranton, Pa.: International Textbook Company, 1969.

Hewitt, Carter E., "What We Did Before the President Came," *Junior College Journal,* 38, No. 8 (1968), 20.

Hostrop, Richard W., "Interviewing Presidential Candidates," *Junior College Journal,* 38, No. 2 (1967), 13.

Johnson, B. Lamar, ed., *The Junior College President,* Occasional Report No. 13. Los Angeles: University of California, May, 1969.

Morgan, Donald A., *Perspectives of the Community College Presidency,* Occasional Report No. 14. Los Angeles: University of California, March, 1970.

Praetor, Ralph, *The College President.* New York: Institute for Applied Research in Education, Inc., 1963.

Rauh, Morton A., *The Trusteeship of Colleges and Universities,* chap. 3. New York: McGraw-Hill Book Company, 1969.

Saunders, Robert L., Ray C. Phillips, and Harold T. Johnson, *A Theory of Educational Leadership.* Columbus, Ohio: Charles E. Merrill Publishing Co., 1966.

Wing, Dennis R. W., *The Professional President: A Decade of Community Junior College Chief Executives,* Topical Paper No. 28. Los Angeles: University of California at Los Angeles, ERIC Clearinghouse for Junior Colleges, January 1972.

6

Recruiting, Organizing, and Training the College Staff

With the selection of the president, the responsibility for personnel recruitment shifts from the board to the newly appointed chief administrator. A community college is a group of human beings who should be in positive interaction with each other. In the period before the first students arrive, this group consists of the administrators and of the instructional and noninstructional personnel who together form the growing staff team of the new college.

Of the myriad decisions facing a new president, none is more immediate or pressing than the identification of key positions in the emerging college, and the search for qualified persons to fill them. However, before he rushes off to hire deans, secretaries, faculty, and custodians, the president and his board must face and resolve some complex questions, or at least decide how to resolve them.

1. What kind of community college are we planning to build? Will it be comprehensive in terms of programs, and open to all residents who can profit from attending? Or will it be a selective institution?
2. What is the philosophic base of this new college? What are its long-term and immediate goals?
3. Will the college be located on a single campus, multiple campuses, or will it be dispersed throughout the community in various locations?
4. Will the college open in temporary facilities while the question of location is pondered?
5. What instructional strategies will be employed at the college? Will most students be educated by traditional classroom lecture methods or will a systems approach to instruction be implemented?
6. What is the timetable for opening the college to students?

The president and the board have essentially two choices. They can solve basic questions like these and then begin to recruit the staff, or they can hire additional key staff members, on the recommendation of the president, and then deal with the basic issues as additional professionals arrive to lend their inputs.

The optimum solution involves a modicum of early key decisions by the president and the board, and a deferral of as many goal and policy decisions as possible until more staff members join the team. (Chapter 7, concerned with development of philosophy, goals, and policies, therefore follows this chapter on staff recruitment and organization.)

However, it is necessary for the board, under the guidance of the president, to state some fundamental tenets so that prospective deans, for example, will be able to decide if their philosophy is compatible with that of the new college. Such a statement might include the following:

1. This community college will be comprehensive, offering a variety of programs to serve initially high school graduates and adults over eighteen years of age.
2. The college will be dedicated to excellence in student learning, using and applying the latest research in teaching and learning. A variety of instructional strategies will be permitted, and all learning sequences will be carefully designed to enable maximum individualization of instruction. Strong learning resources support is envisioned.
3. The community service function of the college will be emphasized through positive involvement with various groups in the community.
4. All aspects of student development will be stressed, including counseling, placement, and meaningful student participation in governance.

The president's personal philosophy will strongly influence any basic statement of principles. However, it is important that prospective staff members know the general philosophical positions of the board and particularly of the president. Such a statement does not and should not reflect a rigid stance. Rather it should be viewed as a position statement that will be tested in the crucible of team decision making as the staff expands.

Recruiting by Functional Areas

One of the first things a new president has to learn, if he doesn't know it already, is that he cannot and should not try to run all aspects of a growing community college from his office. He must carefully select his subordinates and delegate to them considerable authority and responsibility for their areas. This is effective administration that brings out the talents of each leader. Careful attention, of course, needs to be given to identification of the functional areas of a community college, and to an optimum method of administering them.

Most community colleges, regardless of their developing philosophies, require an administrative structure that will enable the essential tasks to be accomplished. Since typical administration charts always seem rigid and tend to emphasize line relationships rather than the more important staff interaction, the classifications in Figure 6-1 may help to identify the basic functional areas of a typical community college.

Some of the assignments of function are debatable. For example, in some organizations a separate learning resources division reports directly to the president's office. However, learning resources are such an integral part of the instructional process that the indicated placement in Figure 6-1 is most defensible. Often long-range planning and campus development are handled by the president, especially in the early stages. Studying the different community college organization charts in Appendix 3, p. 290, will make some of the various administrative patterns that have evolved more understandable.

At this point in the development of a new institution the president must decide on the key administrative officers who will be recruited to assist in the building of the college program and facilities. It is recommended that three deans be recruited in the functional areas of academic affairs, student affairs, and administrative services. It is extremely desirable, if not essential, that these officers join the team at least a year before the college opens for students. If computer services and institutional research are important elements in the developing philosophy of the college, then a fourth dean should be added during the year before opening. The same is true of community services; a dean or director should be recruited in this area if a full initial program involving the total community is anticipated. Usually the president handles public information and long-range planning in the early stages.

In the recruitment of these key administrators, the following principles should be observed:

1. Set salary ranges realistically geared to attract highly qualified and experienced candidates. Make studies of surrounding colleges and states.

2. Develop comprehensive job descriptions that will be valid for several years. These are top executive positions, and it is a mistake to hire a minimally qualified business manager, for example, expecting that he will grow into a dean of administration. (See representative job descriptions in Appendix 4, p. 300.)

3. Look for candidates who are skilled in human relations. This is one of the most important criteria for selection. These top administrators need to work well together as a team and will ultimately be supervising large staffs of their own.

4. If at all possible, secure deans who have had some community college experience. An academic dean from a private four-year liberal arts college may not understand the diversity of the typical community college programs and the range of students they serve.

As these key administrators join the staff, the president discusses fully with them the scope of their job responsibility and authority. The job description, of course, is the basic document for each position, and a file should be established immediately, with new job descriptions written and added as each new staff position emerges. Some colleges are going beyond the typical job description and are developing management objectives for each administrator, which are then reviewed quarterly by each manager and his subordinates to ascertain the degree of accomplishment of the agreed-upon objectives.

The president immediately organizes a working team, welcoming new staff members to the group as they arrive. It is imperative that the small, but growing group of administrators develops close, warm, friendly relationships, for there will be much give and take during the formative months. Under the leadership of the president, the administrative team can profitably conduct an inservice workshop on the principles of team action. Galen Drawry's monograph would be especially useful for a study guide.[1]

The remainder of this chapter will deal with each of the major functional areas of the college (See Figure 6-1, p. 75) and the process of recruiting, organizing, and training the staff in each area.

Academic Affairs

Staffing beyond the dean can be considered in the area of instruction only after basic decisions have been made regarding the organizational structure for teaching and learning. Community college faculties are typically organized either by departments, by broad interdisciplinary divisions, or by departments within divisions. According to Tillery's research, the trend nationwide is toward divisions only or to departments within divisions in larger institutions.

> . . . a high proportion of presidents reported preferences for division structures solely or *with* departments. . . .
>
> Interdisciplinary structures are clearly preferred to traditional subject matter areas, and the department is no longer the preferred pattern of organization. Nevertheless, departments seem to have new credibility when conceived as subordinate units to more broadly conceived divisions. Nevertheless, there is great interest across the country in interdisciplinary programs and half or more of the presidents in the various states and state groups being reported prefer such a conceptual basis for organization.[2]

The broad divisional structure is the soundest basis for organizing the instructional program and staff in the community college. Departments should be avoided because they typically result in small enclaves being established, with

---

[1] Galen N. Drewry, *The Administrative Team: What It Is and How It Works* (Athens, Ga.: University of Georgia Press, 1967).

[2] Dale Tillery, *Variation and Change in Community College Organization* (Center for Research and Development in Higher Education, University of California, Berkeley, California, 1970), pp. 15, 41.

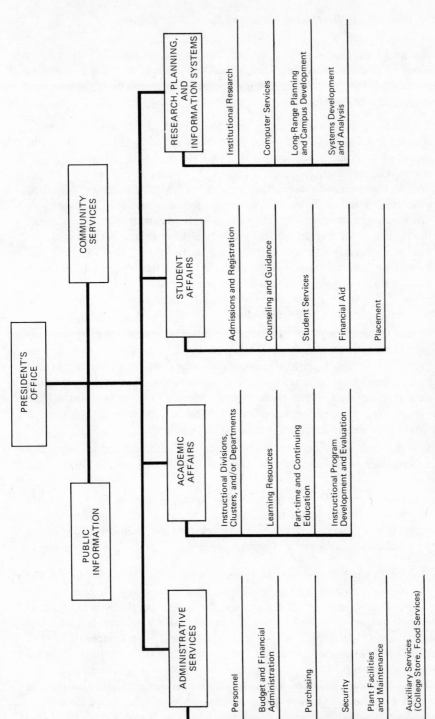

FIGURE 6-1 Major Functional Areas in a Comprehensive
Community College

groups of faculty focusing narrowly on their own disciplines. Interdisciplinary thinking should be encouraged throughout the college, and this can best be accomplished by the divisional organization. The following principles and practices should be established:

1. Divisions should include faculty who teach both the students planning to transfer to a four-year college and those taking the two-year career programs. A complete intermix of faculty is imperative to avoid the formation of narrow cliques based on subjects taught. Too often in community colleges faculty members who teach the transfer students "look down" on their colleagues who teach in the vocational-technical fields. Comprehensive divisional organizations will help to avoid this false snobbery. For example, the faculty in the humanities and fine arts division would teach all students, including music majors and those taking music appreciation to satisfy the general education requirement for graduation. The business and technologies division would include courses, students, and faculty members in the first two years of a four-year business administration major as well as those in the two-year secretarial science curriculum.

2. Instead of organizing departments within divisions, consider the appointment of coordinators of subject areas as the divisions grow. For example, an English coordinator might be appointed when the English staff in the humanities division expands to eight or ten members. The coordinator would be a teaching staff member who is given released time for coordinating the subject area. In very large community colleges, departmental organization within the divisions might be considered.

3. Division chairmen should be given considerable authority and responsibility to lead their faculty, manage the divisional budget, and provide instructional leadership.

4. Assistant or associate deans for career, technical, or transfer programs should be avoided. Such administrative staffing will emphasize differences among students and programs, rather than encourage all staff members and students to feel that they are a part of the total college.

Division Chairmen. It should be apparent from the preceding discussion that the recruiting of strong, well-trained, and sensitive division chairmen is one of the primary responsibilities of the dean. If the budget permits, it is desirable to have the chairmen on board six to eight months before opening day. This will enable them to participate in policy formation and in the recruitment and training of their divisional faculty. The job description for division chairman found in Appendix 4, p. 300 indicates the scope of responsibility for this position. The best candidates are usually those persons with graduate work in administration and extensive teaching experience in a community college. Experience as a coordinator or department chariman is highly desirable. Comparable experience in public school or four-year college teaching and administration may be accepted if appropriate, and if the candidate seems to be in tune with the developing philosophy of the new college.

When he arrives on the job, the division chairman should become an integral part of the dean's team and participate in all decisions regarding the instructional program and faculty planning.

The new college's emerging approach to teaching and learning will determine to a great extent the kind of personnel required after the division chairmen. Questions such as these must be faced and answered before instructional and support personnel can be hired:

1. Is a systems approach to instruction planned, or will all faculty members and divisions go their own way?
2. Are alternate instructional strategies or learning modes contemplated, involving perhaps mediated large group lectures, seminars, independent study, and open audio-tutorial laboratories? Or will the traditional college lecture syndrome prevail?
3. Is differentiated staffing a viable possibility in the teaching-learning process?
4. How important are educational technology and media?

In other words, the approach to instruction that is adopted will determine the number and type of teaching and support personnel required (see Chapters 8, 9, and 10).

Coordinator of Learning Resources. Depending on the emerging instructional philosophy of the college, a coordinator or director of learning resources or library services will be needed early in the planning stages. If at all possible, this professional should be working with the dean a year before the college opens. Initiating a strong book and nonbook media program is a formidable task (see Chapter 10). The coordinator of learning resources has to work closely with the dean and division chairmen in the identification of the programs of instruction and the courses to be offered. Only then can the coordinator begin to acquire basic collections of books and hard media. It is imperative that selection, purchasing, and cataloging procedures be established by the time faculty begin to arrive and to contribute their inputs to the selection process. (Refer once again to Appendix 4, p. 300, for a typical job description for the coordinator or director of learning resources and other positions described in the remainder of this chapter.)

Assistant Dean for Instructional Program Development. If the new college is adopting some form of a systematic approach to instruction, the division chairmen and the faculty will need considerable assistance from the beginning in the techniques of curriculum development, including the writing of learning objectives, the selection and implementation of instructional strategies, and the evaluation of learning results. An assistant dean or two for educational program development and evaluation might be considered as soon as feasible under the budget. Unless the dean is a miracle worker, he will need this assistance well before the college opens, regardless of his personal knowledge and expertise in curriculum design and implementation. There simply will not be time for him to work with the entire staff in these vital areas of instructional planning and evaluation.

Director of Part-Time and Continuing Education. Although it is possible to get along in the first year of operation with the dean or a division chairman handling the part-time programs, it is recommended that a director be employed at least six month before the college opens for students. There are several important reasons for this suggestion:

1. A truly comprehensive community college serves all citizens who can profit from its programs; and many prospective students can take work only in the evenings, on weekends, or part-time during the day.
2. The initial image of the community college is important, and a strong part-time program will give the new institution much more visibility in the community it serves. Courses are often conducted in local high schools or other community facilities to bring the college to the people.
3. Part-time programs are a good source of budget income, and therefore should be developed early. These programs help to facilitate maximum use of the college plant and thereby give the taxpayer a good return on his investment in campus construction.

The Instructional Staff. The recruitment and training of the teaching faculty, instructional assistants, and other personnel associated with teaching and learning is one of the most important responsibilities of the dean of academic affairs in the months before the college opens. Some presidents like to take an active role in the selection of the pioneer faculty; however, this task should essentially be carried out by the dean, with intensive involvement of the division chairmen as soon as they report to the college. The dean and the chairmen are most closely identified with the emerging instructional program and they need to establish close rapport with the faculty. Consequently, their role in recruitment and preservice training should be dominant. After the first year, all faculty ought to be involved in the selection process for the next year.

To insure recruitment of the best possible individuals to serve on the faculty, and to make sure that the philosophy of the college and that of the applicants are in harmony, a well-planned program from initial contact through the beginning of the college year is essential. The following specific suggestions are offered.

1. Write up specific job descriptions for each type of position, e.g., instructional assistant, assistant professor of English, or laboratory assistant.

2. Determine if faculty rank is to be established. There is wide variance in practice throughout the nation. It is usually best to adopt the practice of the state or region in which the new college is located. For example, rank is universal in New Jersey community colleges and rare in California. Applicants who are concerned about rank will want to know if the college plans to adopt the system. Another option is to delay a decision regarding faculty rank and involve the new staff members in making the determination.

3. Prepare an attractive, informative recruiting brochure that includes: the purpose of the college; its philosophy and objectives; the approach to teaching and learning; opportunities for preservice and inservice training; student services; outline of the instructional program; a description of interim and permanent college facilities; the college calendar; and information about the area in which the college is located. (See Appendix 5, p. 321 for a sample recruiting brochure.)

4. Recruit nationwide. Send letters and recruiting brochures to university and college placement offices, and to graduate institutions that train community college personnel. Some new colleges make the mistake of hiring most of their initial staff from local schools and colleges. It is desirable in a new institution of higher learning to recruit a cosmopolitan faculty from various sections of the country, and with different backgrounds. Each will contribute uniquely to the new staff. It may be considered safer to hire local talent, but the president and dean must decide what kind of faculty the new college needs. Of course, some qualified local persons will usually be employed, but they should not be given preference over other candidates simply because they live or work in the area. Furthermore, the college will quickly establish poor relationships with its feeder school districts by stealing a number of the best elementary and high school teachers.

5. Design a comprehensive yet simple application form, and establish sound clerical procedures for acknowledging inquiries and for processing applications.

6. Develop an effective screening process for applications and credentials.

7. Arrange interviews with the candidates who seem best qualified. If recruiting nationwide, it is desirable—and more economical for all concerned—for the dean and division chairmen to fly to certain key points in the nation. Then applicants from a reasonable radius can be scheduled for interviews in a motel or local college placement office.

8. After final selection and approval by the president and board of trustees, each successful candidate should receive a personal letter from the president along with his contract. (The college attorney will assist in designing the contract form; this is dependent on state laws pertaining to nontenured

faculty and other such considerations.) Some colleges do not issue contracts; however, a formal contractual agreement spelling out the responsibilities of both parties is both desirable and necessary.

9. Between contract and reporting time the dean should make occasional mailings to the new faculty, including information on fringe benefits, insurance programs, college procedures, and other pertinent areas. If there has been time to prepare a faculty handbook incorporating such information, this should be mailed to all new faculty members. If not, such a handbook should be put together by the earliest possible date, and certainly by the beginning of the preservice program. (Existing handbooks can be obtained from other community colleges to provide ideas on content and format.)

10. A two- or three-week preservice training program is essential for new faculty each year. The college should pay a stipend to all staff members attending the workshop. Topics to be covered will include: orientation to the college; getting to know each other; learning about the instructional approach; examining data on the incoming students; learning to use the resources of the college; and other pertinent matters. (An outline for a two-week preservice program may be found in Appendix 6, p. 325.) It is always valuable to have the participants evaluate the preservice program so that it may be improved the following year.

11. Continuing inservice programs should be planned during the year. Especially in a systems-oriented college, time will be needed for curriculum development, including the skills of writing learning objectives and developing instructional media. If at all possible, reduced teaching loads should be employed during the first year to provide released time for faculty members to attend inservice programs and to take part in curriculum work.

Student Affairs

The main functions of student personnel services are:

1. To admit the student to college.
2. To set up and keep a records system for him.
3. To provide him with counseling to assist in career, personal, and instructional decisions.
4. To organize and administer a program of student activities with full student participation.
5. To involve the student meaningfully in the governance of the college.
6. To organize and operate work-study and financial aid programs.
7. To aid in career placement and in transfers to senior colleges.

All student services and programs must be correlated carefully with the developing instructional program. The deans of student affairs and academic affairs need to develop a close and continuing working relationship.

The key personnel reporting to the dean of student affairs will be the director of admissions and registration, the director of counseling and guidance, and the director of financial aid and placement. A staff of counselors, or student development specialists, as they are designated in some community colleges, will round out the personnel complement in student affairs for the first year. There should be sufficient budget moneys to hire counselors in a ratio of one to not more than 250 full-time students. One or two of the counselors would normally serve as advisers to the student government and the activities program, as they develop.

The Director of Admissions and Registration. This director plays an essential role in the months before the college opens. He should be on the staff eight to twelve months before students arrive for instruction. Admissions and registration procedures must be carefully developed to provide accurate records and an efficient yet compassionate system for receiving and processing student applications. Some experience in admissions and registration is essential as a prerequisite for this position. If full computer services are envisioned at the college, then the director of admissions and registration needs to understand the support that will be available to him and the college from this source. The computer has proven a very valuable tool at community colleges for record keeping, advanced registration, master scheduling, developing student profiles, and a host of other data. The admissions director will be a part of all policy decisions during this formative period, for example, those on open-door admissions; on the nature of contacts with the local high schools; on the development of the student data bank and the application form; and on the student registration system.

The Director of Counseling and Guidance. This position might well be filled after the college opens. The dean of student affairs can assume the responsibility of supervising the counseling staff as he recruits them. It is well for the dean to observe the performance of the counselors for a period, and then involve them in helping to select one as coordinator of director.

It is important for the president's staff to discuss fully the nature of expected counseling services for students so that the dean may be guided in his recruiting. A community college needs well-trained, experienced, sensitive persons who are people-oriented. Many, if not most, community college students need considerable help in finding their personal and vocational goals in life, and in solving their personal concerns and problems. The success of a student in a comprehensive community college is dependent, to a large degree, on the assistance he gets in thinking through his problems, challenges, and concerns. The counselor is indispensable in this process of human interaction.

The suggestions for recruitment and preservice training of the instructional staff presented earlier may be applied to counselor recruiting as well. All new personnel should participate in the same preservice programs, since they will be working together in implementing the total learning processes at the college. For example, instructional staff members will usually be involved as faculty advisers to students, assisting them in the selection of courses. To function effectively in this role, faculty members will need to work closely with the counselors to determine areas of responsibility. Often the dean of student affairs or one of the counselors will present an inservice program on faculty advising of students.

The Director of Financial Aid and Placement. This official will be a part-time counselor the first year. His main administrative duties are the organization of policies and procedures for making financial aid such as work-study, loans, and scholarships available to students. He also will be planning ahead for placement of the first graduates in business, industry, and the professions. The placement function sometimes includes assisting students in transferring to four-year institutions. Sometimes a transfer counselor is designated to assume this responsibility as part of his counseling load.

Administrative Services

The dean of administration or administrative services will normally be the only professional employed in this area during the planning and early operational stages of the college. For this reason, he must have a broad background in such fields as budget making, accounting, purchasing, plant construction and maintenance, and personnel. It is a serious mistake to hire a less qualified person in this position and expect him to grow into it.

During the year before opening the dean will have to develop the budget with the president's staff, set up a basic accounting system, organize purchasing procedures, develop procedures for employing the noninstructional staff, and get out the payroll. Depending on the nature of the campus and its location the first year of operation, the dean must plan for security, operating the college store, providing food services to students and staff, organizing telephone and mail communications, and maintaining the physical plant.

The total program of administrative services is discussed in Chapter 11. These functions are all supportive of the main purpose of the college—to provide educational programs and related services for students.

The minimum staff required by the dean during the start-up year will include an accountant, strong secretarial assistance, and possibly a construction coordinator, depending on the status of the permanent campus building program. Prior to the opening of the college for students in either interim facilities or on the permanent campus, the following personnel will be needed: security officers, manager of the college store, manager of food services, and maintenance and custodial personnel.

Research, Planning, and Information Systems

As indicated earlier in this chapter, the president usually will be the long-range planner during the early stages of the college, working with the architect, writing educational specifications, and directing campus planning and design up to the awarding of contracts. Some colleges contract with planning consultants to assist with this phase. During the first or second year of operation, these responsibilities may be delegated to the dean of research, planning, and information systems.

Chapters 9 and 10 emphasize the importance of institutional research and computer services in a modern community college. Indeed, if a college expects to achieve excellence in teaching and learning in the 1970s and beyond, the institution must stress internal research that will help to evaluate the achievement of specific goals and objectives. Likewise, a community college that aspires to excellence in this technological age needs the support of a well-staffed, well-equipped computer center.

The president will be searching initially for a competent, experienced administrator who knows the science and technology of data processing and its unique educational applications. This person must be thoroughly competent in systems development and analysis, since he will be organizing the basic data systems on which many programs of the college will be built. He might also have the research and planning background that will enable him to grow into the position of dean of research, planning, and information systems. This is not essential, however. The most important initial skills are those vital to the organization of the data processing function. Another person can be recruited as dean during the opening year of the college if it is not possible to find all these attributes in one administrator.

Community Services

In Chapter 13 the community services dimension of the community college is discussed. The new college, as its name implies, is an integral part of the community it serves. Citizens will come to the college for various activities and services, and the college will extend throughout the community to provide needed educational, cultural, and recreational programs.

If the college intends to be serious about its community identity and responsibilities, a director or dean of community services should be employed prior to the arrival of students. Many studies need to be made, programs must be planned and organized, and the initial activities of the college in this whole area must be carefully thought out. Dr. Ervin L. Harlacher's book on community services is a most valuable resource for planning.[3]

[3] Ervin L. Harlacher, *The Community Dimension of the Community College* (Englewood Cliffs, N.J.: Prentice-Hall, Inc., 1969).

Public Information

With regard to staffing, the president and his secretary will usually handle the initial public information and public relations activities. Regular news releases, occasional news conferences, and speaking engagements in the community are all part of the president's job in the early years. By corresponding with the news media and with church, civic, and service organizations in the community, the president can announce his availability to speak on the newly developing community college. He will want to meet with groups of government, industrial, business, and professional leaders to get their suggestions on the new college and its programs.

If the budget permits, the president might on a part-time basis hire a person with a journalism background to write up several news releases per week and begin to develop other public information activities. As the college moves into the first year of operation, a full-time position in public information and public relations should be budgeted.

Conclusion

In this chapter the key staff positions required to organize a community college were outlined. Suggestions were made for recruiting, organizing, and training the staff. Obviously, the organizational patterns are suggestive only. No two community colleges are exactly alike in their administrative approaches. However, the major areas of responsibility were identified, and viable models described.

Again, it is recommended to study the administrative organization charts and job descriptions in Appendices 3 and 4. Community college catalogs should be consulted as well. Visits to community colleges and conferences with presidents and deans regarding organizational and staffing patterns are invaluable. The president will then recommend to his board what seems to be the most sensible staffing pattern for the new college, considering all pertinent factors such as projected enrollment, educational programs, student services to be offered, the place of the computer in the college, and the emerging instructional program.

As each new staff member arrives and becomes an integral part of the administrative team, his contributions will help to modify future planning, and in this way initial staffing plans will constantly be modified and improved.

Summary

The selection of key staff members in the emerging college is one of the immediate and pressing tasks facing the president. Together with the board of trustees he must enunciate some fundamental tenets, so that prospective administrators and faculty will understand the basic philosophy of the new college and the president. However, early key decisions should be kept to a minimum and as many goal and policy decisions as possible deferred until there are more staff members.

The president, with the approval of the board, will identify the major functional areas in the emerging college and develop an appropriate administrative structure. Three or four deans will then be recruited—in academic affairs, student affairs, administrative services, and possibly in research, planning, and information systems. As these key administrators join the staff, the president immediately involves them in a working team relationship.

In academic affairs, organization by broad divisions is recommended. The recruiting of strong, well-trained, and sensitive division chairmen is one of the primary responsibilities of the dean. The new college's emerging approach to teaching and learning will determine to a great extent the kind of personnel required after the division chairmen. If a systematic approach to instruction is envisioned, with strong learning resources support, a coordinator of learning resources and an assistant dean for instructional program development should be employed well before the college opens. It is advisable that a director of part-time and continuing education be hired at least six months before students arrive for instruction. The recruitment and training of the teaching faculty, instructional assistants, and other personnel associated with teaching and learning is one of the most important responsibilities of the dean of academic affairs and the division chairmen. A well-planned program of recruitment, from initial contact through the beginning of the college year, is essential. This should include: specific job descriptions, recruiting brochures, a nationwide recruiting plan, an effective application and screening process, and a carefully planned preservice training program.

The key personnel to be hired in student affairs consists of the director of admissions and registration, the director of counseling and guidance, the director of financial aid and placement, and the counselors.

The dean of administrative services will normally be the only professional in his area during the planning and early operational stages of the college. He will require a minimum staff including an accountant, secretarial assistance, and possibly a construction coordinator. Prior to the opening of the college, the following personnel will be needed: security officers, manager of the college store, manager of food services, and maintenance and custodial personnel.

In research, planning, and information systems, the president will usually be the long-range planner during the early stages of the college. If institutional research and extensive computer services are considered important for the new college, an administrator competent in these fields should be employed during this planning phase.

If the college intends to be serious about its community identity and responsibilities, a director or dean of community services should be employed prior to the arrival of students. In the area of public information, the president's office usually handles the initial activities. A full-time position in public information is recommended sometime during the first year of operation.

Suggested Activities and Problems

1. You are the newly elected president of a comprehensive community college and have to recommend initial administrative staffing patterns to the board of trustees. Conduct a depth interview with at least two community college presidents; then develop a plan for key personnel to be employed the year before your college opens.

2. Select one of the administrative or instructional positions described in this chapter for which a job description is not included in Appendix 4. Write one.

3. Defend or refute this statement: "The broad divisional structure is the soundest basis for organizing the instructional program and staff in the community college."

4. Interview a dean of student affairs in a community college, with the aim of developing a proposed staffing structure for student services.

5. Outline a detailed plan for community services in a new community college.

Selected Readings

Cohen, Arthur M., *Dateline '79: Heretical Concepts for the Community College,* chaps. 2, 3, 4, 5, 11, 14. Beverly Hills, Calif.: Glencoe Press, a division of The Macmillan Company, 1969.

——— et al., *A Constant Variable: New Perspectives on the Community College,* chaps. 2, 3, 4. San Francisco: Jossey-Bass, Inc., 1971.

Johnson, B. Lamar, *Starting a Community Junior College.* Washington, D.C.: American Association of Junior Colleges, 1964.

Koehnline, William A. and Clyde E. Blocker, "The Division Chairman in the Community College," *Junior College Journal,* 40, No. 5 (1970), 9-12.

Port, Stephen M., *Guidelines for the Recruitment and Selection of Community College Faculty.* Gainesville, Fla.: Institute of Higher Education, University of Florida, 1971.

Richardson, Richard C. Jr., Clyde E. Blocker, and Louis W. Bender, *Governance for the Two-Year College,* chaps. 4, 5, 6, 7, 8. Englewood Cliffs, N.J.: Prentice-Hall, Inc., 1972.

Thornton, James W., Jr., *The Community Junior College,* chaps. 9, 10. New York: John Wiley & Sons, Inc., 1966.

7

Developing the Philosphy, Institutional Objectives, and Policies of the College

---

There are at least several theories regarding written statements of institutional philosophy and objectives.

"Most colleges have them in the catalog so we better come up with something."

"The accrediting association always expects such a statement, so we need to get one together."

"When citizens and other visitors come to the campus, it is desirable to have a sheet of philosophy and objectives to hand out, if requested."

"It is imperative to think through the philosophical base on which the college should be built, and to state rather specific objectives and means of accomplishment to carry out the philosophy."

The first three "theories" have a measure of truth in them, but the last one is the most compelling reason for addressing the question. A community college represents an enormous investment in human and financial resources, and the early decisions regarding the purposes of the college will affect countless generations of students as well as the community at large. No board of trustees or college staff can afford to take lightly its collective responsibilities in this critical area of concern. Philosophical decisions must be faced and decided—at least for the early years of the college. It is hoped that the process of developing and revising institutional philosophy and objectives will be ongoing, reflecting changing values and needs in the society to be served.

Developing Initial Philosophy and Institutional Objectives

Timing is one of the critical questions. When, in the planning process for a new college, should this issue be faced? There are several possibilities, with advantages and disadvantages to each.

1. The president can research and write up a statement of philosophy and objectives and present it to the board for approval.

   Advantages: All new staff members will know where the college stands philosophically as they join the team. This is a simple approach, involving as few people as possible; it is the most efficient way to get the job done.

   Disadvantages: There is no real staff involvement in determining basic thrusts of the college. Furthermore, there is too much reliance on the input of one professional.

2. The process can be delayed until most of the initial professional staff is hired; then a committee would be appointed to report back to the total staff with recommended philosophy and objectives.

   Advantages: This is the most democratic procedure, providing for full involvement. The input of all can be considered.

   Disadvantages: The college would probably be operating for several years without a statement of philosophy and objectives. Too many other pressing matters would crowd out this effort as opening day draws near. If completed, the statement would likely be hurried and ragged.

3. The president can begin the initial research and thinking on philosophy and objectives. As key members join the staff they can immediately be involved in discussions on this highly important topic. Early in the year preceding opening of the college a statement can be ready for board approval.

   Advantages: The college will have a philosophical position before basic decisions in, for instance, curriculum and staffing have to be made. This is, of course, preferred. Otherwise programs are planned with no reference point as to their validity. Another advantage is that this procedure is democratic to the extent that the complete present staff is involved. Also, the purposes of the college will be well known to the community before opening day.

   Disadvantages: This plan does not provide for full staff involvement on a matter of basic importance.

Experience shows that the last suggestion is the most viable, considering all factors. It is imperative to have the philosophy and institutional objectives developed before other major decisions are made. For example, developmental programs for marginal high school graduates can hardly be planned unless it has been decided philosophically that the college will be an open-door institution, committed to serve all those who have graduated from high school.

It is suggested that the initial statement of philosophy and institutional objectives be approved to serve the college through accreditation (see Chapter 14). At that time the full staff can be involved in a thorough review and possible revision of both philosophy and objectives.

The process of developing institutional philosophy and objectives is a critical one and deserves high priority on the list of start-up activities. The following suggestions should prove helpful to the president, his staff, and the board of trustees as they approach this formidable task.

1. Acquire statements of philosophy and objectives from other community colleges throughout the nation. (These are often found in the college bulletin or catalog.) Read the statements as background for the task ahead. Stoutly resist the temptation to cut and paste, thereby shortening the arduous but necessary process of determining the new institution's goals and purposes.

2. Working as a committee of the whole (including all staff members present and several members of the board of trustees), study the community as carefully as possible to discover existing educational needs. Review the basic feasibility study that led to the formation of this community college. Organize conferences with groups of civic, business, industrial, and professional leaders. Seek out representatives of the disadvantaged and of the common citizens, as well as of the acknowledged leadership groups. Through extensive contacts, do everything possible to get ideas on the new community college, and on what the citizens expect it to be.

3. Organize several open forums where citizens are invited to come and talk with the leadership of the college and the board of trustees. Involve the local news media in helping to publicize these forums, whose aim is to get additional ideas from concerned citizens regarding the purpose and function of the new college.

4. Confer with members of the council for higher education, who were initially involved in the plans for establishing the college. They will be able and willing to provide valuable input. (Incidentally, this group is often ignored after the college is organized. It is a wise president and board who continue to involve those who were instrumental in forming the institution.)

5. Begin to write drafts of the philosophy of the college. These should be critically reviewed by the committee and the entire board until all are

FIGURE 7-1

satisfied with the basic philosophical statement. This is then formally approved by the board of trustees.

6. Spell out specific institutional objectives designed to implement the philosophy of the college. If the staff and board are thinking of developing any kind of systematic approach to the instructional process, here is the place to begin. Institutional objectives can be stated in precise, measurable terms that make the college accountable for its efforts from the beginning. Some statements of objectives also list the means of accomplishment, often in performance terms.[1]

Developing Board Policy and Administrative Procedures

Building on the philosophy and institutional objectives just adopted, the president and the board now direct their attention to the writing and approval of basic policies. It is important to note several principles here:

1. There must be a clear understanding between the board and the president regarding their respective roles. The board's main task is to establish general policies for the college; the president's responsibility is to administer the insti-

---

[1]See Appendix 7, p. 327, for statements of philosophy and institutional objectives from several community colleges.

tution, carrying out the established policies. Many boards, colleges, and presidents have come to grief because of the board's involvement in administration. If the institution is to remain healthy and vigorous, this must not be permitted. No president worthy of the position will tolerate board interference in administrative processes. On the other hand, the president should not try to dictate basic board policy. This is the domain of the board members as representatives of the citizens.

In actual practice, the most workable arrangement is one in which the president, because of his experience, recommends proposed drafts of policies to the board. After due consideration, debate, and revision, the board finally approves the policy statements, and they are incorporated in the policy handbook. It is then the president's responsibility to develop, with his staff, the necessary administrative procedures to carry out the basic policies.

2. Another principle is the matter of timing. The arguments on timing of philosophy and objectives enunciated earlier apply here. It is best to develop a good body of basic policies and procedures before the college opens. As administrative, instructional, and noninstructional staff members are hired, they are immediately involved in the formulation of policy recommendations under the leadership of the president. After policies are approved, the staff assists the president in writing appropriate administrative procedures to carry out the policy provisions.

There is a school of thought that holds: "No policy shall be written until the full staff is present, and until the college has some experience in operation." The theory is that policy can best be formulated in the crucible of experience, and that a more meaningful, better written policy will emerge, given the valuable inputs of faculty and students. Perhaps—but experience indicates that so many decisions are made by so many persons during the developmental stages of a college that basic policy formulations are essential to avoid chaos. Can you imagine five key administrators each making decisions regarding admission of students, eligibility for financial aid, staff placement on a salary scale, selection of learning resources, travel expenses and conditions of employment, without some common policy to guide them?

It is best to carefully write a solid body of basic policies and administrative procedures that will serve the college during its early years. These policies and procedures can be modified as the need becomes apparent. But it is far better to have a base from which to operate in a new community college. Such a body of policies and procedures, if cooperatively developed by president, staff, and board, will provide a stable setting for launching the full operations of the college.

The process of developing board policy and administrative procedures can best be learned by reference to typical documents from selected colleges and from practical suggestions that emerge from experience. For the remainder of this discussion reference is made to the excerpts from community college board policies and administrative procedures in Appendix 8, pp. 336. The following suggested guidelines and recommendations are intended to be of practical assistance in developing and organizing policies and procedures.

1. Decide on the divisions of policy and procedure. Either a two- or three-level system may be used. The simplest form is the two-level arrangement, in which each board policy is implemented by a concomitant administrative procedure, detailing how the policy is to be carried out. The three-level system inserts an administrative policy statement, so that the flow is:

Board policy → Administrative policy → Administrative procedure.

With either system, board policies should not be written in isolation. Administrative policies and/or administrative procedures are essential to complete the action called for in the board policy. Matching numbers should be used for easy reference. For example, board policy no. 100 should have a corresponding administrative procedure no. 100.

2. Determine an effective and attractive format for compiling and publishing policies and procedures. A loose-leaf binding is recommended, so that future additions and revisions can easily be made without reprinting the entire manual.

3. Secure policy and procedures manuals from several community colleges similar in projected size and philosophy. These are very useful in helping to identify areas in which policies and procedures are needed. Also, often the wording of various sections can be adapted to meet local needs. Although policy and procedures manuals should not be copied any more than philosophies and institutional objectives, it is extremely helpful to have several admissions policies on hand, for example, when attempting to verbalize the policy that has been decided upon for the new college.

4. In writing policy and procedure it is necessary to keep the entire area of collective negotiations in mind. The college attorney should carefully review all policies and procedures before they are adopted. It is a foregone conclusion that the contents of the policy and procedures manual will become a prime arena for negotiation with the faculty, administrative staff, noninstructional staff, or any other segment of the college community that may formally organize for collective bargaining. If a negotiating unit likes a particular policy, they will opt for including it in the upcoming contract; if they do not like it, the negotiators will be angling for a change. In any event, write *all* policy and procedure with an eye to collective bargaining implications.

5. Identify basic areas for policy determination and work with the staff as a

committee of the whole or with concerned persons. All recommended policy should be tentatively approved by the president's staff, and then presented to the board for its consideration.

Following is a listing of basic areas in which policy and procedures usually are developed:

Salary guides or schedules, including ranges, criteria for placement. Needed for administrative, instructional and noninstructional personnel.

Instructional personnel policies and procedures, including initial assignment, rank, working conditions, contractual periods, renewal and nonrenewal of contracts, salary and wage administration, promotional policy, fringe benefits, absences, leaves, vacations, retirement program, evaluation of personnel, grievance procedure, travel expenses.

Noninstructional personnel policies and procedures, including initial assignment, conditions of employment, evaluation of job performance, grievance procedure, salary and wage administration, fringe benefits, absences, leaves, vacations, retirement program, promotional policy.

Job descriptions for each position on campus.

Academic freedom and responsibility.

Learning resources selection.

Academic standards relating to probation and disqualification from full-time enrollment.

Admissions policy.

Formation and operation of student clubs and organizations.

Plan for involvement in governance of the college.

Referral of students.

Student financial aid.

Confidentiality of student records.

Budget preparation and adoption.

Purchasing.

Use of college facilities.

Public relations.

Sponsored research and grant programs.

Insurance.

Patent and copyright policy.

College calendar.

Code of student conduct.

Forms management and control.

Although not exhaustive, the above list indicates the magnitude of the task facing the president, his staff, and the board of trustees in developing a comprehensive set of initial policies and procedures.

Developing a Plan for Involvement in Governance

One of the basic areas noted above for development of policy and procedure is involvement in governance of the college. The need for facing this issue squarely and early cannot be emphasized too strongly. In the planning stages a tentative or interim plan for involvement of all persons in the decision-making processes of the college should be evolved. As with all other policies and plans, this can then be modified as the college opens and grows.

The basic question, of course, is how much to involve staff members, students, and citizens in the decisions that traditionally have been made by the administration and the board of trustees. It is important that all concerned persons be democratically involved in the decision-making process. And it must be *real* involvement; students and faculty alike can see through superficial plans that provide only for token participation. All members of a college community should have a chance for meaningful involvement in the life and governance of the institution.

A new institution has a unique opportunity to develop a governance plan based on research and experience. The first step is to identify the characteristics desired in a plan. The Handbook of Stockton State College in New Jersey states:

> The prospects for campus governance at Stockton will be enhanced if it has the following among its characteristics:
>
> 1. A simple structure.
> 2. Avenues for participation by the basic constituencies of the college.
> 3. Openness of operation.
> 4. A quick pace of activity.
> 5. Willingness to see each decision as a step along a continuing path.
> 6. Readiness for changing itself.
> 7. The knack of combining seriousness of purpose, dignity of conduct, humility, and a sense of humor.

The Stockton Handbook then identifies the following basic assumptions underlying a system of governance:

> . . . A governance system depends largely on the goodwill and sense of responsibility of its constituents.
>
> . . . A governance system should match structure to function.
>
> . . . A governance system should include manageable groups subject to some checks and balances.
>
> . . . A governance system should minimize exclusivity and maximize a sense of community.
>
> . . . A governance system should allow ready identification of and easy access to persons responsible for policy decisions.
>
> . . . Persons who participate in the formulation of decisions affecting their lives are most likely to accept them.

. . . Opportunities to contribute directly or indirectly to policy making should be available to all members of the college community.

. . . An all-college, single body system simplifies governance, eliminates duplication, and fosters unity.

. . . Legal authority and accountability rest with the President, the Board of Trustees, and the State.[2]

In designing an interim plan of governance, the staff must recognize that at best it is a complex task. There is no single pattern that is appropriate for all community colleges. Some of the options are as follows:

1. An all-college council or legislature, with recommending powers to the president, or with legislative responsibility.
2. A multi-council structure, covering major areas such as Curriculum and Instruction and Student Affairs. Recommendations are made by each council to the president for action (see Appendix 9, p. 349).

In developing any plan for involvement in governance, it is important that the four major constituencies of the college be represented on all councils: students, instructional staff, administrators, and noninstructional or classified staff.

Another basic principle is the matter of ultimate responsibility, and it must be dealt with. A council or committee cannot and will not assume responsibility for decisions. In any college the role of the president as a strong, yet sensitive leader has to be recognized. The board of trustees holds him responsible for the administration and operation of the college. He then must have the right to accept, modify, reject, or send back for further study all recommendations that come to him. Some plans of governance may provide for override of the president's veto on certain actions. In such cases, the matter would go to the board of trustees for final decision.

A workable plan for involvement in governance will help to develop the sense of community that is so important on the college campus. If all persons have a direct participatory role in the decision-making process, the negative effects of unionism and the extremes of hard nosed collective bargaining may be mitigated. This, in itself, will make the strenuous effort at involvement worthwhile. Richardson, Blocker, and Bender's *Governance for the Two-Year College* presents comprehensive treatment of structures of governance and the dynamics of human interaction in the two-year college.

Summary

It is imperative to think through the philosophical base on which the college should be built, and to state specific objectives and means of accomplishment to

[2] *Handbook, College Year 1971-72* (Pomona, N.J.: Stockton State College, 1971), p. 15.

carry out the philosophy. The process of developing and revising institutional philosophy and objectives should be ongoing, reflecting changing values and needs in society.

With regard to timing, development of a statement of philosophy and objectives early in the year before the college opens is recommended. The philosophy and institutional objectives must definitely be developed before other major decisions are made.

The process of identifying and writing elements of the philosophy and objectives includes study of statements from other community colleges, examining the community and the original feasibility study that led to the formation of the college, conferences with people from all segments of the community, community forums, and, finally, actual writing of the college philosophy and institutional objectives.

The next step is the development of basic policies and administrative procedures. The board's main task is to establish general policies for the college; and the president's responsibility is to administer the institution. In practice, the president usually recommends drafts of policies to the board, which are debated and approved. Then the president, with his staff, develops the necessary administrative procedures to carry out the policies. Such a body of policies and procedures will provide a stable setting for launching the full operations of the college.

In the developmental stages of a college, a tentative or interim plan for involvement of all persons in the decision-making processes should be evolved. This may include an all-college council or legislature; or a multi-council structure. Any plan should provide for representation of students, instructional staff, administrators, and noninstructional or classified staff.

Suggested Activities and Problems

1. Write a statement of philosophy for a new community college.
2. Design a set of institutional objectives based on this philosophy.
3. Examine a policy and procedures manual of a community college. Write a critique of the manual.
4. In a paper, discuss the potential relationship between emerging board policy and collective negotiations.
5. Outline a governance plan for a community college, indicating how each constituency will be represented.

Selected Readings

The Assembly on University Goals and Governance. Cambridge, Mass.: The American Academy of Arts and Sciences, 1971.

Graves, Thomas A., Jr., "Crisis in University Governance," *Collegiate News and Views,* 24, No. 3 (1971), 1-3.

Keeton, Morris, *Shared Authority on Campus.* Washington, D.C.: American Association for Higher Education, 1971.

Plan for Involvement in the Governance of the College. Pemberton, N.J.: Burlington County College, 1971.

Representative Legislature of Brookdale Community College. Lincroft, N.J.: Brookdale Community College, 1971.

Richardson, Richard C. Jr., Clyde E. Blocker, and Louis W. Bender, *Governance for the Two-Year College.* Englewood Cliffs, N.J.: Prentice-Hall, Inc., 1972.

Riess, Louis C. "Institutional Attitudes Relating to Faculty Participation in California Community College Governance." Unpublished study. Pasadena, Calif.: Pasadena City College, 1970.

Smith, G. Kerry, ed., *Agony and Promise, Current Issues in Higher Education, 1969,* chaps. 17-20, 26. San Francisco: Jossey-Bass, Inc., Publishers. © American Association for Higher Education, 1969.

——, ed., *The Troubled Campus, Current Issues in Higher Education, 1970,* chaps. 11-16. San Francisco: Jossey-Bass, Inc., Publishers. © American Association for Higher Education, 1970.

8

Designing
the Educational Program

"What kind of educational institution are you planning?" The board of trustees, the president, and the growing staff must continually ask this question, and particularly as they approach the design of the educational program of the college. The emerging philosophy and objectives (Chapter 7) will determine, to a great extent, the directions of the educational programming. And there are really only two options, although there may be slight variations on the themes.

Play It Safe. Build a traditional two-year college with emphasis on the liberal arts transfer program, since the community will best understand this approach, and the college will be more respectable. Cut up a few standard college catalogs, set up the usual courses, and schedule them three times a week. Plan the typical lecture-classroom format for instruction, and hire traditional faculty who are committed to *telling and testing*. Turn them loose on their classroom islands in full possession of their so-called academic freedom, and you will be assured of a traditional, fragmented, and mediocre educational program. If you are ready to settle for this safe, well-furrowed approach, you do not have to continue further in this chapter. If, on the other hand, a forward-looking, innovative curriculum, based on the best findings of educational research is envisioned, the next option is the only viable alternative.

Take a Bold, Dynamic Stance. Plan to build or develop a community college that will truly serve its constituents into the twenty-first century. Defined as a really comprehensive institution of higher learning, the college will open its doors to all high school graduates and other adult citizens interested in initiating or continuing their college education. There will be a great range of students and an equally impressive range of programs to meet their educational needs. The curriculum designers must plan flexible programs that can change as society and the needs of the individual learners change. The following programs, among others, will be offered day and evening, on and off campus, year round: developmental or remedial, transfer, technical, and paraprofessional.

A systematic approach to curriculum and instructional development and the teaching-learning process will be employed to assure that the students are challenged with appropriate, relevant learning experiences. The best and most promising instructional strategies will be employed, utilizing the most modern technology and plant facilities. The college will employ innovative faculty and support personnel who are willing to experiment with new ideas and research in the learning process. Staff commitment to planned experimentation and change is essential.

The remainder of this chapter consists of a step-by-step approach to the systematic design of a dynamic educational program for a modern, learner-centered community college. It is assumed that each staff member, as he is employed, will be intimately involved in all of the suggested activities. It is desirable that a considerable number of faculty and other staff be hired early enough in a new community college to actively participate in program design. In an established college, it is of course imperative that all staff members be involved in ongoing evaluation and revision of the instructional program.

Step 1. Identify needs of the community that can be met by college programs. This may mean updating the studies outlined in Chapter 2. It will probably involve some new surveys of business, industry, and the professions. (Use forms in Appendix 2, p. 273 for guidance.)

The board chairman, president, and other staff members can initiate conferences with leaders of the community, and with other citizens who can contribute to the updating of the needs study.

The leaders of other agencies that offer educational programs around the level of community college offerings should be consulted to avoid overlapping. For example, is the local hospital building up or phasing out its nurse training program? Would the hospital board and administrator welcome the college moving into an associate degree nursing program? Or are the needs already being met? As another example, is the local vocational-technical high school offering post-high school electronics technology, or is the program strictly high school level? The community college has to know the extent of the curricula of other nearby educational institutions before launching new programs of its own. As a third example, what is the scope of the four-year state college and university extension offerings in the area served by the community college? What does the state master plan provide regarding regionalization of curricula? Or are there guidelines from the state department? If so, these must be studied carefully.

Step 2. Determine the basic philosophic approach to instructional development and the teaching-learning process that will undergird the educational programs of the college. A systematic approach to the entire process that involves careful scientific planning every step of the way is recommended. A position paper should be prepared at this stage so that the community, the board of trustees, and new staff members are well attuned to the basic instructional philosophy of the institution. Naturally, all staff members currently present should contribute to this document, but the president or academic dean should take the leadership in writing the various drafts and conducting discussions on them. The following statement is excerpted from such a document, prepared after two years of operation of a new community college. From experience, it is suggested that a preliminary position paper such as this be written the year before opening a college; it can then be revised as the college program evolves.

Instructional Systems for Student Learning: the Burlington County College Approach[1]

Burlington County College has, since its inception, been dedicated to implementing a systematically designed approach to instruction and student learning. The core elements of the systems approach can be concisely stated:

1. From the identified values and needs of society, a basic philosophy for the college is developed.
2. General institutional objectives are specified.
3. Curricular programs are selected and basic goals stated.
4. For each course or learning sequence, outcomes that are to result from the teaching-learning process are defined in advance.
5. An orderly plan or scheme is devised to move from definition of outcomes to their attainment.
6. Feedback is planned as part of the system so that evaluative information may be employed in modifying the system.

The educational endeavor in which we are engaged is a unique one, for it is an *institution-wide experiment* with a particular type of educational innovation. There are presently no perfected systems for us to emulate. As a new institution, we have faced the tremendous task of developing our own educational design. Such experimentation means hard work and problems as well as the satisfaction of accomplishment.

Those who founded and organized the college chose to implement a systematic approach to student learning primarily because educational research has indicated that considerable learning gains can be achieved through the use of such a process. Also, the general public, who supports the college financially, and many people within the educational establishment as well, have become

[1] Position paper issued by Burlington County College, Pemberton, N.J., June, 1971.

increasingly concerned about the outcomes of education in relation to the constantly rising costs. We in education have for years concentrated on instructional process rather than on learning outcomes because of the supposedly vague and indefinable nature of our product. However, if we are to command continuing support, we must define our objectives and exhibit the results of our endeavors. This is accountability, and we have been committed to the concept at Burlington County College long before the term became an educational byword of the 1970s.

How, then, does a systems approach improve learning? The systems approach helps because it is based upon objectives—i.e., well *defined, measurable outcomes*. Why are such objectives important? We cannot prove that we have done anything until we explicitly define what it is we are trying to help the learner accomplish—and then show whether he accomplished it or not.

In our recruiting we have emphasized that the systems approach does require a kind of commitment on the part of the teacher to the tenets of certain educational theorists such as Skinner, Bloom, Mager and Popham, and to rather explicit instructional practices designed around behavioral learning objectives. We have discovered through experience that this approach to learning calls for a substantial change in the teacher's professional role concepts and his traditional supremacy in the classroom, and it also demands a great deal more time and effort in planning and preparation, and in work with individual students. It is true that commitment and extra effort are necessary for successful experience in an institution such as ours, but the role of the teacher, though changed somewhat from the traditional, is *not diminished*. The system cannot function without the master teacher, although his role is certainly different and more challenging.

Let us examine some of the implications, for both faculty and administrators, inherent in this new approach. We are asked to view learning not in terms of some vague and mysterious subjective process, but rather in terms of some objective and observable indication on the part of the student that he has acquired some new knowledge, capability, or attitude that he did not possess before exposure to the system. We are also asked to modify our traditional role expectations concerning teaching—from that of a triweekly, center stage performer and information dispenser to that of a planner, strategist, and instructional manager, using the facilities and resources of the institution, and our special knowledge and skills to bring about the desired changes in student behavior.

Instructional management, as the term is used above, refers to a program of deliberate activities leading to a form of systematic instruction. As the system evolves and our managerial skills improve, greater proficiency in defining outcomes and designing instructional strategies will be attained. The goal of systematic instructional management is to more objectively define, achieve, and measure instructional outcomes in terms of learner behavior.

At Burlington County College a number of instructional strategies using different modes of instruction and various learning resources are available to the teacher or instructional manager. The aim is to individualize instruction as much as possible through the appropriate modes, such as seminar, independent study, and large group instruction. All courses cannot and should not be designed to use all available instructional modes, nor are all instructors expected to employ the same methodologies in the same way. However, budgetary realities require a balancing of large group, laboratory, classroom, independent study, and seminars to achieve a mix that can be supported economically, and that will individualize instruction at the same time.

Much work also remains to be done in the area of evaluation. Changes in student cognitive and affective learning, and attitudes toward learning, are not always easily assessed. Many of our efforts at evaluation are and will continue to be quite primitive—but that is understood. Let it be said here that miracles are not expected, and none of us who has honestly tried, yet failed, to fully measure student change need despair. Experimentation is always fraught with some failure and further challenge. This is accepted as part of the experimental process at Burlington County College. Yet we must continually attempt to measure student change.

Many educators, including some at Burlington County College, fear that technology may dominate and dehumanize learning within a rigid systems framework. Yet we can prevent the medium from becoming the message (to paraphrase Marshall McLuhan). If the college is student-oriented, and specific objectives are written with student learning needs in mind, then the various learning modes available on the new B.C.C. campus can be humanistically employed to help achieve the objectives. Some of the modes will involve various media, the computer, and other technological aids. Our campus is designed for the employment of a variety of instructional strategies. For example, educational technology can be very efficiently utilized in teaching many basic cognitive skills. *Such efficiency at this level can free the instructor for the kind of teacher-student interaction that only human beings can employ. If the teacher can be freed to inspire, motivate, and enable the individual student to learn, then educational technology will have justified its existence.*

An educational system is no better than the people who design and implement it. No amount of paper planning and electronic gadgetry will accomplish the objectives of an institution unless the *people* involved have a unity and commitment to the system and to the objectives. It is realized that in asking for a reexamination of the basic concepts of the teaching-learning process, with an eye toward acceptance of new values, more may be requested than can be delivered in a year or two from the opening of a new college. Again, miracles are not expected, although some have been performed at Burlington County College since September, 1969. It is expected, however, that everyone give the systems approach a chance to work by honestly trying it. Our obligation to the philosophy and institutional goals of the college demand such a commitment, and we should strive for reasonable progress each year. One question that always comes to mind is, "Why did I come here?" All of us are part of an institution that is committed to breaking with tradition in the teaching-learning process. It is probably true that most of us came to Burlington County College because we were dissatisfied with many of the traditional approaches to education. We chose to break with tradition and to experiment with a particular type of educational innovation. Collectively, this has meant a large commitment in terms of human resources, time, money, and campus facilities.

The process that we have begun here is an exciting one and it will always be challenging. Educational theory is not easily turned into institutional fact. When we chose to undertake this venture, all of us were asked to make a commitment to the institution's philosophy and goals. This request still stands. In the final analysis, an educational system is the persons who comprise it—and it is no better than these people choose to make it. Our rewards here at Burlington County College will be commensurate with our efforts.

Step 3. From the results of Steps 1 and 2, identify the basic educational programs to be offered by the college. In a comprehensive community college, they will include, but will certainly not be limited to, the following.

1. *Two-year career programs* leading to the associate degree in such fields as computer technology, secretarial science, electronics, and medical laboratory technology (to mention a few examples of curricula in this technical and paraprofessional area) are offered in most community colleges. Many of these programs are expensive to initiate, and the new college should make certain that the research studies and surveys suggested earlier in this chapter provide rather conclusive evidence (a) that there will be sufficient student interest in a particular curriculum and (b) that there will be jobs for graduates in the regional labor market area. The staffing for each program must also be carefully considered. There are cost factors here, that is, in staff-student ratios required by certain accrediting organizations. Also, the availability of qualified staff may be a problem in some geographic areas. The presence or absence of supporting facilities in the community is a real factor in deciding to initiate career programs. For example, adequate hospital support is essential to most allied health programs. The college cannot usually afford the clinical facilities, and, furthermore, actual student participation in real situations is a necessary part of a good curriculum. In conclusion, it is best to select several basic career programs that have a good chance of success rather than initiate a number, of which some are questionable.

2. *Transfer programs,* which enable the community college graduate to transfer to a four-year institution for his last two years of a baccalaureate degree, are usually offered by comprehensive community colleges. Major areas of emphasis such as liberal arts, sciences, preengineering, preeducation, and others are selected—again on the basis of the need studies among prospective students

and the other surveys previously completed. College officials will want to carefully study the catalogs of four-year institutions to which the community college graduates will most likely transfer. Conferences among administrators of all concerned colleges and universities are highly desirable. These are sometimes organized by the state department. If not, any president or group of presidents can initiate such articulation talks. Sometimes informal organizations of regional college presidents entertain each other at dinner every month or two to discuss such matters as community college students moving into the upper divisions of the state colleges.

In the sixties and seventies, much greater understanding has developed between two-year and four-year institutions. Most senior colleges and universities will now accept the graduates of community college transfer programs on the basis of certification by the sending college. Many state systems of higher education provide for automatic movement of community college transfer graduates into the upper division institutions.

The curriculum designers at the two-year college level need mainly to insure that their evolving freshman and sophomore transfer programs are at least equivalent in quality and scope to the comparable lower division programs in the four-year institutions.

3. A comprehensive, open-door community college will offer strong *developmental or remedial programs* if it is interested in keeping its open door from becoming a revolving door. A college simply should not admit all high school graduates and then offer only one level of English or mathematics to freshman students. Yet, this is still occurring in many so-called comprehensive community colleges.

Carefully designed basic courses in such areas as reading, English, and mathematics need to be individualized to meet the tremendous range of needs of entering freshmen—especially those who have not been very successful learners in high school. Entry pretests, for example, will help to screen slow readers or those deficient in certain reading skills. Basic reading sequences are then required to upgrade the student's skills before he founders and drops out of college. Some community colleges are designing developmental courses in areas other than the basic skills—for example, in social sciences. In this way the student can use programmed multimedia sequences to learn his fundamental concepts in economics while he is improving his reading skills. Usually credit for graduation is not given for developmental or remedial courses, although this is certainly an issue open for extensive debate.

4. *Continuing education* should be part of the initial offerings of any two-year college claiming to be comprehensive. Many persons will want to work part time on a degree or certificate program. Others will take courses for enjoyment, or for learning about a new discipline, or for upgrading vocational skills. Full-time students at other colleges will take summer work at the local community college. Homemakers will drop in for a course or two during the day.

Police officers will be interested in a part-time program in law enforcement that will lead eventually to an associate degree, but which they can take while still retaining their full-time police assignment. The list is endless. Continuing studies need to be made in the community to determine the needed part-time offerings. The program will be varied and inclusive. Students may take the transfer, career, and developmental programs on a part-time basis. In addition, other credit and noncredit offerings will be made available to other prospective students. Short courses and seminars may be planned for business executives and industrial workers. Part-time programs may be presented anywhere in the community where there is a demand—in storefronts, high schools, community centers, or on the main campus.

5. A comprehensive community college will usually include *certificate programs and noncredit offerings* in its curricular repertoire. Such programs are planned to meet specific needs that are not being satisfied by existing educational and community agencies. It is important to coordinate noncredit and certificate offerings with other schools and groups. It is often desirable to establish a countywide coordinating council to involve all educational institutions and agencies, such as the high school adult night schools, the vocational-technical school, the community college, and any four-year collegiate institutions offering programs or courses in the area. Such a group can help avoid overlapping and duplication of effort in both noncredit and credit offerings. The community college president may assume leadership in getting such a council organized.

Step 4. An optional step at this point might be the organization of a general citizens advisory committee and several special advisory committees in the career program areas. All these groups, to be appointed by the board of trustees, would consist of outstanding and knowledgeable citizens who could contribute valuable ideas to the various developing educational programs of the college.

FIGURE 8-1

Such committees are invaluable to an established community college. However, there are pros and cons on initiating advisory groups at this point. These are presented below; you may determine the optimum timing in a specific situation.

Advantages. It is essential to get solid community input at the earliest possible time to assist in the educational program decisions that must be made. For example, if business management is one of the career programs in the new college, valuable input can be obtained from a representative committee of business and industrial leaders regarding proposed learning sequences and experiences to be introduced into the curriculum. An advisory committee in computer technology will advise the administration and board on the latest developments in this fast-moving field that have implications for a data-processing curriculum.

Another advantage of early advisory committees is the positive effect of substantial citizen involvement and subsequent interest in the college at a time when the new institution has low visibility in the community. Advisory committee members usually become strong supporters of the college.

Disadvantages. At this point in the development of a college, the staff is already busy with a multitude of vital activities leading to the opening of the institution. It is too much to expect the academic dean or the division chairmen (if they are there) to take on this added time-consuming responsibility. And the members of the faculty who often work with citizens advisory committees are probably not yet employed.

Another disadvantage could be disillusionment or discontent among the advisory committee members if their advice is not fully accepted. This is always a calculated risk, but especially at this time in the life of a college, when all the good will one can muster is needed.

Also, some advisory committee members tend to equate themselves with the policy-making members of the board of trustees who appoint them. If there is not sufficient time to carefully organize and orient each committee regarding its *advisory* role, this can be a disadvantage.

Step 5. Identify the basic learning sequences for each educational program selected in Step 3. These sequences of subject matter content and instructional methodology are traditionally called *courses.* However, an ideal goal is to develop a continuum of learning in each program so that student entry and progress can be individualized. The end result of such a policy would be a *semesterless* and *courseless* college (see Chapter 9).

Whether learning experiences are grouped in typical course packages or in a learning continuum, the next decision involves the identification of common learning experiences to be introduced to all students. This is usually known as the general education core; it is discussed in Chapter 9. Since a community college serves a variety of students with diverse educational goals, it is generally agreed that a common body of learning in such basic areas as communication, the social sciences, and the humanities is essential for all educated persons to interact in society.

Next, graduation requirements in each program must be determined. With a typical course and credit hour structure, completion of a degree program usually involves the satisfactory attainment of a stated number of semester or quarter hours, with certain courses being required. If the learning continuum concept is adopted, graduation requirements are met in each program through satisfactory demonstration by the student of the accomplishment of performance objectives in each required and optional learning sequence.

Still another decision must be made in a new college. Are initial courses or learning sequences to be developed for the two years of associate degree programs, or for the freshman year only? Experience shows that it is usually best to open the college for freshmen *only* during the first year of operation. This is particularly advisable if a systematic approach to student learning is adopted. Curriculum development is a difficult and demanding task. The new staff will do well to complete sufficient courses or learning sequences for the wide range of freshman student abilities.

Step 6. Complete personnel and logistical support plans for the process of instructional development. First, sufficient supervisory personnel need to be available, such as the dean of academic affairs, division chairmen, and, if possible, an assistant dean for instructional program development. At least one of these persons should be an expert in curriculum development, and he must be available to provide leadership to the faculty. Second, the actual curriculum writers are identified and employed. Two basic options are available:

1. Employ faculty members in the summer and provide intensive pre-service training; then organize them as functional teams for curriculum development.
2. Employ full-time curriculum-writing specialists to design the learning sequences or courses, and to continually revise and update them, working with the faculty.

This, of course, is a basic personnel decision, and its implications need to be seriously considered. Do you want a permanent cadre for curriculum development, or are you prepared to provide the necessary released time during the academic year and/or funds for summer work to enable the regular faculty teams to accomplish the ongoing task? In general, the latter alternative deserves preference in most colleges. Reason: faculty members who interact with students and manage the learning process directly are usually eager to design the learning objectives and strategies. And they will usually do a very creditable job, given the proper supervisory assistance, time, and logistical support.

Facilities and materiel support are crucial. They should include the following before the curriculum project gets underway:

1. A well-stocked professional library, with research materials available in all fields to be developed. This can be an area in the college library or, preferably, a separate space designated *Instructional Development Center* can be set aside near the faculty work areas. This effort will require at least a part-time librarian, and available materials should be attractively displayed for ready use by the curriculum teams. The collection should include lists of learning objectives in the various disciplines, sample curriculum guides from other similar institutions, research findings in each field, and training media such as films and filmstrips on the systems approach, for example. The librarian also must have available up to date bibliographies and other sources of book and nonbook media for each discipline.

2. Quiet working areas for curriculum workers are essential—separate offices, if possible, and attractive conference areas for small group work.

Step 7. Launch the systematic process of instructional development for each learning sequence or course. The first task of the curriculum worker is to select and organize the content to be included in the course. This should be chosen

FIGURE 8-2

with reference to the learning needs of the students, as closely as these can be identified.

The following excerpt may assist in the process of identifying content in any subject area:[2]

2 Ross L. Neagley and N. Dean Evans, *Handbook for Effective Curriculum Development,* pp. 206-9. Copyright ©1967 by Prentice-Hall, Inc. Reprinted by permission.

Truly Representative Content Should Be Chosen. Since it is possible to select for instruction only major concepts, skills, ideas, and generalizations in any subect field, make sure that those selected are typical of the curriculum area under study. Phenix has emphasized this point:

> . . . from the large resources of material in any given discipline, those items should be chosen that are particularly *representative* of the field as a whole. The only effective solution to the surfeit of knowledge is a drastic process of simplification. This aim can be achieved by discovering for each discipline those seminal or key ideas that provide clues to the entire discipline. If the content of instruction is carefully chosen and organized so as to emphasize these characteristic features of the disciplines, a relatively small volume of knowledge may suffice to yield effective understanding of a far larger body of material.[3]

A consultant in the subject area could make a major contribution at this stage of the committee's work. A mathematics specialist will be able to outline, for example, the major ideas, concepts, and skills that are stressed in the principal modern math programs. When these are viewed side by side and available research findings are applied, the mathematics team can begin to identify representative ideas, generalizations, principles, and skills that will become a major part of the content to be taught.

This process of selecting representative content can be expedited by looking for unifying elements or principles in the subject matter under consideration. Goodlad defines these as "organizing elements":

> Effective patterns of curriculum organization contain a unifying element—a concept, principle, generalization, skill, or value—to tie the various parts together into a meaningful whole. These elements are . . . defined as "organizing elements." Then there are topics, problems, units, events, or focal points designed to stimulate appropriate behavior on the part of the students—the components of the organizing elements, so to speak. These are defined as "organizing centers."[4]

To bring this flight into curriculum theory down to earth, consider the selection of a portion of content in the social sciences. A worthy objective might well be "to develop an understanding of mankind's attempts to attain collective security in the modern world." In searching for *representative content* to achieve this objective, the social sciences team will perhaps conclude that it is impossible to cover all of the European alliances that preceded World War I. Under the guidance of a history consultant the committee might select the concept of international cooperation as envisioned in the League of Nations and continued

[3] Philip H. Phenix, *Realms of Meaning* (New York: McGraw-Hill Book Company, 1964), p. 11.

[4] John I. Goodlad, *School Curriculum Reform in the United States* (New York: The Fund for the Advancement of Education, 1964), p. 53.

through the United Nations. This would become the *organizing element*. Several units or problems then might be selected as *organizing centers* for the teaching of the big idea or concept. These could include: "Causes and effects of U.S. refusal to join the League of Nations," "Comparative organization of the League and the UN," and "The effect of United Nations involvement in specific crises on man's quest for global security and peace."

Methods of Study or Inquiry Are More Important Content Sources Than What Is Learned. No one can learn even a small portion of the factual content of a subject area. But the major methods of inquiry can be learned, and these can lead to further learning at a later date. According to Phenix:

> ... content should be chosen so as to exemplify the *methods of inquiry* and the modes of understanding in the disciplines studied. It is more important for the student to become skillful in the ways of knowing than to learn about any particular product of investigation. Knowledge of methods makes it possible for a person to continue learning and to undertake inquiries on his own.
> ... The methods of a discipline are generally more stable than are the results of inquiry. Knowledge continually undergoes modification. New discoveries are made, requiring revision of older ideas that may have been developed by essentially the same methods. Therefore, while it may prove impossible for a person to keep pace with the advancing tide of knowledge in a discipline, he may be able quite satisfactorily to remain abreast of the methods of inquiry in it.[5]

Pursuing the social sciences objective discussed above—developing an understanding of collective security in the world—the consultant at this point should be able to offer an appropriate *method of inquiry* for consideration as part of the content. For example, would it be desirable for high school students to learn the methods historians use to analyze causes and effects of historical events and forces? Could they apply this knowledge in the future to help them better understand relationships among men and nations?

Organizing Content in a Subject Area

In moving from selection to organization of content, one must take into account the theories regarding the importance of *structure* in the subject fields. Beginning with the report of the Woods Hole conference in 1959,[6] there has been increasing pressure for all curriculum workers to consider the structure of content as an important organizing principle for any subject area.

Saylor and Alexander have defined *structure* as follows:

[5] Phenix, *Realms of Meaning,* pp. 11, 334.
[6] Jerome S. Bruner, *The Process of Education* (Cambridge, Mass.: Harvard University Press, 1960).

The structure of a discipline is the set of fundamental generalizations, principles, rules, propositions, or basic abstractions that binds a field of knowledge into a unity, organizes this body of knowledge in a cohesive interrelated wholeness, fixes the limits of investigation and inclusion of knowledge for the discipline itself, and provides the basis for discovering what else exists within the field. Structure defines and limits a field of study, organizes it for comprehension and manipulation, and generates new propositions and knowledge.

Structure enables all who must use knowledge from a field to grasp the essential principles, concepts, and fundamental relationships needed for understanding.

. . . Let us state the reasons why structure is an important base for organizing content.

1. Structure facilitates the use of knowledge.
2. It provides for better mastery of a domain of experience.
3. A knowledge of the structure of a discipline enables the individual to revise his understanding of a field as new facts and data become known or as old concepts and principles are proved to be inadequate or erroneous.
4. It enhances memory.
5. It facilitates use of the knowledge in new stimulus situations.
6. Structure is the basis for making discoveries of new knowledge appropriate to the domain.
7. Structure enables the curriculum worker to make the best selection of content for study in the disciplinary subjects.
8. Organized knowledge constitutes a powerful potential to do, a capacity to act.[7]

Outlining the basic structure of the subject area would seem to be an important step in any curriculum project. However, the task is somewhat complex in many cases. Scholars in the same academic discipline, for example, are often unable to agree on the structure of their subject. . . . Structuring of content should be useful in the process of selection and organization of subject matter if the potential difficulties are recognized and resolved.

To assist the faculty in curriculum development, Burlington County College, Pemberton, N.J. produced a *Three-Phase Systematic Instructional Development Model* (Figure 8-3).

The following procedure describes for the curriculum worker at Burlington County College the process of instructional development, using this model. Excerpted from a position paper entitled *Instructional Systems for Student Learning,* (See Footnote 1, p. 100) the process described below is one viable route to systematic curriculum design and implementation.

[7] J. Galen Saylor and William M. Alexander, *Curriculum Planning for Modern Schools* (New York: Holt, Rinehart & Winston, Inc., 1966), pp. 166-69.

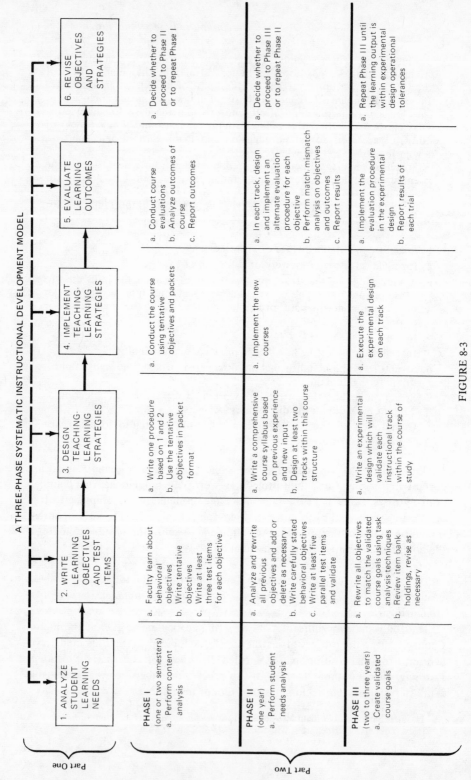

A THREE-PHASE SYSTEMATIC INSTRUCTIONAL DEVELOPMENT MODEL

FIGURE 8-3

112

Systematic Instructional Development

From early in this institution's history our goal has been to provide meaningful and productive learning experiences for our students. As a corollary to this goal it has been assumed that in order to provide quality in the learning process there must be systematic instructional development. Instruction should be a purposeful experience which employs the most effective learning devices and procedures available. Systematic instructional development is not an end in itself; it is a means to the end of effective and efficient learning for our students.

To clarify what is meant by systematic instructional development, a model is attached to this paper which outlines rather precisely events that should be completed, and a suggested order for the accomplishment of these events. (Please refer to this model as you read the rest of the paper.) The model is called a "Three-Phase Systematic Instructional Development Model." It is divided into two parts. Part 1 outlines the activities which must be completed in organizing and executing any course of study—every time that it is offered to students. Part 2 outlines the activities that must be completed at three different levels of sophistication in the instructional development process. Phase 1 is the simplest, most straightforward level; Phase 2 represents extended activities in the area of validation, and Phase 3 is a highly sophisticated procedure in which the instructional development is handled in a controlled, experimental framework. An instructional development project which proceeds through each level could be expected to last from three to five years and would produce one of the most comprehensive and flexible learning procedures available for our students.

Let's analyze each part of this model and determine exactly what you, as an instructor, would do at each level. Part 1 is a function level analysis of what a teacher should do when offering a course of study to his students. It starts with an analysis of student learning needs—a fundamental curricular function. Factors to be considered at this level are: content relevant for the student, societal needs being met by the course, and content requirements. These are fundamental decisions, not to be treated lightly. You have your own experience and training to draw upon, however, as well as the literature in the field and the experience of your colleagues and divisional chairman. The learning needs analysis is basically a research and review procedure which should culminate in a written statement of goals to be accomplished in the course of study. This process must be completed before any other work is done.

Using the outline of concepts and attitudes which were identified in the learning needs analysis, you are now ready to begin writing learning objectives. Each of these objectives should be directly linked to a concept or attitude stated in your needs analysis. The specificity of each objective will vary depending on which development phase is being pursued, but at all times the objectives should be written in such a way that the student has a clear idea of what he must do to accomplish the objective.

FIGURE 8-4

Cognitive objectives involve simple recall or remembering, but also can include reasoning, problem solving, and concept formation. Affective objectives are expressed as interests, attitudes, appreciations, and values. The psychomotor objectives emphasize some muscular or motor skill or act which requires a neuromuscular coordination.

Well-written behavioral objectives state: (1) the behavior that the learner will be able to demonstrate to indicate that he has achieved the objective; (2) the conditions under which he will demonstrate his achievement of the objective; and (3) the specific criterion or standard of performance.

An integral part of each objective should be the test items or evaluative device which is necessary to determine if the objective has been accomplished. These test items or procedures should be written immediately upon completion of the objective. Writing the objectives and test items simultaneously has the advantage of providing an instant internal checking device. Good and bad objectives and items are usually spotted by the developer at this point and are included or scrapped immediately.

Writing objectives and test items is an ongoing instructional development activity. You should plan to spend up to eight hours per week in writing and reviewing objectives and. items. Plan to make considerable use of the support personnel who are provided for you, including your division chairman, appropriate coordinators, and the instructional development officer.

The third function which you should perform is the designing of appropriate teaching-learning strategies for the level of development in which you are engaging. A Phase 1 project, for example, would basically entail constructing one instructional track which would be followed by all of the students in a course. This might make use of a number of instructional modes such as large group, directed independent study, and seminar. More advanced projects will later be constructed using a multi-track approach which will have different students engaged in different learning activities as they accomplish the common objectives of the course. Different approaches may include highly mediated large group or independent study activity, self-paced learning using programmed materials, student contracts in which the student may use his own strategy to reach a mutually agreed-upon objective, or any number of modes and techniques which you may design. This is real individualization of instruction.

In developing content and teaching-learning strategies, the instructor is faced with difficult decisions of selecting from the mass of knowledge that is rapidly accumulating in each discipline. In most cases he will do well to stress the method of inquiry in the particular discipline. This enables the student to learn how a physicist solves problems, for example, so that he can continue to learn and solve problems after he completes the present learning sequences. By stressing the method of inquiry the student sees that real learning involves the processes of inquiry and discovery that lead to exploration, experimentation, questioning, and debate. In building instructional sequences it is important to include opportunities for observation, reflection, and problem solving. Learners become more self-motivated as they discover opportunities to form their own concepts, generalizations, and insights. The learning process, then, ought to involve dynamic methods of inquiry and ways of thinking which are self-generating and self-motivating, and which help the learner to identify and follow his own purposes, and relate them to the stated objectives. It is important to help the student to develop the skills of investigation and inquiry that will enable him to continue to educate himself.

While the student is developing his skills leading to the goal of self-directed education, it is the instructor's responsibility to provide meaningful learning opportunities.

Faculty activities in designing teaching-learning strategies may include writing course syllabi, learning packets, or modules; writing scripts and storyboards; identifying and ordering commercially available materials and components for instructional programs; writing self-instructional packages; and working with the support personnel within the institution. Your division chairman will be a major asset to you, along with the instructional development

FIGURE 8-5

officer in the dean's office and the personnel of the Division of Learning Resources.

The implementation stage of instructional development is the closest you will come to engaging in "teaching" activity. Here you subject the product of your work to the pragmatic test—does it work with students? This is sometimes a shattering but very revealing experience.

Although students may be working with your materials at any time during the course, you usually should spend no more than a third of your effort in implementation type activities. These will include lecturing to groups, leading seminar discussions, monitoring laboratories, or meeting with individuals or small groups for individualized instruction. At Burlington County College, faculty members are consistently asked the very hard question, "How much of your time must be spent directly with students in order to make *their learning* an effective and meaningful experience?" You will probably discover that as you proceed into more advanced instructional development projects, you will spend less time in actual implementation and more time in development and revision. The purpose is not to remove teachers from students but rather to put students and teachers together when the contact is most advantageous to the students. Very often, implementation type instructional activities can be carried out by paraprofessional and technical people and, as our needs develop in this direction, the idea of differentiated staffing will become more workable. Probably the greatest assistance in the implementation step of instruction will be from the staff of the Division of Learning Resources. This group is specifically charged with the responsibility of servicing faculty requests for instructional support and has the facilities, resources, and personnel to assist you.

Evaluation, the next step in systematic instructional development, is one of the most crucial parts of the whole procedure. Evaluation is a two-pronged process. First, the faculty member is responsible for evaluating the student learning as it occurs. Second, it is essential to evaluate the effectiveness of the instructional design and to report the conclusions. Learning outcomes are measurements of how well the students mastered the objectives. This is determined by evaluating the responses to the test items which were constructed to match the objectives. Measuring learning outcomes may be more subjective when objectives in the affective domain are used.

Evaluating the instructional process becomes a more complicated procedure. To assist in making this evaluation, it is necessary to devise a data-collecting mechanism for each instructional sequence. This mechanism can take many forms, from an anecdotal type journal or log to a precise error rate indicator. The level of sophistication of the project will help to determine which kinds of evaluation devices will be needed.

An overall goal of the evaluation process is the systematic movement toward validated instructional sequences. Validation will become more important to the instructional developer as he proceeds into Phases 2 and 3.

Evaluation is an ongoing instructional development activity. At the end of a course of study the time spent on this activity will increase significantly while you are analyzing, summarizing, and reporting your evaluations, but it should be noted that during this period, design and implementation activities will be sharply curtailed.

The report which you prepare as the final evaluative activity will be submitted to your division chairman. You will have the assistance of your chairman in creating this report and you should call upon the instructional development officer as well. The report is intended to be an accurate indicator of where you are in the development of a course of study based on your most recent tryout. The extent of the report and the time it requires for completion will vary with the complexity of the instructional development project and with the individual.

The final step in the functional level of the systematic instructional development model is basically a decision point. The decision you must make is directly related to the level of curriculum development in which you are engaged. You must decide, based upon the work you have done and the data which you have generated, whether or not to repeat the course at Phase 1 or 2 or to advance to the next phase of development. This decision should be made with a good deal of thought. Again your chairman and the instructional development officer should be involved in this decision.

This has been a brief overview of Part 1 of the "Three-Phase Systematic Instruction Development Model." Let's turn to Part 2 and a discussion of the activities and implications of each of the three phases.

Please examine Part 2, noting the activities that are suggested in each phase as they relate to the activities outlined in Part 1.

As you can see, the steps in each of the phases relate directly back to the functions outlined in Part 1. This means that each time you proceed through one of the phases of instructional development, you will be repeating the same functions but at a more complex level of sophistication. In this regard, instructional development must be considered a cyclic, spiraling phenomenon, in which each cycle is based upon the previous cycle, but is distinct in terms of complexity and exactness.

Phase 1, for example, is a relatively simple procedure which closely resembles a traditional course structure. There are significant differences, however, particularly in the experimental attitude which the instructor-developer must use in completing the project. For example, each step is carefully documented and these documents become the foundation upon which the remainder of the entire project will be built. Objectives are written using behavioral terminology as much as possible. Test items are constructed to match objectives directly. Packets are written to communicate to the student what learning is expected of him and what he must do to demonstrate that this learning has occurred.

A Phase 1 project is usually designed with only one instructional track. Instructors may use different instructional modes but every student in the course will generally perform the same learning activities in reaching the objectives of the course. Evaluation of a Phase 1 project usually centers on such factors as drop-out rate and grade distribution, but an important new factor is how well the students mastered each of the stated objectives. This analysis furnishes the foundation for deciding to repeat Phase 1 the next time the course is offered or to proceed to a Phase 2 instructional development project.

Phase 2 is a much more precise, experimental type of instructional development. It is characterized by the concept of validation. Each step is predicated upon the idea that the learning experiences provided should prove themselves to be valid when they are carefully reviewed. Each part should function adequately to insure that acceptable levels of learning are being attained.

The process in Phase 2 starts with a student needs analysis which is based upon the content analysis from Phase 1 compared with the student reactions which were also generated in the first phase. From this analysis a more valid student needs statement can be written, based on content and student input. With this new needs analysis, the instructional developer can then write a much more valid set of objectives. Because of the total experience of the Phase 1 activities, the instructor-developer can also write the objectives in a much more precise form. When writing the objectives for a Phase 2 project, considerable attention should be given to the level of complexity of both the cognitive and affective objectives.

Two other elements which characterize a Phase 2 instructional development project are a comprehensive course syllabus and a multiple track instructional design. These two developments occur in the new design for teaching-learning strategies. The syllabus is a rather explicit statement of knowledges, skills, and attitudes which are to be developed during the course of study. The syllabus is also explicit as to how the course is organized and the activities which a student must accomplish in order to complete the course.

The development of multiple tracks is one of the most challenging development activities. Based on the behaviorally stated objectives, each instructional track must be carefully outlined to be parallel but not similar. Different modes of instruction may be utilized on each track but the principle behind the idea of tracking is to allow the student to select a pathway which is most suited for his learning needs and style. Some tracks may be very traditional in structure, others may be quite open to student design, but the terminal product of each track should be equivalent learning, based on criteria-oriented evaluation techniques.

Evaluation of a Phase 2 instructional development project will be a rather extensive match-mismatch procedure which compares outcomes directly to objectives. The skill of the instructional developer will be even more essential here because evaluation of learning outcomes will be a very objective procedure.

Finally, at the end of evaluation of a Phase 2 project, a decision must be made. There is always the possibility of modifying and repeating the project. The other option is to move to a Phase 3 project and the refining procedure which this kind of advanced project requires.

Phase 3 is a highly experimental procedure in which the entire development process is completely reviewed, and research and experimental techniques are utilized at the application level. Learning needs are assembled in terms of institutional philosophy and goals, appropriate content, student input and societal impact. Validated course goals are generated which take each of these factors into consideration.

From these goals course objectives are written which are behavioral in format and adhere to a defined hierarchy in both the cognitive and affective domains. Task analysis techniques should be used to generate the course objectives and careful documentation should be kept on the effectiveness of each objective and instructional procedure which spins off the objective. Each of the objectives written will specify the operational tolerances which will be acceptable and the process will be refined until these tolerances are being consistently maintained.

Teaching-learning strategies should be generated to complement a precisely written experimental design. This experimental design should have internal checking components which will automatically monitor the progress of the student as he proceeds in his learning tasks. Again, multiple tracks will be employed to guarantee that a student is not hindered by the form of his learning experience. A good deal of individualized attention will be necessary in order to determine the effectiveness of the experimental design in light of the specified operational tolerances.

Although evaluation is an ongoing activity at every phase of instructional development, it will be particularly evident in a Phase 3 project. Because of the nature of an experimental design, considerable evaluative data will be generated constantly. It will be necessary to devise procedures to properly interpret this data and to translate it into a form which will lead the developer to make revisions. Through this feedback and revision process, the instructional developer will be able to tune the course of study on each of the instructional tracks until student performance is consistently within the acceptable operational tolerances range.

Time is a major consideration in systematic instructional development. A new attitude toward lead time is necessary for the kind of instructional development that has been outlined in this paper. The time frames suggested on the model should be reviewed again here. These time frames are cumulative. Phase 1 projects will take one or two semesters. Phase 2 projects will take one or possibly two years, depending on how often the course is offered. Phase 3 projects are definitely long-range propositions. They often will take two to three years to complete. Availability of time and resources for instructional development projects will affect the suggested time frames.

Summary

In designing the ecucational program, the college has two basic options: the safe, traditional stance, or the forward-looking, innovative approach. A comprehensive, flexible, experimental community college will meet the needs of its constituency in this century as well as the next. There will be a large range of students and an equally impressive range of programs to meet their educational needs.

A systematic approach to curriculum development and the teaching-learning process will be designed to assure that students are challenged with appropriate, relevant learning experiences. The best and most promising instructional strategies will be employed, utilizing the most modern technology and plant facilities. The college will hire innovative faculty and support personnel who are willing to experiment with new ideas and research in the learning process. Staff commitment to planned experimentation and change is essential.

A step-by-step approach to the systematic design of a dynamic educational program for a modern, learner-centered community college is indicated. The steps may be summarized as follows:

1. Identify the needs of the community that can be met by college programs.
2. Determine the basic philosophic approach to instructional development and the teaching-learning process that will undergird the educational programs of the college.

3. Identify the basic educational programs to be offered by the college.
4. Possibly, organize a general citizens advisory committee and special advisory committees in the career program areas.
5. Identify the basic learning sequences for each educational program.
6. Complete personnel and logistical support plans for the process of instructional development.
7. Launch the systematic process of instructional development for each learning sequence or course.

Suggested Activities and Problems

1. List the basic elements in a systematic approach to instruction. Critically evaluate each one.
2. Interview the academic dean of a young community college to discover the problems encountered in the development of the educational program. Write a paper summarizing your findings.
3. Outline a plan to determine the basic curricular programs to be offered by a new community college.
4. Defend or refute in a paper the following proposition: "Citizens advisory committees should be organized during the process of initial instructional development, before the college opens."
5. Critically evaluate the three-phase systematic instructional development model presented in this chapter.

Selected Readings

Cohen, Arthur M., *Objectives for College Courses.* Beverly Hills, Calif.: Glencoe Press, a division of the Macmillan Company, 1970.

———, *Dateline '79: Heretical Concepts for the Community College.* Beverly Hills, Calif.: Glencoe Press, a division of the Macmillan Company, 1969.

——— et al., *A Constant Variable: New Perspectives on the Community College,* chaps. 7, 8, 9, 10. San Francisco: Jossey-Bass, Inc., 1971.

Johnson, B. Lamar, ed., *The Improvement of Junior College Instruction,* Occasional Report No. 15. Los Angeles: University of California, Los Angeles, 1970.

Mager, Robert F., *Preparing Instructional Objectives.* Belmont, Calif.: Fearon Publishers, 1962.

Neagley, Ross L. and N. Dean Evans, *Handbook for Effective Curriculum Development,* chaps. 6, 7, 8, 12. Englewood Cliffs, N.J.: Prentice-Hall, Inc., 1967.

Reynolds, James W., *The Comprehensive Junior College Curriculum.* Berkeley, Calif.: McCutchan Publishing Corp., 1969.

Thornton, James W., Jr., *The Community Junior College,* chaps. 12-16. New York: John Wiley & Sons, Inc., 1966.

9

How New
Will the New College Be?

This entire text is concerned with innovative approaches to planning and building community colleges. This chapter will attempt to stimulate planners to check on their own practices and to set their sights ever higher as they peer into the future. Nothing suggested here is beyond the realm of possibility. A number of the practices mentioned are being utilized somewhere, at least to a limited degree, right now, but they are far from commonplace. In some instances where the location of the innovation is known the sources are given, whereas in other examples some mind reading has been done. Although it is repetitious, each section will close with a series of questions that can serve as a checklist to determine the newness of the various facets of any given community college.

Innovation and Change

Resistance to innovation and change seems to be deeply inbred in human beings. When prototypes have been established in the minds of men, they are difficult to eradicate or change. Since its inception, the community college prototypes have been the liberal arts college on the one hand and the public secondary school on the other. Innovation and change have merely breathed down the neck of liberal arts colleges. Secondary schools have been somewhat more responsive.

In order to envision the *new* community college as an institution that truly is responsive to the needs of all persons in the community being served, a new image is needed, or rather, many new images are required because no two community colleges will resemble each other.

A very encouraging movement has been the organization of the League for Innovation in the Community College, which was formally organized in January, 1968. It was incorporated under the laws of California in 1969 and at that time linked thirty-eight colleges with an aggregate population of more than 350,000 students.[1]

The league proposes to accomplish its purposes by cooperative work between and among its members, which will assist them to:

1. Experiment in teaching, learning, guidance, and other aspects of junior junior college operation.
2. Share results of experiments.
3. Share conceptual planning and learning objectives.
4. Exchange instructional materials and procedures designed to enhance learning.
5. Examine the relevance of various modes of college administration to experimentation in teaching and learning.
6. Provide a common base for research on the effects of varied innovative practices by gathering and sharing data on students, programs, and modes of organization.
7. Evaluate the impact of the institution's practices on its students and community.[2]

If community colleges are to meet the challenges of the 70s this movement and others like it must continue to grow. Perhaps the community college movement is one in which the key word can truly be cooperation rather than competition. This is what the world sorely needs. It would be marvelous if community colleges could point the way toward cooperative effort.

How New Is the Administration?

Although administrative officials will probably continue to have titles for some time to come, the hierarchial administrative structure of the bureaucratic model will soon be as dead as a dodo. Atwell and Watkins emphasized the modern trend when they wrote:

> It is readily apparent that our society has come to depend to an increasing degree on work which is performed by groups and teams rather than by individuals working alone. The days of isolated individuals and independent living have long since disappeared from the scene. In view of

[1] B. Lamar Johnson and Richard D. Howe, "Toward Change and Improvement," *Junior College Journal*, 40, No. 4 (1970), 9.
[2] Ibid., pp. 9-10.

this increased organizational complexity of life, the importance of groups organized to accomplish the myriad tasks faced by our society has become evident.[3]

The philosophy expressed in the above statement is consistent with the demands of both faculty and students that they become involved in helping to make decisions that affect them. This trend will continue, and it *should* in a democracy. The question is no longer whether or not faculty and students should be involved, but rather, how their talents can be utilized to the best advantage. Parents and other lay citizens and community groups also will continue to demand a larger share in the administration of the community college. Likewise, representatives from government, industry, and business will have to play a much greater role if the colleges are to become truly community oriented.

This shift from the authoritarian role to that of the leader of a team has given many community college administrators a feeling of inadequacy. They know that the authority and prestige of their title may no longer be taken for granted, but they also realize that they still are held accountable for seeing that the organization accomplishes its purposes. Actually, many community college administrators are not certain what their new role should be.

Richardson, in a very cogent article, attempts to assist in the resolution of this dilemma by suggesting that community college administrators must no longer think of their function as that of *coordination,* but rather as that of *problem solving.* He bases this assumption on the following premise:

> ... that the two-year college with respect to its educational program (including all services rendered by the professional staff) requires only a minimum of coordination. Such coordination can be achieved through the class schedule, prescribed procedures for formulating and implementing budgets, and such other personnel policies as may be jointly developed by members of the professional staff and approved by the governing body.[4]

Ovsiew takes the point of view that the central function of administration is *planning* when he writes as follows:

What might other assumptions be for developing a theory that would explain and predict the phenomena of the behavior of educational administrators? Using Griffiths'[5] format of statements as a basis, the following assumptions are suggested:

---

[3]Charles A. Atwell and J. Foster Watkins, "New Directions for Administration," *Junior College Journal,* 41, No. 5 (1971), 17.

[4] Richard C. Richardson, Jr., "Needed: New Directions in Administration," *Junior College Journal,* 40, No. 6 (1970), 19.

[5] See Daniel E. Griffiths, *Administrative Theory* (New York: Appleton-Century-Crofts, 1959), pp. 71-74.

1. Administration is a generalized type of behavior to be found in all organizations.
2. Administrative behavior has both a substance and a process. The substance of administration is forming the general and specific purposes, goals, and objectives of the institution, and the strategies for their achievement. The process of administration is to direct and control the work of people in the organization.
3. The central substantive function of administrative behavior is planning, and controlling the decisioning processes is the central process function.
4. The administrator works with others, in groups, or with individuals with a group referent, or sometimes as individuals whose countervailing power constrains his power.

. . . Planning is more than a decision-making process. There are elements in planning that are not decisioning procedures, even though deciding (making choices) is a pervasive procedure, by definition, in the practice of administration.

. . . *Evaluation* is one of the elements of planning. It is a continuous administrative responsibility. As the ultimately accountable person in the organization, the chief executive must always be able to make judgments about how effectively college operations are achieving organizational purposes. But legal accountability aside, the necessity for education is that the chief executive has the responsibility to achieve what the organization is committed to achieve (maintenance) and, no less vital, to reconsider what goals and objectives it should be achieving and how it should be achieving them (improvement). While it is true that some planning is needed simply to guarantee the organization's capability for maintaining its operations, major planning efforts are occasioned by the need to change, and that need is revealed by evaluation.

When evaluation shows the probable advantage of course change—in purpose, goal, objective, operation, or process—planning begins. Webster says, "a plan always implies mental formulation." Call it *formulating* or *conceptualizing,* the core product of planning is a statement which gives form and expression to an idea (or construct of ideas, program or project) about the organization's work. Though decision making is implied (this rather than some other formulation!), it is not the decisioning process that is the characteristic activity of making a plan. The substantive activity is *conceptualizing,* formulating an idea. This is the substance of administrative behavior.[6]

Another trend in administration that will be applied to the community college field is the use of theory in administration. As more experience is gained

[7]Leon Osview, "Assumptions for a Theory of Educational Administration" (Unpublished manuscript, March 1969), pp. 3-6.

in its use, theory will become the most practical approach to community college administration.

The computer increasingly will be called upon in problem solving by the use of simulation. This versatile instrument already is being utilized extensively in many other aspects of community college administration. After studying best practices in a number of two-year colleges, Stevenson developed a model for an electronic data-processing system for selected administrative areas. The model included the following ten subsystems: manpower inventory, payroll, business functions, admissions, registration and records, financial aid, counseling, test marking, alumni records, and institutional research.[7]

FIGURE 9-1

Community college leaders who are interested in keeping up with the trends will want to give careful consideration to the following questions raised by Atwell and Watkins:

1. Does your institution embody an administrative team concept in its organizational configuration?
2. From an organizational leadership focus, how do the members of the administrative team view the individuals who make up your college staff?

7 William Stevenson, "The Development of a Model for an Electronic Data Processing System for Selected Administrative Areas in Two-Year Publicly-Supported Community Colleges" (Doctoral dissertation, Temple University, 1971), p. 2.

3. How effectively is your college functioning to allow staff members, individually and collectively, to recognize and develop their capabilities to the fullest extent possible?
4. How effectively is the creative potential of your staff being utilized?
5. What organizational provisions are made for raising and responding to questions of a critical nature?[8]

The following additional questions are suggested:

1. Do the members of the administrative team have a knowledge of and a healthy respect for theory in administration?
2. Is educational planning being emphasized in administration, and if so, to what degree?
3. Are all appropriate uses being made of the computer as an aid to administration, including decision making?

How New Are the Facilities?

This discussion is not concerned with the dates on the cornerstone of each building, but rather with the question of whether the planners took into account all that is presently known about planning and housing community college programs. Also, after being exposed to this discussion, the reader will hopefully be stimulated to seek more imaginative solutions to building problems.

In Chapter 12 the need for diversity in educational facilities is pointed out. Community college facilities of the future will and should be quite different. As emphasized in the same chapter, the architectural firm will be carefully selected well in advance of the project; the staff, students, and community will be involved in planning; and interim facilities will increasingly be used. In the "new" college, educational specifications for all facilities will be carefully written but they will not be too prescriptive.

Phased construction, fast track building, systems building, and building systems will be used extensively.

The total environment will be carefully planned with detailed attention being paid to the spacial, climatic, visual, sonic, and aesthetic aspects of the environment.

To prevent that they will be out of date before they are opened, the facilities of the new college will be planned for great flexibility, with many open spaces. Provisions will be made everywhere for present and future electronic teaching and learning devices. Computer terminals will be easily available for administration and instruction.

Many new colleges will elect to use short-lived facilities such as portables, membrane structures, and rented spaces. Shared facilities with business and

[8] Atwell and Watkins, "Directions for Administration," p. 19.

FIGURE 9-2

industry and public buildings throughout the community will be common practice.

As two examples of membrane structures, Antioch College is creating a satellite campus in the downtown section of the new city of Columbia, Maryland. The entire campus will consist of an acre of leased ground enclosed by a 44,000 sq. ft. inflated bubble. La Verne College in California has a much more ambitious plan. Its membrane structure will cover some six to eight acres that will enclose a physical education center, student union activities, fine arts and drama programs, and health services, plus outdoor recreation and leisure time spaces, all in a parklike setting.[9]

Cohen foresees in the city dispersed and short-lived facilities when he writes:

> The college is of the city; the campus on the hill outside the town is no more. The image of higher education as a retreat from life stemmed from a time when all knowledge was carried in the minds of elders. . . . Conceptually the community college is not a place apart from the "evil influences" of the city, but it is actually a part of the community. It appears to be a decentralized college; actually its campus has expanded to include the confines of the entire community. . . .
>
> Each center enrolls between 900 and 1,500 students. They are located in rented stores, in spaces that formerly were office buildings, and in old mansions that had outlived their original purposes. Easy access by numbers

[9] *EFL College Newsletter 10* (New York: Educational Facilities Laboratories, Inc., September, 1970), pp. 2-3.

of students and economy of physical-plant operations are the chief criteria by which locations are determined.[10]

Community college officials interested in knowing how new their facility planning is might consider the following questions:

1. Was a competent architectural firm selected in advance of the project?
2. Were administrators, faculty members, students, and citizens involved in planning the new facilities?
3. Were competent consultants utilized?
4. Was the use of interim and short-lived facilities considered?
5. Was the architect given a set of carefully written educational specifications?
6. Were provisions made for all types of electronic learning aids?
7. Was a maximum amount of open space planned, and flexibility provided?
8. Was the learning resources center strategically located?
9. Were ample provisions made for individualized instruction?
10. Were building systems and fast-track construction procedures used?
11. Were computer-simulated laboratories considered as a substitute for costly laboratory spaces?
12. Were environmental controls planned to the best advantage?
13. Was adequate consideration given to the use of the latest construction materials?
14. Were high rise buildings planned if the site was limited in size?
15. Did the planners refrain from duplicating costly facilities that could be made available by business and industry?

How New Are the Curriculum and Instruction?

If the community college is to truly serve the community and meet the needs of all its citizens, it must be prepared to take the leadership in seeing that instruction is available in any subject for which individuals have a need or desire.

Curriculum. Educational institutions on all levels have experienced a sort of revolution in the curriculum during the 60s and early 70s. In a companion text, we made the following predictions concerning the trend in curriculum in the elementary and secondary schools:

> Until certain basic issues are resolved, the curriculum of the nation's schools will continue to fluctuate between an emphasis on content and an

[10]Reprinted with permission of Glencoe Press (Beverly Hills, Calif., a division of The Macmillan Company), from Arthur M. Cohen, *Dateline '79: Heretical Concepts for the Community College*, p. 9. Copyright © Arthur M. Cohen, 1969.

emphasis on method. In spite of the present opinion that the discovery approach to learning should be stressed, the content of the disciplines is receiving the most emphasis. By the 1980s the pendulum will once again swing the other way and disciplines as separate entities will be less important. The use of knowledge, the discovery of new knowledge, and an understanding of the interrelationships and commonalities of the disciplines will then be stressed.[11]

The backbone of the curriculum of the new community college likely will continue to be general education for postsecondary-age youth. However, many students who must of necessity enter the labor market as early as possible will require technical and vocational education programs. As suggested in the to require technical and vocational education programs. As suggested in the previous section, these programs should be offered by business and industry under the supervision of the community college. Similar programs will be necessary for older workers who must update their skills or learn new ones.

Many short-term courses will be offered. The concept of the semester will become obsolete. In fact, individuals will be encouraged to proceed at their own rate of learning.

Appendix 10, pp. 353-59, offers a firsthand look at representative innovative programs and ideas that thirteen junior college districts (comprising the League for Innovation in the Community College) are adopting to improve their total learning environments. A number of these innovations will be highlighted throughout this section. The reader is referred to Appendix 10 for the others.[12]

Chicago City College has developed a handbook on the role of the Indian in various periods of American history, a child development curriculum, and a black thought and culture course. Cuyahoga Community College has inaugurated Afro-American studies, audiotutorial learning, computer-assisted instruction (CAI), and integrated humanities courses. Foothill Junior College in California has developed an interdisciplinary course on minorities in America. The course encompasses anthropology, history, political science, and sociology. Kern Junior College District, also in California, is offering a contemporary concerns seminar. The discussions are concerned with readings relevant to topics that change from semester to semester. Seattle Community College has a family life education department and preschool laboratory. It also has established a regional training center for the deaf and hard of hearing, as well as a floating marine science laboratory. The Dallas County Junior College District is providing space in the physical education complex at each college for a physical fitness laboratory, which has far-reaching implications for community services and for the student program.

[11]Ross L. Neagley and N. Dean Evans, *Handbook for Effective Curriculum Development* (Englewood Cliffs, N.J.: Prentice-Hall, Inc., 1967), pp. 294-95.

[12]Appendix material is from "Emphasis-Innovation on the Campus," *Junior College Journal,* 40, No. 4 (1970), 3, 5. (The entire issue is devoted to the topic with separate articles on each member college.)

Finally, Peralta Junior College District of California is offering a "Body Shoppe" Class in which overweight individuals can shed their excess pounds. This three-day-a-week, one-credit class uses the group-psychology method, followed by physical activities, and advice on beauty and fashion.

Community colleges that desire to remain new will be experimenting and innovating continuously with their curriculum offerings. New courses will be born regularly and others will die when they are no longer relevant.

Even more important than the variety of learning experiences offered will be the increased emphasis on the achievement of objectives set up for each learning unit. Regardless of the length of the learning unit, behavioral objectives will be written for each one and students will be held accountable for achieving them to a reasonable degree. For example, in Santa Fe Junior College, Florida,

> Educational objectives are stressed in out-of-class activities as well as in formal courses. All student activities are approved only after objectives are stated in behavioral terms consistent with the purposes of the college. Each activity is cooperatively evaluated by students and faculty, and decisions are made regarding its continuation or modification on the basis of its progress toward the achievement of its objectives.[13]

In order to keep the curriculum relevant and up-to-date, curriculum study and revision must become a continuous process. Following are examples of how two community colleges insure that their curricular offerings are kept current.

Seattle Community College has organized a faculty-oriented committee (four faculty members and three administrators) on curriculum innovations and

FIGURE 9-3

[13] Joseph W. Fordyce and Ann Bromley, "Santa Fe Junior College," *Junior College Journal,* 40, No. 4 (1970), 46.

planning.[14] Los Angeles City Community College has established a roving position for curriculum study. The full released-time position is assigned to one department for a semester, then to another, and so on.[15]

Instruction. Instruction in the new community college will take into consideration everything that is known about learning and the different learning patterns of individuals. It will also include all known methods of instruction, and attempts will be made constantly to improve them and to discover additional methods. As mentioned in the previous section, behavioral objectives will be formulated for most learning experiences and individual progress will depend upon the achievement of these objectives at a specified level of competence. Faculty members as well as students will be held accountable for the success of the learners.

To provide for individual differences in learning patterns of students, opportunities will be provided for individuals to utilize their peculiar cognitive and emotional styles in the various learning experiences they elect to pursue. This may be accomplished in at least two ways. In his look into the future Cohen suggests the following pattern:

> In its attempt to resolve many such problems, the (*new*) college offers six distinctly different types of instructional sections in each course (though not for each unit). Each section has its own reason and style; each one is based on a specific instructional form—yet all sections lead to similar course goals.
>
> The six types of sections offered in each course are categorized by the different media employed. These varied media are not simply different reading lists or types of lectures given by different people; each one is a distinct design for instruction that is built on a distinct rationale. Most units in each core course are offered in lecture, discussion, independent-study, tutorial, audio-tutorial, and computer-assisted sections. The sections run concurrently throughout the year in staggered time sequences.[16]

The second way is a modification of Cohen's suggestion. Courses will be organized and taught within each section, so that opportunities are provided for the utilization of all the six above forms of instruction. In other words, differentiation of instruction will take place within a given class section rather than having separate sections for each form of instruction.

It is assumed that in the new college efforts constantly will be made to provide the necessary equipment, materials, and know-how to make each instructional form as efficient as possible. For example, under the lecture form

[14] See Ed K. Erickson, "Seattle Community College," *Junior College Journal*, 40, No. 4 (1970), 50.
[15] See T. Stanley Warburton, "Los Angeles Community College District," *Junior College Journal*, 40, No. 4 (1970), 36.
[16] Cohen, *Dateline '79, pp. 24-25.*

of instruction, use will be made of the latest type of student-response system and all types of audio-visual equipment and materials will be employed freely. Television will play an increasingly important role in the lecture-presentation method.

The computer will continue to grow in importance as an aid in instruction and learning. Elsewhere in this chapter the computer-assisted science laboratory has been mentioned. Costly science laboratories will no longer be necessary when students can obtain similar experiences with chemical reactions on the computer. Through simulation, business-management experiences also will be possible. In fact, the hardware is now available for the effective learning of almost any subject in the community-college curriculum. All that is still needed is the software. Computer programs have just not kept pace with advancing computer technology.

FIGURE 9-4

In the *new* college the computer will serve another purpose in the instructional program. Although in its infancy, individually prescribed instruction (IPI) will make it possible to tailor each student's program to his special needs and rate of learning. It also will contribute to the achievement of course objectives at an acceptable performance level.

Illustrative of some of the instructional trends at innovative institutions are the following (see Appendix 10, p. 353):

Delta College, Michigan, has instituted independent study with variable credit offerings for advanced students specializing in certain academic areas. It also has developed a number of interdisciplinary travel seminars during the summer months under the direction of regular full-time faculty members.[17] El Centro

[17]See Don Carlyon and Martin Wolfe, "Delta College," *Junior College Journal,* 40, No. 4 (1970), 23.

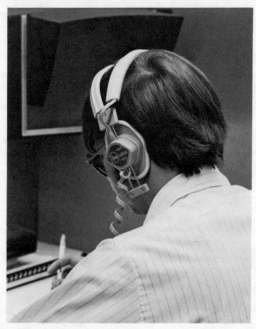

FIGURE 9-5

Junior College, Texas, established the *mini-college*. This is an instructional unit in which five instructors are responsible for teaching five courses (English, history, art, psychology, and mathematics) to a group of 180 students. The services of a counselor, reading specialist, media specialist, data-processing director, and curriculum coordinator also are available to the *mini-college*.[18] Orange Coast Junior College, California, is using computer-assisted learning in management games, elementary surveying, and several mathematics and chemistry courses. The same institution has funds made available by the district to finance faculty fellowships in support of innovative and developmental work. Faculty members may work individually or in groups to develop improved learning experiences for students.[19] American River Junior College, California, has an instructional resources committee to review innovative proposals and assist faculty members with the development of particular program ideas.[20]

Community college officials can check how up-to-date their curriculum and instructional programs are by responding to the following questions:

[18] See H. Deon Holt, "Dallas County Junior College District," *Junior College Journal,* 40, No. 4 (1970), 21.
[19] See Norman E. Watson and Bernard J. Luskin, "Orange Coast Junior College District," *Junior College Journal,* 40, No. 4 (1970), 41-42.
[20] See Walter T. Coultas, "Los Rios Junior College District," *Junior College Journal,* 40, No. 4 (1970), 38.

1. Have any students in the service area been turned down because the course or program they needed was not available?
2. Are the technical and vocational education programs offered by business and industry planned cooperatively with the college?
3. Are a number of short-term courses being offered?
4. Has a curriculum council been organized and granted the proper authority to act and make recommendations?
5. Is curriculum revision and study a continuous process, with released time or extra compensation in the summer provided for staff members to participate?
6. Are behavioral objectives formulated for most courses and standards of competency set?
7. Are experimentation and innovation in the curriculum and instruction encouraged?
8. Is the instructional program based on a thorough knowledge of the learning process and an understanding of different cognitive, affective, and emotional styles of learning?
9. Are a variety of forms of instruction utilized and are they constantly being improved?
10. Are adequate equipment, learning materials, and spaces available at all times?
11. Is the computer being utilized for computer-assisted instruction (CAI) and for individually prescribed instruction (IPI)?
12. Is theory being utilized in curriculum and instruction?

Is Research Being Conducted?

It is difficult to imagine that the curriculum and instruction can be kept up-to-date unless research is regularly being conducted by the new community college.[21] An adequate educational program depends upon continuous investigation in order to determine its strengths and weaknesses. It is not possible to plan for improvement adequately without supporting data, and these essential facts are discovered only through study and research. The learner also must be under continuous scrutiny if the learning objectives and methods are to be improved.

The new college has an adequately staffed research office, which is concerned with assessment of the product of the college. Utilizing a variety of procedures, follow-up studies are made of students to determine whether or not objectives are being attained.

The research office stimulates, encourages, and assists faculty members to participate in research, both of the action type and at a more sophisticated level.

[21] See John E. Roueche and John R. Boggs, *Junior College Institutional Research: The State of the Art* (Washington, D.C.: American Association of Junior Colleges, 1968).

The administration lends its support by providing funds and released time for participating members of the staff. Some of the more gifted staff members may be fortunate enough to obtain grants from foundations and the federal government to conduct their research.

Finally, the administration and teaching staff have a healthy respect for research, and they make important educational decisions only after familiarizing themselves with available research on the topic.

Community college officials who admit that research is important in the new community college may wish to answer the following questions:

1. Has an adequately staffed research office been established?
2. Is continuous evaluation of the curriculum and instruction being conducted?
3. Are follow-up studies made of students in the various programs to determine whether or not objectives are being attained?
4. Are faculty members encouraged and assisted to conduct action research?
5. Are faculty members encouraged and assisted to obtain research grants?
6. Do the administration and teaching staff utilize the findings of research in making important educational decisions?

Is the College Involved with the Community?

The new community college will become more deeply involved in the life and work of the community. It not only will be responsive to the educational needs of the youth and adults of the area it serves, but it will use the community as a learning laboratory. Many of the community's problems will become the content for study and discussion in the college classes, and real solutions will be sought and applied.

Many opportunities will be provided for field experiences of both the observational and work type. Merchandising will be experienced in local stores; other vocational and technical skills will be learned in factories; and business education will take place in offices and banks, all under the supervision of the college.

Students, as part of their curriculum, will become involved in political campaigns, city government, antipollution drives, antidrug campaigns, anticrime drives, redevelopment projects, and a host of other real-life situations that have meaning for them at the time.

College facilities and resources will be shared with the community. In some instances community services will be housed in the college buildings. The library, gymnasium, swimming pool, playing fields, auditorium, and dining areas will be used by the community. Colleges with large sites will have nature trails and picnic areas that may be shared with the community.

Cultural activities and events will be conducted and sponsored on and off campus by the college for the benefit of the community.

All of the above is in addition to the many opportunities the college will provide by offering a wide variety of courses of a recreational and avocational nature. It is to the community college that many adults will turn for this type of activity. As earlier and earlier retirement ages become a reality, the community college must be prepared to assist in filling the void in the lives of individuals retiring in the prime of life.

As a check on the newness of the college in respect to working with the community, college planners might answer the following questions:

1. Does the college have a standing committee on community services with personnel from the college and the community?
2. To what extent are vocational and technical courses housed in factories, shops, and business establishments in the community?
3. To what degree are opportunities provided for students to become involved in the solution of community problems as part of their educational program?
4. How many community services are handled in college facilities?
5. How many of the special college facilities are available for community use, and how frequently are they used?
6. How many cultural activities and events did the college conduct or sponsor for the community, and how well were they attended?
7. How many courses of a recreational and avocational nature did the college offer during the past year?

There are other facets of the community college that might be utilized to test the newness of a college; however, in a work as brief as this, the five areas discussed should suffice to set the sights of the reader.

Summary

If the community college is to serve its unique mission, innovation and change must be the rule rather than the exception. Groups of colleges must band together and share ideas with each other. Cooperation rather than competition must become the keyword.

The administration of the new college will use the team approach and the hierarchical model will disappear. Faculty, students, and citizens will participate in making decisions that affect them. The new roles of college administrators will be those of planning and problem solving. The use of theory in administration will be commonplace and the computer will play an increasingly more important role in college administration.

Variety will be the rule in community college facilities. Architects will be selected early and a host of new services will be provided by them. Systems building, building systems, and fast-track construction procedures will not be out of the ordinary. The total environment will be carefully planned. Flexibility and open spaces will continue in vogue. New techniques will be developed to provide for electronic teaching and learning aids.

In urban areas, colleges will continue to occupy modernized industrial, commercial, educational, and government buildings. In many cases there will be shared occupancy of facilities. New buildings will increasingly be high-rise.

Short-lived facilities such as portables, membrane structures, and rented spaces will increase in popularity.

Curriculum study and revision will be a continuing process with ample funds and released time to support the activity. The backbone of the curriculum will continue to be general education for middle-income families, and technical and vocational education for those students who must make an early entrance on the labor market. Many short-term courses will be offered on any subject for which there is a reasonable demand.

There will be an increased emphasis on the use of behavioral objectives; reasonable levels of competence will be established for each learning unit.

Instruction in the new college will be based on a thorough knowledge of the learning process and an understanding of the differences in learning patterns of students. To meet these individual differences, all known teaching and learning techniques will be available to students and faculty. A variety of teaching and learning aids, including the latest electronic learning devices, will be regularly utilized.

Individualized instruction, where students are permitted to progress at their own rate, will increase in popularity. The computer will be used widely for computer-assisted instruction (CAI) and individually prescribed instruction (IPI).

Research will play a more important role in the new community college; changes made in the curriculum and instruction will be based on research. In administration, research will be utilized in problem solving. A special office will be established in the new college to conduct some of this research, to encourage faculty members to participate in research and to utilize the findings of research in their work.

The new two-year college is not merely *in* the community; it is *part* of it. The students use the community as a learning laboratory and the citizens uses the facilities and resources of the college for educational, vocational, avocational, and recreational purposes.

Suggested Activities and Problems

1. Select two facets of the new community college not discussed in this chapter and make predictions for the future.

2. Prepare a discussion guide and interview a college president to obtain information concerning his view of the community college of the future.

3. After extensive reading, write a paper that predicts what the probable effect of the computer will be on one of the following: (1) college administration, (2) curriculum and instruction, and (3) research.

4. Read a number of references on individually prescribed instruction. Write a paper indicating the contributions you believe this innovation can make to the instructional program in the community college.

5. Formulate a questionnaire that will elicit responses concerning the status of research in community colleges. Secure responses from a minimum of five institutions and write a paper on your findings.

6. Write a case study on a community college that has established many of the relationships with its community mentioned in this chapter.

Selected Readings

Bushnell, Don D. and Dwight W. Allen, *The Computer in American Education.* New York: John Wiley & Sons, Inc., 1967.

Cohen, Arthur M., *Dateline '79: Heretical Concepts for the Community College.* Beverly Hills, Calif.: Glencoe Press, a division of The MacMillan Company, 1969.

EDP and the School Administrator. Washington, D.C.: American Association of School Administrators, 1967.

Eurich, Alvin C., ed. *Campus 1980.* New York: Dell Publishing Co., Inc., The Delacorte Press, 1968.

Johnson, B. Lamar, *Islands of Innovation: Changes in the Community College.* Beverly Hills, Calif.: Glencoe Press, a division of The Macmillan Company, 1969.

——, ed., *The Experimental Junior College,* Occasional Report No. 12. Los Angeles: University of California, 1968.

Mager, Robert F., *Preparing Instructional Objectives.* Belmont, Calif.: Fearon Publishers, 1962.

McMurrin, Sterling M., *Innovations in Education: New Directions for the American School.* Washington, D.C.: Committee for Economic Development, 1968.

Moeller, Gerald H., and David J. Mahan, *The Faculty Team.* Chicago: Science Research Associates, Inc., 1971.

Roueche, John E. and John R. Boggs, *Junior College Institutional Research: The State of the Art.* Washington, D.C.: American Association of Junior Colleges, 1968.

10

The Impact
of New Media

Educational Technology in the
Community College[1]

The great playwright George Bernard Shaw was more of a prophet than he realized in 1949 when he told the writer that radio had revolutionized the education of the masses and brought the world into little villages like his Ayot St. Lawrence, nestling in the Hertfordshire hills some twenty miles from London. As Shaw alluded to the electronic infant, television, and spoke of his belief in the effective use of educational motion pictures and other audio-visual aids in the classroom, he was indeed anticipating a technological explosion that was to transform society and the educational process in the second half of the century.

Whereas Shaw referred to the great changes in his village, Marshall McLuhan proclaimed some twenty years later that man lives in a global village created by the instantaneous world of electronic media. From relative isolation in many separate cultures and societies, man has dramatically and rapidly evolved to an awareness of the other "villages" in his world. He has been thrust into involvement with peoples and lands once quite distant from his own both geographically and culturally.

If one accepts to some degree a major McLuhan premise that "any technology gradually creates a totally new human environment,"[2] then there are

---

[1] Some of the content in this chapter has been quoted and adapted from Ross L. Neagley, N. Dean Evans, and Clarence A. Lynn, Jr., *The School Administrator and Learning Resources: A Handbook for Effective Action* (Englewood Cliffs, N.J.: Prentice-Hall, Inc., 1969), pp. 1-2, 38, 54-60, 68-81, 83, 138-39.

[2] Marshall McLuhan, *Understanding Media: The Extension of Man,* 2nd ed. (New York: McGraw-Hill Book Company, 1966), p. viii.

serious and challenging implications for all educators. In a world that has suddenly become much smaller and more intimate through the development of communications satellites, intercontinental color television, and supersonic jet airliners, many traditional concepts of educational institutions are rapidly becoming obsolete.

Education Yesterday and Today

Educators, like all human beings, find some comfort in reverie about the "good old days." In terms of teaching, learning, and curriculum, this means an era when almost everything a student was expected to know could be found in the pages of a basic textbook. After this major resource was selected, the college administrator could rest secure in the thought that the instructor, dutifully following the text, and supplementing it from his own background, would probably succeed in covering the required material. The students were required at intervals to regurgitate selected facts on a test paper, and the "learning" process continued into the next chapter. Simply digesting facts from a basic text was thought to be adequate education at one time, but any modern-day proponent of such a curriculum would face a formidable task indeed. With the sum total of man's knowledge doubling every few years in most academic fields, it is impossible to catalog all facts, let alone teach them.

By the 1950s and 1960s, many educational institutions had thrown off the shackles of a rote curriculum designed for group consumption. Research into the learning process made it apparent to more educators that all students did not learn at the same rate and could not profit from the same curriculum. "Individual differences" and "individualization of instruction" became popular terms in the professional literature. Learning aids such as supplementary books, filmstrips, motion pictures, and recordings were used by many instructors; however, it was still difficult to help the individual student to learn according to his needs as long as only group instruction was utilized. The instructor who understood that he should individualize instruction was often unable to do so. Large group lectures were planned to free more teacher time for smaller seminar discussions and some individual work. But the problem of the teacher-student ratio always prevented the real individualization of instruction—until the technological explosion of educational media in the late sixties. Here was a breakthrough in methods and materials of instruction that held at last the promise of Mark Hopkins on one end of the log and the student on the other.

It is easy to become enamored with the fascinating world of color television, random dial access, computer-assisted instruction, and other capitvating media. Indeed many colleges throughout the nation have introduced various learning resources into the instructional program in recent years. Oldsters take beginning French via TV; freshmen in study carrels dial sequences in chemistry; and science classes visit the city museum of natural history. Health education students view a color film on human reproduction; city students visit a farm; and future social service students slide single-concept social science films into their own projectors.

"Isn't it marvelous?" the casual observer is likely to exclaim. "The days of the dull single textbook are gone; the learning environment is so much richer today!" *Or is it?* The mere introduction of a variety of educational media and experiences is no guarantee of a sound instructional program. Learning resources do not have intrinsic value in themselves. A college administrator who builds a TV studio, a dial access system, and a film library into the new community college may not be contributing anything significant to the learning processes of the students. Far too many institutions are leaping into the new media without considering where they are going or how they propose to get there. We dare not adopt the new gadgetry simply because it is on the market and in the educational literature.

Technology is making a great contribution to the work of the community college in ways other than instruction and learning. As mentioned in Chapter 9, the computer is being utilized by these institutions for alumni records, admissions, business functions, counseling, financial aid, manpower inventory, payroll, registration and records, research, and test marking. The community college that lacks a data-processing system capable of providing the above services is outmoded and, as a result, will be severely handicapped.

Getting the Most from the New Technology

The extent to which the new media-educational technology will have an impact on the community college must be determined during the early planning stages of the institution. The selection and orientation of the administration and staff toward educational technology, the type of facilities planned, the budgetary provisions made, and the opportunities provided for research and experimentation, all condition the initial and continued use of these new tools.

Administration and the New Technology

If the new technology is to make a real impact in the new community college, all members of the administrative and instructional staff, as well as personnel in supportive services, must be sympathetic toward and, to the degree needed, competent in the use of the new media-instructional technology. Those concerned must also understand, and be able to make intelligent use of, the computer for all purposes previously enumerated. This must be kept in mind in the selection of staff. In addition, opportunities must be provided for staff members to constantly upgrade their knowledge and skill in the application of technology to education.

Chapter 5 described the selection, qualifications, and job of a president and Chapter 6 the recruiting, organizing, and training of the college staff. This section will emphasize certain personnel attitudes and competencies as they relate to new media and educational technology.

The College President and the New Technology. A dynamic, alert, intelligent community college president is the key to successful utilization of the new technology in the administration of the college and in the instructional program. Although he will have little time to participate directly in media selection, production, or use, his attitudes and actions as head of the college profoundly influence teaching methods and resources. The president's obvious interest in the latest instructional and administrative applications—involving computers, for example—is bound to carry over to the other members of the administrative team and, hopefully, to the entire staff. A truly dynamic president sets the tone for the college philosophy and practice.

The community college president, then, can do much to encourage the use of educational technology in the college. He can direct the development of a sound learning resources program by demonstrating positive, democratic leadership in the following ways:

1. Analyze the budget to determine total funds expended for various instructional media in the several subject and program areas. Such a study should show differences in expenditures between general and specialized education. The administration will then know exactly what the media dollars are buying.

2. Read as much as possible in the field and route pertinent articles and books to other members of the staff. Keep up-to-date on new developments.

3. See that the agendas of the administrative staff or instructional affairs council provide for periodic discussions on learning resources.

4. Support budget requirements for various media that grow out of current curriculum studies in the college and are recommended by the academic dean.

5. Work with other institutions in the area and state to provide or expand needed cooperative services in learning resources.

6. Visit innovative educational institutions and learning resource centers at least two or three times a year. It is easy to get into a rut, and getting out of the office for such field trips is a healthy experience for any college president.

7. Spend considerable time in the classrooms and learning centers to observe the role of media in many teaching-learning situations.

8. See that the board of trustees gets periodic reports on the learning resources program and its contribution to the fulfillment of instructional objectives. Invite key personnel, such as the director of learning resources, to make visual presentations to the board on occasion.

9. Make sure that professional contracts provide released time for participation

of all staff members in the program of curriculum development, including selection of appropriate instructional media.

In summary, the community college president's main task is to provide top-level support for the learning resources program. This is evidenced by his enthusiasm, his expanding knowledge of the field, and his coordination of all instructional activities in the college. His most important personnel decision concerns the administrator to whom he delegates the responsibility and authority for the development of the instructional program and supporting media.

In a similar manner he can assume leadership in the application of technology to the administrative aspects of the developing community college.

The Academic Dean and the New Technology. The dean of academic affairs should become the key figure in the administration of the learning resources program. Indeed, his responsibilities encompass supervision and coordination of the entire instructional process in the community college, including curriculum development. He is, of course, assisted by the chairmen of instructional divisions and/or departments. He also relies heavily on the director or coordinator of learning resources.

The dean of academic affairs directs the development of the new media-instructional technology in the following ways:

1. He keeps up-to-date on the latest research and technical developments in the field of learning resources. The academic dean will rely primarily on the director or coordinator of learning resources and the chairmen of instructional divisions or departments to discuss with him new trends and experiments in such fields as dial access retrieval and programmed instruction by computer. But he must include in his professional reading enough articles and books on educational technology to be conversant with current streams of thought and action. This will require the scheduling of certain definite working hours for reading, study, and personal "hands-on" testing of new learning aids.

2. As the leader of the instructional team, the dean of academic affairs meets regularly with all of those administrators who report directly to him. This group is part of the college instructional affairs council, which often makes major decisions regarding the instructional program and its supporting media. Such a council should meet weekly or biweekly, depending on the stage of curriculum development in the college. It is suggested that large blocks of time be set aside for in-depth discussion on such matters as the proposed experimental introduction of computer-assisted instruction, or the development of an interdisciplinary course. Normally, the chaimen of instructional divisions or departments will present recommendations from their faculty for

consideration by the instructional affairs council. However, the floor should always be open for freewheeling, brainstorming discussions on the state of the learning resources program in the college and its obvious relationship to the developing curriculum and the instructional program.

The academic dean may be the catalytic agent in this council of key instructional leaders. Indeed, to be successful in his major leadership role, he must rise to the challenge of coordinating the dynamic, democratic group action that will emerge from such a group.

3. The dean of academic affairs delegates considerable responsibility and authority to the director or coordinator of learning resources and expects him to work cooperatively with the division chairmen in exploring new thrusts or changes in instructional aids. In the media field, the director or coordinator of learning resources is obviously the right arm of the academic dean, who relies heavily on him for guidance in making the ultimate decisions regarding introduction or modification of media systems and resources in the college.

4. The academic dean personally spends time in the various divisions and departments, talking with chairmen and instructors and participating in the instructional program as an observer and resource person. There is no substitute for active involvement in the learning experiences of students; an office-bound administrator soon loses touch with the realities of teacher-student interaction.

5. The chairmen work closely with the academic dean, keeping him informed of the evolving instructional program in their divisions. He sits as a participant with faculty in the subject areas or disciplines and knows the current status of each curriculum study. He also lends his own resource assistance to the deliberations.

6. The dean of academic affairs keeps the president informed on all major instructional projects, especially possible changes or experiments being considered by the divisions or the instructional affairs council. This is particularly important if there are budget considerations involved, for instance, in the introduction of new educational technology. The community college president should never be surprised by a question like this after a rotary club speech: "Dr. Brown, what do we hear about the college contemplating the purchase of additional computer terminals to teach science?" If the academic dean is doing his job in this respect, the president will always be fully informed.

7. After full deliberation by the division faculties and the instructional affairs council, and after recommendations by the director or coordinator of learning resources, the academic dean will need to make some final decisions regarding curriculum, instruction, and learning resources for the next budget year. For example, if there is a strong recommendation that comprehensive environmental studies course sequences be developed and supported by

instructional materials, how much will all of this cost? And must this need be weighed against others of equal or greater importance? At this point, after due consultation with his subordinates, the academic dean prepares his budget recommendations for the president.

8. Beyond the college, the academic dean has a major responsibility, with the director or coordinator of learning resources, for determining the extent of college participation in county, regional, state, and federal programs for learning resources.

The Dean of Administration or Administrative Services and the New Technology. The individual who assumes this important post influences the use of the new technology in the developing college from several viewpoints. First, he has a role in personnel selection; second, he is in charge of budget and financial administration as well as purchasing; third, he participates in plant planning and maintenance; and fourth, he utilizes the computer in much of his work connected with the other three responsibilities. As a consequence of the latter, this dean must cultivate good working relationships with the office of the dean of research, planning, and information systems.

The dean of administrative services works in a staff relationship with the dean of academic affairs on matters pertaining to budgeting, purchasing, and other items involving finance. Optimum administrative organization suggests a president's cabinet or administrative council that would include all administrators reporting to the president. Developing the college budget is the joint concern of these administrators and their subordinates.

With regard to learning resources, the dean of administrative services participates in major budget conferences. He meets regularly with the other top administrators, both in cabinet and individually. He keeps himself informed on the changing learning resources field, mainly through his contacts with the dean of academic affairs.

Since the media-educational technology budget is inextricably tied to the developing curriculum and the objectives of the entire instructional program, the major decisions regarding proposed expenditures should be based on curricular needs. The dean of administrative services, therefore, should not oppose a budget item simply because of its cost. The financial requirements for media naturally grow out of the professional decisions made in the instructional affairs council, and in the office of the dean of academic affairs. The dean of administrative services can play a valuable role in citing figures and percentages from the current budget, in presenting cost analyses, and in summarizing other financial data that may be required. Under no circumstances, however, should he have sole decision-making power over line items, especially in the instructional areas. In summary, his function in the budget-making process for curriculum and learning resources is supportive and advisory.

Once the college budget is adopted, the dean of administrative services has the important job of purchasing materials and services. Here again he relies on the professional judgment of those competent in instruction to prepare the specifications for such items as slide projectors, learning carrels, or new library books. He then orders the recommended learning resources, within the various budget categories.

The dean of administrative services supplies each administrator with a monthly budget analysis, showing expenditures in each category to date. It is his job to inform individuals and divisions or departments of their spending rate. For example, assume that the college library is allocated a budget of $100,000 for new acquisitions, and that it spends $94,000 in the first seven months of the budget year. It is the responsibility of the dean of administrative services to inform the librarian that there is a $6,000 balance in that category for the remaining five months.

The Dean of Research, Planning, and Information Systems and the New Technology. This administrator is responsible for institutional research, computer services, long-range planning and campus development, and systems development and analysis. From the above job description it is readily discernable that this dean will also exert considerable influence on the use of technology in the college in all of its different aspects.

His responsibility for institutional research and computer services makes him a regular user of the new technology. The dean of academic affairs and faculty members interested in research and innovation constantly will be seeking his aid and advice. The extent to which computer-assisted instruction (CAI), computer-mediated instruction (CMI), and individually prescribed instruction (IPI) are utilized will depend a great deal upon a good working relationship between the dean of research, planning, and information systems and the dean of academic affairs.

In long-range planning and campus development as well as in systems development and analysis, the computer will be an indispensable tool.

The Dean of Student Affairs and the New Technology. The individual serving in this position also requires extensive use of computer services. Charged with responsibility for admissions and registration, counseling and guidance, student services, financial aid, and placement, it is doubtful if he could perform all these functions without the assistance of the new technology. Here again there is a need for excellent working relationships between this office and those of the academic dean and the dean for research, planning, and information systems.

Instruction and the New Technology

Learning resources should be considered within the total process of curriculum development and instruction. Therefore decisions regarding media are best made only after extensive progress in curriculum design. Media-educational technology cannot be considered separate from the educational program. It is part and parcel of the total offering of the new community college.

The Role of Media and Method. It is imperative that learning resources and techniques of instruction be designed to aid in accomplishing the objectives of learning sequences. For instance, even the best documentary film on Adolf Hitler and the Third Reich must be related to the behavioral outcomes and content of the appropriate unit in modern world history before the film becomes relevant as a learning resource.

FIGURE 10-1

Also, modern concepts of the nature of the learning process, as discussed in Chapter 8, require considerable imagination and flexibility in the use of instructional materials and methods. (1) For example, if students are really to have the opportunity to inquire, to exchange ideas with their instructor and with each other, and to debate various issues, there must be ample opportunity for confrontation in small groups of ten to fifteen. Perhaps the only learning aid required here would be a chalkboard. The method obviously is group discussion or seminar. (2) To meet other learning objectives, students can study on their own in carrels, using materials previously prepared and stored electronically. In this way true individualization of the learning process can be achieved. (3) These two methods are often preceded or supplemented by large group instruction, where major concepts introducing a unit of instruction can be presented to several hundred learners at one time. Through the selective use of such media as overhead transparencies, 16 mm film clips, closed circuit television, and various student-response systems, a skilled lecturer can effectively reach 200 students instead of the 30 he might have in a regular classroom. Following is a more detailed description of how such a multimodal learning environment may operate in a community college.

FIGURE 10-2

The student in the new college is confronted with learning in a variety of places and formats. Learning takes place in large group assemblies, small group sessions (seminars), and individual study carrels, to name a few.

During the large group assembly the instructor presents a carefully prepared

FIGURE 10-3

and rehearsed program based on one or more objectives of the unit being studied. The instructor utilizes a variety of presentation devices and media. At selected points during the program, the students will be asked to respond to questions flashed on the screen. The master control will tabulate these responses and provide immediate feedback to the instructor, who can continue with his presentation or branch to an alternate path presenting the material in a different format.

At the end of the large group assembly, the 200 or more students continue with specific assignments relating to the unit, which they now study as individuals. These assignments may consist of a series of articles culled from various magazines, a chapter from a book, or a session in the individual study center, where the student will dial a prepared program from his carrel or plug in a slide-tape presentation.

After the student has completed these tasks, he may meet in a group of ten to fifteen with the instructor in a seminar room to discuss, inquire about, and debate the issues brought forth during the large group and individual study sessions. Once the instructor is satisfied that a student understands the issues and has met the established objectives, he certifies him for the next unit of study.

The learning process thus becomes a program in which technology, resources, and the instructor are brought together, each functioning in the best way— technology taking over many of the routine chores of teaching, continuously evaluating individual students, and providing quick access to knowledge; learning resources bringing the world into the classroom, taking verbal abstractions and making them concrete; and the instructor leading and guiding students on an individual and small group basis into abstract areas of knowledge.

FIGURE 10-4

Since all or most of the instructors in the college will be utilizing the above and other methods in a variety of patterns, it becomes apparent that a vast number of instructional materials, some rather sophisticated hardware, and a new type of service organization will be required. Such a modern learning resources center will be described later in this chapter.

This section on instructional modes would be incomplete without a brief reference to the use of the computer in instruction. Increasingly, the computer is being utilized as a teaching-learning device that, according to its advocates, has a real capability of adapting the instructional environment to the characteristics and needs of the individual learner. There seems to be general agreement that computers hold considerable promise for individualizing instruction at any level. In the usual installation, terminals are connected to a central computer in which the curriculum content is stored on magnetic disks or tapes. There actually is no limit to the number of courses or units that can be programmed and stored. Modified "typewriters" are used for two-way communication between the student and the computer.[3]

The above procedure is known as computer-assisted instruction (CAI). The computer also is utilized for programming and prescribing the program of individual students. In the literature this is described as individually prescribed instruction (IPI).

Individually Prescribed Instruction (IPI) is a far cry from traditional college teaching. It places the instructor in an entirely new role in his relationship to his students. Instead of being the final authority and the dispenser of information in his subject matter field, the instructor's role in IPI is to organize a system of instruction, diagnose learning problems, prescribe instructional remedies, and coordinate the educational assistance required by the student.

An excellent operating description of IPI may be found in the 1966 Yearbook of the National Society for the Study of Education, Part 2. The following material has been adapted from the operating principles developed by Bolvin and Lindvall and reported in the above publication.

Basic Assumptions of IPI

1. Individually prescribed instruction is the notion that learning is something that is ultimately personal and individual learning takes place only on an individual basis.
2. Curriculum sequences must be developed in such a way that they represent a long-term development process which ignores guidelines.
3. If students are progressing individually, questions about grouping, classification, or housing are irrelevant.

[3] Adapted from Ross L. Neagley and N. Dean Evans, *Handbook for Effective Supervision of Instruction,* 2nd ed. (Englewood Cliffs, N.J.: Prentice-Hall, Inc., 1970), p. 270.

Critical Elements in Implementation of IPI

1. The objectives to be achieved must be spelled out in terms of desired student behaviors.

2. To the extent possible, instructional objectives should be ordered in a sequence which makes for effective student progression with a minimum number of gaps or difficult steps and with little overlap or unnecessary repetition.

3. If students are to work through a curriculum on an individual basis, it is essential that instructional materials be such that students can learn from them without constant help from an instructor and can make steady progress in the mastery of the defined objectives.

4. In individualized instruction care must be taken to find out what skills and knowledge each student possesses and to see that each one starts in the learning sequence at the point which is most appropriate for him.

5. For individualized instruction, conditions must be provided which permit each student to progress through a learning sequence at a pace determined by his own work habits and by his ability to master the designated instructional objectives.

6. If instruction is to be effective, it must make provisions for having the student actually carry out and practice the behavior which he is to learn.

7. Learning is enhanced if students receive rather immediate feedback concerning the correctness of their efforts in attempting to approximate a desired behavior.

8. The final criterion for judging any instructional sequence must be its effectiveness in producing changes in students, and feedback concerning student performance should be used in the continuing modification and improvement of materials and procedures.[4]

The Total Learning Resources Center

Have you looked at a learning resources center lately? Under the traditional system the learning resources center consisted of two separate operations. First, there was the library. Just what happened in the college library? The books were stored neatly on its shelves; some students could be seen milling around looking for books; others were seated at tables writing reports. The librarian could be

---

[4]C. M. Lindvall and John O. Bolvin, "Programed Instruction in the Schools: An Application of Programing Principles in 'Individually Prescribed Instruction,'" in *Programed Instruction,* Chap. 8. Sixty-sixth Yearbook of the National Society for the Study of Education, Part 2, ed. Phil C. Lange (Chicago: University of Chicago Press, 1967), pp. 233-50.

observed cataloging some new acquisitions, or perhaps preparing a bibliography for an instructor.

Next, there was the audio-visual department. What happened here? The films, filmstrips, and tapes were all stored neatly on the shelves; some students might be seen looking at a filmstrip over there in a corner. The A-V director was occupied cataloging some new films or perhaps preparing a transparency for a teacher.

In order to determine the true nature of a total learning resources center, let us examine more closely the activities occurring in each of the above areas.

*Students seem to be coming to these areas to study.

*Some are reading books; others are viewing films or filmstrips or listening to tapes.

*Instructional materials are being stored in each area—books and other printed matter in one—projected materials and audio devices in the other.

*Materials are being acquired, produced, and cataloged, and professional consultations are being offered in both to faculty and students.

Under the traditional system we had two separate organizations within the same institution, each performing identical operations, the only apparent difference being the medium upon which the operation was being performed. How this dichotomy of function came into being will not be discussed here. However, the new community college will not be able to tolerate this division, since it perpetuates the following:

1. A teaching-learning process that depends upon verbalism in a world in which the student (outside the college) has been learning through a rather sophisticated media system.
2. A dependence by the instructor and learner upon the printed page, primarily because of the emphasis placed on the traditional library and the textbook in the educational program.
3. Lip service to other forms of communications systems, simply because it is in vogue to have them.

Needless to say, the organization described above has proven to be very inefficient and highly uneconomical.

The learning resources center for the modern community college must become an instructional support organization responsible for the development, implementation, dissemination, and evaluation of information transmission systems. These systems must be developed around: (1) the stated philosophy, goals, and objectives of the institution, and (2) the objectives of the students and faculty in terms of the curriculum.

If the student himself is to be responsible for more and more of his own learning, where can he accomplish this? If there is any single facility in educational institutions today that is designed for independent study and searching for information while providing the necessary professional personnel to assist and guide the student in his quest for knowledge, it has to be the learning resources center. The college learning resources center must be the focal point of the individual student's learning. It must therefore be designed around the needs and activities of the student who will use it.

If the learning resources center is to provide the required services to faculty and students, proper facilities, materials, and equipment will be necessary. For example, space must be provided for a large number of students to study independently. This will require study carrels placed unobtrusively throughout the learning resources center. Small-group meeting rooms should be provided. Areas will be needed where students can view films and other projected materials or listen to tapes and watch programs through the audio-video dial access system or other distribution systems.

FIGURE 10-5

No longer can the library be thought of as a room with book stacks along the walls and a few tables and chairs provided for study purposes. Rather, the library must be a *large and comfortable* area where the student will want to learn. The floor should be carpeted and comfortable chairs provided in pleasant surroundings. "Floating" book stacks should divide the collection into various reading areas. The library, in fact, must become the student's home away from home.

However, the library is only a part of the total learning resources center. As was mentioned earlier, the center is also responsible for the development and evaluation of information transmission systems. Therefore, space must be allocated for such services as the acquisition, production, and testing of instructional materials.

Facilities and services can only be determined by the total educational program of the school. Following is a description of the services—with related facilities—needed if a total communications system is planned.

Production Services. The local production of materials developed to achieve the specific objectives and goals of the curriculum is imperative. In many instances commercial materials will be available to meet these objectives. However, the college must be prepared to produce its own materials, particularly where they will be utilized in independent study.

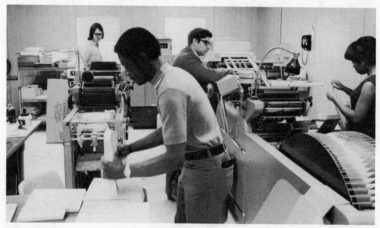

FIGURE 10-6

Facilities should be anticipated for:

1. Printing and duplicating: offset presses, spirit duplicator, copiers, plate making, stapling, collating, binding, storage.
2. Photography: film studio, darkrooms, drying rooms, film-loading room, microfilm production, photographic reproduction area, and storage.
3. Graphics: Production room, layout room, copying area, model shop, storage.

Electronic Communications Service. The use of television, audio recordings, and radio for the transmission of educational programs is becoming more prevalent in systems-oriented colleges. Careful planning and proper design of these facilities is of great importance. Provisions should be made for the following:

1. Television: studio, control room, video-tape room, distribution center, set construction, dock, maintenance, and storage.
2. Radio and audio recording: recording booth, control room, audio-dubbing and duplication room, transmission center, storage.

Central Storage and Distribution. Although many programs will be distributed throughout the college electronically, a centralized area will still be required for the storage and distribution of:

1. Equipment: projectors, recorders, microreaders, cameras, and so on.
2. Materials: maps, globes, films, filmstrips, books, periodicals, records, and many others.

FIGURE 10-7

Library Technical Services. In this area all learning resources are processed for distribution to the classrooms and laboratories within the college. Facilities will be needed for:

1. Acquisitions.
2. Cataloging.
3. Maintenance and binding.
4. Storage.

The above services and facilities may appear extensive to some college administrators; however, the process of curriculum development and student learning envisioned in the future will be seriously curtailed if they are not provided. In some cases, several institutions can develop a cooperative approach to the provision of these services.

Staffing the Learning Resources Center

With the establishment of any instructional support program, whether it be computer services, curriculum consulting, counseling services, or a learning resources program, the provision of specially trained and qualified professional, technical, and clerical personnel is essential.

Since the services to be offered by the center are somewhat complex and require a number of personnel with varied training and ability, careful consideration must be given to the activities in which the staff will be involved. Many of these activities will be determined by the programs to be offered in the college.

Although only key personnel will be discussed here, it should be apparent that the professional staff of the learning resources center will be a team of specialists concerned with the communications program—relative to the learning process—of the entire college. As such, they are responsible for the efficient design and utilization of all carriers of information, and the effect of these upon the learner.

Organization of the Learning Resources Center Staff. The staff needed by the college will be determined by the number of services to be provided. A learning resources center organized and staffed as follows will enable the college to basically provide the services discussed.

The Director of Learning Resources is responsible for the administration and supervision of the entire learning resources program of the college. Reporting to the dean of academic affairs, he is expected to maintain close contact with the president, all deans, division and department heads, and faculty members. He will take the initiative, with the academic dean, in developing a sound philosophy regarding the role of learning resources in the instructional program.

Along with other members of the center's staff, he is responsible for:

1. An inservice training program to bring about an effective utilization of all types of learning resources.
2. Development of effective procedures for the evaluation and selection of book and nonbook media and equipment.
3. Preparation of the learning resources budget to be submitted to the dean of academic affairs, as part of the total instructional budget.
4. Development of a program to train technicians, clerks, and students in the production of certain learning resources and the operation of instructional equipment.
5. Continuous evaluation of the learning resources program based on the philosophy and objectives of the college.

The qualifications for this position include training in audio-visual communications, a background in curriculum development, successful teaching experience, training in research, skills in the areas of production, and successful experience in learning resource administration.

The Coordinator of Library Services will administer and supervise the book media program of the college. Reporting to the director of learning resources, he also is expected to maintain close contact with all administrators, division and/or department chairmen, and instructors. As a member of the learning resources team, he will meet with all curriculum development teams and take the initiative in developing a sound philosophy of the role of the library in the college's instructional program. With other members of the library staff, he is responsible for:

1. Assistance with the learning resources center's inservice program relative to library services.
2. Preparation of the library budget to be submitted to the director, as part of the total learning resources budget.
3. Development of effective procedures for the evaluation and selection of printed materials.
4. Development of procedures and hiring of personnel for the acquisition, cataloging, and maintenance of all learning resources.
5. Development of a program to recruit and train technicians, clerks, and students to assist in the library technical service area.
6. Assistance in the preparation of bibliographies of book and nonbook materials for distribution to faculty and students.
7. Continuous evaluation of the library program based on the philosophy and objectives of the college.

The qualifications for this position include training in library science, successful teaching experience, a background in curriculum development, and successful experience in library administration.

The Coordinator of Media Services will administer and supervise the college's nonbook media program. He, too, is expected to maintain close contact with other administrators, division and/or department chairmen, and the teaching staff. As the third member of the learning resources team he will meet with the curriculum development teams and take the initiative in developing a sound philosophy for the role of nonbook media in the college's instructional program.

With other members of the media staff he is responsible for:

1. Assistance with the learning resources center's inservice program dealing with the utilization and production of materials and the electronic distribution of programs.
2. Preparation of the media budget to be submitted to the director as part of the total learning resources budget.
3. Planning the production of television programs.
4. Scheduling the distribution of television programs.

5. Coordinating the production of all instructional materials.
6. Supervising the media distribution service.
7. Development of a program to train technicians, clerks, and students to assist in the production of instructional materials.
8. Continuous evaluation of the media program, based on the philosophy and objectives of the college.

Qualifications for this position include extensive knowledge of electronic communications, skills in areas of production such as photography and graphics, a background in curriculum development, and successful experience in media administration.

In addition to the key professional personnel discussed above, the learning resources center must also provide adequate support personnel for nonbook media.

Technicians. These should be employed to:

1. Maintain and repair audio-visual equipment owned by the college.
2. Make continuing inventories of equipment and materials.
3. Clean and repair instructional materials.
4. Assist in the scheduling and distribution of materials and equipment.
5. Check and process new materials for circulation.
6. Assist in the production of instructional materials, including printing and duplicating, TV production, and audio recording.

Clerical Personnel will:

1. Assist in the procurement of materials for preview and acquisition purposes.
2. Type letters, reports, and other items.
3. Maintain the files and records of the learning resources center.
4. Schedule all equipment and materials.

Graphics and Photographic Personnel will design and produce the artwork for materials used in the instructional modes and for television and photography.

Figure 10-8 depicts the organizational structure and required staffing for a learning resources center serving a systems-oriented community college with 1,550 full-time and 1,100 part-time students.

Building for the New Technology

Chapters 9 and 12 both refer to this topic. It is evident to anybody interested in educational facilities that the new media-educational technology has had and will continue to have a great impact on the planning and building of all facilities used for educational purposes. It should be sufficient to remind the reader that

DIVISION OF LEARNING RESOURCES ORGANIZATION PLAN

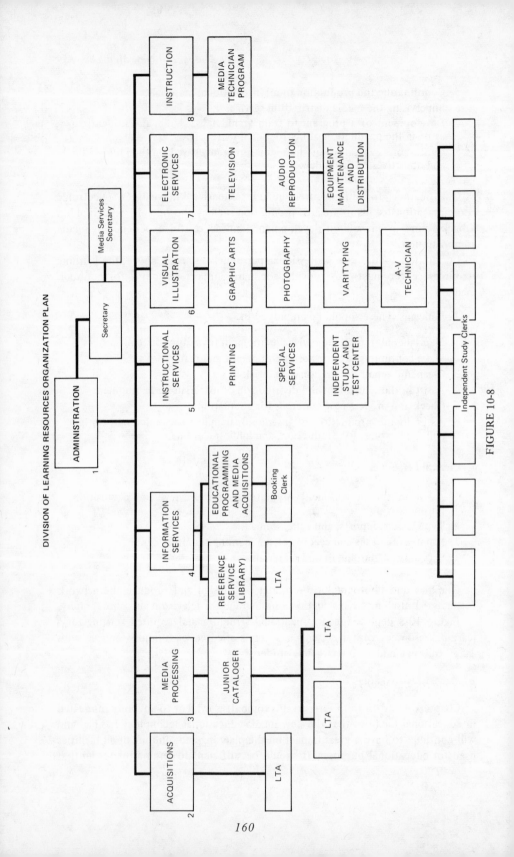

FIGURE 10-8

the growth in educational technology is taking place so rapidly and the cost is becoming so competitive that the "hardware" and its corresponding speed of acceptance in educational institutions has outstripped the know-how to provide adequate plant facilities in which it is possible to make optimum use of these new learning resources. New educational plants must be built and old ones modernized to take full advantage of the most advanced teaching and learning technology known today and, to the extent possible, dreamed of for tomorrow. Particular attention must be directed to the many past errors made in respect to such critical factors as viewing angles and distances; visual, sonic, and thermal environments; and storage and distribution systems. A new look must also be taken at the design of facilities for other supporting functions including origination, production, video taping, and recording. Finally, new educational facilities must be planned with such programs as computer-assisted instruction (CAI) and individually prescribed instruction (IPI) in mind.

FIGURE 10-9

Budgeting for the New Technology

Budget allocations, like space assignments, depend upon the educational program. Therefore, with the focus on procedures rather than on budgetary details, the following principles of budgeting and financing the new media-educational technology programs are enumerated:

1. An educational media program should operate from a central budget which is prepared and defended by representatives of the educational media services.

2. An educational media program should be financed entirely from regularly appropriated institutional funds.

3. A community college should have clear-cut policies concerning allocation, income, and charges against the educational media budget.

4. The budget of an educational media program should be based on both the college's long-range goals and immediate educational media needs.

5. Long-range budget planning should provide for improvements to be made gradually until the full media program goals are realized.

6. Long-range financial plans should include provisions for the expansion of media services as required by the improvement of the quality and scope of the instructional program.

7. The budget of an educational media program should provide for increased scope of services, expansion of services to meet increased enrollments, and the needs created by the addition of new structures.

8. There should be a definite plan for gaining administrative and community support for the media program. The plan should include evaluation of the program, determination of media needs, long- and short-range planning, and presenting facts about media needs to administrators and governing boards.

9. All costs relating to procurement or production of materials, purchase of equipment, and employment of staff for use in the college's educational program should be completely subsidized through a centralized budget.

10. The selection of all materials and equipment for purchase by the educational media center should be based on predetermined specifications formulated by the media staff, with input from the instructional staff.

11. Provisions should be made in the educational media budget for systematic replacement of obsolete or worn-out media.[5]

The above eleven principles should receive serious consideration by all individuals responsible for budgeting and financing an educational media program.

In 1971, a committee of learning resources directors in New Jersey community colleges made an exhaustive study of media financing in these institutions. Their conclusions and recommendations should provide useful guidelines for budget preparation.

1. For initial book collections in new community colleges, the committee recommended the American Library Association guidelines of 20,000 volumes for the first 1,000 full-time students, and 5,000 volumes for every 500 students thereafter. The average price of a hard cover book in 1970 was

---

[5] W. R. Fulton, *Criteria Relating to Educational Media Programs in School Systems* (Norman, Okla.: University of Oklahoma. Developed as part of a study performed pursuant to a contract with the USOE, Department of Health, Education, and Welfare, under provisions of Title VII, Public Law 85-664, mimeographed, n.d.), pp. 8-9.

$11.66, up from $8.43 in 1967; consequently the committee noted that these unusual inflationary cost factors must be taken into consideration in building budgets.

2. Noting the trend toward large nonbook media collections, the committee recommended that a sum equal to 30 percent of the cost of the initial book collection be allocated for nonbook media in new community colleges. However, "nonbook media collections tend to grow very rapidly as soon as courses are well established. Indeed, there seems every possibility that media centers may soon be spending just as much for nonbook media as for books. For example, Burlington County College budgeted $50,000 for books during the 1972 fiscal year and $38,000 for nonbook media during the same period."

3. The committee reported that New Jersey community colleges spent an average of $45.00 yearly per full-time equivalent student on all media from 1969 to 1971. It was recommended that continuing annual media budgets (after initial acquisitions) should be devised as follows: Multiply the number of FTE students by the average sum spent on media per FTE by all community colleges for the past two years, and add the annual inflationary percentile reported by the Association of American Publishers. Determining the split between books and nonbook media would be the responsibility of the local college, based on the status of its developing instructional programs and the resulting media requirements.[6]

There should always be a contingency item in the learning resources budget to allow for unanticipated needs by instructors, librarians, and media personnel. Even with careful budget preparation, the rapidly changing media field demands some flexibility in budgeting. Instructors and learning resources personnel are unable to completely assess the learning needs of next year's students when they participate in the budget-making process. Decisions regarding the re-allocation of contingency funds will be made mainly by the dean of academic affairs, the director of learning resources, and other concerned division or department chairmen and instructors.

Research, Experimentation, Innovation, and the New Technology

The new media-educational technology has influenced research, experimentation, and innovation in educational institutions to a considerable degree. In the first place, the introduction of new teaching-learning techniques via the new technology has placed responsibility on the faculty members who use them

---

[6] Report of the Committee to Develop a Formula for the Purchase of Library Books and Nonbook Materials, Association of County Community College Presidents of New Jersey, September, 1971.

to demonstrate by experimentation and research that the new procedures are superior or at least equal to the former methods of instruction. In the second place, the computer has proven to be a valuable tool in conducting this research. Use of the computer enables the researcher to do a more sophisticated type of research in a considerably shorter period of time.

In addition to research in instruction and learning, the computer facilitates major institutional research as well. The community college that desires to remain in the forefront will make wise use of the computer in research of all kinds.

Summary

A community college staff must be well organized to administer the new media-educational technology effectively. Instructors, division chairmen, and administrators need to have a clear conception of their function in the entire educational process, including curriculum development.

A dynamic, alert *president* is the key to a successful learning resources program. He will have little time to participate in the actual media selection, production, or use, but his attitudes and actions profoundly influence the other members of the staff. He also is influential in encouraging the utilization of computer technology.

The *dean of academic affairs* too is an important figure in the administration of the new media-educational technology program. He is a line officer, to whom the division or department heads and the director of learning resources report. He is the team leader for instruction and therefore sets the tone for curriculum development. He coordinates the whole instructional media program through cooperative action with other administrators and other personnel concerned with instruction.

The *dean of administrative services* participates in major budget conferences involving instruction. Decisions on proposed expenditures for media-educational technology are based on curricular needs. This administrator serves as an adviser on the instructional budget. His main function, after budget approval, is control of expenditures within limits adopted.

The *dean of research, planning, and information systems* influences the new technology's impact on the college. As the individual responsible for institutional research, computer services, long-range planning and campus development, and systems development and analysis, he is in a key position to exert considerable influence on the use of technology in the college.

The office of the *dean of student affairs* makes extensive use of computer services for registration, counseling and guidance, student services, financial aid, and placement. These functions are closely related to academic affairs, and excellent working relationships among all the deans are imperative.

It is important to consider learning resources within the total process of curriculum development and instruction. Decisions regarding media are best made only after extensive progress in curriculum design. Media-educational technology cannot be considered separate from the educational program. It is imperative that learning resources and techniques of instruction be designed to aid in accomplishing the objectives of the learning sequences.

The modern community college will provide a multimodel learning environment including, for example, provisions for large group instruction, independent study, small group seminars, and computer-assisted instruction. The implications for sophisticated learning resources support are many and complex.

The learning resources center for a community college geared to the future must be an instructional support organization responsible for the development, implementation, dissemination, and evaluation of information transmission systems. These systems must be developed around institutional goals and the specific learning objectives of the curriculum. The modern learning resources center must provide a variety of learning spaces including independent study carrels, small group rooms, and a large, comfortable library.

Provision of the following services is essential: printing and duplicating, photography, and graphics; electronic communications, including television, radio, and audio recording; central storage and distribution of A-V equipment and materials; and library technical services.

Key staff members in the modern learning resources center include the director of learning resources, the coordinator of library services, and the coordinator of media services. Depending on the organization of the college and the center, various technical, clerical, and specialized personnel will complete the staff requirements.

The new media-educational technology has had a profound influence on construction and modernization of educational facilities. Careful planning is necessary in order to facilitate the maximum use of the new educational technology. The visual, sonic, thermal, and aesthetic environments are critical in all areas in which specific environmental conditions are required for the most advantageous use of learning resources.

Careful attention must be given to budgeting for the new technology. The learning resources budget grows out of the needs of the educational program and includes provisions for book and nonbook media, as well as financial support for the personnel needed in the learning resources center. In new community colleges the budget must provide adequately for initial media acquisitions; in established institutions formulas have to be developed to provide continuing annual support for both book and nonbook media.

Community colleges should take advantage of the impetus that has been given to experimentation, research, and innovation by the new media-educational technology.

Suggested Activities and Problems

1. Interview a dean of academic affairs in a community college to ascertain his leadership role in the area of media-educational technology. Write an analysis of the position in respect to this phase of the job and show its relationship to other staff positions concerned with media-educational technology.

2. Interview a division or department chairman and an instructor in the same division. Get their individual points of view regarding the involvement of instructors in the area of media-educational technology. Do all staff members participate in curriculum development and the selection of learning resources? Compare the results of both conferences.

3. Read several articles on the use of computer technology in the community college. Develop a model for computer use that you consider to be ideal. Give the reasons for your recommendations.

4. Interview a community college director or coordinator of learning resources to determine how he keeps abreast of the new media-educational technology. Write up your findings.

5. Investigate the possibilities of securing aid from a foundation or local industry for a research project involving the use of the new media-educational technology. Prepare the necessary proposal.

6. Examine an educational-media budget for a community college. Interview an appropriate college official to determine the steps followed in its preparation. Write a short critique of the budget and of the procedures used in its development.

Selected Readings

Brown, James W. and Kenneth Norberg, *Administering Educational Media*. New York: McGraw-Hill Book Company, 1965.

Fusaro, Janice, "Toward Library-College Media Centers," *Junior College Journal*, 40, No. 7 (1970), 40.

Joyce, Bruce R., *The Teacher and His Staff: Man, Media, and Machines*. Washington, D.C.: National Education Association, 1967.

Loughary, John W., *Man-Machine Systems in Education*. New York: Harper & Row, Publishers, 1967.

Neagley, Ross L., N. Dean Evans, and Clarence A. Lynn, Jr., *The School Administrator and Learning Resources: A Handbook for Effective Action*. Englewood Cliffs, N.J.: Prentice-Hall, Inc., 1969.

Ofiesh, Gabriel D., *Dial Access Information Retrieval Systems: Guidelines Handbook for Educators*, Project No. BR-1042. Washington, D.C.: Department of Health, Education, and Welfare, 1968.

Weisgerber, Robert, ed., *Instructional Process and Media Innovation*. Skokie, Ill.: Rand McNally & Co., 1968.

Wheeler, Helen R. *The Community College Library—A Plan for Action.* Hamden, Conn.: Archon Books (Imprint of Shoe String Press), 1965.

Wiman, Raymond, *Mediaware: Selection, Operation and Maintenance.* Dubuque, Iowa: William C. Brown Company, Publishers, 1969.

11

Organizing
Administrative Services

The achievement of the academic goals of a modern community college requires extensive supporting services. Many of these are usually organized and provided under a division or department of administrative services, with a dean in charge. (See Chapter 6, p. 82 for a review of the initial staffing required in this area for a new college.)

As previously discussed, there are various options open to the president and his staff in organizing the essential functions and services of a community college. A review of the organization charts in Appendix 3, p. 290 will underline this statement. Consequently, the organizational structure for providing administrative services will vary from one institution to another, depending on the assignment of functions and services.

Figure 11-1, p. 169 depicts a typical plan for the provision of administrative services in a community college. The functional areas are listed under the administrator in charge. Note that this gives the dean of administration a span of control of seven persons reporting to him. (Research recommends a range of from three to nine, depending on the levels of responsibility and other pertinent factors.) Figure 11-1 depicts the administrative services organization for a comprehensive community college in its third year of operation, serving approximately 1,550 full-time and 1,100 part-time students. The remainder of this chapter consists of a discussion of the functional areas in administrative services, with suggestions for organizing each area to support the goals and programs of the community college.

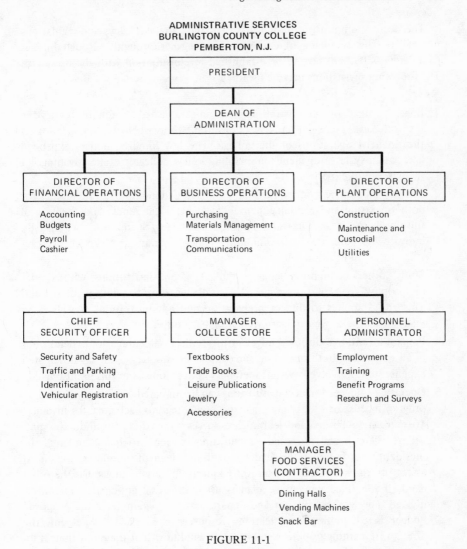

**ADMINISTRATIVE SERVICES
BURLINGTON COUNTY COLLEGE
PEMBERTON, N.J.**

FIGURE 11-1

Financial Operations

One of the first and most basic tasks in finance is the development of the college budget. This procedure will vary, depending on different circumstances. For example, is a new building program contemplated or underway? Does the local board of trustees prepare the budget and levy the necessary taxes, or does the board recommend a budget to the governmental agency? Is tuition to be charged, and if so, how much?

The dean of administration will have to study the state laws and regulations relating to the financing of community colleges thoroughly. Rough budget parameters will then have to be established in consultation with the president. The following suggestions may be useful:

1. Engage a dean of administration from an established community college in the state on a per diem basis as a consultant to assist in the organization of the financial operations of the college. The few hundred dollars expended here will pay large dividends in enabling a new college to take advantage of the wisdom of experience.

2. Identify all income sources, including available federal funds; state monies for both operating and capital expenses; available local funds; and the typical tuition charge, if any, in state community colleges. Such a study will usually indicate the percentage of community college operations to be financed by state, local, and tuition sources.

3. Study other community college budgets from institutions with similar philosophy, goals, and programs. "It is not necessary to reinvent the wheel." This adage applies to budget preparation and administration, as well as to many other areas. We can learn well from each other.

4. Prepare a tentative outline budget giving typical percentages of expenditures in all categories, both operating and capital. Be sure to include all anticipated expense items; involve key staff members in decisions from this point on.

5. Operating budgets for new institutions can be prepared inductively—based on program needs—or by assigning a fixed percentage to each area, for instance, 10 percent to library and learning resources support. If the inductive procedure is used, and proposed expenditures exceed anticipated income, the president's staff, under the leadership of the dean of administration, must assess priorities and cut the budget requests in various areas. On the other hand, if the fixed percentage plan is used, the total anticipated income is divided among each division and department. For example, if the proposed budget is $1 million, and learning resources is assigned 10 percent, the director of learning resources and his staff will know that they may budget up to $100,000. Maximum delegation of budget-making responsibility should be given to each division within the agreed-upon limits.

6. Capital budgets are usually designed for a specific phase of campus construction and supported by a combination of state, federal, and local funds. Some state and local procedures provide for annual capital budgets to supply needs such as furnishings, instructional supplies, and site development. In other states and localities such items must be included in the annual operating budget.

7. The dean of administration should set up cost accounting procedures as early as possible. These will enable the development of actual cost figures by

college program, so that the institution can move to some form of pro-grammed budgeting. It is recommended that the entire administrative staff study cost accounting and budgeting by program, under the leadership of the dean of administration and perhaps an outside consultant.

Insurance is a key area of financial operations. The board of trustees should authorize the dean of administration to identify and recommend an insurance broker in the college service area to develop and administer the total insurance program. Such a broker can be selected through a series of in-depth interviews with leading insurance agents in the area. Needless to say, the final selection should be based on competence, experience, and ability to serve the college, rather than on political considerations. A modern, comprehensive community college has complex insurance needs and should insist on the best professional service available.

The establishment of a basic *accounting system* is essential, including the maintenance of all records of receipts and disbursements, accounts receivable and payable, fund balances, and ledgers.

Budgetary controls are required to assure availability of funds in the proper budget accounts and to maintain allocation controls. The recording of budget encumbrances and expenditures can be handled on the computer.

The payroll function is one of the first financial operations that must be launched. It includes, of course, the preparation and distribution of payrolls for all personnel. This function includes the various types of deductions, fringe benefits, and reports, and the preparation of tax returns.

Business Operations

The functional areas of purchasing, materials management, transportation, and communications may be included in business operations.

In *purchasing,* it is of the utmost importance to develop policies and ad-ministrative procedures that will enable the college to procure goods and services of high quality at the lowest possible cost. As a public institution, the com-munity college owes the taxpayer the most for his money. Accordingly, there should be no room in purchasing procedures for favoritism, graft, or kickbacks. All procurement should be based on existing law and on clear-cut and fair policies that are known to vendors and suppliers. (See Appendix 11, p. 360 for typical policy and administrative procedures.)

The purchasing department is responsible for procurement of goods and services for all divisions and departments of the college. It is important to centralize this function to avoid waste, duplication, and excessive cost.

Materials management involves the receipt, accountability, storage, delivery, and issue of materials, equipment, and supplies. As the college grows, a receiving and distribution department will be required. Stockrooms and appropriate inventory control records are needed.

The *transportation* function is responsible for scheduling and coordination of use of college vehicles, and for rental or leasing of needed transportation.

The *communications* function provides intracampus mail services and handles incoming and outgoing mail. The campus telephone service is also a part of communications.

Plant Operations

This area includes coordination of the interim or permanent campus construction program, responsibility for building maintenance and custodial services, and operation and servicing of all utilities.

The dean of administration will usually supervise campus construction from the awarding of contracts until occupancy. When extensive building is initiated, a director of plant operations should be employed to coordinate the construction program, to assure compliance with specifications, and to monitor the critical path from ground breaking to project completion. Even if the architect provides a full-time construction supervisor (and he should), the college will benefit financially and materially from having its own coordinator to keep everyone else honest.

In addition to construction experience, it is desirable if the director of plant operations has supervised maintenance, custodial, and utilities functions, since these areas are usually under his direct control. They involve repair, cleanliness, and upkeep of all college buildings, grounds, equipment, and facilities. Operation and maintenance of the electrical, water, heating, lighting, air conditioning, and sewage disposal facilities all are part of plant operations.

Security and Safety

The security force is responsible for safety on the campus and for the security of college buildings, grounds, and equipment. Control of all vehicular and pedestrian traffic, enforcement of parking regulations, and motor vehicle registration are further responsibilities of the security department.

Two main options are open to a new college. (1) Contract with a commercial organization to provide security services. (2) Hire a well-qualified security chief and build your own force. Generally the second option is to be preferred for the following reasons: Persons employed by the college for this function take more interest in the institution and usually feel more identified with it. They are able to establish a closer rapport with students and staff, since they are an integral part of the college community. The administration can maintain tighter and more intimate supervision of the entire operation when the chief security officer is an employee of the college, who reports to the dean of administration.

It is imperative that a positive, cooperative attitude be fostered among the security officers, students, and staff. In this way, crisis periods can be weathered more smoothly—for example, when a crackdown on drug pushers must be instituted, and members of the college community are involved.

The College Store

An attractive and well-organized store is a real practical and aesthetic asset to any college campus. In addition to text and trade books, college stores usually handle jewelry, gifts, greeting cards, souvenirs, accessories, and miscellaneous merchandise. In general this operation should be handled as a nonprofit auxiliary

FIGURE 11-2

enterprise, with a budget of its own. The goal of the store should be to break even; good management will result in the lowest possible prices for students and staff. The college usually provides the space and utilities for the operation of the college store.

Food Services

This should be another nonprofit operation, providing good food at reasonable prices for the members of the college community. Food services may be provided by the college hiring its own staff, or through a contractual arrangement with one of the corporations specializing in institutional food service. There are advantages and disadvantages to each alternative.

College Operates Food Services

Advantages: Institution maintains complete control of operation; local people may be employed, who are interested in the college; more flexibility is possible in handling special events.

Disadvantages: More costly kitchen equipment is usually required to cook everything from scratch; the college has all the employment problems: turnover of personnel, labor relations, and so on; the college must hire a manager for food services.

College Contracts for Food Services

Advantages: Less capital equipment is needed, since some food is pre-cooked off campus; there are no direct personnel problems, since all employees work for the contractor; local persons are often sought and hired by the contractor; an experienced, professional organization is operating the food services.

Disadvantages: Contracts usually call for certain minimum profit; in a bad year the college has to make up the difference. The institution has no control over personnel assigned or hired for the operation. Special events may be more difficult to arrange.

In taking either route, the pros and cons must be studied carefully. A few of them are listed above. There is no substitute for visiting other campuses and discussing the alternatives thoroughly. If outside contractors are being considered, examine their offers very carefully, and check them out in colleges where they are already operating. Proceed carefully in this area because a pleasant, clean, and appetizing eating facility is essential to the good health of the campus community.

Personnel Administration

As the college grows, an administrator is usually added to handle all non-instructional personnel employment, training, and recruitment. Also, the personnel files for all college employees are maintained in this office.

The actual hiring of noninstructional persons should be a cooperative effort between the personnel office and the employing administrator. For example, if a division chairman needs a new secretary, candidates would be screened by personnel and sent to the chairman for interviewing. He then makes the final decision on employment.

Conclusion

The staffing of administrative services, discussed briefly in Chapter 6 and in this chapter, will be dependent on the growth rate of the college. An experienced dean of administration will plan the development of this area to insure the provision of administrative services as they are needed by the college.

Summary

Many necessary supporting services are usually organized and provided under a division of administrative services, with a dean in charge. The major functional areas include: financial operations, business operations, plant operations, security and safety, the college store, food services, and personnel administration.

The staffing of administrative services is dependent on the growth of the college.

Suggested Activities and Problems

1. Interview a dean of administration or comparable administrator in a community college. Determine his major areas of function. Write a paper summarizing his responsibilities.
2. Select one of the options for developing a budget that is presented in this chapter. Defend your choice.
3. Write a critique of the purchasing policy and procedures found in Appendix 11, p. 360.
4. Interview a construction coordinator or director of plant operations in a community college that is engaged in, or has just completed, a large building program. What were the major problems encountered during the project? Explain how you would try to avoid these problems or solve them if you were just taking charge of a construction project.
5. Defend or refute the following proposition: A community college should organize and operate its own food services.

Selected Readings

Hartley, Harry J., *Educational Planning-Programming-Budgeting.* Englewood Cliffs, N.J.: Prentice-Hall, Inc., 1968.

Johnson, B. Lamar, *Starting a Community Junior College.* Washington, D.C.: American Association of Junior Colleges, 1964.

School Management Institute, *PPBS (Planning, Programming, Budgeting System) for People Who Don't Understand PPBS.* Worthington, Ohio: School Management Institute, 1971.

Van Dyke, George E., ed., *College and University Business Administration,* rev. ed. Washington, D.C.: American Council on Education, 1968.

12

Planning
the Interim and Permanent
Facilities

Mark Hopkins may have been able to conduct school on a log, but community college students require a roof over their heads. Buildings cost money—a lot of money—and it takes time to plan and build new ones and to renovate and adapt other types of buildings for educational purposes.

In some areas of our nation, land is at a premium and adequate size college sites are just not available. Colleges and branch centers opened in the inner city may have to be satisfied with small sites or none at all, except the ground on which the building is standing. These problems and others connected with planning community college facilities will be discussed in this chapter.

Will Interim Facilities Be Utilized?

The first decision that the board of trustees and the new president must make in respect to housing for the college is whether or not to open the college in temporary quarters while the permanent facilities are being planned and constructed or renovated. Some boards prefer to delay opening the college until permanent facilities can be constructed; others are anxious to serve the youth of their area at the earliest possible moment.

Types of Temporary Quarters

Boards of trustees desiring to open their colleges as soon as possible have a number of options available to them. Usually these options fall into the following categories: (1) double occupancy; (2) abandoned school, industrial, business, and government buildings; and (3) relocatable structures.

Burlington County College, New Jersey, exercised two of the above options. During the first year of operation it shared the facilities of the Lenape Regional High School, whereas in the second year it utilized six demountable buildings erected on the eastern section of its 225-acre permanent site. Although the main student body moved into the new permanent facilities during the third year of operation, these fully air conditioned and carpeted interim buildings continued to serve the needs of the expanding college during the period of planning and construction of the subsequent stages of the permanent campus.

The Philadelphia Community College chose a center city renovated department store as its first quarters, and did not plan to occupy a new campus until five or more years later. The interim facility will continue in use as a branch campus for a number of years in the future. Montgomery County Community College, Pennsylvania, utilized an abandoned high school building while its new campus was being planned and built.

If the involvement of the faculty and students in the planning of a permanent campus is as desirable as school planners claim, opening the college in interim facilities should receive serious consideration by all boards of trustees. It is under this procedure that the staff and student body can have the greatest input in the planning of the facilities. When the opening of a college is delayed until permanent facilities have been planned and constructed, only a very limited number of regular staff members have the opportunity to assist in the development of the curriculum and the educational specifications based on it. Frequently, the planning team consists only of the president, dean of academic affairs, dean of student affairs, and dean of administrative services, together with the board of trustees and whatever consultative help is engaged.

Another obvious argument for opening the community college in interim facilities is that the college can open at a much earlier date. As previously mentioned, Burlington County College students would have lost two years and Philadelphia Community College students at least five years of educational opportunity.

There are, however, some pitfalls in the use of interim or temporary facilities. According to a recent government publication the following pitfalls should be carefully noted:

1. Temporary facilities frequently become too permanent, some continuing in use for 20 years or longer.
2. Temporary facilities sometimes give the wrong image by suggesting that the quality of instruction is on par with the inferior facilities.
3. The habit of getting along with inferior facilities sometimes causes the board, the administration, and even the faculty to willingly continue to accept what is available as sufficient.

4. Temporary college facilities, especially those in a high school, deter many students from continuing their education in the local area.[1]

The same publication makes the following suggestions for avoiding pitfalls that have been found in the use of temporary facilities:

1. Begin a master plan for the development of the permanent facilities before going into temporary facilities.
2. Make sure that the faculty, students, and community are thoroughly acquainted with the master plan.
3. If the master plan shows that a certain building is to be available by a certain time, accept this as a definite commitment and not as a vague promise.
4. Exercise caution in providing temporary facilities. The buildings should be reasonably adequate without entailing such great cost for construction or renovation as to seriously affect the quality of the permanent facilities.
5. Budget time and money for planning and constructing the permanent facilities in accordance with the master plan.[2]

To Build or Renovate

Although most boards of trustees, community college presidents, and the residents of the area that the colleges will serve would probably prefer to have new college campuses planned from scratch, the wisdom of this procedure may be questionable. This is particularly true in heavily populated areas. Instead of erecting new facilities on limited sites from which substandard housing or old commercial buildings have been razed, it might be far better to renovate existing structures for use as permanent community college facilities. Even if at a later date new campuses are established within a city, boards of trustees should consider establishing branch centers in existing facilities. These facilities must, of course, be renovated and modernized for the programs they are to house. The same careful planning done for new structures should be utilized when renovation and modernization are contemplated.

Illustrative of urban community colleges that are using renovated buildings as part of their multi-campuses are the following: (1) Portland, Oregon is using a former elementary school and an industrial building, (2) Kansas City remodeled two former public school buildings as an anchor for a permanent downtown campus, (3) Dallas County Junior College, Texas, rehabilitated a nine story department store in the downtown area, (4) New York City Community College renovated a Navy Test Laboratory for permanent quarters, and (5) Philadelphia

---

[1] *A Guide for Planning Community Junior Colleges* (Washington, D.C.: Department of Health, Education, and Welfare, 1969), p. 38.
[2] Ibid., pp. 38-39.

plans to continue to use the remodeled department store after the development of its other campuses.[3]

Shared Facilities

A recent trend in this country is the construction of school and college facilities as parts of other building complexes in the community. This makes it possible for the community to share certain facilities with the school or college. It also brings the college to the community and uses it as a laboratory for the students.

An excellent example of the above is the Fashion Institute of Technology in New York City. As a specialized college serving the garment industry and a part of the community college system of the State University of New York, it is located at the heart of the garment industry. The Fashion Institute plans to eventually occupy an entire block. It not only will prepare young people for the fashion industry, but it anticipates becoming a landlord in a high-rise building that will include apartments on levels above those that will house the community college programs. The college will provide recreational facilities for its students, housing, and commuter lounges, and all the ingredients that provide a situation conducive to learning.[4]

The Inner City Community College

Everywhere cries are heard concerning our dying cities. We are constantly reminded through the news media of crime, unemployment, poverty, inadequate schools, financial problems, and a host of other catastrophes facing large cities. If community colleges are truly community-oriented institutions, they should be able to tackle some of these problems. This raises a question concerning the location of the main city campus and its branches or perhaps several main campuses each with branches and "beachheads." Weidenthal makes the following comments on the subject:

> The idea of the "beachhead campus" is an appealing one. These small centers of learning in churches, neighborhood schools, storefronts, and even in small new buildings in urban renewal areas, could attract those who, for one reason or another, decline to venture from their own neighborhoods.
>
> In Seattle, the basement of a church, a warehouse on the docks, and aircraft factories have been successful sites for classes. Similar locations have worked in other cities. These may serve as feeder or outpost

---

[3] See Bob Reed, *The Urban Community College 1969* (Houston, Texas: Caudill Rowlett Scott, 1970).

[4] Bob H. Reed and William A. Harper, *The College Facilities Thing* (Washington, D.C.: American Association of Junior Colleges, 1968), pp. 5-6.

campuses, providing intensive counseling, some basic courses, and enough excitement to whet the appetite for more learning on the central campus. Thus the process of social transition is carried on.

And the central campus, too, should reflect the new dimension of higher learning.

It must become a home away from home for the student who will spend most of his working hours on campus and merely sleep at home. He will commute in reverse. This is a major facilities challenge.

It means more library and study space, more cultural and recreational opportunities, and more of the atmosphere that stimulates hope and inspiration. This and nothing less must be our aim.[5]

Planning New Facilities

Regardless of whether a new campus is being planned, a new building added, or a factory or other building renovated for community college use, certain individuals and groups must be responsible for the planning function.

The Tasks and the Planners

In order to intelligently select these individuals and groups, the tasks to be performed must be delineated and understood. Priest and Holt suggest in the following broad terms the job specifications of planning office personnel, when coordinated with governing board, chief administrative officer, and business office functions:

1. Evaluation and selection of architects.
2. Evaluation and acquisition of site(s).
3. Establishment of general architectural character, if the board desires to provide any guidelines in this regard.
4. Identification of master planning and initial construction guidelines and limitations in such areas as enrollment capacity, budget, average class size, footage allowances, etc.
5. Determination of functional relationships of different facilities to each other on the proposed campus—the general orientation of such elements as major building complexes, parking, and athletic facilities.
6. Coordinate work of faculty and consultants in development of educational specifications—translating the educational program into a description of space needs.
7. Cooperation with architects in review, refinement, and approval of campus master plan, schematic design, and preliminary drawings.
8. Approval of final plans and specifications.
9. Bidding and awarding of contracts.

[5] Bud Weidenthal, *The Community College Commitment to the Inner City* (Washington, D.C.: American Association of Junior Colleges, 1967), p. 11.

10. Continuous liaison with architect to make necessary decisions whenever problems and questions arise during the construction period.
11. Continuous inspection throughout construction period and acceptance of finished job.
12. Development and approval of specifications and arranging for purchase and installation of equipment and furniture.[6]

A discussion of each of the above twelve planning tasks would constitute a volume by itself. The remainder of this chapter, therefore, will be selective in its approach.

Priest and Holt also suggest the following administrative structure for accomplishing the above planning tasks. They believe that a key planner responsible directly to the chief administrative officer should be engaged. For long-range building programs involving several campuses, they would add a specialist in educational specifications, at least one technical assistant with architectural and/or engineering training and experience, and several persons as inspection personnel during the construction period.[7]

Another solution has been suggested if the new campus is started from scratch with no planned curriculum, regular staff, or other personnel. In Chapter 3 it was recommended that the council for higher education establish at least four task forces to develop preliminary plans for the organization and building of any proposed college. It was to be clearly understood that the purpose of these task forces is to generate sufficient data to enable fairly accurate cost projections, not to preempt the future authority of the board of trustees and the president of the new college.

Two of these task forces are of special concern in this chapter; namely, the philosophy and program task force and the facilities planning task force. The membership of the philosophy and program task force was to include one or two members of the council, a college or university administrator, a school superintendent or high school principal, and several members from business, industry, government, and the professions.

The recommended membership of the facilities planning task force included an architect, a county planning official, one or two business-industry executives with building experience, a facilities development administrator from a community college or four year institution, one or two members of the council, and a public school plant administrator.

In Chapter 5 the recommendation was made that the president be employed several years before the college is expected to open. If the dean of academic affairs, dean of student affairs, and dean of administrative services are also engaged at an early date, they can become the nucleus of the actual planning

---

[6] Bill J. Priest and H. Deon Holt, "How to Organize for Facilities Planning," *Junior College Journal*, 37, No. 6 (1967), 31.
[7] Ibid.

team that will work with the task forces in the accomplishment of the twelve tasks enumerated above. If the budget is not sufficient to engage all of the suggested personnel several years in advance, some may be selected and employed as consultants during the initial planning period.

There is no reason why recruitment for key faculty members cannot also begin several years in advance of the opening of the college. Since they will be holding full-time jobs elsewhere, they can serve as consultants in the planning process on a per diem basis. Future faculty members will be delighted to assist in planning the educational facilities in which they expect to work.

Consultation also should be carried on with individuals who represent the other services to be provided and utilized by the new college, and with potential students, their parents, and other interested citizens.

Some boards of trustees may prefer to utilize an external planning firm for the development of the educational master plan. This has proved to be a highly successful procedure in a number of instances.

The possibility of utilizing task forces of consultants as planners who are managed by the institution should also receive serious consideration as another alternate.

In both of the above solutions, however, the planners must maintain close relationships with the administration, representative staff, potential students, and residents of the college service area to insure sufficient input and understanding on their part.

Educational Specifications Are Important

It is a trite but accepted truism today that educational planning must always precede facility planning. Architectural firms experienced in the planning of educational facilities will not place a pencil on their drawing boards until a clearly written set of educational specifications is placed in their hands.

Tadlock and Ebey reflect this trend when they state:

> The good architect has every right to expect that the college administration and faculty have been as industrious and exacting in their preparation of the educational plan as they expect him to be in the architectural plan.[8]

Developing the Educational Specifications

Educational planning probably is more crucial in respect to community colleges than it is for any other type of educational facility because of their newness and uniqueness. Architectural firms are being asked to create something

[8]Max Tadlock and George Ebey, "'Pound-Wise' Planning," *Junior College Journal*, 38, No. 3 (1967), 28.

that many of them do not even understand. It is likely that many persons employed by community colleges themselves do not see some of the ramifications of this greatly accelerating educational movement.

There can be no standard plans for community colleges. Their diversity is one of their most significant characteristics. Each community college must be tailored to meet the needs of its own community. In theory no two colleges should be the same if each is oriented to the particular individuals and geographic region it is expected to serve.

Educational Specifications: A Cooperative Effort. One of the very important tasks in planning is the development of educational specifications for each facility. Here is a task in which there should be as much staff, student, and community involvement as possible. The dilemma faced by many boards of trustees and community college administrators is that they are asked to prepare educational specifications before a full staff has been employed. This has been used elsewhere in this chapter as one argument for interim facilities. It is sufficient to mention here that, within reason, the longer the period of educational planning and the greater the involvement of interested individuals, the more likely it is that satisfactory facilities will result.

If the planning is beginning from scratch, procedures for involving potential professional and nonprofessional staff suggested under general planning procedures should be followed in developing educational specifications.

Assuming that the college is functioning in interim quarters, who should be involved in the planning of the permanent campus facilities? The best answer to this question is that the entire human resources of the staff, student body, and community should be tapped, together with as many experts and consultants as are needed. In a companion work, we have stated the following concerning the planning team:

> The highly technical aspects of planning must be done by experts, and the educational specifications must be written by the professional personnel. The planning of areas of the plant that have implications for custodial services, cafeteria services, secretarial services, and health services should be done in consultation with the individuals responsible for these services. The students who will be living and learning in the new facilities have their contributions to make, as do their parents and other citizens who will pay for the new facility.[9]

For the purpose of this discussion, "educational specifications" are defined as *the document containing the educational requirements for the new facility or for one to be modernized, prepared for the design team of architects and engineers.*

[9]Adapted from Ross L. Neagley and N. Dean Evans, *Handbook for Effective Curriculum Development* (Englewood Cliffs, N.J.: Prentice-Hall, Inc., 1967), p. 253.

What guidelines are needed for writing educational specifications? The following basic information is recommended:

1. The educational philosophy and objectives of the community college.
2. The educational aspirations of the community.
3. Data concerning the number and ages of the students to be housed.
4. A brief explanation of the educational programs to be offered and the instructional procedures to be used.
5. A list of the number and kinds of facilities that are required, including future expansion.
6. Suggestions concerning the qualitative aspects of each space and area.
7. Affinities and relationships of the various facilities.
8. Activities that will take place in each area.
9. A list of the furniture and equipment for each space.
10. Special requirements of instructional and supervisory personnel.
11. Types and amounts of tack board, chalkboard, storage, and similar needs.[10]

The Document. Educational specifications are usually written by one person after many individuals have contributed the information to be included in them. During the collection of this information and the writing of the document, frequent consultation with the architect will insure better specifications. Likewise, at all stages of the development of the educational requirements, consultation with the planning specialists should continue as questions arise.

The individuals responsible for developing educational specifications may obtain a clearer understanding of the types of information that should be included in the document by contacting several other community colleges that have had similar building programs. College administrators who recently have completed building programs are usually proud of their accomplishments and are willing to share copies of their educational specifications with individuals facing similar building projects.

Visits to a number of new campuses are an absolute *must* before educational specifications are written. During the visit, time should be provided for securing information concerning the procedures used in writing the educational specifications and the main items in them. Valuable visiting time can be saved if copies of the specifications are secured and read prior to the visit. Unless the facilities are viewed as the embodiment of an educational program, the visit may be a fruitless one.

Although the persons involved in this process will want to secure copies of educational specifications that are current at the time they are involved in planning, it seems desirable to include excerpts here from several sets of educational specifications that have resulted in college facilities that have proven to be highly satisfactory.[11]

[10] Ibid., pp. 254-55.
[11] Ibid., pp. 255-56.

Figure 12-1 is a facsimile of several pages from the Burlington County College document as an example of the importance of well written institutional objectives in educational specifications.

Figure 12-1
Section of Educational Specifications
For Burlington County College, New Jersey*

*Institutional Objectives with Educational
and Architectural Implications*

1. Provision of the best possible teaching-learning experiences is a central aim. Individualization of instruction and provision for independent study are imperatives.

    Instructional implications: The administrative and teaching staff recognize that learning is more than traditional teacher-centered class contact. Rather, student-centered learning experiences will be continually stressed. The classroom lecture-textbook-recitation syndrome is recognized as inadequate. Teachers first identify course objectives in behavioral terms and then stress learning by inquiry and discovery. Active student participation is essential. To enable this type of learning experience, there must be a close working relationship between the teaching staff and the learning resources and library personnel. Technical personnel must be available to support the teaching staff in the preparation of visual aids, recordings, and printed matter. The Learning Resources Center, including the library, will play a central role in curriculum development and teaching-learning. The goal is to lead students to assume more responsibility for their own learning, under the skillful guidance of the instructor.

    Architectural implications: The Learning Resources Center should be the focal point of the campus. Areas for books and non-book learning aids must be provided. Flexibility is the key, because of the rapid changes in electronic and other learning resources. Spaces for teachers and technical personnel to work and confer are needed. Many individual student carrels are required.

2. The college is dedicated to innovation and experimentation based on sound principles.

    Instructional implications: No teaching method or learning resource is sacred. All staff members continually strive to improve their teaching by trying new ideas and applying promising research. Nothing is static in course outlines or in learning sequences. Evaluation is constant.

    Architectural implications: Space needs for instruction may be entirely different several years after a building is constructed. Creative, flexible planning is the keynote.

*Used by permission.

3. Many county citizens of all ages and educational backgrounds will be served.

   Instructional implications: Day and evening courses will be varied and comprehensive. The college will offer any needed educational program that is not being adequately provided by another institution or agency. A changing array of liberal arts and science and career programs will be offered through the years. There will be credit and noncredit courses, day and night, winter and summer.

   Architectural implications: Campus must be designed for day and evening, all season use. Adequate service, food, and parking facilities will be needed.

4. There will be nothing in the building or campus design or administrative practice of the college that will cause or encourage to be caused a development of a "status hierarchy" of student groups according to the curriculums in which students are enrolled.

   Instructional implications: Opportunity is provided for all students to learn according to their aptitudes and abilities. No major area is considered superior to another. Career programs and those in liberal arts and sciences are all college level majors, and a student is a student. In the life of the college, all have equal status.

   Architectural implications: Career programs will be offered in the same buildings as the liberal arts and sciences. No segregation by major should be permitted. Student lounges and food service should be provided only in the campus center, which then becomes the meeting point for all students regardless of curriculum.

5. To assist all in seeking their own careers and identity, guidance and counseling of students is a vital concern of the college. The aim is to humanize education by enabling many staff-student contacts.

   Instructional implications: Each student will be assisted in finding an educational program best suited to his aptitudes, interests, and abilities. The needs of society also will be served through counseling of students into various careers for which they are suited. A reasonable ratio of counselors and students is imperative. The teaching staff also is vitally concerned with the guidance function.

   Architectural implications: Provide many opportunities for staff and students to meet. Plan one office for every faculty member and counselor. Locate offices in all buildings where they are accessible to students. Provide numbers of spaces for small groups to congregate.

6. The physical, emotional and social growth of all students is an important goal.

   Instructional implications: Emphasis will be on a variety of lifetime sports, student activities, and other individual pursuits that are designed to involve all students.

Architectural implications: Plan areas for indoor and outdoor activities such as volleyball, squash, isometrics, basketball, swimming, handball, softball. Provide many areas for students to meet for study and recreation.

7. In every sense the college will aim to be a community center.

Instructional implications: Unique opportunities are present for the college to plan activities such as concerts, plays, and seminars to enhance the cultural life of the area it serves.

Architectural implications: Large group spaces such as an auditorium-theatre are needed for many community affairs. Multi-purpose facilities may be planned.

The library-learning resources center has grown to be one of the most important parts of many educational facilities today. Figure 12-2 is a facsimile of a section from the specifications for this facility in Somerset County College, New Jersey.

Figure 12-2
Section of Educational Specifications
For Somerset County College, New Jersey,
By Dr. Henry J. Evans, Dr. Saul Orkin,
and Richard Samuelson *

The Library-Learning Resources Center

Introduction

The library at Somerset County College is the central element in the educational program of the College. It should be, in essence, a laboratory and a workshop for students in all curricula. The library should supplement the course work of all students. Modern learning resource and instructional material facilities and programs will attract and stimulate the individual to self-education.

Although this is not a research library, it should have sufficient research facilities and resources to allow the faculty to develop innovations in their fields and to undertake experimentation.

The library-learning resources center should be designed to encourage maximum use. Space flexibility is necessary to accommodate growth and change. At the same time, a warm and pleasant environment should be maintained during the transitions from one phase to the next.

Dial-access systems from audio, video, and film sources are vital. The library should be designed to take advantage of many new developments in computerized instruction, audio-visual techniques, and programmed learning.

*Used by permission.

A. Vestibule

The Vestibule should be large enough to prevent congestion. This is a convenient place for a bookdrop and a directory. It serves the further purpose of reducing drafts in the lobby.

It is recommended that a separate entrance be provided from the outside to other areas used for non-library purposes.

B. Lobby Area

The Lobby Area will house the circulation desk. It should be spacious and designed as an exhibit area, furnished with carpeting. Staff rest rooms will be located near the circulation desk.

The Lobby will have ample bulletin board space, lounge-type seating and browsing shelves for new books. For a dramatic esthetic effect an island of some kind—plantings, fireplace, or fountain—is suggested.

An unattended cloak room will be located off the Lobby. The room will be equipped with twenty-four lockers which return deposit money, as well as with open bins.

1. The *Main Card Catalog,* easily seen, should be located near the main entrance and the circulation desk. The area should be 500-750 square feet.

2. The *Circulation Desk* will be constructed as a series of interchangeable units bolted together, about 40" high.

    a. Slot bookdrop into depressable trucks.

    b. Space for automated circulation chargeout.

    c. Tray section for cards with movable shelves on top to conceal cards.

    d. A typewriter with portable sound cover. Also space for a wide carriage typewriter as well as one manual typewriter with Gaylord Se-line label unit.

    e. Small repair and supply storage counter.

    f. Storage space for personal effects (pocketbooks) for staff members.

    g. Under-counter storage for library book trucks.

    h. General storage shelves.

    i. Microfilm storage and checkout.

3. The *Circulation Office*—one room adjacent to the Circulation Desk, 300 square feet. Adjacent should be a glassed-in area for a copying machine and a clerk's station.

C. Reserve Book Area

The Reserve Book Area will be adjacent to the Circulation Desk. It should be equipped with stacks sufficient to store 2,000 volumes and also carrels and tables for a total of 75 stations.

D. Reference Area

The Reference Area should have an office of 300 square feet equipped with a sink and should be located adjacent to the Reference Area which will contain space for approximately 5,000 reference books and eighty pupil stations.

E. Periodicals Index Area

This area should be 500 square feet located near the bound periodicals with seating for 20-30 students.

F. Current Periodical Display and Reading Area.

Lounge seating for twenty.

G. Technical Processing, Receiving, Loading-Unloading Area

1. *Loading and unloading area.*
2. The *Mail and Receiving Room* of 500 square feet, adjacent to the Technical Processing area, should have counters along the wall with adequate door space in and out of the room. There should also be an elevator in or near the Technical Processing Area.
3. The *Order and Acquisition Department* should be adjacent to the Cataloging area and should have adequate work space.
4. A *Cataloging Department* with required work area.

H. The library seating should accomondate 25% (750 stations) of the total student body of 3,000.

I. Provisions should be made for:

1. Custodial services and supply room.
2. Public lavatories.
3. Dead storage area.
4. Public telephones.

J. The Learning Resources Center

The Learning Resources Center will include a dial-access system, complete storage, repair, distribution and listening facilities for AVA equipment, a graphic arts production area, and appropriate administrative space.

If practicable, the Learning Resources Center should be located to minimize traffic in the library quiet areas.

Some boards of trustees prefer to utilize the services of a firm of consultants in the writing of educational specifications. Figure 12-3 is a facsimile of several pages from the *Educational Requirements and Specifications* for Brookdale Community College, New Jersey, prepared by the Educational Services Division of General Learning Corporation. The pages are from the Science Module of the

Health and Sciences Cluster. Additional material in the specifications on the module includes general requirements, special requirements, diagrams, and a space summary.

Figure 12-3
Section of Educational Requirements and Specifications
For Brookdale Community College, New Jersey,
Prepared by Educational Services Division,
General Learning Corporation.*

3.5 Health and Sciences Cluster

The Health and Sciences Cluster includes the following modules:

Sciences
Allied Health
Recreation

3.5.1 Sciences Module

Traditionally program needs in the Sciences Module would dictate separate laboratory spaces for each specialization. At Brookdale, however, it is appropriate to group all laboratory spaces except the physiology laboratory into "core" facilities.

The basic core laboratory will include the utilities and equipment normally found in the following:

Physics Laboratory
Chemistry Laboratory
Earth Sciences
Zoology Laboratory
Botany Laboratory
Biology Laboratory (See Phase II Report, Figure 2-4, page 2-54L.)

The "core" laboratory facility, although clearly defined as having particular characteristics necessary for each area of specialization, can be organized to reflect the needs of many of the students whose programs will require a survey approach in the sciences. Individual specialized laboratory spaces will provide support for a program of greater depth which will be needed by transfer oriented students.

The composition of the core laboratory facility must provide for common

bench, tables (heat and chemical resistant)
gas, electric, water services
cabinet and storage space
outlets for instructional media

---

*Used by permission.

Because of ethics and social mores regarding cadavers, the physiology laboratory, which is associated with careers rather than general education, is separated from the other spaces. It is, however, close enough to use and be used by the rest of the Cluster. Program accommodations will be determined by the administration.

3.5.1.1 Description

The modern courses in science are predominately laboratory centered, and more time must be spent in properly equipped laboratories. In addition to career oriented courses, there is a trend toward the presentation of post high school vocational courses, transfer oriented courses such as biology, botany, zoology, chemistry and physics, earth science, geology, and physiology, and community services needs.

Facilities are being designed to allow the student, when he has reached a particular level of readiness, to be more self-directed in regular course work (as with the audio-tutorial system developed by Postlewait at Purdue). Space should be provided for students to carry on individual research and store their work without interfering with regular classes. Trends toward flexible scheduling permit greater opportunities for students to achieve an individually paced rate of progress.

3.5.1.2 Operational Requirements

Through inquiry and laboratory discovery, students in the Science Module will not only be exposed to a logical and integrated picture of contemporary science but will also have the opportunity to conduct their own research. They will engage in a variety of independent learning activities for the greater part of their time. These independent activities will be augmented by large group or seminar instruction.

Approximately 30-40 percent of a student's time in Science will be devoted to work in the laboratory. This percentage of time will undoubtedly increase to 50 percent or more as more emphasis is given to laboratory experiences in "unitized" learning packages that are currently being developed.

Individual study will require resources such as books, written teacher materials, monographs, audio tapes, single concept films, records, programmed learning materials, and film strips. Students will need easy access to these materials as they pace themselves to complete the prescribed curricula.

Laboratory activities will be individual in nature and will be attempted as the students reach a level of readiness. As many as seven to ten different laboratory activities may be going on simultaneously in the "core" laboratory facility. Students will often work in clusters of two or three when they find they are working on the same problem or work as a team on a particular research project (team learning or "some-pack" instruction). *

---

*"Some-pack" instruction in this report refers to groups of four, six or eight students working together in a directed learning environment.

Science tables that support the various activities and group sizes will be needed. These tables should provide built-in storage with portable "tote-drawers" for individual student use. They should be spaced far enough apart so that students can have freedom to move about the area or gather materials and consult with other students.

Small groups will frequently meet for tutorial instruction. At times, however, small group instruction will be heuristic or task and problem centered. Thus, it will be necessary to move the furniture to fit different types of group activity. Fifteen should be the maximum number of students involved in such small group instruction.

Students in the sciences will also receive large or medium size group instruction. Lecture halls will accommodate the viewing of films or the presenting of general information to a large group of students (90-120) and will be found in the college commons areas. Medium sized group instruction (30-50 students) will focus predominantly upon teacher demonstration activities. This area will also support project demonstrations that can be left in one place for a period of time and be accessible to students for study or testing.

Self testing will be an important activity included in the learning packages. Individual work spaces will facilitate the development of a successful testing program. Students will move in and out of testing situations very frequently.

A small percentage of students will be capable of handling advanced projects in the biological sciences. These projects are generally quite complex and require longer use of the laboratory facility. Students will work on these projects at particular times of the day or evening. Utilization of a flexible approach to scheduling would allow students to use the area during times when they are not scheduled for a specific learning activity. Advanced projects will require a self-contained laboratory or easy access to laboratory equipment and supplies.

3.5.1.3 Facilities

Space Requirements

Facility	Area Range in Sq. Ft.
Area # 1	
Individual work area	1,400
A multipurpose room for independent work	
Students will write up test data and work individually at carrells	
Seating for 60 students	
Area # 2	
General laboratory area (80 stations)	2,800

General purpose laboratory
A total of 80 stations, using appropriate laboratory bench
tops

Area #3
Storage and preparation room   2,100
  A storage and preparation room equipped to serve the
  laboratories, erected in such a manner as to permit student
  access
  Adequate space for up to four people working simultaneously; however, primary objective is a maximum of
  storage and counter areas.

Area #4
Cold storage area   250
  A walk-in facility which is connected to the storage
  and preparation area

Area #5
Multi-purpose demonstration/project area   950
  An area for demonstration to medium size groups

Area #6
Physiology laboratory   1,500
  A physiology laboratory and cold storage for cadavers
  Physiology laboratory for 24 students
                                               Total   9,000 sq. ft.

It is important to remember that educational specifications must not be so detailed that there is no room for the architect to utilize his creative talents. Too frequently, educators try to play architect. It should be remembered that good educational specifications are descriptive and not prescriptive.

Educational specifications are extremely important, and great effort should be expended to provide the architect with good ones. However, they do not always guarantee results. We emphasized this in another publication as follows:

> Excellent educational specifications do not automatically result in a superior . . . plant. In the first place, the cost of meeting the demands of the specifications may far exceed the available funds for the project. In the second place, architects are frequently unable or unwilling to interpret the educational specifications in terms of bricks and mortar. In the third place, it is difficult for those who developed the educational specifications to visualize what they will look like when they are embodied in a building. As a consequence, the results may prove to be disappointing.[12]

[12] Ibid., p. 263.

Selecting the Architect

The first job specification of planning previously enumerated is the evaluation and selection of the architectural firm. Regardless of whether new facilities are to be planned or existing facilities adapted for community college use, the selection of the right architect is extremely important to the success of the enterprise.

In order to intelligently select an architect, the board of trustees should be aware that coordination of the entire project is a very important part of his job. Many specialists are involved in planning community college buildings and the architect must coordinate all of their work. Engineers, equipment and communications consultants, site planners, landscape architects, and lighting specialists are utilized, and even anthropologists, psychologists, and sociologists are consulted at times.

Choosing and Utilizing Architectural Services

There are many factors to consider in the selection and utilization of architectural services. One very important decision is the stage in the project that the services should be engaged. The criteria to be used in the selection and also the weight given to each criterion are important. Finally, the services to be expected from the firm that is engaged form another important consideration.

Time of Selection. Architectural services should be engaged as early in the project as possible. The architect can play a vital role in site selection and in the development of the educational specifications for the campus. He also can get an earlier start in the design phase. In a period of rising costs, time means money saved.

If several sites are available, the architect can determine on which site it is most economical and feasible to build. He can recognize potential site problems that the board of trustees and members of the staff would not notice. During the writing of the educational specifications, the architect can gain a lot of information, which will assist him in designing a better structure. During that time he can also serve as a resource person and make valuable suggestions to insure that only the necessary information is included. As stated previously, architects need to be furnished with *description,* not *prescription.* Without the help of the architect, educators could make serious mistakes.

Criteria Used in Selection. One of the first dilemmas frequently faced by boards of trustees is whether or not they should engage a local architectural firm. Sometimes undue political or other pressures are exerted to get the contract for a local firm.

Although present day modes of travel make it possible for architectural firms to work over a wide geographical area, the local firm generally has several points in its favor. Because the members of the firm are local residents, they will have a certain local pride in the new college. If mistakes are made, the local architect must live with them and correct them.

Another plus value is that the proximity of the firm's offices to the job saves on communications and travel, and the members of the firm are immediately available to their clients.

A number of architectural firms have gained national and, in several instances, international recognition in the school and college field. Since fees are largely standardized, boards of trustees may be tempted to engage a celebrity firm. Of course, there is nothing wrong with such a choice, providing the disadvantages are considered along with the prestige sought.

Travel and communication are the first things to bear in mind. Even though the firm may have a branch office reasonably close by, the board of trustees may find that it has little direct contact with the prestige members of the firm. This does not mean that an inferior product will result, but it largely depends on the project architects assigned to the local job. Their experience, creativity, and design ability are critical concerns.

On the plus side, an architectural firm with a national reputation has great resources and much experience to bring to its clients. With a wide variety of buildings to its credit, it is a simple matter to check on both its products and its method of operation.

Irrespective of whether a local or more distant architectural firm is being considered, the following qualifications should be examined:

1. Registration and reputation.
2. General experience and in particular experience in community college or other college designing.
3. Resources available, both human and material.
4. Methods of operation.
5. Amount of interest shown in project.
6. Past performance in terms of quality of work.
7. Reputation for designing good buildings that can be constructed at a reasonable cost.
8. Opinions of former clients.

More recently, the willingness and ability to design for phased construction (fast track) has become an important consideration. Where it is legally permissible, the fast-track method initiates construction as soon as site work and foundations drawings are completed instead of waiting until a set of working documents is ready before starting to build. This can result in saving both time and money; however, the final cost of the project cannot be determined exactly until the last contract is let.

Selection Procedures. Some community college trustees have had experience in building projects in connection with their other activities. If one or more members have had a successful experience with a particular architectural firm, they may recommend this firm for the present construction program. In other instances, a firm may be highly recommended by a board of trustees of another community college, a board of public education, or by some influential individual or group. Finally, as previously mentioned, the board may select a firm based on its national reputation.

When an architectural firm is selected for one of the reasons mentioned above, the procedure is referred to as the *direct appointment procedure.*

Another selection procedure, rarely used for schools and colleges in the United States but quite common in certain foreign countries, is the *design competition procedure.* Johnson explains this process as follows:

> . . . architects are invited to submit their solutions for a design project that is clearly described in the official program for the competition. A jury of competent people is chosen to judge these submissions and to select a winner. The winner is then awarded the commission and continues with the development of the plans for eventual construction of the project.[13]

It is interesting to note that in Switzerland the school building designs are displayed in a public place, and the voters choose the winner by public ballot.

The most typical procedure used in selecting architectural firms for educational facilities in the United States is known as the *comparative selection procedure.* In this process the architectural firm is selected from a number of interested parties who have made available information and supporting materials that will enable the client to judge their fitness for the job.

The list of firms from which information will be solicited may be prepared by a member of the college administration. To avoid criticism, it may be desirable to include all architectural firms in the area on the list.

The basic information concerning the architectural firms may be collected by using a questionnaire. Although boards of trustees have the privilege of asking any questions they desire, time may be saved and the essential information gathered by making use of a form similar to the "Standard Form of Questionnaire for the Selection of Architects for School Building Projects."[14]

The following types of information are needed:

1. Name, address, and type of organization.
2. Brief history of the firm, including date established, record of growth, types of work, and any specialties.
3. List of principals and key staff, with the professional background, registration, and affiliations of each.

---

[13] Marvin R. A. Johnson, *The School Architect-Selection-Duties-How to Work with Him* (Washington, D.C.: Administrative Leadership Service, 1968), p. 14.

[14] This form may be obtained from either the American Institute of Architects, 1735 New York Ave. N.W., Washington, D.C. 20006, or the Council of Educational Facility Planners, 29 West Woodruff Ave., Columbus, Ohio 43210.

4. List of projects completed in recent years, giving type, size, cost, location, and dates.
5. List of references, including clients, contractors, and financial institutions.
6. Statement of philosophy and approach to the design and construction process.
7. Statement of policy in the handling or procedure of a project; participation of principals, assignment of personnel to project, engineering services, and other specialized services.
8. Copy of firm's brochure plus plans and photographs of completed buildings.[15]

Architectural firms invited to submit qualifications for evaluation should be given as much pertinent information about the client and the project as possible. The following list constitutes the minimum information prospective architectural firms need to determine their interest in the project:

1. Name, address, and responsible administrative office of the client.
2. Name and phone number of the individual who will act as negotiator or contact.
3. Description of the project (or projects) under consideration, giving the size in terms of number of students, location, area required, and other information normally included in the educational planner's statement on program and space needs.
4. Time schedule proposed for the project(s).
5. Brief statement about the planning procedure to be used, the people to be involved, and the proposed assignment of responsibilities representing the client.
6. Description of the community, the educational system, and the resources available.
7. Brief statement of the educational philosophy on which the architectural planning should be based.[16]

After all the information submitted by interested architectural firms has been carefully examined and screened, a number of firms should be selected for a personal interview. There is no magic number, but it is likely that the client will desire to select at least three and, at the outside limit, not more than six firms to interview.

The interviews should not be rushed and they should be conducted in an atmosphere of genuine interest and mutual respect. The setting should be pleasant and the dialogue cordial, brief, and informative.

Some architectural firms are known for their showmanship in making

[15] *CEFP Guide for Planning Educational Facilities* (Columbus, Ohio: Council of Educational Facility Planners, 1969), p. 41.
[16] Ibid., p. 41.

presentations to potential clients. They appear for the interview with a very well organized, visually augmented presentation of an hour or more in length. Firms should not be ruled out because of their public relations pitch; however, boards of trustees must not be overwhelmed by the mechanics of the presentation. The board is looking for hard, cold facts to determine the relative qualifications of the finalists in a carefully screened group of architectural firms. If the method of presentation contributes to this objective, it may prove to be of great value. If not, it is so much window dressing.

In addition to the information gathered in the initial screening and during the interview, the board of trustees or the college administrators should visit some of the recent projects completed by the finalist firms and talk with their previous clients. Something of value likewise might be learned by talking with contractors who have constructed these projects. Another worthwhile procedure is to visit the office of each firm to get a firsthand picture of the establishment and the manner in which it operates.

After carrying out the above procedures, the board of trustees should be in a position to select an architectural firm in which it can place the greatest confidence and with whom it can be assured of both an excellent working relationship and an outstanding job.

Formulating the Agreement. When an architectural firm has finally been selected, it is time to draw up a formal agreement. Although it is acknowledged that architectural firms and college officials are partners in constructing the best possible facilities, the relationship established is strictly a sound business proposition. The agreement must be in writing in a formal, forthright, and honest form. It should be carefully and clearly worded and all individuals concerned must be certain that they understand the full implications of every line of the document. It is too late to discover that omissions or misinterpretations have occurred after the agreement has been signed.

Too frequently, clients concern themselves only with the services and responsibilities of the architectural firm and forget to read carefully the part of the agreement concerned with the owner's obligations and responsibilities.

Since agreement forms have been largely standardized—as, for example, AIA Document B131 "Standard Form of Agreement between Owner and Architect on a Basis of a Percentage of Construction Cost"—the agreement per se will not be discussed here. However, the college attorney should approve the wording and form of the contract.

The next section of this chapter will list and comment on some of the services the architectural firm may be expected to perform.

Services of the Architectural Firm. The services the architectural firm can perform are divided into two categories. The first category includes basic services, which most firms agree to render for the basic percentage fee. All other services, sometimes designated as special services, require an additional fee. The basic services include the following phases:

1. *Predesign planning.* This phase is not always included as basic, but architects are increasingly rendering this service. Predesign planning consists of assisting the client in the preparation of the educational specifications for the project(s). The importance of this service was stressed earlier in this chapter.

2. *Schematic design.* This is the phase in which the architect begins the translation of the educational specifications into design documents such as drawings, sketches, words, models, and whatever other methods will enable the client to understand the relationship of the building(s) to the area in general and to the site in particular. This phase also reveals the degree to which the educational specifications are being met. There is much give-and-take during this phase and compromise is necessary. Finally, a schematic design is agreed upon by the planning team and it, hopefully, is approved by the proper authorities.

3. *Design development.* In this phase the documents are prepared that illustrate the major decisions concerning floor plans, the structural system, mechanical and electrical installations, services and equipment, building materials, and form and appearance of the building(s).

This also is the phase in which a more detailed cost estimate is made and in which plans are usually submitted to governmental agencies for their approval. Once again, the final plans are presented to the planning team and to the designated authorities for their review and approval.

4. *Construction documents.* During this phase, the complete working drawings and construction specifications are prepared. To differentiate, the work drawings establish quantity: sizes, shapes, locations, and relationships, whereas the construction specifications are concerned with quality: standards, types, and manufacturers. The bidding and construction information also is included in these specifications.

During this phase, earlier cost estimates are reviewed and updated. Any required approvals of government agencies not previously obtained are also sought. The completed construction documents are now ready for final approval and authorization to receive bids.

5. *Bidding.* This is the phase in which the architectural firm renders assistance to the owner in securing bids and awarding contracts. Cooperatively they determine procedures for bidding and the eligibility of contractors, although in public projects answers to these questions are usually established by law and interpreted by the institution's attorney. In fulfilling the above role, advertisements for bids are prepared, published, and a date established for receiving bids. Assistance also is received in the preparation of contracts.

6. *Construction.* This is the final phase of the basic services performed by the architectural firm. During this phase progress bulletins, change orders and

certificates of payment are issued; continual on-site supervision is provided to monitor the progress of the work; interpretations of the contract are made; and dates of substantial and final completion are established.

In addition to the basic services, there are a number of other services that an architectural firm is prepared to perform for an additional fee. The following are illustrative only and do not represent a complete list:

1. Financial feasibility studies.
2. Planning surveys and site selection.
3. Preliminary work necessary before additions are planned.
4. Revisions of drawings and documents after original approval.
5. Detailed estimates of construction costs.
6. Special interior design and furnishing services.

If increases in construction costs continue, many of the larger architectural firms will probably expand their services considerably in order to speed the process of construction. The title for these comprehensive services is *construction management.* In a recent brochure a Philadelphia firm describes this new technique as follows:

> The building industry has been exploring many new approaches to speed the process. At Nolen and Swinburne, we are sure one of the most promising time saving methods is Construction Management. Essentially a new management technique, Construction Management uses the best combinations of the many recent developments to unite the process of design and construction in a single effort that speeds progress and maximizes all cost saving potentials. This comprehensive service allows the owner to manage the entire process of design and construction through a single professional organization.[17]

These broad services naturally would change the present fee structure for architectural services.

Selecting and Developing the Community College Site

The second job specification enumerated earlier in this chapter for the planning group was the evaluation and acquisition of the community college site(s). The following discussion will be concerned with that task and will add another dimension, namely, site development.

Site Selection

Selecting a site for a community college is an extremely important task. In many instances it is a difficult and frustrating experience. If community colleges

[17]*Directions—Construction Management* (Philadelphia: Nolen and Swinburne Partnership, Spring 1971), p. 1.

are classified as rural, suburban, and urban, the picture is somewhat as follows. There are probably numerous rural sites still available with a considerable price range per acre, depending upon the section of the country in which the college is to be located. It is much more difficult and certainly more costly to secure even a moderate size suburban site. In the city, sites will be small, costly, and difficult to find. In fact, the dispersed site may prove to be one of the better solutions.

The Selection Team. The overall planning team as previously enumerated under several types of organization may wish to participate in the site selection procedure or designate a smaller group to represent them. In any event, the team should include representatives from the board of trustees, college administrators, and the architectural firm selected to design the facilities.

Criteria for Site Selection. Numerous criteria have been suggested for the selection of sites for educational facilities, ranging from five to twenty or more items. As a minimum list of criteria for the selection of community college sites, Finlay and Lahti suggest the following: (1) Cost. (2) Location within community. (3) Size or area. (4) Availability of public utilities. (5) Access to major streets.[18]

A much longer list of criteria, applying to sites of all types of educational facilities, is recommended by the Council of Educational Facility Planners. This list includes the following twenty-one items:

1. Size and shape adequate for present and future enrollment.
2. As near as possible to center of pupil population, avoiding long travel distances.
3. Location to avoid traffic hazards, disturbing noises, smoke, dust, and odors.
4. Accessibility.
5. Availability of utility services.
6. Suitability of soil for building foundation and for vegetation.
7. Cost is reasonable—land optioned well in advance, if possible.
8. Contour fairly level, sloping away from buildings to assure good drainage.
9. Consideration of present and future school and community programs.
10. Environment.
11. Topography.
12. Aesthetic appeal.
13. Zoning and city planning regulations.
14. Preservation of vegetation, including trees.
15. Proximity to other educational and recreational institutions.
16. Proximity to safety facilities.
17. Suitable for construction.
18. Ample space on site for parking.

[18] Louis E. Finlay and Robert E. Lahti, "The Demands of Effective Site Selection," *Junior College Journal, 37, No. 8 (1967), 17.*

19. Availability for use in the educational program.
20. Industrial and commercial expansion.
21. Orientation in relation to climate.[19]

It should be obvious to the reader that, although important, all the above criteria are not of equal merit. Each selection committee, in terms of the geographical location of the college, number of available sites, and time period allotted for selection must choose those criteria that are considered vital and apply them to the sites under consideration.

In an attempt to look in the future Raymond C. Schneider, a recognized authority on school sites, made the following challenging comment:

> We are using these techniques to select and plan sites for facilities which must accommodate changes beyond our imagination. Our tools for conducting these investigations need sharpening or replacing. Hardware exists today which will accommodate millions of bits of information. I suspect that before the next few years are past, someone will have devised a site or land data bank from which all factors may be retrieved and assessed in future—and faster—site selection studies. They must also devise ways of up-dating these data.[20]

Site Development and Planning

In this era of tremendous expansion of community college facilities, many new colleges will be founded and existing institutions of higher learning will be moved to new sites. Fortunate indeed are those who find that they are able to start from scratch in planning the development of a brand new site.

The more difficult problem is how to expand and use an existing site. This requires master planning of a quality that will tax the skill, experience, and ingenuity of the wisest planners. Two characteristics of a community college, namely, *length of use* and *constant change,* make it imperative that a long-term plan be developed. A plan should be developed for the arrangement of the campus that anticipates the general plant development for a period of approximately fifty years.

Whether the site is old and already filled with many buildings or new and undeveloped, a painstaking site analysis should be made. Creating a plan for site development of a community college campus is part and parcel of the planning of the various building units. An acceptable site plan should encompass the total campus and should indicate future developments in the same manner that future building additions are shown.

[19] *CEFP Guide,* pp. 61-62.
[20] Raymond C. Schneider, "Setting Your Sites for Century 21," in *Planning Community Junior College Facilities,* eds. Floyd G. Parker and Max S. Smith (East Lansing, Mich.: Proceedings of a Conference Sponsored by College of Education and Continuing Education Service, Michigan State University and Council of Educational Facility Planners, 1968), pp. 26-27.

FIGURE 12-4 *(Donald M. Stephenson, photographer.)*

Principles of Site Development

As previously stated, site planning cannot be separated from total planning. The same steps including the involvement of many individuals are necessary for both site and building planning. Certain principles are also applicable to both. A well formulated plan for the proper development of a community college site would be concerned with:

1. Economy of construction, operation, and maintenance.
2. Safety and convenience in operation and use.
3. Attractiveness in overall appearance.
4. Adequate provision for the needs of the total man.
5. Facility groupings and affinitives.

Economy. Site development with economy in mind will find many ways of saving money without impairing the safety, usefulness, or aesthetic values of the campus. Savings may not only be effected in the original cost of development, but operation and maintenance economies may be realized over the years.

Proper placement of buildings can reduce excavation and foundation wall costs, expenses for special footings and special drainage, and it can also limit the length of utility and drainage lines. Good planning can reduce erosion, divert surface water that might damage building foundations, drives, and parking lots, and reduce the quantity of paved areas that must be maintained.

Safety and Convenience. A site developed with safety and convenience in mind will locate service drives near storage rooms, kitchens, stages, and other points to which deliveries must be made. Most campuses are "walking campuses." Although strategically placed parking areas should be provided, emphasis should be placed on walking between classes rather than driving. In the development of roads on the site, care should be taken to eliminate as much of the pedestrian-auto conflict as possible. If students can walk between most of the buildings on the campus without crossing a street, excellent circulation has been accomplished. Playfields should be located within reasonable distance from the exits through which the users will leave the building.

Attractiveness. Attractiveness and overall pleasing appearance of the entire college campus should be the objective of the planner in this respect. Form of architecture, placement and relationships of buildings, drives, parking areas, and playing fields all contribute to the aesthetic values of site development. However, the important finishing touch to site development is the planting of the campus or newly developed area. Planting must receive attention from the early stages of planning. The soil composition, grading, and existing plantings must receive early consideration.

As is the case in all matters of modern functional design, planting of a campus should be approached from the standpoint of utility as well as aesthetics. Initial cost as well as maintenance must be kept in mind. Plantings may be beautiful, but at the same time prevent soil erosion; they may form an attractive setting for the cafeteria and yet serve as a screen for the service yard. In like manner, plantings serve as windbreaks on cold, windy days, and as protection from the sun's rays during warm weather. On the community college campus planting may be valuable for actual instruction in nature study, botany, ecology, and conservation.

Campus plantings should consist of reliable varieties that will resist adverse conditions. It is essential that the soil be properly prepared before planting. In many cases overplanting is done rather than underplanting. Another common mistake is to plant too close to the building. A well planned visual environment can quickly be destroyed by too much outside shade. Climbing plants should also be avoided because of the maintenance required and the harm to the building that may result.[21]

Needs of the Total Man. In planning educational facilities, too frequently overemphasis is placed on the intellectual man and the other aspects of the total man receive less attention. The concept of campus planning and development to

---

[21] Adapted from my writings in *Planning Facilities for Higher Education* (Columbus, Ohio: Council of Educational Facility Planners, 1960), pp. 31-33.

meet the needs of the total man were expressed very well by Erickson and Kump when they wrote:

> The junior college campus is not a package for people nor a monument for posterity. It is a dynamic learning environment. Just as a cathedral induces reverence and worship, so does creative college architecture have a profound effect on learning. Campus design is all-embracing because a junior college is a microcosm of man's total environmental and social needs. The college campus must provide for the gathering of groups of many sizes and purposes. In addition to classes, lectures, and seminars, it must accommodate dining, recreation, research, office, living, library, maintenance, art, drama, vocational work, and in some cases, worship. Virtually every type of building and space is included on the junior college campus. All will affect, for good or ill, the total learning environment.
>
> The complete conception of a college plant involves profound and intense collaborative effort of many minds, through a carefully ordered sequence of steps, beginning with basic premises and unfolding through successively more specific development phases until every detail is determined. The architect and the educator must recognize that campus design encompasses every physical element of the college—buildings, grounds, circulation, landscaping, interior furnishings, and equipment.[22]

FIGURE 12-5

Symbolism. A truly functional building serves more than physical function; it must also be planned to serve an emotional function as well. Community college buildings are made for human beings. They are used by young men and women at one of their most crucial and formative periods of their lives. During

---

[22] Clifford G. Erickson and Ernest J. Kump, "Campus Design and Learning Environment," *Junior College Journal,* 38, No. 4 (1968), 27.

their college years young people are to a large degree free from the more serious responsibilities of adulthood, which makes these years, in their later memories, the most wonderful time of their lives. When as alumni they return to their Alma Mater, there is in each case a reidentification with some individual, object, or spot that enables the graduate to relive a memory of a particular time or event. The more the college planner takes this necessary symbolism into account, the happier the students will be, not only during their college years, but in the years that follow. The master planner makes every effort to achieve the correct balance between functional architecture and opportunities for the display of healthy and natural emotions of students and alumni.

Facility Groupings and Affinities. Planners have found it desirable to further divide the main campus area into the academic, student activity, and housing zones.

The academic zone includes the classrooms, laboratories, library-learning resources center, administrative suite, faculty offices, and auditorium. The architectural character and planning of this zone should be in keeping with all of the best tradition and formality of the early universities and yet possess enough of the freshness and vigor of the present to stimulate youth to continue their search for truth. The academic zone should be the quietest section of the campus and needs the least service requirements. The provision of outdoor courts for meditation and outdoor laboratories for experimentation would be highly desirable in this zone. A parking area should be provided convenient to this area, but it should not be too conspicuous.

The academic zone should have primary relationships to the student activity zone, because these are the only two zones used by all persons at the college, namely, faculty, boarding students (if there are any), day students, and evening students.

The student activity zone includes the field house, student center, meeting rooms and cafeteria. If properly planned, this zone functions to unite the various divisions of the student body into one complete whole. In this area, social gatherings vary from two students eating and drinking at the snack bar to the entire student body assembled in the field house. Within this zone revolves the social life and student services of the college.

The architectural character of this zone is extremely important. The key note should be one of friendliness and informality. Campus planning in this zone should include outdoor social courts and terraces. Maximum service, parking, and noise levels should be provided in this area. It is also essential to provide ready access from this area to the academic zone and to the housing zone (if one is required).

In community colleges with boarding students the housing zone includes the dormitories, lounges, and game rooms. The physical environment of this area should be homelike. There should be an atmosphere of relaxation, informality and friendliness. Areas should be planned and furnished in such a manner that there will be created an awareness of aesthetic appreciation and a desire for a high personal standard of living. Service and parking requirements are maximum in this zone and highly controlled noise levels needed. This area should be convenient to the outdoor physical education facilities and have direct access to the student activity zone.

Within the various zones mentioned and in specific buildings certain facilities must be close to each other because of the functions they serve. Locker and shower rooms must be near the gymnasium and also convenient to the athletic fields. It is also helpful to have the instrumental music room near the stage.

The location of the library-learning resources center is also of some importance. College instruction depends to a great extent upon this facility. It should logically be in a central location, but the right atmosphere for study and learning must be present. There are many other functional affinities to be considered and some areas that should be definitely separated such as noisy areas from the quiet ones; however, these should all be worked out during the planning stages in terms the educational program and the desires of the planners.[23]

Environmental Controls[24]

The community college planner knows the tremendous influence that environment plays in shaping lives. He knows that the total environment influences what an individual is and what he does—that it contributes to the shaping of his aspiration, beliefs, and values. The community college campus and its buildings should, therefore, be inviting places in which it is a real joy to work, to walk, or to linger. He is also aware that he must produce an environment that adequately provides for the health, safety, and comfort of the students and faculty.

This section of the chapter, therefore, will be concerned with space, air conditioning, light, sound, and aesthetics as environmental factors. No attempt will be made here to treat the technical aspects of each of these factors. The reader is referred to the many excellent publications dealing with these areas, several of which appear in the bibliography.

Space As an Environmental Factor

Civilized and perhaps uncivilized man has always demanded space in which to move and live. The very nature of man requires plenty of "elbow room" as stated by the early frontiersman. Give individuals ample room in which to move and breathe and they show all the desirable attributes of civilized man, but herd

---

[23] Adapted from *Facilities for Higher Education*, pp. 34-35.
[24] Most of this section was adapted from *Facilities for Higher Education*, pp. 19-20, 94-97.

them together in cramped quarters and the undesirable characteristics soon assert themselves.

This fact has serious implications for the community college planner. Overcrowded classrooms not only make variation in teaching techniques difficult if not impossible, but the psychological bar to learning is tremendous. In boarding colleges, placement of four or more students in dormitory rooms planned for only two may impose impossible handicaps on some students.

Procuring an inadequate size site or absorbing needed free space on an already crowded campus means that for generations students will live, work, and play in a cramped outdoor environment. Nowhere will a student be able to find solitude on the campus.

The college planner, therefore, will make every effort to see that the site is ample, that the buildings are properly grouped, and that some secluded areas are available. In planning the various buildings he will provide ample free floor space in classrooms and laboratories so students will not feel cramped. He will insist that rooms be adequately planned and maximum class size for each room set and discourage college administrators from adding additional seating.

Air Conditioning As an Environmental Factor

Research indicates that students learn best when the condition of the air and surrounding surfaces is most conducive to physical and mental well being. Although it is possible for the human organism to adjust itself to a wide variety of environmental conditions, this adjustment is made with a considerable expenditure of energy, which distracts the student from learning in an uncomfortable environment. Factors that must be considered in this respect are air temperature, radiant temperature, relative humidity, air motion, odors, dust and dirt, and atmospheric contaminants.

Because community college buildings are used around the clock and during all seasons, total climate control is an absolute necessity. In planning for this environmental factor every effort should be made to convince the architectural firm that this area is not the place to cut corners financially.

Light As an Environmental Factor

Because of less rigid standards and control, many post-secondary school plants have not kept pace with the research in school lighting and color conditioning. Too many students sit in unattractive, poorly lighted classrooms, which places a strain on their eyes and reduces their efficiency. Lighting has recently received more attention in educational literature than any of the other environmental factors. It is now widely accepted that the brightness-balance concept of school lighting is more important than intensity alone for the production of proper seeing conditions.

As the principles of brightness-balance have become better understood, there has developed an increasing awareness of the importance of a good visual environment for learning. At present it is a known fact that the elimination of glare and the provision of a balanced-brightness environment can help a student or instructor to see classroom tasks with more comfort, more speed, and more accuracy.

Of perhaps even greater importance are the research findings that indicate that a good system of lighting lessens the expenditure of energy required for students and instructors to carry on visual tasks in classrooms. Research indicates that a balanced visual environment reduces fatigue, restlessness, and in attention among students and contributes to the conservation of energy for other needs.

Studies have shown that the number of eye defects increases as students progress through school. By the time they enter community colleges, a fairly large percentage of the students have substandard vision. When it is realized that adequate balanced lighting improves the visual performance of people with substandard vision, the need to provide a better than minimum quality visual environment becomes apparent. A good visual environment is important, too, because it helps create an aesthetically pleasing environment for learning.

Sound and Noise As an Environmental Factor

In this age of stress, strain, and innumerable distractions, sound conditioning is as important as air and sight conditioning. In the community college learning takes place through lecture, discussion, study, and research. In all these activities the sonic factor is of utmost importance. Undesirable and conflicting sounds produce a negative influence on verbal communication between instructor and student and between student and student. In order to learn, students must not only hear distinctly, but they should be protected from distracting and nerve-jangling, extraneous sounds. This is particularly important during study and research. Experimentation has clearly established that efficiency increases as distractions are minimized. The strain and excessive expenditure of energy necessary to carry on oral communication in a noisy environment are familiar to most individuals.

Colleges and their surroundings produce many sources of sound. Some of these sounds are desirable; others are distracting and consequently undesirable. Environmental control, in this respect, involves facilitating the propagation of desirable sounds and the tempering or muffling of the undesirable sounds.

In sound conditioning educational spaces, one or both of these actions are used; however, usually both actions are provided for simultaneously.

External Sonic Distractions. A well located site removed from airports, railroads, highways, or noisy industrial plants contributes greatly to the reduction of external noise coming from sources beyond the site. Unfortunately, these sources of external distraction frequently come after a college has been built. However, if the site is extensive enough, some of these noises may be made less distracting by placing the various buildings properly on the site. A wooded area on the site or large screen plantings will also serve as sound barriers.

External sounds originating *on* the site may be made less distracting too by the proper placement of buildings on the site and by screening. As previously mentioned in this chapter, zoning of the campus areas is exceptionally important. The academic zone should always be in the quietest section of the campus. This zone should also be somewhat removed from the student activity zone and the eventual housing zone.

Internal Sonic Distractions. All buildings should be designed to prevent noise from reverberating within the various spaces and to reduce noise transmission from one space to another.

Faulty structural design is one cause of excessive noise transmission. This is a highly technical matter, which requires specialized engineering consultant services.

Ventilating and air-conditioning ducts are common offenders in transmitting sounds. It is not uncommon for students in adjoining classrooms to be able to hear both instructors at the same time. The use of separate ducts, adequate baffles, and sound absorbing materials should be considered in order to minimize this type of sound transmission.

Each area has its own acoustical problems and should receive the attention of experts. Classrooms, corridors and stairways, administrative offices, the learning resources center, gymnasium, auditorium, music rooms, and cafeterias individually need study and treatment if internal sonic distractions are to be eliminated.

Aesthetics As an Environmental Factor

A building properly conceived and well planned is the result of the appropriate blend of the aesthetic and the practical. Beauty in a structure is the result of the proper mixture of symmetry and imagination.

These aesthetic qualities are not a result of visual satisfaction alone. They are derived from the total reaction an individual feels through all his senses and the kinds of emotional satisfactions he gains from working or living in a truly functional architectural creation. The difference between an environment that is cheerful rather tham somber, lively rather than dull, or calm instead of restless comprises this total reaction of the individual.

Designing Community Colleges for Optimum Use of Learning Resources

The effectiveness of any learning resource, be it the simple slate and copybook of yesteryear or the most modern electronic teaching device available

FIGURE 12-6

today, is influenced by the physical conditions under which it is used. Environmental conditions as near ideal as possible should be provided in the various learning areas and spaces. Ways of providing ideal visual, sonic, thermal, and aesthetic environments should be studied carefully before final decisions are made in planning or modernizing community college facilities (see Chapter 10).

Maximum use of learning resources may also be hindered by an insufficient number of, and/or poorly located power receptacles. Electrical circuits must be planned to carry the initial demand as well as any anticipated future load safely. In view of the many new technological devices to be installed in the future, ample open conduits should be provided throughout new buildings so that electrical wires may be pulled through economically at a later date to serve these devices.

Adequate size, built-in screens should be provided in each area where projection will take place. Ample bulletin board and other display facilities should be carefully planned, and the chalkboards must not be overlooked as possible teaching aids. Off-white chalkboards, utilizing colored writing materials, also double as projection screens.

Special attention must be paid to facilities for individual, small-group, and large-group instruction and learning. Accommodations for teachers and students to carry on independent study and to plan with each other must receive serious consideration in initial planning.[25]

Summary

Planning interim and permanent college facilities is an extremely important assignment. The use of interim facilities speeds up the opening of the college and makes the staff and student body available for planning the permanent facilities. Interim facilities may include double occupancy; abandoned school, industrial, government, and business buildings; and relocatable structures.

Decisions must be made whether to build new facilities or to renovate existing buildings. In the big city renovation is frequently elected, even though later new campuses may be built and the renovated structure utilized as a branch campus.

Some community college facilities are being constructed as sections of other building complexes. The development of community college facilities requires expert planning and the involvement of a great many people. Tasks such as selection of the architectural firm, acquisition of sites, and development of educational specifications require careful planning and a lot of hard work. To the extent possible, the administration, instructional and noninstructional staff, students, and lay individuals, together with a host of specialists, should be involved in planning.

Carefully formulated educational specifications are of extreme importance. Architects expect an educational blueprint that will enable them to design the kinds of facilities that will meet the needs of the students, faculty, and community.

An important first task of the planning group is the selection of the architectural firm. Early appointment makes it possible for the architect to assist in site selection and in the development of the educational specifications.

Architectural firms are usually selected by direct appointment or by comparative selection based on a number of criteria. Information concerning the qualifications of each firm is collected and the less desirable ones screened out. Up to six firms are then invited to make presentations before the selection committee. Finally, the successful firm is given the contract.

Another important task of the planning committee is the selection of the college site or sites. In certain areas adequate sites are increasingly difficult to find and very expensive.

It is of the utmost importance that the architectural firm participates in the selection of the site. Twenty-one criteria have been suggested to be used in the selection procedure.

Site development also deserves considerable attention. The potential of many excellent sites has never been realized because they were not developed properly.

The community college planner must be aware of the tremendous influence that environment plays in living and learning. He knows that proper attention must be given to space, air conditioning, light, sound, and aesthetics as environmental factors.

Finally, the community college must be designed for the optimum use of learning resources.

Suggested Activities and Problems

1. Interview the president of a community college that opened in interim facilities to determine the advantages and disadvantages of this procedure. Write a paper on the topic and give arguments for and against the use of interim facilities.
2. Read extensively on the use of shared facilities by community colleges. Write a paper describing the various arrangements.
3. Recommend the personnel you believe should assist in the planning of community college facilities. Give the reasons for your choices and indicate the role each team member should play.
4. Visit an architectural firm that has recently completed a community college building program. Interview members of the firm to determine their reactions to their relationships with the college planning group.
5. Secure a copy of the educational specifications for a community college building program and write a critique of them, based on what authorities say should be included in the specifications.
6. Examine a community college site and utilize the twenty-one criteria in the text to evaluate it.
7. Discuss the effect of open spaces on environmental controls.

Selected Readings

Bricks and Mortarboards. New York: Educational Facilities Laboratories, 1966.

Castaldi, Basil, *Creative Planning of Educational Facilities*, Chap. 14. Skokie, Ill.: Rand McNally & Co., 1969.

CEFP Guide for Planning Educational Facilities. Columbus, Ohio: Council of Educational Facility Planners, 1969.

Center for Architectural Research. *Facilities for Educational Technology*. Troy, N.Y.: Rensselaer Polytechnic Institute, School of Architecture, 1971.

A College in the City: An Alternative. New York: Educational Facilities Laboratories, 1969.

Griffin, C. W., Jr., *Systems—An Approach to School Construction.* New York: Educational Facilities Laboratories, 1971.

A Guide for Planning Community Junior Colleges. Washington, D.C.: Department of Health, Education, and Welfare, 1969.

Johnson, Marvin R. A., *The School Architect—Selection—Duties—How to Work with Him.* Washington, D.C.: Administrative Leadership Service, 1968.

Joint Occupancy. New York: Educational Facilities Laboratories, 1970.

Merlo, Frank P. and W. Donald Walling, *Guide for Planning Community College Facilities.* New Brunswick, N.J.: Rutgers—The State University, Graduate School of Education, 1964.

Parker, Floyd, G., and Max S. Smith, eds., *Planning Community Junior College Facilities.* East Lansing, Mich.: Proceedings of a Conference Sponsored by College of Education and Continuing Education Service, Michigan State University and Council of Educational Facility Planners, 1968.

Planners and Planning. Palo Alto, Calif.: Stanford University, Community College Planning Center, 1966.

Reed, Bob H., *The Urban Community College 1969.* Houston, Texas: Caudill Rowlett Scott, 1970.

13

Organizing
Special Programs and Services

Decisions concerning the special programs and services to be provided are among the most crucial to be made in planning and starting a community college. Although special programs and services are important in all educational institutions, they should be given particular attention in the community college because of the nature of the institution. Since it is an open-door college, admitting students from a variety of backgrounds with considerable range in abilities, motivation, achievement, age, and vocational interests, the need for all types of student affairs services is greatly accentuated. If the daily needs of such a heterogeneous student body are to be met, expertise of the highest order in planning will be required.

If attempts are to be made to meet the intellectual, physical, social, and emotional needs of all individuals the community college serves, a careful program of institutional research must be planned, conducted, and continuously improved. Only in this manner can the strengths and weaknesses of the various aspects of the educational program and special programs and services be evaluated and upgraded.

The unique function of the two-year college as an instrument for community improvement and the need for community understanding and support make it necessary to establish strong public information services in the new institution.

If the community college is to live up to its name, the community services aspect must be carefully planned, inaugurated, evaluated, and constantly improved.

These, then, are the topics to be discussed in this chapter under the heading of special programs and services.

Student Affairs Services

Student affairs services begin with admission and end with placement and follow-up procedures. In between are a host of services that if properly administered can make a lasting impression on the lives of the students affected by them.

The types and quality of student affairs services available in a community college reflect, probably more than any other aspects, the real attitude of the administration and staff toward the students. If the services are maintained at a high level, it indicates that the students really count. Contrariwise, inadequate student personnel services create the impression that the administration and staff are not too concerned about the welfare of the students.

The student personnel program is as important as the instructional program. As can be seen in Figure 6-1, p. 75, the position of the dean of student affairs is at the same level as that of the dean of academic affairs. Both officials are responsible directly to the president of the college.

The importance of this key position cannot be overemphasized. An individual highly qualified in student affairs should be employed to head these services at least a year before the college opens.

Admission, Retention, Placement, and Follow-up

It has been the avowed purpose of the community college to make some form of higher and continuing education available to all persons within the service area if they can benefit from it. The fulfillment of this great promise requires a wide variety of curricular offerings, liberal admission policies, excellent guidance and counseling services, and careful follow-up procedures.

The Open-Door Policy. More has been written than done about making the community college a truly open-door institution.[1] This is one of the first basic decisions that must be made in the initial planning of a community college. An open-door college must be very different from a college that is selective in admissions and retention. Much of the total planning of the institution from start to finish depends upon the answers to the following two questions:

1. Will all post-secondary school age students, both high school graduates and others, who can benefit from the educational offerings be admitted to the new community college?
2. Will the same policy apply to adults of all ages and educational levels?

Hopefully planners of community colleges will answer the above questions in the affirmative because the true function of the community college is to meet the needs of all individuals who wish to improve their education. However, in a

---

[1] For a status report, see John W. Huther, "The Open Door: How Open Is It?" *Junior College Journal,* 41, No. 7 (1971), 24.

system of community colleges some of the units may wish to be selective in their admission policies. The important point is that every individual has the opportunity to improve his education within a reasonable distance from his domicile.

The open-door policy is thus a reflection of the philosophy of the administration and staff. It, therefore, is imperative that in the selection of staff members (see Chapter 6) there is general acceptance of a liberal admissions policy. A community college that pretends to subscribe to an open-door policy but does not practice it, or that has a liberal admission policy and then flunks or forces out students who cannot make the grade, causes irreparable harm to the involved students and to the community college cause.

Meeting the Needs of All Entrants. An open-door policy not only implies open access for all individuals who can benefit from post-secondary school education, but it also assumes that programs, courses, and activities will be available to meet the needs of all individuals who enter the open door. If students are to be retained until the successful completion of the program or courses for which they entered the community college, provisions must be made for compensatory education. Many of the individuals eligible for entrance under the open-door policy will have deficiencies in certain skills that are necessary for further learning.

Excellent guidance and counseling services also are of paramount importance if students are to select the programs and courses for which their aptitudes best fit them. These services will be discussed later in this chapter.

Although the open-door policy allows all high school graduates and otherwise qualified students to enter the community college, it does not guarantee that they will be eligible to enter all programs. Neither does it guarantee that all students will be successful. For example, students desiring to enter the transfer program will be expected to meet certain minimum entrance requirements or be accepted on probation until they have taken the necessary compensatory education to qualify. Likewise, they will be expected to meet the minimum requirements for graduation if they plan to continue their education in a four-year college.

Another factor affecting both the admission and retention of community college students is that of funds for both tuition and living expenses. Although ideally community college education should be free to students, in reality it mostly is not. For many potential community college students, entrance is dependent upon some form of student loan. Planners who desire to meet the needs of these individuals must consider some type of student loan program, or many possible applicants will either not be able to enter college or drop out shortly after admission.

The retention of students is directly related to the grading system that is used. If it is highly competitive, there will be more failures and dropouts than if the more humane pass-fail system is used. If behavioral objectives have been carefully formulated for the various learning experiences and much of the instruction has been individualized, there would seem to be no need for competitive grades in the new community college. Planners should seriously consider the pros and cons of removing the threat of a competitive grading system from students.

Placement. Placement of graduates is another important service that must be rendered to community college students. Students who desire to continue their education beyond the two-year college must be assisted to locate four-year colleges and universities that will admit them. Individuals who are ready to enter the job market likewise need assistance in securing positions in vocations for which they have been prepared.

Checking on the Effectiveness of the Programs. No community college can hope to continuously improve its programs unless it establishes good student follow-up procedures. To be truly effective, it has to ascertain the degree to which each of the programs has met the needs of the individuals who were in it. It is not enough to study only the effectiveness of the college transfer program. If the new community college is to accomplish its avowed purposes, the college administration and staff must learn how successful each of its students has become.

Follow-up studies are among the tasks of institutional research. Plans should be made to conduct them regularly and not just periodically or only as part of the evaluation procedures.

Counseling and Guidance Services

Considerable controversy has been waged over the kinds and extent of counseling and guidance services necessary to meet the needs of community college students. The relative roles and responsibilities of professionally trained counselors and regular instructors, and the use of paraprofessionals in the counseling process, have all been topics for discussion and debate. Each of these areas will be treated in the following discussion.

Counseling by Professionals. To assist students in the new community college in making intelligent decisions in matters related to vocational choice, educational planning, and personal problems, a staff of professionally trained guidance personnel is essential. However, instructors and paraprofessionals can be very helpful as well.

Administrators, likewise, can make their contributions to the guidance and counseling services. In addition, the public information system contributes by enlightening parents and prospective community college students concerning educational programs and vocational educational opportunities at the college.

In the employment of counselors, efforts should be made to select individuals who come from the various ethnic groups and social classes represented by the students who will attend the new community college. Counselors who do not understand students' backgrounds have difficulty in communicating with them. At least one counselor should have considerable knowledge about vocational guidance.

In several places in this text, the employment of personnel prior to the opening of the college has been recommended. Here again, it would be advantageous to engage the counselors during the spring and summer before the college is scheduled to open. If they were selected early during the second semester, they could continue in their present position and work for the college part-time. Their full-time employment could then begin in the summer.

The value of early counseling for "future students" has been demonstrated in a study reported by Garneski and Heimann. In their study a summer program was designed to provide comprehensive group counseling prior to matriculation to give students a longer period to consider their vocational goals and the educational means of attaining their objectives.

When the students who received summer group counseling were compared with a similarly motivated control group at the end of the first semester and again at the end of the first year, the counseled groups achieved at significantly higher levels than the control group upon all criteria with the exception of the number of semester hours earned. The criteria examined were percentage of dropouts, mean grade point average, and mean semester hours earned.[2]

Another strong argument for employing counselors prior to the opening of the new college is advanced by Roberson as a result of his experience in Illinois Central College. He cites the following rewards from involving counselors in curriculum development:

1. The counselors thoroughly understand the rationale of the school's curriculum and have greater knowledge of the curriculum of other colleges.
2. There developed respect for and comprehension of the technologies, business, and other terminal career programs.
3. Faculty members have sincere appreciation and respect for the supportive roles that counselors play in the educational milieu.
4. An *esprit de corps* is developed that is possible only through men working in concert and successfully overcoming obstacles.[3]

It would seem that both of the above writers would favor using counselors in academic advisement. Arguments pro and con are enumerated later in this chapter.

Although every community college is unique and, consequently, should plan its own counseling and guidance services, it might prove helpful to the new

[2]Thomas M. Garneski and Robert A. Heimann, "Summer Group Counseling of Freshmen," *Junior College Journal,* 37, No. 8 (1967), 40.
[3]Glenn Roberson, "The Counselor and the Curriculum," *Junior College Journal,* 39, No. 6 (1969), 74.

college to examine what other institutions have done. As an example, elements of the counseling program planned for William Rainey Harper College located in a northwest suburb of Chicago are listed below. The rationale for each element can be learned by reading the entire article.

1. Professionally trained counselors will be hired on a 300:1 ratio.
2. The counselors will do the academic advising.
3. Counselors will be assigned to a division of the college and will specialize in advising majors in that division.
4. Each counselor will (in addition to the specialized majors) be assigned a group of undecided students and a group of developmental students.
5. The counseling function will be decentralized and counselors will be officed in divisional suites throughout the college.
6. The counselors will be used in the college orientation program.
7. Most academic advising will be done during the summer.
8. Good mental hygiene will be stressed and serious problems will be referred.
9. The college will develop a counseling-placement center.
10. The college will use terminals and a computer in the counseling process.[4]

It should be noted from the above elements that the counseling services described depend largely upon professionally trained counselors and that there is little involvement of the instructional staff in the academic advisement process. One of the most important decisions that the planners of community colleges must make in respect to guidance and counseling services concerns the respective roles of professional counselors and instructors.

The following arguments favor the use of professionally trained counselors in the academic advisement process:

1. Academic advisement is a complicated procedure that requires full-time professionally trained personnel.
2. In practice, counselors do a better job in providing students with current information concerning course requirements, probationary policies, graduation requirements, transfer procedures, and other academic areas of concern.
3. Contacts made during academic advisement provide opportunities for counselors to discover students who are in need of other types of counseling.

Educators who are opposed to having counselors serve as academic advisers give the following arguments against the practice:

1. The assignment of academic advisement to counselors is too costly because a larger staff of counselors will be needed.

4   James Harvey, "The Counseling Approach at Harper College," *Junior College Journal,* 38, No. 2 (1967), 38-40.

2. If counselors spend their time in academic advisement, vocational and personal guidance might be neglected.
3. Counselors who participate in academic advisement are categorized in that role, and students are less likely to seek help from them in other areas of concern.

Regardless of whether or not counselors assume responsibility for academic advisement, they have other important tasks to perform. Counselors are experts in vocational guidance and, generally, can be more objective in this area than college instructors who might try to persuade students to choose their specialty. In helping students to make vocational or educational choices it is often necessary to assist them with personal adjustment problems. Conflicts with parents or other authority figures, problems related to the opposite sex, financial problems, and health problems all affect students' chances for success in the new community college.

There is general agreement that counselors should not pose as psychotherapists; however, they do have enough training and are in a good position to assist students with minor adjustment problems and to recommend additional help when needed. Counselors, likewise, can alert instructors when students in their classes have problems with the hope that more humane treatment will result.

One problem the college faces is that when counselors do discover more severe cases of maladjustment, the students concerned are reluctant to seek help outside the college. Jones suggested a solution to this problem when he wrote:

> In view of the fact that substantial numbers of junior college students are in need of psychotherapeutic help, some colleges may wish to consider the possibility of including one or more doctoral-level clinical or counseling psychologists as members of their counseling staffs. These highly trained psychologists could serve both as consultants in the mental health area for the total college community and as resource persons accepting referrals from counselors who are either less well trained or who do not wish to work with difficult personal adjustment cases. This type of arrangement would seem to offer promise in facilitating the implementation of referrals.[5]

It should be noted that in the above recommendation there is an overlap of the counseling and guidance services with the health services. The necessity for overall coordination of pupil personnel services should by now be apparent to the reader.

There is little disagreement over the fact that professionally trained counselors can play an important role in the new community college. The question is whether or not they will perform as expected.

[5] Twyman Jones, "The Counselor and His Role," *Junior College Journal,* 40, No. 7 (1970), 11.

It, therefore, is extremely important that the philosophy and objectives of the counseling system are carefully formulated and the roles of the counselors delineated before the new college opens. The example of Harper College cited earlier in this section represents this type of thoughtful preplanning of the counseling approach.

Counseling by Instructors. The arguments previously enumerated *against* the use of professionally trained counselors as academic advisers could all be used as arguments *for* using regular college instructors as advisers. Likewise, the arguments supporting the use of counselors as academic advisers can be accepted as good reasons for *not* asking instructors to serve in this capacity. These arguments will not be repeated here. There, however, are several pros and cons in respect to the use of instructors as academic advisers not previously mentioned.

Community college administrators who favor utilizing instructors in the academic advisement process make the following additional claims:

1. Many regular college instructors have both interest and talent in counseling, which should be encouraged by the college.
2. Utilization of instructors as counselors encourages improved relationships between the instructional program and the guidance and counseling services.
3. Instructors in the various curriculum areas have a better knowledge of their specialty than counselors can be expected to acquire.
4. Instructors have regular contacts with students in their classes and thus have frequent opportunities to counsel students informally or arrange a conference with little delay.
5. The supply of professionally trained counselors is so limited at present that they must be assisted by either regular instructors, aides, or both.

Arguments not previously mentioned against the use of regular staff members in advisement are:

1. Because of their lack of preparation for the advisement task, instructors may cause irreparable harm to students by giving them the wrong advice.
2. Many instructors are not really interested in counseling and some who *are* interested do not have the type of personality that lends itself to advisement.
3. If student advisement represents part of the faculty load, instructors' time—for which they are compensated—could be more expertly and efficiently utilized by the assignment of extra classes.

A good student personnel program should involve professionally trained counselors, regular instructors, and counselor aides. The team approach to advisement and counseling should be utilized with each of the three groups performing on levels equivalent to their knowledge and training. Just as regular counselors are professionally prepared for high-level performance and counselor aides trained as paraprofessionals, instructors who are assigned advisement responsibilities must be given in-service education to assist them in becoming increasingly proficient in the advisement phase of their jobs.

Counselor Aides. The criticisms of the services rendered by counselors in community colleges mentioned earlier in this section are frequently unjustified because counselors are expected to perform miracles. Student personnel services in most community colleges are greatly understaffed and counselors are given impossible workloads.[6] One way to improve this situation is to prepare paraprofessionals to serve as aides to counselors. Collins describes the counselor aide and his work in the following manner:

> The counselor aide envisioned here would be a paraprofessional, not a clerk. He would need fundamental understanding of the entire function of the counselor just as the surgical nurse needs an intimate understanding of the work of the surgeon. The counselor aide would not be a counselor, but he would be the counselor's alter ego. He would be a knowing team member. He would prepare the counselee for the professional work of the counselor. He would perform many of the carry-through tasks and give the finishing touches after the counselor had done the truly professional work.
> . . . The well-prepared aide, working with a truly professional counselor, would be constantly stretched to reach higher, to handle tasks and progressively demand more skill, more knowledge, more wisdom.
> The journeyman counselor would use the aide like an advanced apprentice. He would have him conduct induction interviews; provide an immediate ear to the drop-in counselee who cannot be worked into the counselor's schedule; contribute his peer perspective; translate and maybe even interpret across the generation gap, or the gap of caste and class; administer, score and rough out the general meaning of group tests; secure and prepare needed data for the counselor; help the counselee to search out needed occupational and educational information; fill in the details of the broad educational plan sketched by the counselor; negotiate referrals to on-campus specialists or off-campus agencies; do the legwork of the follow-up plan designed by the counselor; assist the counselor in student characteristics studies and in evaluation research.[7]

In order to perform the above tasks, Collins believes that the training program should consist of a two-year associate in arts degree program that would encompass a core curriculum, and specialized courses topped by an internship. He further adds that special efforts should be made to recruit individuals previously discriminated against. This includes blacks, students from lower-class families, and women.[8]

[6]See Charles C. Collins, *Junior College Student Personnel Programs: What They Are and What They Should Be* (Washington, D.C.: American Association of Junior Colleges, 1967).

[7]Charles C. Collins, "Giving the Counselor a Helping Hand," *Junior College Journal,* 40, No. 8 (1970), 19.

[8]Ibid.

Collins's suggestion holds great promise not only for assisting the professional counselor and thus permitting him to function on a higher level, but also for increasing the supply of badly needed professionally trained counselors. Many of the paraprofessionals may discover that they have an intense interest in and aptitude for student personnel services and they may decide to continue their schooling and obtain degrees in counseling.

Planners of community colleges should seriously consider using paraprofessionals as counselor aides. It could pay large dividends.

Health Services

Health services usually have been the stepchild of the student affairs services in community colleges. Although public elementary and secondary schools and four-year colleges have set good examples by maintaining good health services, community colleges, for the most part, have not followed their lead.

Good mental and physical health are among man's most cherished assets. Good health also contributes to improved learning; therefore, it is the responsibility of every community college to provide health services that will maintain the mental and physical health of students at the highest possible levels.

Organizing Health Services. As the first step in planning the health services program, community college planners must be convinced of their responsibility for providing these services. Unless the board of trustees and college administration are deeply committed to the need and value of health services, the new college is not likely to make adequate provisions for them.

As an aid in organizing the health services, answers to questions similar to the following will prove helpful:

1. Who will be eligible to receive health care?
2. Will physical examinations be required of all students and employees?
3. What type of pupil health records will be kept and where will they be housed?
4. What relationships will the college health services have to the various community health services and agencies?
5. What relationships and obligations will the college health services have to the community law enforcement agencies in respect to the drug problem?
6. What relationships will the health services have to the other student-affairs services?
7. What will constitute an adequate staff for the health services?
8. What responsibilities will the health services have for insuring a safe and healthful college environment?
9. What responsibilities and relationships will the health services have in respect to formal health instruction?

10. What procedures for first aid and for handling more serious emergencies must be set up?
11. How will the health services be financed?

Every new community college must plan its own health services in terms of its specific needs. However, it is always helpful to have guidelines as suggested by persons in the field. Alice Thurston, former dean of students at Cuyahoga Community College, Ohio, and two of her associates believe that an effective health service incorporates the following elements:

Organization:
1. As an important arm of a student personnel program in a community college, the health service is the responsibility of the dean of students. The nurse in charge should be a fully functioning member of the student personnel staff. She should have faculty status, serve on faculty committees, and participate in the faculty senate.
2. Preferably there should be a part-time medical director who assumes medical responsibility for a health program for the total college community. Otherwise, a consulting physician is needed; in this case, considerably more medical responsibility is assumed by the nurse in charge.
3. A psychiatrist or psychologist should be within regular consulting distance to provide in-service training for nurses and counselors, to be available for diagnosis and referral, and to serve as a resource for the total college community.
4. College nurses should have at least a baccalaureate degree. Administrative, psychiatric, emergency room, and public health experience are all of great value.
5. College nurses should be encouraged to belong to professional groups, attend appropriate institutes and workshops, and utilize every opportunity for professional growth.
6. All areas involved in health—paramedical education, physical and health education, counseling, and others—should work closely together.
7. Top administrative understanding and support is needed.

Health Service Functions:
1. The basic objective of the health service is to maintain and to improve the health of students, especially as it relates to their educational achievement.
2. The ultimate responsibility for health care is the students'. In communicable disease control, however, the health service must assume a more active role.
3. While students are the first concern, faculty and staff should also be eligible for service and should be encouraged to participate in all health programs.

4. Health counseling is a major role. Students are helped to identify their health problems and obtain proper care in the community, to accept their physical limitations, and to understand their feelings about their illnesses. Independence and maturity in health habits are encouraged.

5. Through various educational media such as symposia, posters, pamphlets, other resource materials, and individual and group work, students are helped to understand what behaviors affect health.

6. Temporary treatment of minor illnesses is available under standing orders of the physician. First aid for injuries is provided. Aspirin and band-aids are useful door openers which permit the nurse to accomplish the functions listed above.

7. Individual student health needs are assessed by studying required health examinations, and follow-up is conducted. Auditory, visual, diabetic, and other screening programs are sponsored, often in cooperation with community agencies.

8. Environmental health and safety is explored collaboratively with other responsible departments of the college to identify and resolve potential health hazards.

9. Like other aspects of student personnel work, continual self-study and evaluation is conducted.[9]

It should be noted that answers to a number of the questions raised at the beginning of this section can be found in the above discussion. Others remain to be answered.

Student Participation in Governance

If the flood of student activism is a barometer, student government has not proven to be an effective device for improving the communication between students and the administration. Likewise, many serious questions are being raised concerning the kinds of experiences that should be made available for students in the activity or cocurricular program.

In starting a new community college a fresh look should be taken at both the student government and the entire cocurricular program before any commitments are made. A new institution like the community college has the opportunity to avoid some of the pitfalls that secondary schools, four-year colleges, and universities have experienced.

Student Government. If properly organized and run, the student government or student council can provide an excellent vehicle by which students: (1) can

⁹ Alice Thurston, Lynne Norrie, and Joan Venable, "Health Services: Who Needs Them?" *Junior College Journal*, 40, No. 8 (1970), 34.

exercise control over their activities, (2) communicate effectively with the administration and faculty, and (3) gain experience in the skills of self-government.

How can the student governing organization be properly organized and run in the new community college? First, it is essential that the board of trustees and administration are in agreement concerning the duties, responsibilities, and areas in which the student government may operate. It must be clearly understood under what circumstances and conditions the student government has a *budget of power* and when their deliberations result only in recommendations to the administration.

The old model of student government, in which a few chosen representatives went through the motions of playing at governance, will no longer be tolerated by students today. Unless the student government has real authority, is well integrated with the total institutional governance, and can win and hold the respect of the student body, there is little use trying to organize one.

However, student government can be revitalized and made to work if new patterns of participation in policy formulation and decision making are formed. The new college must be innovative and willing to experiment with different forms of organization in student government. The traditional model consisting of a hierarchical system—with the students at the bottom of the totem pole, the faculty in the middle, and the administration at the top—must be replaced. The new model must guarantee participation by students, faculty, and administration so that special interests all are represented, but at the same time the welfare of the total college is considered to be paramount.[10]

To the extent possible, representative future students and faculty members should be involved in all deliberations concerning the participation of students in governance and planning the cocurricular program. This will require a series of widely publicized meetings to which potential future students and available faculty members are invited.

When decisions have been agreed upon and approved by the board of trustees, they should be put in writing in the form of a constitution and bylaws. Some writers on the topic suggest that the student government organization should be given a charter that clearly spells out the limits within which the students may operate and contains provisions for administrative veto power over certain types of actions.[11]

To make sure that the student government may be properly organized and may continue to function well, individuals responsible for planning and supervising the pupil personnel services should be aware of what is happening in other similar institutions. A study of student government made by McAnich in the

---

[10]For some suggestions see William L. Deegan et al., "Student Participation in Governance," *Junior College Journal,* 41, No. 3 (1970), 15.

[11]See James W. Thornton, Jr., *The Community Junior College,* 2nd ed. (New York: John Wiley & Sons, Inc., 1966), p. 261.

North Central Accrediting Region in which 110 administrators and 105 students responded revealed the following interesting practices:

1. Fewer than two-thirds (62.8 percent) of the respondents indicated that candidates were nominated by petition.
2. A large majority (89.1 percent) of the respondents reported that elections were by secret ballot.
3. A large majority (84.4 percent) responded that the term of office was one full year.
4. Almost all (97.3 percent) respondents indicated that the student government was operating under a written constitution.
5. Fewer than two-thirds (62.7 percent) of the participants in the study reported that weekly meetings were held.
6. A slightly larger number (65.5 percent) indicated that the administrator had final veto power.
7. More than half (58.2 percent) of the respondents reported that orientation in the college philosophy was provided student government members.
8. There was no general agreement on the number of members. Slightly more than one-third (34.9 percent) of the respondents indicated that the student government had ten to nineteen members, and less than one-third (27.5 percent) reported twenty to twenty-nine members.[12]

In the same research report the following somewhat surprising findings were reported:

1. Approximately 11 percent of the colleges did not select their student representatives by secret ballot.
2. Approximately 42 percent of the colleges failed to provide orientation in the philosophy of the college.
3. In only 15.5 percent of the colleges the student government had sole responsibility for activity fee expenditures and in more than 25 percent of the institutions studied, the student government organization had no control at all over determining activity fee expenditures.
4. More than 40 percent of the institutions indicated that the student government must conduct fund-raising activities in order to supplement its budget.[13]

When a comparison was made of the opinions of students and administrators as to the desirability of selected practices used in organizing and administering student governments, they were found to be in general agreement except for two crucial areas. There was a significant difference among the opinions of administrators and students in the following two key areas: training student government

---

[12]Harold D. McAnich, "Can Students and Administrators Communicate?" *Junior College Journal*, 39, No. 6 (1969), 112.
[13]Ibid.

members in the philosophy of the school, and the veto power of the administrator over student government decisions.[14]

Community college planners and students of community college administration should consider the implications of the above study for organizing and operating an effective student government. It should be kept in mind, however, that common practices are not necessarily best practices.

In summary of this section on student participation in governance, the following recommendations should be given serious consideration:

1. Planning sessions with representative future students and faculty should be held before classes are in session, to make initial plans for the student government organization.
2. Planning should not be in terms of the old hierarchical model of student government but, rather, in terms of student participation in the governance of the college.
3. As part of the planning process, copies of the *Joint Statement on Rights and Freedoms of Students* should be secured and studied.[15]
4. The writing of a preliminary constitution and bylaws should be one of the first tasks in the organization of a student government.
5. Elections for student government should be conducted by secret ballot.
6. Every effort should be made to assist the students in realizing the need for providing orientation sessions in college philosophy as part of the training of student government members.
7. Sufficient internal funds should be made available for the operation of the student government. It should not have to engage in moneymaking activities to provide any of these necessary funds.
8. The student government should have the authority to determine the expenditure of funds for its necessary operation.
9. Attempts should be made to arrive at a clear understanding and agreement between the students and administration in respect to the veto power of the administration.

As a consequence of student activism, a new student official is appearing on the educational scene. In a number of colleges and universities the office of ombudsman has been created. This term was borrowed from Scandinavian countries where a government official occupying this office investigates citizens' complaints against public officials.

In colleges having an ombudsman the office has proven to be an effective procedure for keeping the lines of communication between the students and administration open. Planners of community colleges would be wise to give serious attention to the idea.[16]

[14] Ibid., p. 114.
[15] See Jane E. Matson, "Statements on Student Rights," *Junior College Journal,* 38, No. 3 (1967), 38.
[16] For status of the ombudsman, see Frank B. Pesci, "The Ombudsman Concept in the Two-Year College," *Junior College Journal,* 41, No. 8 (1971), 30.

The student handbook can be a valuable aid in the orientation of students both during the beginning and continuing stages of a community college. To be most effective, students, instructors, administrators, and parents should all play a part in deciding upon its contents. There is no place for a student handbook written by administrators and forced upon students. If the handbook is to serve effectively as a guide for students during the time they are on campus, they must have a large say concerning the guidelines it contains. The student government will play an important role in determining the contents of the initial student handbook and in keeping it current.

The development of the student handbook can begin before the college opens, with future students contributing their ideas. The actual preparation of the handbook can take place during the first year of college operation. Many excellent ideas may be obtained from handbooks collected from other community colleges. However, handbook writing is much more than copying items from the publications of other colleges. If particular items seem appropriate to use and are approved by the students, a check should be made with the colleges from which the handbooks originated to determine the worth of the particular items to be adopted.

Cocurricular Program. The new community college faces the same problems in this area that have plagued secondary schools for years. One decision that must be made early in the life of the community college is concerned with whether or not activity periods should be provided during the regular college schedule.

The best solution probably is to provide time for a reasonable number of cocurricular activities, some of which are included in the regular college schedules. Provisions must be made so that prime time is not taken from the

FIGURE 13-1

regular instructional schedule. Plans also should be made so that married students and others normally not interested in cocurricular activities have opportunities to utilize this time in a manner they believe to be constructive.

Another serious problem is related to the position the new college will take with respect to intercollegiate athletics. Certainly, regardless of their eventual scope, they should be very limited during the initial years of operation. During this period, intramural sports programs largely should provide the athletic competition needed to develop enthusiasm in the new college.

On a long-term basis careful consideration should be given before total commitment is made to a costly athletic program in which a small number of students participate while the rest shout and wave flags.

The community college is unique in many respects, one of which is that it is a two-year institution. In high schools and four-year colleges the coaching staff works with the players over a three- or four-year period.

FIGURE 13-2

The community college provides a marvelous opportunity for introducing students, both young and old, to the types of cocurricular activities that can be lifelong pursuits. Music, art, dramatics, dancing, golf, bowling, handball, tennis, jogging, and swimming are among the types of activities that should be encouraged and promoted rather than team sports. However, as previously mentioned, intramural sports might be included in the program.

Requests doubtless will be made for many other worthwhile types of cocurricular activities, some of which will be an outgrowth of the instructional program. Whenever possible these requests should be honored.

A well-planned program of cultural activities and entertainment should be part of the offerings of the new community college. Some of these activities should be for the benefit of only the students, others for the community, and a few for both.

Institutional Research

The term *research* has been associated with colleges and universities in the United States for many years, but it has not been institutional research. It has been largely *basic* research or *applied* research, where the application of the findings is made outside the institution. Institutional research is a newcomer on college and university campuses. As discussed here, institutional research is defined as: *A problem oriented, action type of research performed within institutions of higher learning with the main focus upon current issues and problems of concern to the institution for the purpose of providing data necessary to make intelligent administrative decisions in order to successfully maintain, operate, and improve the institution.*

Ideally, the community college is a natural site for good institutional research. The institution is so new, its programs so varied, and its characteristics so unique that there is a never ending series of issues and problems that must be researched; the solutions must be tested and then researched again.

All aspects of the community college are under constant scrutiny. Continuous attention must be paid to the objectives of the institution and to staff utilization in order to meet the changing needs of society. The instructional program, learning resources center, student personnel services, public information services, community services, financial support, and administrative organization and effectiveness should all be topics for institutional research as the need arises.

In a review of junior college institutional research made by Roueche and Boggs they reported the status of this type of research as follows:

> Four traditional methodologies are represented by junior college research reports. First, there are "observational studies," which obtain data from records or surveys. These studies, the most common, allow for educational decision making that employs more adequate evidence than was available before the study. For example, the counseling of transfer students is improved by the results of a survey of transfer policies of senior institutions. Also, the value of a given vocational curriculum can be more accurately assessed through the use of a survey report of graduates from that curriculum.
>
> A second traditional approach represented in junior college institutional research is the use of "group comparison." The following procedures are typically used: (1) the comparison of groups matched on some characteristic; (2) the comparison of randomly selected groups; and (3) the comparison of "natural" or already existing groups. Group comparisons are used to observe the effects of a given treatment (e.g., instructional procedure) upon various kinds of groups, as well as the effects of various treatments upon the same kinds of groups. When natural or existing groups are used, differences in the characteristics of the groups are often analyzed to determine factors that may account for the behavioral or other differences between the groups. An example is the analysis of parental aspirations of over- and underachievers. The value of group comparisons is dis-

closed by the statements of contrast that result. The following may be examples of such statements:

In this situation, students learn more English with the programmed material than with the conventional text. For this course, a difference in class size is not reflected in student performance.

"Correlational studies" represent a third approach. Frequently, correlation studies are used in the junior college to improve predictions of college success or failure on the basis of standardized tests or locally constructed test scores. These studies are designed particularly to improve the accuracy of selecting students for special programs, classes, or counseling.

A final research approach, most typically employed for evaluation, is the "pre- and postobservation." Pre- and postobservations are used to assess student changes during a single class, a given program, or a total two-year experience. An example of this approach would be the administration of a test before and after a remedial English class, to determine the increase in student reading comprehension.

These four methodologies are among those most often used by junior colleges to study a variety of problems.[17]

The increasing respect held by two-year colleges for institutional research is evidenced by the summer institute held at the Kellogg-sponsored Junior College Leadership Center at the University of Florida. Administrative teams from thirty-eight colleges convened in a workshop training program to plan for institutional research. By the end of the workshop each administrative team had developed the design for a study to be utilized as the basis for the formulation of a specific institutional policy. Typical of the types of problems studied are the following:

1. To investigate a trial program designed to qualify for admission certain applicants not otherwise qualified for admission.
2. To determine the relevance of class size as a contributing factor in learning writing.
3. To discover if the results of student rating of faculty by honor students would correlate significantly with rating(s) done by the total student body.
4. To ascertain whether there are significant nonintellective differences between students who succeed in being admitted in the fall and persist successfully through the freshman year, and those who are admitted in the fall from the on-trial program but who do not complete the freshman year.
5. To determine the most optimum time for advising incoming students on their academic programs.[18]

Institutional research has a very important role to play in the community

---

[17]John E. Roueche and John R. Boggs, *Junior College Institutional Research: The State of the Art* (Washington, D.C.: American Association of Junior Colleges, 1968), pp. 7-8.

[18]Moses S. Koch, Jr. and Willis A. LaVire, "Institutional Research for Decision-Makers," *Junior College Journal*, 37 No. 8 (1967), 13-15.

college. The reader is again referred to Figure 6.1, page 75, picturing the major functional areas in a community college. It should be noted that here again the individual responsible for research, planning, and information systems will report directly to the president. The selection of the person to head these important services is crucial. Unless the person chosen is action research oriented, little research of this type will be conducted.

Finally, although community colleges are unique, they do have similar problems. Therefore, community colleges have the added responsibility of sharing with each other the problems, research designs, and findings of their institutional research. However, wholesale application of outcomes from research in one institution to similar problems in another is not advisable. Rather, other colleges should thus be stimulated to research the same and other problems in their own institutions.

Public Information Services

In Chapter 2 the need for a comprehensive program of public information in the establishment of a community college was discussed. Chapter 5 detailed the role of the college president as a public relations expert, and Chapter 6 suggested the eventual need for a specialist to head the public information services. This discussion will be limited to establishing the need for the above position and to describing the job of the public information office.

Need for a Specialist in Public Information Services

In many instances examination of the causes of campus unrest throughout the nation revealed a definite absence of good communication lines in all directions. To a degree, the involvement of instructors, students, parents, and other interested lay persons in decision making will improve communication. This, however, is only a beginning. There are many other avenues of communication that need to be opened and regularly used.

The president can and does perform public relations functions as described in Chapter 5, but as the college grows larger he becomes less effective, particularly in respect to internal communication. In these days of negotiation the college is frequently split into two camps—administration in the one and faculty and students in the other. Sometimes the students are in a third camp. As a consequence, there is a need for an official to represent administration, faculty, and students—someone who will report all issues fairly and squarely, so that each faction receives an honest public hearing.

The public information officer should report directly to the president. In cases of emergencies and deadlines, a third party does not have to be involved. The public information officer can contact the president directly to secure permission for releases of news. This gives the public information officer a certain amount of prestige with the community and with the communications media. As spokesman, he saves the president much valuable time that would be lost if everyone insisted on seeing him.

Job Description of the Public Information Officer

Community colleges are of many sizes and are organized differently, both externally and internally. Some institutions have single campuses; others have branch campuses. Many have beautiful new buildings, whereas others are operating in temporary quarters or permanent remodeled factories, stores, and schools. There are many other differences and so each new college must determine its own shape, form, and destiny. But the new college must have some place to start—some point of reference from which to depart. Consequently, this text has given planners of community colleges examples of ways in which other institutions have solved the problems of starting and administering a college. Therefore, it seems appropriate to reproduce here a model job description for the public information officer as developed by the Michigan Association of Community College Public Information Officers and reported by Mitchell Tendler.

1. Prepare releases for and maintain continuing liaison with representatives of press, radio, and TV.
2. Prepare a college newsletter for internal and/or external distribution.
3. Coordinate college publications excluding student and instructional materials.
4. Prepare the college annual report.
5. Prepare and distribute a digest of board proceedings following each official board meeting.
6. Sit with press at board meetings and have copies of all handouts for distribution to press and other visitors.
7. Respond to selected presidential correspondence.
8. Prepare selected reports for president.
9. Serve as member of president's cabinet.
10. In the table of organization, report directly to the president.
11. Hold a twelve-month contract.
12. Hold administrative rank comparable at least to academic dean.
13. Develop long-range institutional public relations programs.[19]

The same source recommends that in order to do an effective job, the public information officer must be assigned a minimum of one competent assistant,

[19] Mitchell Tendler, "Case for the Public Information Officer," *Junior College Journal*, 40, No. 5 (1970), 52.

whereas in a multicampus college at least one full-time professional assistant should be assigned to each installation.[20]

The best public information services cannot do the job alone. The image of the college portrayed by the administration, students, faculty, and other personnel sometimes speaks much louder for or against the college than any news releases via newspapers, radio, or television. The students themselves constitute the most potent single agent for spreading the news—good or bad. If the students believe that they are treated fairly as human beings and they are pleased with the educational offerings, student affairs services, and their voice in governance, a good image of the college will be portrayed in the community.

Programs, activities, and events held at the college to which the public is invited also play a role in school–community relations. Provisions made to meet the educational needs of individuals who are beyond college age can also invite good will.

Finally, the extent and caliber of community services can serve as a powerful medium to reinforce the public information services.

Community Services[21]

The extent to which the new college will be able to serve its total community determines whether or not it deserves to be called a community college. Too many community colleges are *in* the community but not *of* the community. The other functions of the community college, namely, preparing students for advanced study (transfer), providing occupational education (terminal), general education, and guidance and counseling are all important responsibilities, but they do not qualify an institution to be designated as a community college. Its community services function admits the institution to the select group of colleges known as community colleges.

The community college is uniquely qualified to offer a wide variety of services to its community. The following characteristics support the above contention:

1. The community college is a community-centered institution with the primary purpose of providing service to the people of its community. Its offerings and programs are planned to meet the needs of the community and are developed with the active participation of citizens.
2. The community college claims community service as one of its major functions. . . .

[20] Ibid., p. 50
[21] In addition to the footnoted direct quotations, many of the ideas in this section on "Community Services" have been adapted from Ervin L. Harlacher, *The Community Dimensions of the Community College* (Englewood Cliffs, N.J.: Prentice-Hall, Inc., 1969), pp. 19-34. By permission of the publisher.

3. Since the community college is usually a creature of citizens of the local community or area, and since it is most frequently governed by a board of local citizens, the community college is readily capable of responding to changing community needs.
4. Most community colleges are operated by a local district which encompasses several separate and distinct communities. . . .
5. The community college is an institution of higher education, and as such can draw upon the advanced resources of its staff in assisting in the solution of the problems of an increasingly complex society.
6. The community college, as a relatively new segment of American education, is "unencrusted with tradition, not hidebound by a rigid history, and in many cases, new and eager for adventure." Thus, it is able, without duplicating existing services in the community, to tailor its program to meet local needs and conditions.[22]

Although the community college made great strides in the 60s in meeting its obligation to the community, it will become an even more dynamic force in affecting the lives of the residents in the college community during the 70s. There has, however, been some confusion concerning what actually constitutes the community services aspects of the new college. In his recent book on the subject Harlacher defines them in the following manner:

> . . . community services are educational, cultural, recreational services which an educational institution may provide for its community in addition to its regularly scheduled day and evening classes.[23]

The first step to insure intelligent planning for the community services in the new college is to make a cooperative community survey involving college officials and citizens of the college community. The purpose of this survey is to determine the areas of greatest need. The college should not duplicate services already being offered in a satisfactory manner by other agencies in the community.

As a second step, it is recommended that objectives be formulated for the community services program. As an end product of a survey of related literature, the results of a nationwide study, and another investigation of sixty-five community college districts operating 104 campuses in nineteen states, four major objectives of community services were identified. They are offered here as a guide to planners of these services.

1. To become a center of community life by encouraging the use of college facilities and services by community groups when such use does not interfere with the college's regular schedule.
2. To provide for all age groups educational services that utilize the special

[22]Ervin L. Harlacher, "New Directions in Community Services," *Junior College Journal,* 38, No. 6 (1968), 13-14.
[23]Harlacher, *Community Dimension of the Community College,* p. 12.

skills and knowledge of the college staff and other experts and are designed to meet the needs of community groups and the college district at large.

3. To provide the community, including business and industry, with the leadership and coordination capabilities of the college, assist the community in long-range planning, and join with individuals and groups in attacking unsolved problems.

4. To contribute to and promote the cultural, intellectual, and social life of the college district community and the development of skills for the profitable use of leisure time.[24]

It can be noted from the above definition and objectives of community services that they are the services that the college performs in addition to the regularly scheduled classes, evening as well as day.

What are the kinds of activities the new college should plan to engage in and what relationships must it establish with the community in order to meet each of the four objectives enumerated above?

Use of College Facilities and Services

Included under the first objective area of the program of community services are the use of the college physical plant and services, cosponsorship of community cultural and recreational programs, community use of library facilities, and campus tours.

Most communities need a center to serve as a gathering place for many community functions. In some communities the public school buildings partly fulfill this need, but in areas served by community colleges they can discharge their most useful function by serving as a center for community activities and events.

The new college must decide what community services it will offer to meet the first objective before the college physical facilities are planned. The educational specifications must clearly indicate the areas of the buildings and college site that are to be utilized by the entire community.

One very tangible piece of evidence of the success of the community services program is the extent to which members of the community of all ages use the college facilities. The playing fields, courts, ice rinks, picnic grounds, nature trails, gymnasium(s), and swimming pool should ring and reverberate with the shouts and laughter of happy children, youth, and adults from the college community whenever these facilities are not required for the regularly scheduled classes and events of the college.

Under the same conditions, the auditorium, little theater, outdoor theater, music rooms, conference rooms, cafeteria, and other spaces should be made available for use by community organizations for a great variety of educational

[24] Ibid., p. 19.

activities such as meetings, institutes and conferences, lectures, forums, concerts, films, dramatic productions, exhibits, and dinners.

Some of the events and activities suggested above will be jointly sponsored by the college and the community. Under these circumstances it is usually customary to waive charges for the use of the college facilities and services.

If the new college decides to open the library for use by citizens of the college community, it must be carefully planned to serve its dual purpose. A direct entrance can make the facility more accessible to the community.

Campus tours also are included under the first objective. Tours acquaint the community with the college campus. They begin during the dedication open-house ceremonies and continue throughout the life of the college. Some colleges have special attractions such as farms, arboretums, and museums.

Educational Services to the Community

Under the second objective planners of community services must provide for noncredit courses of short duration, seminars, workshops, in-service training, college credit extension courses, community counseling and consultation, human resource development training, special radio and television programs, and use of college staff and students as speakers, performers, and assistants on civic projects and community development.

Education is now recognized as a continuous process from the cradle to the grave. Post-secondary education is no longer the prerogative of youth alone, nor is the educational program of the community college confined to formal instruction in the classroom. The services rendered to the community under the second objective are designed to meet the needs of all age groups on the campus and also out in the college community. The new college must plan to reach out to: professionals as well as to those in search of a profession; executives, and individuals desiring to fill this role; the disadvantaged who have been denied opportunities for higher education; housewives and husbands; children and high school youth alike.

Noncredit short courses must consist of a great variety of workshops, symposia, institutes, seminars, conferences, and special demonstrations and lectures designed specifically to meet the needs of various groups and individuals in the college community. These short noncredit courses range in length from one-day events to a series of meetings covering several weeks.

In order to bring the resources of the college within the reach of all who need its services, planners of community colleges will aggressively develop multiservice outreach programs according to one authority. He makes the following prediction:

> Through the use of extension centers, empty stores, portable units located on vacant land, mobile units, churches, schools, libraries, museums, art galleries, places of business and other community facilities,

the community college will establish communications links with all segments of the college district community, encouraging a free exchange of ideas and resources. The community college, stable yet unfettered by the permanence of buildings, will move in physical location in response to shifting needs.[25]

Inservice training both on and off the campus must be planned. With the tremendous increase in knowledge and the rapid development of new technology a continuous program of retraining is necessary in government, business, and industry. Planners of community services must expect their institutions to be the central agency for upgrading the personnel in these agencies and companies through both instruction and consultation.

To meet the counseling and consultation facet of the second objective the new college must plan to offer educational and vocational guidance and counseling services for individuals in the college community who have not had access to these services as day or evening students. This service will be concerned particularly with retraining and dropout problems of the community. Services that should be provided are individual and group counseling and guidance, periodic occupational conferences, a broad testing program, guidance publications, and in-plant consultation, counseling, and testing.

Under the heading of human resource development the community college should plan for: retraining programs; basic education programs for the functionally illiterate; short-term occupational and basic skills programs for disadvantaged persons; and special programs due to the increased leisure of senior citizens and others. Many of the federally financed programs for the disadvantaged also belong in this category.

If the new community college plans include an educational FM radio and/or television station, these could be used for special programming for public events to be held on the college campus, community development, and self-improvement. The stations also may be utilized for television teaching. If radio and television stations are not part of the campus proper, local educational radio and television outlets can be utilized.

Community Development

The third objective, community development, may be thought of as the college and its community uniting their resources to attack unsolved problems. The knowledge and skills possessed by the college staff are made available to assist the citizens in making important decisions about local affairs.

The services to be rendered by the college include advisory assistance; research and planning; surveys, polls, and studies; conferences, institutes, and workshops; and participation in the organization and coordination of community councils and other required community agencies and groups. This is the

[25]Harlacher, "New Directions in Community Services," p. 14.

area of community services in which the two-year college has its best opportunity to integrate with the community.

Community development has been one of the most neglected areas of community services. Therefore, the planners of community colleges would be wise to place it high on their list of priorities.

Cultural and Recreational Activities

The fourth objective goes hand in hand with the first one. Many of these activities are experiences by the community through the use of college facilities and services. They include the arts, lectures, and film series; field trips and cultural tours; gallery programs; physical activities; festivals; community performing groups; and community science services.

The new two-year college can plan an important role in the cultural development of its community and region. It has the implicit obligation to lift the level of living in its community by raising the standards of recreation and entertainment. Particularly a community survey to ascertain its needs is crucial in respect to this area of community services. Before cultural and recreational activities are planned, it is of vital importance that the new college identify the services that are already available in the community in order to avoid unnecessary duplication.

Leadership for Community Services

A program of community services as comprehensive as the one sketched in this section requires the full-time leadership of an individual on the same academic level as the other deans. Colleges that have tried to combine this position with that of director of the evening school program have not been able to offer the variety of services found in colleges with full-time deans of community services.

If the new college is unable for financial reasons to engage a full-time staff member to provide leadership in the community services area, the responsibility can, during the early years of the college, be assigned to a staff member on a part-time basis. This, however, should be a temporary measure only and the position should become a full-time one as soon as possible.

Regardless of whether the position is full-time or part-time, a committee should be organized to work with the coordinator in order that there be college-wide participation in planning and program development. Representatives from the community should also be included on this committee.

Summary

Planning for all special programs and services should begin before the college opens. Decisions concerning special programs and services set the tone for the institution even more than the academic program. Decisions relative to admission, retention, placement, and follow-up determine whether or not institutions truly are open-door colleges fulfilling their declared purposes of bringing some form of higher and continuing education within the reach of all individuals who can benefit from it.

In order to meet this American dream, expert counseling and guidance services must be made available to all students, potential students, and the community at large. A staff of professional counselors must be selected, regular instructors must be used in counseling, and counselor aides must be trained and utilized.

Good health services also should be provided in the new community college. Too frequently, they have been neglected to the detriment of the student body. The board of trustees and the administration need to be convinced of the importance of this phase of student affairs services.

Planners of health services must make decisions concerning eligibility, physical examinations, health records, relationships to other student affairs services and to community agencies, staffing, extent of responsibility for a safe and healthful college environment and for health instruction, first-aid procedures, and ways to finance the health services.

Planners of community colleges should make a serious study of the role of students in governance and the kinds of experiences that should be made available in the activity or cocurricular program. Future students and faculty members should be involved in seeking solutions to these important problems. Parents should also be consulted. Whatever form the student governance organization takes, opportunities must be provided for the students to play an active part in the governance of the new college. The period when students were satisfied to role play student government is past. They now must experience the real thing.

Communication lines between the administration and the student body must be kept open, so there must be some mechanism for airing students' complaints. In some institutions the office of student ombudsman has effectively performed this function.

The cocurricular program also must be carefully scrutinized and studied. Crucial decisions must be made concerning the balance of intercollegiate athletics and other sports and activities.

A well-written students' handbook can also prove to be an asset in student affairs services. However, students should participate in determining its contents.

A continuous program of institutional research must be planned if the new college hopes to meet the intellectual, physical, social, and emotional needs of all individuals it serves. Community colleges are so new, their programs so varied, and their characteristics so unique that many issues and problems need to be studied continuously if improvements are to be made. No aspect of the community college movement is sacred; all areas should be open to investigation.

New community colleges should carefully plan their public information services. Many of the causes of campus unrest and lack of community support may be attributed to a lack of communication. The responsibility for keeping communication channels open should be shared by the administration, faculty, and students. Parents also can play an important role.

The job of the public information office includes preparing news releases for the press, radio, and television, and liaison with their representatives; writing a college newsletter; coordinating college publications; preparing the college annual report; writing and distributing board proceedings; responding to selected presidential correspondence and preparing reports; and developing long-range institutional public relations programs.

In respect to his status, the public information officer should serve in the president's cabinet, report directly to him, have a twelve-month contract, and hold administrative rank.

To truly fulfill the role of a community college, the new institution must be community oriented. The two-year college is uniquely qualified to provide its community with a wide variety of services.

The planning of community services requires a cooperative community survey to determine the areas of greatest need, and to insure that the college will not duplicate services already being offered by other agencies.

Planners should next formulate objectives for the community-services program. Services resulting from the objectives usually fall into the following categories:

1. Community use of college facilities and services.
2. Educational services to the community.
3. Community development.
4. Cultural and recreational activities.

Although it may not be feasible in the initial years of the community college, plans should be made to designate the leaders of these special programs and services as full-time positions with ranks corresponding to that held by the academic dean. The services and programs deserving this status are student affairs; institutional research, planning, and information systems; public information services; and community services.

Suggested Activities and Problems

1. Examine the admission, retention, placement, and follow-up policies of three community colleges. Write a paper relating the information gathered to the *open-door* concept.
2. After reading widely on the topic, write up a plan for ideal counseling and guidance services in a community college.

3. Interview the person responsible for health services in a community college to determine the major problems he must solve in order to maintain adequate health services. Make recommendations for improving these services.

4. Prepare a questionnaire covering the topic of participation of students in community college governance. Secure responses from a minimum of twenty-five students in a community college. Analyze their responses and write a paper comparing your findings with an ideal situation.

5. Examine the literature on institutional research in community colleges and make recommendations for improving the situation.

6. Interview the public information officer of a community college to determine his status and job. Write a paper comparing what you learned in the interview with the ideas in this text.

7. Contact two community colleges and ascertain the extent of their community services in each of the four categories discussed above.

Selected Readings

Collins, Charles C., *Junior College Student Personnel Programs: What They Are and What They Should Be.* Washington, D.C.: American Association of Junior Colleges, 1967.

Deegan, William L., "Student Participation in Governance," *Junior College Journal,* 41, No. 3 (1970), 15.

DuBois, E. E. and R. J. Frankie, "Community Colleges must Invest in Public Relations Professional to Improve Faculty Image," *College and University Journal,* 10 (March, 1971), 28.

Fitzgerald, Laurine E., Walter F. Johnson, and Willa Norris, eds., *College Student Personnel: Readings and Bibliographies.* Boston: Houghton Mifflin Company, 1969.

Gleazer, Edmund J., Jr., *This Is the Community College,* chaps. 3, 4, and 5. Boston: Houghton Mifflin Company, 1968.

Harlacher, Ervin L., *The Community Dimension of the Community College.* Englewood Cliffs, N.J.: Prentice-Hall, Inc., 1969.

Ivey, A. G., "Information Office Revisited," *College and University Journal,* 8 (Fall, 1969), 27.

Johnson, Dorothy and Mary Vestermark, *Barriers and Hazards in the Counseling Process.* Boston: Houghton Mifflin Company, 1970.

McDaniel, J.W., *Essential Student Personnel Practices for Junior Colleges.* Washington, D.C.: Student Personnel Commission, American Association of Junior Colleges, 1962.

Recommended Standards and Practices for a College Health Program. Evanston, Ill.: American College Health Association, 1964.

Roueche, John E., and John R. Boggs, *Junior College Institutional Research: The State of the Art.* Washington, D.C.: American Association of Junior Colleges, 1968.

Shaffer, Robert H. and William D. Martinson, *Student Personnel Services in Higher Education.* New York: Center for Applied Research, 1966.

Thornton, James W., Jr., *The Community Junior College,* 2nd ed., chap. 17. New York: John Wiley & Sons, Inc., 1966.

Wilkinson, R. D., "Community Relations for Special Programs in Higher Education," *School and Society,* 99, (March, 1971), 70.

Woody, R. H., "Counseling and Health Education" (Bibliography), *Journal of School Health,* 41 (January, 1971), 3.

14
Getting
the Community College
Accredited

Much has been heard in recent years about the need for quality education. The loudest hue and cry went up immediately after the launching of Sputnik by the Russians because we believed that their technology had surpassed ours. The new battle cry is accountability. Both of the above concepts imply that evaluation and appraisal are necessary in educational institutions.

It is interesting to note that this is not by far a new idea in education. Although measurement and quality control are rather recent phenomena in business and industry, educational institutions in the United States have utilized accreditation as a quality control mechanism for approximately half a century.

At first, high schools, four-year colleges, and universities were the only institutions evaluated by accrediting commissions. Now, with the tremendous growth in the number of community colleges, they have joined the ranks. In fact, of all the institutions desiring to be accredited, the community college probably has the most at stake. This is partly due to the fact that in the minds of too many staff members, students, and laymen the community college is considered an institution that is inferior to the four-year college and the university. In their opinion, a high rating by an evaluation committee and subsequent accreditation by the regional commission on higher education serves as a great prestige builder.

One of the important tasks of planners of community colleges, therefore, is to obtain accreditation for the new institution as early as possible. The purpose of this chapter is threefold: (1) to briefly describe the steps that must be taken to apply for and secure accreditation, (2) to assist community colleges to prepare for accreditation, and (3) to make suggestions that will enable the institution to derive the greatest benefits from all phases of the accreditation process. Suggestions will be included concerning what to do about the accreditation report. As background for the above discussion, one very pertinent research project involved in basic assumptions about accreditation will be presented and discussed.

Basic Concepts and Assumptions
about Accreditation

The stated purpose of accreditation is to insure some form of quality control of the services and educational program in the institution that is applying for accreditation. When the name of a community college appears on the accreditation list, the assumption is made that all institutions on the list have met the *minimum* quality requirements. Some persons interpret this as meaning that all colleges on the list are equally good. Those who have been members of visitation committees know that this is not true. They are aware that there are wide variations among institutions on the list.

As educators gained experience with the accreditation process, certain assumptions have been made about it in respect to procedures to be utilized and concerning the value of the experience as a method of improving educational institutions. A number of these assumptions gleaned from the aforementioned research project will be listed here; then throughout the discussion in the remainder of the chapter, suggestions will be made to assist institutions in realizing the benefits implied in the assumptions.

Assumptions concerning Accreditation

In a doctoral study at the University of California, Collins searched the literature for assumptions concerning the accreditation process. He then attempted to test these assumptions by interviewing seventy-two staff members and board members in seven community colleges that had gone through the accreditation process. Each of the assumptions follow, with Collins's findings:

1. *Accreditation requires an institution to make a comprehensive self-study that is an examination in depth into the qualitative aspects of the services and educational program.* Individuals interviewed did not perceive accreditation as an examination in depth into the qualitative aspects of their college.
2. *There should be total involvement of the staff in the self-evaluation.* In the institutions studied there was no total staff involvement. The least involvement was at the department chairman and instructor levels.
3. *Participation in the self-evaluation is a valuable professional growth*

experience for staff members. Individuals interviewed felt that preparation for accreditation is a process rather than an event. There was almost unanimous agreement among the seventy-two participants that their colleges were engaged in a never-ending process of self-evaluation and that formal preparation for accreditation and reaccreditation was of questioned value.

4. *Self-evaluation procedures result in improvement in services and in the educational program.* When questioned concerning educational improvements, respondents agreed only on the point that new avenues of intrastaff communication were created.

5. *Accreditation gives status to an educational institution.* The participants interviewed strongly confirmed this claim.

6. *Accreditation should be viewed as a system of quality control.* The respondents at all ranks confirmed this assumption.

7. *Although accreditation sets minimum standards, it does not encourage conformity.* Respondents viewed accreditation as an upgrading influence that does not force colleges into the bonds of conformity.

8. *Voluntary accreditation by a regional agency is preferable to compulsory evaluation by some governmental agency.* Respondents strongly supported this assumption.

9. *Members of accreditation teams are assumed to be competent to conduct the evaluation.* Respondents did not view these teams as an entity, but rather as a collection of representatives from various levels of higher education. In general, the team visit was viewed as important, but the claim that accreditation teams are composed of competent evaluators was only partly confirmed.

10. *Members of accreditation teams are frequently treated as consultants.* Respondents did not support this claim.

11. *Members of accreditation teams objectively evaluate the quality of an institution during the visitation.* All respondents categorically denied this claim. However, there was almost universal feeling that subjective judgment is used by accreditation teams and that this is a valid means of appraising quality.

12. *Evaluation by a team of individuals from outside the institution to be accredited is a valuable experience for the local staff.* Respondents felt that this was a valuable experience. There was strong sentiment in favor of the contacts made with experienced educators from outside.

13. *The oral report of the team chairman is a valuable experience for the staff.* Respondents attached great significance to this report. In most cases this oral appraisal had greater impact on staff members than the evaluation report that follows months later.

14. *Evaluation reports are given wide circulation internally and externally and*

meaningful use is made of the findings and recommendations in the report. Respondents supported the first part of the claim, but only partially supported the claim that meaningful use was made of the document.

15. *The evaluation report can be used to convince the administration and board of trustees of needed changes.* Respondents only partially confirmed this claim.

16. *Accreditation is a powerful force in improving the quality of services and the educational program.* Most of the respondents did not view the evaluation report as a motivating force that might bring about change.[1]

The findings of Collins' research indicate that all the assumptions were not supported by the respondents in the seven community colleges he studied. This does not mean that the situation cannot be improved if that seems desirable. Individuals responsible for the accreditation process should work with the staff to determine objectives to be achieved by the accreditation procedures, and the means by which they may be achieved should be clearly spelled out.

Procedures Leading to
Accreditation

The United States has been divided into six regions for the purpose of accreditation of secondary schools, colleges, and universities. Community colleges are usually under the direct supervision of a commission of higher education. Much of the material in this chapter is drawn from publications of the Middle States Association of Colleges and Secondary Schools. In addition to the six regional associations there are special accrediting groups as, for example, the National Association of Colleges of Teacher Education (NACTE) and specialized professional accrediting agencies for two-year college programs in areas such as allied health and engineering. State departments of education also accredit specific programs and license colleges for operation.

Because they are multipurpose institutions, community colleges are usually faced with a number of special accreditations. The Carnegie Commission would like this to be changed and gives the following rationale for its recommendation:

> Two-year colleges are accredited, along with other institutions of higher education, on a general institutional basis by the various regional accrediting bodies and on a specialized basis for particular programs by professional associations or specialized accrediting agencies. Although this dual basis of accreditation is generally considered valuable in higher education, it has created problems for the two-year colleges, with their

[1]John J. Collins, "Accreditation—Aims and Perceptions," *Junior College Journal*, 38, No. 4 (1969), 19.

specialized vocational and technical training programs. Thus far only five professions—medicine, dentistry, nursing, engineering, and music—have specialized accrediting agencies for two-year college programs, but the American Association of Junior Colleges is apprehensive about the probable increase in such specialized accrediting agencies with the proliferation of technical and vocational specialties. Such a trend would greatly increase the complexity of the accreditation process and the costs associated with accreditation for the institutions.

The Carnegie Commission believes that although a contribution is made by the specialized accrediting agencies for two-year college programs, this contribution should be made on the basis of cooperation between the relevant professional organizations and the regional accrediting bodies.

The Carnegie Commission recommends a single program of institutional accreditation for two-year colleges and the elimination of accreditation of specialties. The contribution of professional associations in the evaluation of specialized programs should be made through cooperation with the regional accrediting bodies.[2]

These multiple accreditations create problems for community colleges and require special attention, depending on the specific programs offered by an institution. The discussion in this chapter will be limited to the process of accreditation by the regional commission.

Doubtless there are differences in accreditation procedures among the six regional associations in our nation; however, these groups have been coordinating their efforts, procedures, and terminology in recent years. The procedures used by the Middle States Association will be described here as typical. Each community college will of course follow the procedures of the association in its own area.

Accreditation

In a recent document the association describes itself and the work of the Commission on Higher Education as follows:

The Middle States Association is an independent organization of non-profit educational institutions admitted to membership through a process of evaluation and accreditation. ACCREDITATION is an expression of confidence in an institution's actual present performance and in its long-range ability to maintain and improve that performance. The Commission on Higher Education, through which the Association conducts all its work with institutions above the secondary level, publishes descriptions of good practice from time to time but prescribes no quantitative standards. It does not classify its members into

[2] The Carnegie Commission on Higher Education, *The Open-Door Colleges—Policies for Community Colleges* (New York: McGraw-Hill Book Company, 1970), p. 49.

categories. It evaluates each applicant for membership in qualitative terms in the light of that institution's own reasons for existence. Accreditation indicates that in the Commission's judgment an institution has clearly defined and appropriate objectives, has established conditions under which it can reasonably be expected to attain them, appears in fact to be attaining them in substantial measure, and should be able to continue to do so. The Commission seeks to serve the academic community and the public by establishing standards of quality and identifying institutions which achieve them.

Non-profit institutions of higher education in the Middle States region may request appropriate status as described below if they offer two or more years of undergraduate or one year of graduate studies leading to degrees, diplomas, or certificates issued under proper legal authority. At least one principal program should rest upon a base of liberal studies required of all or most students. Before it will be evaluated, an institution must have graduated students who have completed their full programs at the institution.

Eligibility for Consideration for Accreditation

To be eligible for consideration for accreditation an institution should have a charter and/or formal authority from an appropriate governmental agency to award a certificate or associate or higher degree; be a non-profit organization with a governing board representing the public interest; ordinarily offer at least two years of higher education at the undergraduate level or at least one year at the graduate level; have been in existence long enough to have graduated at least one class; require for admission the completion of not less than an appropriate secondary school curriculum or satisfactory evidence of equivalent educational achievement; have its principal educational programs based upon a core of liberal studies required of all or most students.

The Accrediting Process

The steps leading to an institution's first accreditation and membership in the Middle States Association include the following stages:

(1)   *Correspondent   and/or   Recognized   Candidate   for   Accreditation* —depending on its stage of development, an institution may be required to begin as a Correspondent or may be accepted directly as a Recognized Candidate for Accreditation, (2) *Appraisal of Readiness for Evaluation,* (3) *Evaluation,* and (4) *Membership* in the Middle States Association, which follows automatically when accreditation is attained.[3]

The same source describes the first two steps in the following manner:

[3] Commission on Higher Education, *Policies and Procedures Handbook* (New York: Middle States Association of Colleges and Secondary Schools, 1971), p. 15.

Correspondent Status

An institution will find it advantageous to enter CORRESPONDENT status as early as feasible and may do so even before it opens to students. The opportunities and responsibilities of Correspondent status are described below. When accorded by the Commission,

> *Correspondent status attests that an institution has given evidence of sound planning and of having the resources to implement its plans, has indicated its intent to work toward accreditation, and appears to have the potential for attaining this goal. Correspondent status does not imply or assure eventual accreditation.*

Institutions which have been in operation a number of years may choose to omit this step in the accreditation process, going directly to Recognized Candidacy at the discretion of the Commission.

Recognized Candidate Status

An institution in Correspondent status is eligible to become a RECOGNIZED CANDIDATE FOR ACCREDITATION only after at least one year of operation with students in attendance. Recognized Candidacy is an important step in the accreditation process, and it is particularly advantageous to an institution undertaking a comprehensive self-study.

> *Acceptance as a Recognized Candidate for Middle States accreditation attests that the Commission on Higher Education considers an institution to be offering its students, on at least a minimally satisfactory level, the educational opportunities implied by its objectives. In the Commission's view the institution's organization, structure, and staffing are acceptable for its stage of development, its sponsors are committed to supplying its needs and are able to do so, its governing board is functioning properly, and its academic and financial plans are well designed.*[4]

General Criteria

Each regional group has prepared a set of General Criteria covering all phases of the educational program and services offered by the college. The General Criteria headings are as follows:

1. Objectives.
2. Program.
3. Faculty.
4. Library or Learning Center.
5. Students

4 Ibid., p. 17.

6. Student Personnel Services.
7. Plant and Equipment.
8. Finance and Accounting.
9. Administration
10. Governing Board.
11. Evaluation of Results.
12. Innovation and Experimentation.[5]

Although the document includes a series of questions under each category, "... the institution is encouraged to develop a freely-designed narrative report to fit its own needs, including the necessary factual data in the most effective and readable manner."[6]

The Self-Study

Community colleges become eligible for a visit from an evaluation team after they graduate their first class. This would suggest that the self-study could take place as early as the second year of operation, and the evaluation team visit could be scheduled for the third year the college is functioning. However, some institutions may decide to proceed more deliberately, and this is their prerogative.

During the period of self-study, the administration and faculty make an evaluation based on the self-study guide supplied by the Association. Later the self-evaluation is utilized by the evaluation team in making their determinations.

Nature of an Institutional Self-Study. The essential purpose of a self-study is to determine what the institution is attempting to do and whether or not it has the necessary program and resources to accomplish its purposes in a satisfactory manner. The Commission spells out the essential nature of a self-study as follows:

1. What are this institution's *objectives* and what obligations does it have?
2. Are the *objectives appropriate*? Now? Here? For its constituency?
3. Are all the *institution's activities* consistent with its objectives?
4. Are the programs and activities *designed to achieve the objectives?*
5. Are the *resources available* to carry out the programs? Will they continue to be available?
6. Is there reason to believe the *objectives* are being achieved? What is the evidence?[7]

[5] Ibid., pp. 62-70.
[6] Ibid., p. 27.
[7] Commission on Higher Education, *Institutional Self-Study Handbook* (New York: Middle States Association of Colleges and Secondary Schools, 1971), p. 12.

Budgeting for the Accreditation

Although it is only a small item in the total budget, a separate appropriation should be made for this important activity. The college is responsible for all the legitimate expenses of the accreditation. Publications must be purchased and the college pays for travel, meals, and lodging for the accreditation team. Team members in some regions receive remuneration; if so, this is specified by the association. Social activities also inflate the budget. For example, will the entire faculty or a part of the staff be invited to the initial dinner? Funds must be provided for activities such as retreats during the self-evaluation if any are planned.

Organizing for Self-Study. Although staff members usually are anxious to work in a community college that is accredited, they are not always willing to participate in a self-evaluation study. As staff members in a new institution, they have from the first day on the job, been developing a philosophy, writing behavioral objectives, developing a curriculum, and contributing to the writing of educational specifications for the new campus. It is easy to understand why they might not want to go immediately over the same ground again.

One possible way of resolving the above dilemma is to secure copies of the *Institutional Self-Study Handbook* in the initial stages of planning and building the community college. If the *Self-Study Handbook* is utilized from the beginning as a guide for the planning and development of each facet of the new college, it will be a relatively simple matter to write the committee reports during the actual self-evaluation process. If this procedure is followed, it might be possible to complete the self-evaluation during the second and third years the college is in operation and, hopefully, schedule the visitation team for the second semester of the third year or at the latest the first semester of the fourth year of operation.

Whether it is planned in the above manner or new committees are selected to begin from scratch, it is important that a small steering committee composed of interested and dedicated persons and chaired by a competent person be appointed to coordinate the entire self-evaluation. Ideally, the dean of academic affairs should assume the chairmanship of the steering committee. Some community colleges will have an assistant to the president or an assistant dean who could assume this very important role.

Early in the self-evaluation procedure one of the executive secretaries from the Commission on Higher Education should be invited to meet with the steering committee to assist the members in planning the evaluation enterprise.

When the area committees are finally organized, it is important to provide good leadership for them. Community colleges making their first self-study may desire to have two kinds of committees. The one type includes the broad areas other than "Program" listed earlier in this chapter. The other type of committee includes those concerned with subject and program areas. However, the institution usually has great flexibility in designing all aspects of the self-study, including committee structure.

The membership on the first type of committee should consist of persons who have expressed interest in the area to be evaluated and who have some competence in the area. A frequently used procedure is to provide the entire faculty with the opportunity to become acquainted with the *Institutional Self-Study Handbook* and the procedures to be utilized by the local college in conducting the self-study. The faculty is then asked to make three choices of committees in order of priority on which they would be willing to serve.

The personnel on the subject and program area committees will consist of the faculty members who belong in each of the departments or divisions being studied, and others to provide interdisciplinary dialogue.

To the extent possible, members of the board of trustees should be involved in the self-evaluation. The better the trustees understand the strengths and

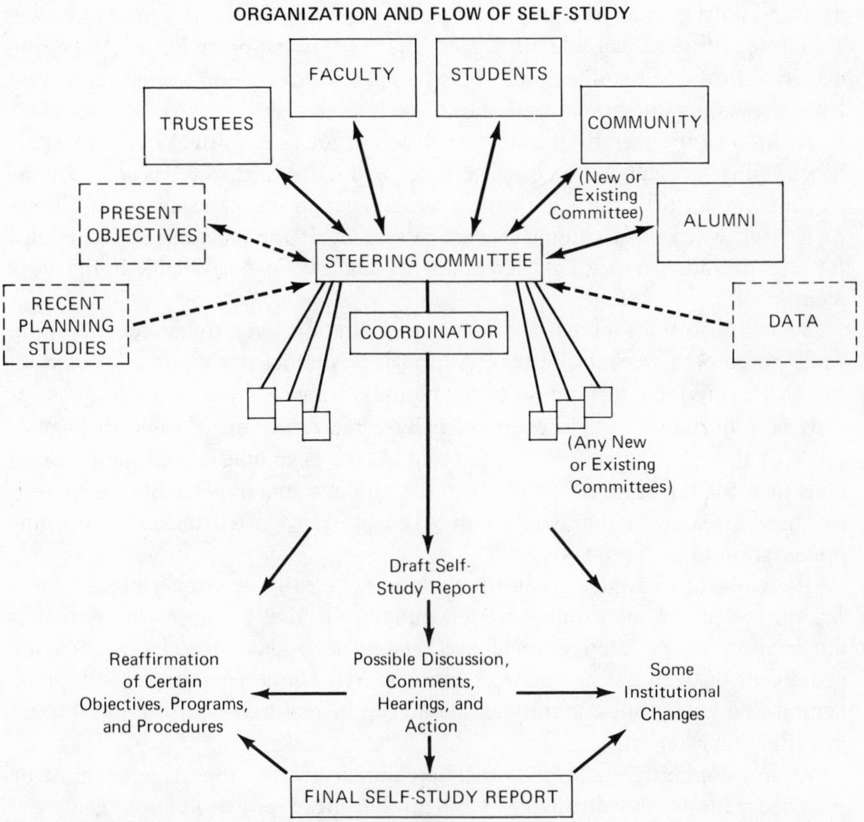

ORGANIZATION AND FLOW OF SELF-STUDY

Figure 14-1. Adapted by permission from Commission on Higher Education, *Policies and Procedures Handbook* (New York: Middle States Association of Colleges and Secondary Schools, 1971), p. 30.

weaknesses of the college, the more likely they want to find solutions to existing problems, and to provide the necessary resources.

The wise community college administrator will make certain that there is student representation on each area committee. With the addition of the twenty-sixth amendment to our constitution, it no longer may be said that eighteen- to twenty-year-olds are not competent to make important decisions. Representation from the alumni also should be included if the self-study is made after the first class has graduated.

It is a smart move as well to have some lay representation on area committees. Not only do laymen have something to contribute, but their representation is a good public relations procedure as well.

Figure 14-1 represents one plan of organization and flow of the self-study that can be adapted to the needs of any institution.

Conducting the Self-Study. Community college personnel are busy people. This certainly is true in a new institution preparing for its first accreditation. Therefore, it seems sensible to suggest that, whenever possible, meetings connected with the self-study should be scheduled in advance on a semester or year basis, depending upon the duration of the self study.

As soon as the membership on the different area committees has been established, a master schedule of meeting times and dates might be drawn up by the steering committee. There are certain advantages to setting aside specific times each week when most committees are in session. If the meetings are scheduled for late afternoon hours, light refreshments might be made available in the work areas.

Some institutions preparing for an accreditation have found the necessary funds to go on a weekend retreat. Although it is rather strenuous, a lot of work can be accomplished in a concentrated period of time.

It is important to get a good start. By whatever means possible the significance of the self-study should be stressed. At the beginning is the time to set up objectives for the study in addition to the ultimate goal of accreditation. This is the time to examine the assumptions. The president often makes an opening presentation to the entire staff.

The work of each area committee consists of clearly describing strengths and weaknesses of the area that is under study, collecting the necessary statistical information to be used as evidence, and making recommendations for improvement. Questions in the *Institutional Self-Study Handbook* will prove helpful as a guide, but committees should not be required to utilize that format in writing their report.

As area committees complete their preliminary work, opportunities must be provided periodically for them to report to the entire local evaluation team or at least to the steering committee so that their suggestions and reactions may be obtained. Committee reports are then revised as a result of the help received from the larger group. After that, the college is ready for the Appraisal of Readiness for Evaluation.

Community colleges must be reaccredited periodically. It would be wise for the college at the close of its first self-study to evaluate the committee organization and procedures used and write any recommendations that might assist future self-study committees to do a better job.

Getting the Most Out of the Self-Study. The first four assumptions presented earlier in this chapter (pp. 247-48) are concerned with the self-evaluation procedure. Assumption 1 indicated that accreditation required ". . . an examination in depth into the qualitative aspects of the services and educational program." If the committees for self-study are carefully organized and the procedures suggested above are followed, the first assumption would be supported.

Assumption 2 is concerned with total staff involvement in the self-evaluation. This was recommended in an earlier discussion and student and lay participation was suggested.

Assumption 3 indicated that self-study has valuable professional growth potential. If this is to be realized, specific behavioral objectives should be formulated and questions similar to the following raised. What desirable behavioral changes may be expected in staff members as a result of the self-evaluation experience? What steps must be taken to insure that the greatest number of changes will take place? Are certain self-study techniques more effective in producing professional growth than others?

It should be evident from the above discussion that if professional growth is to occur as a result of a self-evaluation, it must be planned for from the beginning. Nothing as important as professional growth should be taken for granted or left to chance.

Assumption 4 is a natural outgrowth of number 3. If staff members grow professionally, there is a greater potential for improvement of services and the educational program. These changes in the services and educational program must be planned for too or they probably will not take place. During the self-study, weaknesses in the services and educational program are discovered and recommendations for improvement are made. The next step is to plan procedures for carrying out the recommendations, and the final step is to make the improvements required to correct the deficiencies. Unfortunately, too many colleges don't follow up the last two steps.

The remaining assumptions deal with aspects of the accreditation process other than the self-study. Where appropriate in relation to the particular topic, they will be discussed in other sections of this chapter.

The Appraisal of Readiness[8]

The appraisal of readiness for evaluation is a last-minute checkup by experienced outsiders to determine whether or not the college is really ready for the evaluation team. The date for visitation by the evaluation team is only

[8] Adapted from *Policies Handbook*, p. 31.

tentative until the appraiser's report has been received by the president of the community college.

The appraisal of readiness is actually a consultative service performed by two individuals during a one-day visit to the campus of the college seeking accreditation. The report made directly to the college assists its officers to determine whether to continue with the total evaluation. This enables the institution to try for accreditation at the earliest opportunity by taking away some of the risk, although it does not guarantee that accreditation will quickly follow. On the other hand, an unfavorable appraisal report does not place the accreditation in jeopardy but merely indicates that additional preparation is advisable.

An oral appraisal report is made to the president of the college before the appraisers leave. A written report is received shortly afterwards. The executive staff of the Commission on Higher Education also receives a written copy of the report, so it can assist the college plan the next step. Under normal circumstances, the visit of the evaluation team follows the appraisal report in approximately eight weeks to three months.

The Evaluation Team and Its Work

The professionals who visit the college seeking accreditation are referred to in this text as the accreditation team, the evaluation team, or the visitation committee. The terms are used interchangeably and all refer to the same team.

Just like any other group of human beings, evaluation teams do vary in composition and in the competency of the individual members of the team. Some members may be serving for the first time; others may be veterans on the circuit. It should be remembered that individuals volunteer for service on evaluation teams and that the three- or four-day visit is strenuous. Committees often work far into the night and are on the job again bright and early next morning. They deserve the best facilities and resources that the host college can provide for them during their visit.

Scheduling the Visit. As mentioned earlier, it is not necessary to wait for the completion of the self-study before tentatively scheduling the visit of the accreditation team. Actually, it is desirable to schedule the visit as early as the commission will permit. The impending readiness appraisal and visit of the evaluation team can serve as a powerful incentive for completing a detailed work schedule for the self-study and for adhering to it. However, care must be taken that as the time approaches the pressure does not result in sloppy and superficial work by the local committees. This will only delay the evaluation because if the college is not given the green light in the readiness appraisal, a new date for the visitation by the evaluation team will have to be scheduled.

Depending upon the demand and the availability of personnel, there often is some latitude for the selection of the dates for the visit of the accreditation team. If the college is given an option, the most favorable dates and days of the week should be selected. This, naturally, will vary from college to college.

The accreditation team wants to observe as near normal a situation as is possible. Therefore, visitation dates just prior to or immediately after a vacation period may be less desirable. Examination time also is not a normal situation and should be avoided. Some colleges may prefer not to be visited at the opening of a semester before things have settled down and are running smoothly.

It will be remembered that Assumption 5 indicated that accreditation brings status to the college. It is generally agreed that this is true, so it may be important to the college to note the annual dates on which the regional commission acts to accredit institutions. A fall visitation might result in accreditation the following spring whereas a spring date could mean a delay of another year. The date on which the written report is made available also affects any improvements or changes that are to be made for or during the next year.

In respect to the best days of the week for the team to be present, local conditions too may determine these. In general, Fridays are undesirable. Frequently, the team arrives on Sunday afternoon and completes its work on the following Wednesday.

Selecting the Team. It is obvious that a community college applying for accreditation cannot expect to select the team that will make the evaluation. However, colleges can make requests for individuals with certain kinds of experience and competency to be included on the team.

In Collins' study reported earlier, respondents had great praise for most junior college representatives.[9] Consequently, it is not unreasonable to expect that some of the members of the team will have had experience in community junior colleges. It might be desirable to have one or more community college instructors on the evaluation team. Frequently, the teams are overloaded with administrative personnel.

Colleges usually are given the opportunity to remove names from the list sent to them prior to the visitation. Occasionally, the list will include the name of a person who might be considered either biased or prejudiced by authorities in the college to be accredited. They should not hesitate to request a replacement for somebody considered undesirable for these or other valid reasons. A request for replacements is not likely to be necessary very often because accrediting commissions try to match the teams carefully with the institutions being accredited. However, through lack of information, mistakes could occur. Certainly a person who lost his job when he worked in another institution with the president or dean of the college to be visited is less likely to be an objective evaluator. Names of close friends of administrative officials in the college also should be deleted, for obvious reasons.

According to the Commission on Higher Education, Middle States Association of Colleges and Secondary Schools:

> Teams are composed of six or more carefully chosen professional educators who are currently active members of the faculties and staffs of

[9]Collins, "Accreditation," p. 21.

member institutions, generally from other States than that of the host institutions, or even from regions other than the Middle States. A typical evaluation team would include: Chairman, Three (or more) Liberal Arts Members, Professional Field Experts, Librarian, Finance Officer, and One (or more) Members to address specific problems or interests of the institution.

In effect, each team is tailored to the specific nature and needs of an institution. . . .[10]

The chairman of the visitation committee plays a very important and influential role in the entire accreditation process. Prior to or during the visit he organizes the work schedule and makes area committee assignments. Throughout the visitation days, in his contacts with area committees and individuals, he leaves his imprint upon them. During the meetings of the total committee, he influences many of the decisions that are made. According to Assumption 13, his oral report at the close of the visitation frequently is taken more seriously than the final written report that he also prepares and influences by emphasis, addition, and omission. The better and more experienced the chairman, the more thorough and helpful the report will be. Therefore, the college may consider it desirable with good cause to reject the name or names submitted for the chairmanship—if this privilege is extended by the regional commission.

If the college is concerned with having the best possible accreditation team, makes suggestions, and exerts its veto power, members of accreditation teams will be more competent, and Assumption 9 will be supported.

Preparing for the Visit. The main preparation for the visit is the self-evaluation discussed earlier. Persons in charge of arrangements should be certain that there are enough copies of the self-evaluation report, with sufficient copies of any supporting materials available for the committee. It is usually better to provide more copies than have been requested. Maps of the campus and floor plans of the buildings help the committee members to locate areas they must visit and save them time.

The chairman of the accreditation team might be invited to the college to meet with the staff sometime prior to the date of visitation. If he accepts the invitation, he can explain to the staff the procedures that will be followed during the evaluation visit. Even though the college has been certified as being ready for the visit, he will desire to check on the final details of the visit. He also can become familiar with the plan of the campus, thus facilitating the actual visitation. Another advantage of this preliminary visit is that the chairman can observe the college in action in a more normal situation before the entire committee arrives.

The meeting with the staff gives them the opportunity to size up the

10 Commission on Higher Education, *Evaluation Team Members Handbook* (New York: Middle States Association of Colleges and Secondary Schools, 1971), p. 13.

chairman. Hopefully, he will be able to allay some of their fears concerning the visitation. (Note: The chairman and vice-chairman of the evaluation team are often sent by the commission to make the appraisal of readiness visit. This, of course, accomplishes the desirable outcomes stated above.)

If several members of the staff have previously served on an accreditation team while on the faculty of an accredited institution, they can act as resource persons for the accreditation of their new institution.

The physical accommodations provided for the evaluation team are important. The team should be housed in adequate quarters not too far from the college. Meals and lodging are not the items on which to skimp. A happy, satisfied committee does a more competent job.

At the college a room or suite of rooms should be made available to serve as headquarters for the committee. The room(s) should be furnished so that not only small groups can meet but also so that the entire visitation committee can be accommodated when necessary. Provisions should be made to keep the headquarters open until midnight.

Plans must be made in advance for serving meals to the committee. It is customary to provide lunch and dinner. Breakfast is taken at the hotel or motel where the team is staying. Frequently, the initial dinner is a big affair, with the board of trustees and representative college staff members attending.

In preparing the staff and student body for the visit of the accreditation team, it is important to emphasize that "business as usual" is the slogan. The accreditation team prefers to observe as normal a situation as possible under the circumstances. If a show is put on or any sprucing-up is done especially for the visit, the chairman of the committee and his experienced members will not be fooled. At this point in the process, the best advice is to carry on all the activities of the college in the usual manner.

The Visit. The final phase of the accreditation process consists of a three- or four-day visit to the college campus by a team of six or more experienced educators from accredited institutions, primarily from the association area. The team always includes at least some representatives from institutions similar to the one being visited. The task of the team is to verify and supplement through observation and inquiry the analysis made by the college in the self-study report, and to judge the college's performance and future potential in qualitative terms.

If the self-evaluation has been done efficiently and preparations carefully made for the visit of the evaluation team, things should run smoothly during the visit. As previously noted, the usual procedure is to begin the visit with a social hour and dinner the evening before the first visitation day. Board members and staff representatives have an opportunity here to meet and chat informally with the members of the accreditation team. Self-study committee chairmen are usually invited to this opening affair, as well as the key administrative officers of the college.

During the entire visit, administrative personnel and area committee chairmen should be on call in case the accreditation team needs information or an inter-pretation of the self-study report. Clerical service also must be readily available. If the campus is extensive, information centers, student guides, and transporta-tion should be provided.

Faculty members should understand that they will probably be visited by one or more team members as part of the accreditation procedure. The team must be supplied with schedules for all faculty members. Arrangements also have to be made for team members to interview special service personnel.

In the study by Collins the instructors and self-study chairmen valued greatly the opportunity to spend time informally with team members. They were convinced that much could be gained if more time was scheduled during the accreditation visit for faculty members to meet informally with members of the team.[11]

The accreditation team's schedule is crowded, but with the members' approval it should be possible to increase these informal contacts to a certain extent. An additional social hour might be scheduled before dinner on the first visitation day. Coffee breaks might be held each morning. Key faculty members might eat lunch with the team. This would be a topic that could be discussed with the chairman of the accreditation team during his earlier visit. If these informal contacts are perceived to be valuable, every reasonable effort should be made to provide them.

Opportunities also must abound for members of the accreditation team to meet both formally and informally with members of the student body. These students usually are picked at random by the team. The team will get the kinds of answers it requires if the entire student body has been impressed with the need to give honest answers and opinions.

The Oral Report. At the close of the visitation period, the chairman of the accreditation team makes an oral report on the findings of his team. Usually, it includes some general comments about the college and then a series of commendations and recommendations are given for each area studied by the accreditation team. The chairman also thanks the college at this time for its cooperation and hospitality. Earlier, it was mentioned that the oral report usually makes a big impression on the members of the staff. It would seem desirable, therefore, to arrange for the oral report to be given in a room in which a large number of persons can be accommodated. This would make it possible to include the board of trustees, faculty, administration, student representatives, and citizens from the community.

For an audience of this size, it would be advantageous to have the staff of the learning resources center prepare some visual aids. This expansion of the chairman's report is, of course, contingent on his willingness to speak to a larger audience. Some chairmen prefer to keep the atmosphere cozy and informal so

[11]Collins, "Accreditation," p. 22.

they can "speak off the cuff" at times. In any event, the chairman and the college president usually decide the composition and size of the group to hear the oral report.

If the chairman has no objections, his oral report might be recorded and the transcript of the tape used to obtain an early start in carrying out the recommendations.

In case the chairman intimates in the oral report that several areas are rather weak, the college should be certain that the weaknesses to be corrected are clearly understood. These areas should be tackled first in the improvement program.

Possible Higher Education Commission actions after a Middle States evaluation are, in simplified form:

1. Immediate accreditation . . . with no qualifications or requests for further reports.
2. Accreditation . . . with a request for later visits or progress reports, or both, on specified matters.
3. Deferment of decision for a year or two, to give a new institution time to mature . . . Progress reports, and usually visits also, are stipulated.
4. Critical action:
   a. For an institution seeking initial accreditation, denial. The way remains open to try again, under advisement, and there is no set time interval before another try.

Each member institution is required annually to update its description and data summary on file with the Commission. . . . The form of a re-evaluation depends upon circumstances, particularly upon the degree to which an institution makes habitual and skillful use of self-study techniques on its own accord. . . . The normal interval between reviews is ten years, unless a substantial change in the nature of the institution, question as to its educational effectiveness, or other serious reasons move the Commission on Higher Education to re-examine it earlier. *Initial accreditation is reviewed within five years.* [12]

The Final Written Report. The written report usually arrives several months after the evaluation team departs, depending upon the workload of the chairman and the accrediting commission that is responsible for the report. After receiving the report of the team visit from the chairman of the accreditation team, the commission compiles the final report. This report indicates accreditation, length of term, and includes commendations and recommendations. In colleges in the Middle States Association, the president receives a report of the team's observations and comments at the same time it is sent to the commission. He then has an opportunity to respond in writing to the team's findings before action is taken and the final report received from the commission. The formal process of accreditation ends when this final report is received.

[12] *Policies Handbook*, pp. 25-26.

Assumption 14 indicated that evaluation reports are widely circulated both within and outside the institution and that meaningful use is made of them. The research quoted supported the first part of the assumption but not the second.

The report ought to be made available in quantities for distribution internally and externally. Staff members and students should be encouraged to read and discuss it. It should appear on the agenda of staff meetings and special discussion sessions are in order. Releases may be prepared for the news media and several large meetings might be held to interpret the report to all interested persons.

The term of accreditation as specified in the report can be of some consequence. New community colleges are given terms of from one to three years in some areas of the country and up to five in others. If community colleges go through accreditation procedures before they move to permanent quarters, they usually receive a shorter term of accreditation. This means a repeat of the accreditation process when they occupy their new campuses. This can have discouraging effects on faculty morale. All colleges are hopeful of the longest term for their initial accreditation.

Implementation of the Recommendations

The community college that begins to carry out the recommendations made by the self-study committees has a head start on the implementation of the final report, as do those institutions that begin after hearing the oral report.

Except for improvements that are required for reaccreditation, few changes actually take place as a result of the final report, unless a concerted effort is made. Implementation of the report is much more likely to take place in institutions that make a total commitment to innovation, research, and professional improvement as a way of life. If this spirit was developed during the planning stages of the college and continued throughout the self-study, there should be few problems connected with implementation of the recommendations. The framework for organization is already there from the self-study. This should be modified and utilized.

Usually, there are too many recommendations to tackle all at once. Besides, some cost a lot of money, others require more time to accomplish, and still others may depend upon cooperation with outside persons· and agencies. Therefore, it would seem sensible to establish priorities and to develop a time schedule that will insure most of the recommendations to be at least partially implemented within a period of several years.

Successful completion of the suggested schedule will require the cooperation of all facets of the college and the community. The community, board of trustees, administration, faculty, and students must all carry their share of the load. Only in this manner can the latter part of Assumption 14 and all of Assumption 15 be supported.

Summary

After approximately half a century of experience, a number of assumptions have been formulated concerning attitudes toward accreditation and the value of certain aspects of the evaluation processes. At least one piece of research supports some of these assumptions and refutes others partially or entirely.

The procedures that a new community college must follow in order to receive its first accreditation are complicated. If values other than accreditation are to accrue from the process, they must be planned for at the beginning and leadership of a high quality must be exercised.

The accreditation process includes a self-evaluation by the institution. A handbook containing suggestions for the self-study is provided by the accreditation association. In turn, the self-evaluation is followed by an appraisal of readiness and a visitation by a team of educators who review the self-evaluation and make commendations and recommendations on the various aspects being evaluated. An oral report is made at the close of the visitation period. A written report, followed by the announced term of accreditation, follows in several or more months.

Scheduling the accreditation team's visit, attempting to get the best team possible, preparing for the visit, and insuring that the visit is productive are all of extreme importance to the success of the venture. Careful planning is necessary to accomplish all the above steps successfully.

When the final report is received, all human and material resources of the college and its community must be organized, priorities established, and a timetable drawn up to carry out as many of the recommendations as possible.

Suggested Activities and Problems

1. Search the literature dealing with accreditation on the higher education level and formulate a new set of assumptions. Comment on the implications of these assumptions for institutions in the process of accreditation.

2. Write to three of the six regional accrediting associations and request copies of the procedures for accrediting community colleges. Write a report on the similarities and differences you find in the procedures.

3. Use the assumptions in this chapter or your own list as an interview guide, and interview a staff member of a community college that has recently gone through the accreditation process. Attempt to find out the assumptions he would support and the ones he would reject, and then write up your findings giving his arguments.

4. Write to the accreditation commission in your area to ascertain if there are any set regulations concerning the composition of the accreditation team in

respect to experience, present position, number, and so on. On the basis of your findings, describe the background of each member of a hypothetical accreditation team you would consider to be ideal, and give the reasons for your choices.

5. Secure a copy of a recent community college accreditation report and select ten of the most important recommendations. Write a paper describing the procedures you believe should be used to implement each of them.

Selected Readings

Accredited Institutions of Higher Education, Washington, D.C.: American Council on Education (latest ed.).

Collins, John J., "Accreditation—Aims and Perceptions," *Junior College Journal*, 38, No. 4 (1969), 19.

Commission on Higher Education, *Evaluation Team Members Handbook*. New York: Middle States Association of Colleges and Secondary Schools, 1971.

———, *Institutional Self-Study-Handbook*. New York: Middle States Association of Colleges and Secondary Schools, 1971.

———, *Policies and Procedures Handbook*. New York: Middle States Association of Colleges and Secondary Schools, 1971.

Deferrari, Roy J., ed., *Self-Evaluation and Accreditation in Higher Education*. Washington, D.C.: The Catholic University of America Press, 1959.

Dressel, Paul L. et al., *Evaluation in Higher Education*. Boston: Houghton Mifflin Company, 1961.

Mayor, John R. and Willis G. Swartz, *Accreditation in Teacher Education—Its Influence on Higher Education*. Washington, D.C.: National Commission on Accrediting, American Council on Education, 1965.

Roueche, John E., George A. Baker III, and Richard L. Brownell, *Accountability and the Community College: Directions for the 70's* Washington, D.C.: American Association of Junior Colleges, 1970.

Selden, William K., *Accreditation*. New York: Harper & Row, Publishers, 1960.

Appendixes

appendix 1

Maryland Master Plan for Higher Education

Contents

appendix 2

Delaware County Council for Higher Education
Business-Industry Survey

Name of Establishment or Firm _____
Kind of Business _____Person Reporting_____

This survey is being made to help determine the need for a community college in Delaware County. Its purpose is to secure information on the requirements of business, industry, and community services for trained people and the type of training that will best prepare them for these positions. You may rest assured that the information you give us will be confidential. Neither your firm nor specific information regarding it will be identified in any way in the reports. Your cooperation in answering this questionnaire is greatly appreciated.

* * * * *

1. What is your average number of regular employees? _____
2. What percentage of your employees are engaged in work which requires more than high school training but not necessarily a college degree?_____
3. Will the proportion of your employees requiring training beyond high school increase during the next ten years?____Yes____No _____Don't know
4. Would there be opportunities for employment, in your organization, for people with two years of technical or semi-professional training beyond the high school?____Yes ____No
5. If "Yes" would you check the types of training in the list below which, if

offered by a local community college would be of value to your firm or organization.

_____ 1.   Drafting and Blueprint Reading
_____ 2.   Management, Development
_____ 3.   Labor-Management Relations
_____ 4.   Instrumentation and Plant Control
_____ 5.   Laboratory Technician
_____ 6.   Metallurgy
_____ 7.   Business Management
_____ 8.   Agriculture (Economics, Engineering, etc.)
_____ 9.   Building Trades
_____ 10. Foreign Language
_____ 11. Economics and Government
_____ 12. English and Speech
_____ 13. Mathematics
_____ 14. Literature and History
_____ 15. Industrial Chemistry
_____ 16. Inspection and Quality Control
_____ 17. Engineering Aides
_____ 18. Mental Hygiene
_____ 19. Advertising
_____ 20. Product Design
_____ 21. Purchasing
_____ 22. Law Enforcement and Related Occupations
_____ 23. Photographic Processes
_____ 24. Applied Science
_____ 25. Applied Mathematics
_____ 26. Machine Technology
_____ 27. Welding
_____ 28. Retailing—Merchandising
_____ 29. Plant Protection
_____ 30. Secretarial
_____ 31. Clerical Practice
_____ 32. Business Machines
_____ 33. Sales Representatives
_____ 34. Bookkeeping and Accounting
_____ 35. Air Conditioning and Refrigeration
_____ 36. Electronics
_____ 37. Electric Wiring and Motors
_____ 38. Machine Shop Practice
_____ 39. Technical Writing and Reporting
_____ 40. Apprentice Training (Tool and Die, etc.)
_____ 41. Physics
_____ 42. Mechanics (auto, diesel)

Other _____ Other _____
      _____   _____
      _____   _____

6-A. Are some of your college graduate employees spending a significant portion of their time at less than college graduate level work? ____Yes ____ No

6-B. If so, could employees having two years of training beyond high school replace some of the college graduates in your organization? ____Yes ____No

7-A. Is there an organized training program in your company or organization for less than college graduate level employees? ____Yes____No

7-B. If so, could it be modified ____, or eliminated____, by programs in a community college?

8. Do existing educational facilities in the area meet the employment needs of your organization for less than college graduate level employees? ____Yes ____ No

9. If you have not attached a separate letter on this questionnaire, would you please comment here on your thoughts concerning the need or advisability of developing a local community college, which would include two-year terminal technical-vocational and/or semi-professional training programs.

Other Comments:

May we quote your comments in the letter or above?____Yes

____No

* * * * *

Delaware County Council for Higher Education
Report of Business-Industry Survey

In its continuing study of the need for a two-year public, community college for Delaware County, the Council for Higher Education, in cooperation with the Delaware County Chamber of Commerce, surveyed a stratified sample of two hundred businesses and industries in the County. The purpose of this survey was to secure information on the present and future personnel needs of business and industry in Delaware County.

Of the two hundred survey forms, seventy-two, or 36% were returned. A total of 40,336 regular employees were reported by these 72 firms. The distribution of total number of companies and employees is shown in the following chart.

Number of Employees		Number of Companies Reporting
Over 200	37,660	25
100 to 199	1,233	8
Under 100	1,443	37
No response on this item	–	2
Total	40,336	72

28% of all employees reported are engaged in work which requires more than high school training but not necessarily a college degree.

43 of the respondents indicated that the proportion of their employees requiring training beyond high school would increase during the next ten years. 20 replied that they did not know if there would be such an increase. 17 of those responding in the affirmative were the large firms employing over 200.

Employment Opportunities in Technical And Semi-Professional Fields

61 companies or 84.7% answered that there would be opportunities for employment for people with two years of technical or semi-professional training beyond high school. Of the largest employers (over 200 employees), 23 or 92%, answered this question in the affirmative.

The respondents were asked to check the types of training which, if offered by a local community college, would be of value to their organization. The following charts show the most frequent choices.

No. of firms indicating value of training	*Types of training*
45	Drafting and Blueprint Reading
36	Bookkeeping and Accounting
34	Machine shop practice
34	Secretarial
32	Inspection and quality control
30	Welding
28	Engineering Aides
27	Instrumentation and plant control
26	Machine technology
26	Mathematics
25	Business Management
25	Management and Development
25	Business machines
25	Sales representative
24	Clerical practice
20	Purchasing
20	Apprentice training (Tool and Die, etc.)
19	Electric wiring and motors
18	Laboratory technician
15	Labor-management relations
14	Electronics
13	Industrial chemistry
13	Metallurgy
11	Building trades
11	Product Design
10	Advertising

The 25 larger companies, employing over 200 persons, listed the following types of training needs.

No. of firms indicating value of training	*Types of training*
16	Secretarial
15	Bookkeeping and Accounting
15	Drafting and blueprint reading
15	Engineering aides
14	Business machines
12	Inspection and quality control
12	Machine shop practice
11	Laboratory technician
11	Electric wiring and motors
11	Welding
10	Electronics
10	Machine technology
10	Instrumentation and plant control
9	Apprentice training (Tool and Die, etc.)
8	Management and development
8	Clerical practice
7	Industrial chemistry
7	Business management

21 companies indicated that some of their college graduate employees were spending a significant portion of their time at less than college graduate level work. 18 of these firms said that employees having two years of training beyond high school could replace some of the college graduates.

29 firms stated that there is an organized training program for less than college graduate level employees in their respective companies. 18 of these, including 8 of the largest employers, said that their programs could be modified or eliminated by programs in a community college.

The final question: "Do existing educational facilities in the area meet the employment needs of your organization for less than college graduate level employees?"

The responses: Yes—33   No—25

Ten of the largest companies, employing a total of 23,360 persons answered "No" to the above question.

* * * * *

Comments by
Business Executives and Personnel Directors

Unless other colleges in the immediate Chester-Delaware County area could expand to include 2 or 3 year terminal courses leading to "Associate" degrees, need for a community college along suggested lines would seem indicated, considering heavy concentration of industry in area. This Corporation is presently hiring men with "Associate" degrees for other plants in the country in addition to plants in local area and have been obliged to recruit from other states to fill needs.

Current and future competition for college graduates with full technical degrees will not permit their economical employment in non-technical or semi-technical activities. Growing need for men with 2 or 3 year degrees should develop accordingly.

— — — —

I believe that every community should have such a facility and that Delaware County, with its great variety of industry and business, is in the forefront of those where a real need is evident.

— — — —

We believe any type of educational training will benefit the community and should be an asset for employment for our company.

— — — —

I believe a two-year community college would be of great value to those of our youth who cannot afford to attend a four year school, both from an employment and educational viewpoint. There are many positions available that absolutely do not require a degree, but do require training in addition to that obtained in high school. This could be made available through the two-year junior college.

— — — —

Due to its location our company has various schools to draw from—Drexel, University of Pennsylvania, P.M.C., etc. However, from a community standpoint, a two-year college might be very worthwhile.

— — — —

Appears to be a good idea.

— — — —

We believe it would be an excellent aid to some firms in this area. However, the bulk of our employees do not require higher education.

— — — —

It seems to me that there are quite a few jobs that require more than high school but not necessarily a college degree, and the two-year college would fill that gap. I am all in favor of a two-year college.

— — — —

Our major source for female employees is the housewife. The males employed in the various trades have gained their experience elsewhere for the most part. Younger people with the proper training might be a logical future source.

— — — —

Since we are an educational institution, we feel it helps if employees, particularly office personnel, have a college degree even though the job description doesn't require a degree. Experience has shown that such people enjoy the atmosphere and are apparently satisfied with their job assignments.

— — — —

There seems to be a lack of emphasis by local higher educational facilities on the technical programs. This may be only a result of failure to communicate to prospects the need for technicians. This may further result in insufficient applicants to warrant technical courses. And this may be a further reflection of the "over" emphasis of parents and educators on college degree training.

— — — — —

We feel a community college would be most beneficial in raising the educational level of our high school graduates which in turn would be beneficial to the business community.

We believe it should be of benefit to the community.

— — — — —

It seems obvious that two-year colleges would tend to mitigate pressure on the higher education system. However, it is also obvious that considerable cost is involved in creating another level in our education system. Would these colleges be under the school district, county, or state in administration and tax recourse? In any event, some sort of state aid must be assured, unless enrollment is restricted to those persons residing within the district involved. I am assuming that, at a later date, a complete report of the feasibility of the project will be issued by the Council and other responsible agencies. California has a successful program in operation, and Oregon is instituting a similar project. Both of those programs are administered at the state level, I believe, and both have recourse to tax bases at the state level. I am concerned with the political possibilities.

— — — — —

This could be of considerable assistance to the semi-professional employee; particularly in our area of scientific research.

— — — — —

This institution believes that there is need for a local community college in Delaware County especially in the area of a two-year terminal technical-vocational and semi-professional training programs and will give its support and assistance to the formulation of such an institution. The latter statement represents institutional policy.

— — — — —

Due to plants being automated, particularly in our business, there is great need for men who have good knowledge of electronics and instrumentation.

— — — — —

I am convinced that in every field there is a large opportunity for a two-year college. It is my feeling that you still need practical experience. Every company will teach you their own methods; consequently, there are some jobs where college trained personnel are not necessary.

— — — — —

I believe that the two-year college in this area is of great necessity to fill a gap which exists in the educational field between the high school graduation and the college graduation.

— — — — —

Since we are a small organization, our requirements are not in the highly skilled level educationally, as most of our work is on the assembly basis. A higher education basis required for management, and whether a two-year training or a full college course would be required, would depend on the individual.

— — — —

Unlimited opportunities—Plastics and its related subjects a must.

— — — —

I do feel there is a need for machine shop trainees who have taken a course in basic machine operation. I believe this area does lack a good training program for this type of work. About the only school is the Williamson Trade School and almost 100% of their graduates are taken by industry so I feel this also proves the need for further schooling of this type.

— — — —

Most of our employees were trained at a different machine shop, as we do not have the trained personnel to do the training and we are not a big enough company to go through the experience of this training. We feel that we would get better qualified personnel from a local Technical-Vocational Community College.

— — — —

I feel that such a training would be of value to the business community as a whole.

— — — —

I believe in general good for a community. However, for my employees probably not very valuable. Too many unskilled. To the extent indicated on the first page, increased use of machines will increase need for more skilled men— total number involved only five or six.

— — — —

The idea should have considerable value in assisting our local educational requirements.

— — — —

We require high skill personnel in machine and precision sheet metal. It's much easier to hire a college graduate than a good mechanic.

— — — —

I believe there is a definite need for more vocational training after high school. The present systems taught in high schools do not properly prepare a person for industrial employment.

— — — —

One thing we do not have—that is enough colleges. My feelings toward this is, we should build new colleges not only in our community but through the United States.

— — — —

It is believed that there is a definite need for both academic and vocational high schools in this area. For many valid reasons these schools should be separate institutions for qualified students. Although our college graduates often engage in work below their education level they are frequently called upon to meet with people equal to or above this education level.

— — — — —

Rather than make a personal comment, I would be glad to bring this matter before our Board of Directors or membership at large for their opinion on how this would or wouldn't benefit our type of business if you so desire. My personal opinion is that in the distant future a college degree or its equivalent will be a must in our profession to operate successfully; this would be academic rather than a technical course.

— — — — —

In order to attract more industry to this area and assist industries now here to expand, a growing pool of better educated personnel is a must.

— — — — —

Present schools are fairly adequate, but certainly a two-year community college would result in a significant improvement.

— — — — —

This would be of great value to our community and we sure would like to see this come true. There is a great need for training of the individual dropouts from high school, more so in reference to our present problems.

— — — — —

I believe that a community college would be of great value in this area as it would permit people to attend who have no means of attending this type of school which may be located at a greater distance from the area.

— — — — —

We employ over 13,000 in the Philadelphia Metropolitan Area. Of these approximately 1,000 are employed in Delaware County.

We have organized training programs, without regard to education, designed to prepare the individual to perform the tasks and assume the responsibilities to which he is assigned.

It is unlikely that the type of training we perform would be of general interest or application to industry.

Our business historically has relied heavily upon its own training for the technical development of its employees. We have generally required a minimum of high school education for all entry jobs into the business. We do not see a substantial change from this position in the years ahead. Automation and mechanization, however, have introduced requirement for exceptionally talented employees for such assignments as programmer and engineering technician. For positions such as these we foresee a need for additional employees whose education goes beyond high school but does not necessarily require a college degree.

Our company policy has always been to promote from within, and a sizeable portion of our management ranks is composed of people whose talents and desire to succeed have allowed them to progress from entry jobs to the limits of their ability. This policy, which we feel will remain unchanged in the years ahead, clearly says that we have a continuing need for highly talented, highly motivated people. We recognize that this type of person often is not going to be content with the minimum high school education, but will seek out college or advanced technical training. We will, therefore, be very much interested in those individuals who would seek further education—but because they are the type of employee we seek and want, not primarily because of the technical skills acquired in school.

We are quite concerned with the unemployment problems which loom on the horizon. The high rate of unemployment among the young and the unskilled give us all great cause for concern. It is our feeling that the greatest contribution to be made by a local community college, including the two-year terminal technical training, would be in the preparation of the young untrained worker of limited talent who will be entering the labor market in the years ahead. This program would, of necessity, have to be geared to the locality served by the institution. It seems to us that the encouragement of our youth to remain in school becomes a hollow promise unless we can reasonably assure them that work does, in fact, exist upon completion of the program.

* * * * *

The Council for Higher Education concluded that the findings of the Business-Industry Survey plus the results of the Student-Parent Survey gave positive and solid indication of widespread support for the establishment of a community college in Delaware County. The need was clearly affirmed.

Delaware County Public Schools

Dear Parents:

Will your teen-ager have an opportunity for further education when he graduates from high school? The enclosed booklet may help you to answer that question. We urge you to read it carefully. Enclosed also is a questionnaire for your eleventh or twelfth grader to complete. Will you please discuss the questions with your son or daughter so that we may have your joint thinking? The completed questionnaire should be returned to school immediately.

A new state law in Pennsylvania enables communities such as those in Delaware County to establish two-year public colleges to serve the needs of many high school graduates who otherwise might not be able to attend institutions of higher learning.

Such a community college would be open to most high school graduates, and would offer a wide variety of courses. There would be two-year technical courses for students interested in trades or professions requiring one or two additional years beyond high school. Also, high school graduates could take their freshman and sophomore years in the community college and, if achievement has been satisfactory, transfer to another college or university for the third and fourth years.

The average tuition fee to the student is approximately $300 per year in most community colleges. The remainder of the cost is paid by the state and local communities. Students live at home and thus do not have the expense of room and board.

The response to this questionnaire will help us to determine the interest in and the need for a two-year community college in Delaware County.

To Twelfth Graders and Their Parents:

We realize that high school seniors will not have the opportunity to attend the above proposed community college next year. However, we would appreciate your cooperation in discussing and completing the questionnaire. Your replies will be of great value in developing plans for a two-year college in Delaware County.

G. BAKER THOMPSON
County Superintendent of Schools

Delaware County Public Schools
Community College Survey Questionnaire

This survey of eleventh and twelfth grade students is part of a county-wide study to determine the post-high school educational needs of the Delaware County area.

DIRECTIONS: 1. Please answer all questions and statements.
DIRECTIONS: 2. Check all answers that apply to you. You may need to check more than one space to answer some of the questions.

High School	School District of Residence

Name of Student_____   Age____Sex M____Grade 11 ____
                                                              F____Grade 12 ____

Occupation: Father _____
Occupation: Mother _____

Number of brothers and sisters: In elementary school (grades kinder-garten-6)____, in junior high school (grades 7-9)____, in senior high school (grades 10-12) _____

I. If a two-year community college were available in Delaware County at a cost of $300 per year, would you be likely to attend?____Yes____No

II. If you answer to # I is "yes", please answer these questions:
    A. Why would you choose to attend the community college?
       1. The low cost   _____
       2. To live at home   _____
       3. To keep a job while studying   _____
       4. To be near friends   _____
       5. To improve scholastic record   _____
       6. Other (Please explain) _____
          _____
          _____
          _____

    B. In what type program would you be most likely to enroll?
       1. Liberal arts program for transfer to a four-year college.   _____
          Technical training program. Examples: Chemical, mechanical and electrical technology.
          Terminal professional program. Examples: Nursing, lab techni-cian, dental or medical technician, legal or medical secretary, etc.   _____
    C. Which type of student would you be?
       1. Full-time day student   _____
       2. Part-time evening student   _____

III. Please indicate the occupation in which you are:
     A. Most interested   _____
     B. Somewhat interested _____

IV. If you would not go to college (Even if a community college
were available), please indicate your reason.
A. Getting married _____
B. Want full-time job _____
C. Entering armed forces _____
D. Can't afford cost of college _____
E. Not sure of future plans _____
F. Other (please explain) _____

V. Do your parents want you to continue your education after high school?
_____Yes_____ No

VI. *For seniors only:*
A. Have you been accepted for college, university, or some other form of
post high school education for the fall of 1964?_____Yes_____No
If yes, give name of institution. _____
B. Did you seriously consider one of the colleges or universities located
within commuting distance of your home?_____Yes_____ No
If yes, which one?_____
If no, why not?_____

Student's Signature _____
Parent's Signature _____

(Use reverse side of sheet for any comments you may have.)

RESULTS OF THE COMMUNITY COLLEGE STUDENT-PARENT SURVEY
Conducted by
The Delaware County Council for Higher Education

To help determine the need for a public, two-year community college in
Delaware County, a questionnaire study was conducted among the 17,400
eleventh and twelfth grade students in the public and parochial high schools of
the County. Parents were asked to verify the responses by their signatures.
13,601 valid questionnaires, or 78.2% of the total distributed, were returned to
the guidance counselors who conducted the study in the various high schools.

Usable Questionnaires Returned

Public Schools	9214	76.7% returns
11th grade	4999	
12th grade	4215	
Parochial schools	4387	81.2% returns
11th grade	2262	
12th grade	2125	

Number Interested in Attending a Community College

A total of 7,864 students or 57.8% of those returning the questionnaire,
answered YES to the following question: "If a two-year community college were

available in Delaware County at a cost of $300 per year, would you be likely to attend?"

The following chart indicates the number of interested students from the public and parochial high schools.

	Number answering YES	Total number of valid questionnaires	Percent of total number answering YES
Public School			
11th grade male	1527	2492	61.3%
11th grade female	1294	2507	51.6%
12th grade male	1061	1979	53.6%
12th grade female	1044	2236	46.7%
TOTALS	4926	9214	53.5%
Parochial Schools			
11th grade male	809	961	84.2%
11th grade female	859	1302	65.9%
12th grade male	518	884	58.6%
12th grade female	752	1240	60.6%
TOTALS	2938	4387	67%

* * * * *

The following reasons were given for choosing a community college if one were available.

The low cost	5659 replies
To improve scholastic record	4020
To live at home	3606
To keep a job while studying	2658
To be near friends	1138

Those students indicating an interest in attending a community college were asked to check the program in which they would be most likely to enroll. The responses were as follows:

Liberal arts program for transfer to a four-year college.	3315 students
Terminal professional program, such as nursing, lab technician, dental or medical technician, legal or medical secretary.	2960
Technical training program, such as chemical, mechanical and electrical technology.	1783

* * * * *

6378 respondents said that they would be full-time day students at the college.

1378 indicated interest in being part-time evening students.

* * * * *

Those students not interested in college even if a community college were available were asked to list their reasons, with the following results:

Want full-time job	1967
Not sure of future plans	1846
Can't afford cost of college	1167
Entering armed forces	812
Getting married	329

In answer to the question, "Do your parents want you to continue your education after high school?" 10,888 students, or 80% of the respondents replied YES.

* * * * *

Twelfth graders were asked if they had been accepted for college, university, or some other form of post high school education for the fall of 1964. The responses are tabulated below.

School	*No. accepted*	*Percent of seniors accepted*
Public	1838	43.6%
Parochial	718	33.8%
TOTALS	2556	40.3%

The following institutions were mentioned most frequently: West Chester State College, Temple University, Drexel Institute of Technology, Villanova University, and Pennsylvania State University.

* * * * *

2572 seniors, or 40.5%, seriously considered one of the colleges or universities within commuting distance of their homes. Institutions listed most frequently were: West Chester State College, Temple University, Drexel Institute of Technology, Villanova University, St. Joseph's College, Pennsylvania Military College, LaSalle College, Pierce Junior College, and University of Pennsylvania.

Seniors who did not consider local colleges or universities listed "desire to live away from home" and "cost" as the main reasons.

Comments from Students and Parents

I would only consider a community college if it offered a substantial enough education in my chosen field, so that I could either get a job in that field or go on to higher education in a regular college that maybe I could not have gone to before I went through the community college.

This is a wonderful idea. We have a younger son in Junior High who could avail himself of this new college. I hope it will be functioning at that time.

I think it would be just great! I am only sorry that we will not be able to avail ourselves for this opportunity as Frank is a senior.

Although I, myself, am not interested in a community, two-year college, from my experiences and associations, I feel that it would be very useful to many students and to the community in general.

I do not like the idea of a two-year college. If it were four years, then maybe I would be interested, but do not like the idea of transferring.

I feel that a community college would help Delaware County considerably, but because it is only for two years, I would personally not consider going. I feel others would think the way I do about a two year college.

I feel a community college has many good points. Had it been that this survey had come out a few months ago there would have been many more "yes" votes. I feel that, at this time, most of the seniors have had their minds made up as to what they are going to do, therefore, the thought of changing one's mind is out of the question.

Although I would not take advantage of a community college, the opportunity for further education (inexpensive and convenient) would greatly enhance our community. I can't see how such a college could be anything but a success.

How about a business program for students who are not academically or mechanically inclined like myself? I had to switch to General course with Business subjects.

Am very much interested in a Junior College for my daughter and would look forward to having one in this area.

I believe the community college is excellent for the future students who will be able to take advantage of it.

We all agree that a two year community college is a wonderful idea. However, in our particular case we would prefer the four year college for the following reasons:

a. Living away from home and attending college creates a good intellectual atmosphere.
b. Richard's college expenses have been set aside.
c. We all feel Richard needs the experience of "being on his own." This is a vital factor in growing up.

There are some families who could not afford a four year college, and there are some circumstances that would make a two year community college a tremendous advantage for some students. We sincerely hope this type college becomes a reality in Delaware County.

I have applied at Temple for the Tech school although I haven't been accepted yet I have a sincere desire to attend there. Not because of the school but because of the course they offer.

It's a shame they haven't thought of this sooner.

This project is being planned too late to be of any value for Stephen. However, with four more boys coming along to be educated, we should be most interested in a low cost community college.

Brother in construction business and I plan to go in with him

I feel that a community college should limit its students to those who cannot afford the assinine fees demanded by larger colleges and universities. I feel that this should be the policy of any college not privately owned, otherwise those less financially secure would not benefit greatly. Actually, I doubt whether I would attend any two-year college. The transition to another school for the other two years would be unnecessary and pointless in my particular case.

My answer was "no" because I would like a four year program all at one institution if possible. However, I think the idea of a community college a worthy one.

Am completely in favor. Extremely needed in our vicinity.

I was considering a nursing career, but if I had chosen to go to college, I would have chosen a local college. I would have been able to live at home, so I would keep the cost down.

We are most interested in the establishment of two-year community colleges, knowing that Pennsylvania is already far behind in this matter. Even tho our own children are far enough along so that they will not benefit, we deem it necessary for the many who cannot go away to school. We hope there will be sufficient interest and support in the necessary quarters to bring this plan to fruition.

Although the community college would not benefit us it is a probable necessity to carry on the educational program of the nation. We have educated three through four year colleges.

I feel that a community college is greatly needed in Delaware County. I'm in my senior year in high school and realize now how important a college education is. My high school grades have been very poor and this has made it very difficult for me to get into college. Fortunately I found a Junior College in Virginia that was willing to give me a chance to prove myself capable of college work. I'm sure there are many other students who are in the same position I am and would further their education if given the opportunity.

Mr. Lomis and I have long fought for a Junior College. It is too bad for us that our girls could not have taken advantage of one, however, we are glad that Haverford students will have the choice to attend one in the future.

I think the community college for Delaware County, if it is started, is an excellent idea. It will give the only average student the opportunity to further their education. It is almost essential for boys to go on to some kind of further training beyond high school. A girl should also have an extended education to give her children a good background of learning. Parents must be trained in the best possible way.

A two-year public college is a much needed school in this area.

If this two-year college offered subjects in which I planned to major I would be interested in attending. But, I found it very difficult locating a college that offered Fashion Merchandising.

I think there should be a community college even though I would never consider going. It would enable a great many more students to continue their education because of the low cost and the eligibility requirements.

Because I am interested in a certain type of nursing, the college program does not offer what I want. However, if a community college had been available, I might have changed my mind. My brother (8th grade) is very interested in the community college.

appendix 3

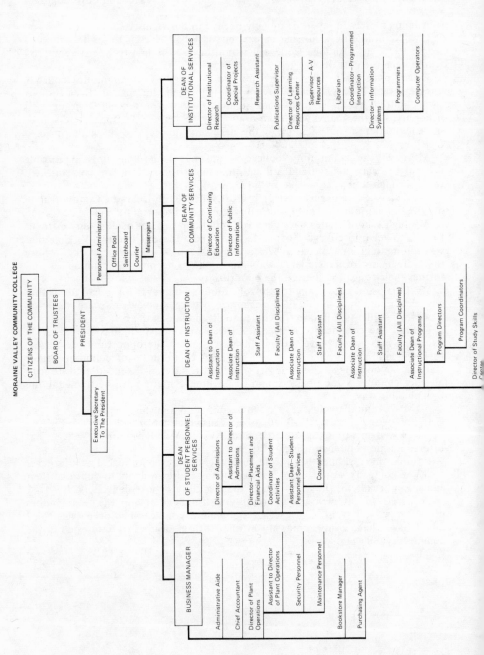

MORAINE VALLEY COMMUNITY COLLEGE

CITIZENS OF THE COMMUNITY

BOARD OF TRUSTEES

PRESIDENT

Executive Secretary To The President

Personnel Administrator
- Office Pool
- Switchboard
- Courier
- Messengers

BUSINESS MANAGER
- Administrative Aide
- Chief Accountant
- Director of Plant Operations
- Assistant to Director of Plant Operations
- Security Personnel
- Maintenance Personnel
- Bookstore Manager
- Purchasing Agent

DEAN OF STUDENT PERSONNEL SERVICES
- Director of Admissions
- Assistant to Director of Admissions
- Director—Placement and Financial Aids
- Coordinator of Student Activities
- Assistant Dean—Student Personnel Services
- Counselors

DEAN OF INSTRUCTION
- Assistant to Dean of Instruction
- Associate Dean of Instruction
  - Staff Assistant
  - Faculty (All Disciplines)
- Associate Dean of Instruction
  - Staff Assistant
  - Faculty (All Disciplines)
- Associate Dean of Instruction
  - Staff Assistant
  - Faculty (All Disciplines)
- Associate Dean of Instructional Programs
  - Program Directors
  - Program Coordinators
- Director of Study Skills Center

DEAN OF COMMUNITY SERVICES
- Director of Continuing Education
- Director of Public Information

DEAN OF INSTITUTIONAL SERVICES
- Director of Institutional Research
- Coordinator of Special Projects
  - Research Assistant
- Publications Supervisor
- Director of Learning Resources Center
  - Supervisor—A-V Resources
  - Librarian
  - Coordinator—Programmed Instruction
- Director—Information Systems
  - Programmers
  - Computer Operators

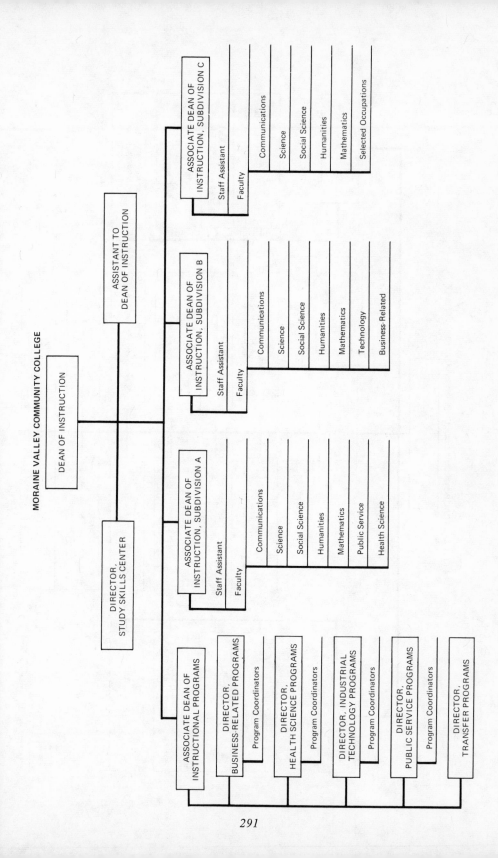

MORAINE VALLEY COMMUNITY COLLEGE

DEAN OF INSTRUCTION

ASSISTANT TO DEAN OF INSTRUCTION

DIRECTOR, STUDY SKILLS CENTER

ASSOCIATE DEAN OF INSTRUCTION, SUBDIVISION A
Staff Assistant
Faculty
Communications
Science
Social Science
Humanities
Mathematics
Public Service
Health Science

ASSOCIATE DEAN OF INSTRUCTION, SUBDIVISION B
Staff Assistant
Faculty
Communications
Science
Social Science
Humanities
Mathematics
Technology
Business-Related

ASSOCIATE DEAN OF INSTRUCTION, SUBDIVISION C
Staff Assistant
Faculty
Communications
Science
Social Science
Humanities
Mathematics
Selected Occupations

ASSOCIATE DEAN OF INSTRUCTIONAL PROGRAMS

DIRECTOR, BUSINESS-RELATED PROGRAMS
Program Coordinators

DIRECTOR, HEALTH SCIENCE PROGRAMS
Program Coordinators

DIRECTOR, INDUSTRIAL TECHNOLOGY PROGRAMS
Program Coordinators

DIRECTOR, PUBLIC SERVICE PROGRAMS
Program Coordinators

DIRECTOR, TRANSFER PROGRAMS

SEATTLE CENTRAL COMMUNITY COLLEGE ORGANIZATIONAL CHART

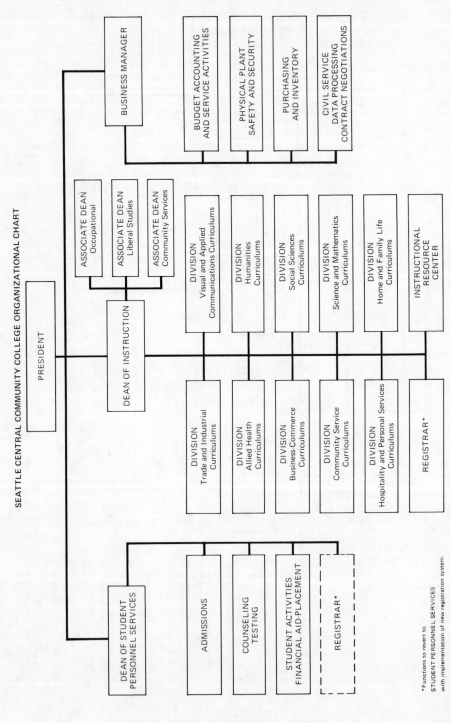

*Functions to revert to
STUDENT PERSONNEL SERVICES
with implementation of new registration system.

292

BURLINGTON COUNTY COLLEGE ORGANIZATION CHART

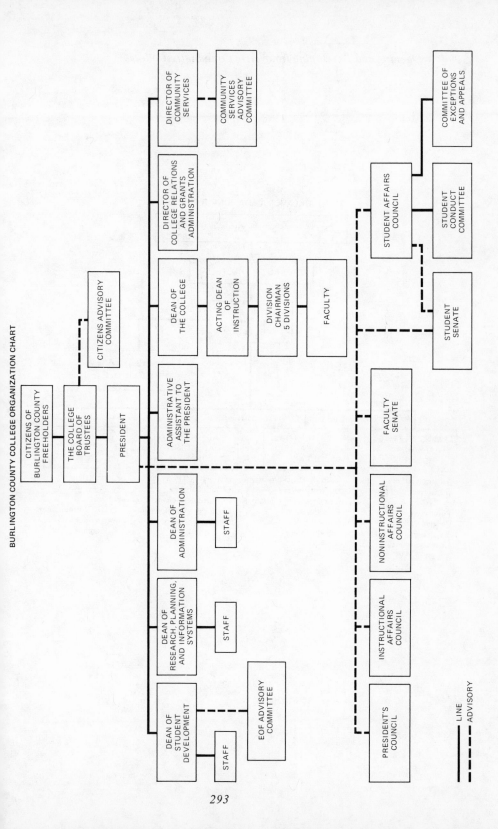

LINE
ADVISORY

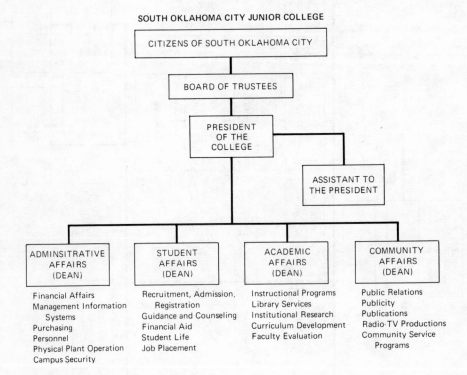

SOUTH OKLAHOMA CITY JUNIOR COLLEGE

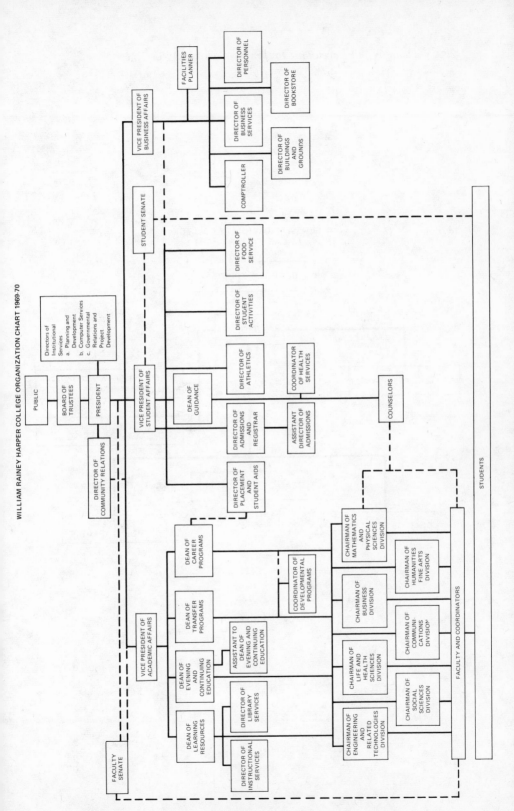

WILLIAM RAINEY HARPER COLLEGE ORGANIZATION CHART 1969-70

PUBLIC

BOARD OF TRUSTEES

PRESIDENT

Directors of Institutional Services
a. Planning and Development
b. Computer Services
c. Governmental Relations and Project Development

DIRECTOR OF COMMUNITY RELATIONS

VICE PRESIDENT OF BUSINESS AFFAIRS

FACILITIES PLANNER

DIRECTOR OF PERSONNEL

DIRECTOR OF BOOKSTORE

DIRECTOR OF BUSINESS SERVICES

DIRECTOR OF BUILDINGS AND GROUNDS

COMPTROLLER

STUDENT SENATE

VICE PRESIDENT OF STUDENT AFFAIRS

DEAN OF GUIDANCE

DIRECTOR OF FOOD SERVICE

DIRECTOR OF STUDENT ACTIVITIES

DIRECTOR OF ATHLETICS

COORDINATOR OF HEALTH SERVICES

DIRECTOR OF ADMISSIONS AND REGISTRAR

ASSISTANT DIRECTOR OF ADMISSIONS

COUNSELORS

DIRECTOR OF PLACEMENT AND STUDENT AIDS

VICE PRESIDENT OF ACADEMIC AFFAIRS

DEAN OF CAREER PROGRAMS

DEAN OF TRANSFER PROGRAMS

COORDINATOR OF DEVELOPMENTAL PROGRAMS

DEAN OF EVENING AND CONTINUING EDUCATION

ASSISTANT TO DEAN OF EVENING AND CONTINUING EDUCATION

DIRECTOR OF LIBRARY SERVICES

DEAN OF LEARNING RESOURCES

DIRECTOR OF INSTRUCTIONAL SERVICES

CHAIRMAN OF MATHEMATICS AND PHYSICAL SCIENCES DIVISION

CHAIRMAN OF HUMANITIES FINE ARTS DIVISION

CHAIRMAN OF BUSINESS DIVISION

CHAIRMAN OF COMMUNICATIONS DIVISION

CHAIRMAN OF LIFE AND HEALTH SCIENCES DIVISION

CHAIRMAN OF SOCIAL SCIENCES DIVISION

CHAIRMAN OF ENGINEERING AND RELATED TECHNOLOGIES DIVISION

FACULTY AND COORDINATORS

FACULTY SENATE

STUDENTS

295

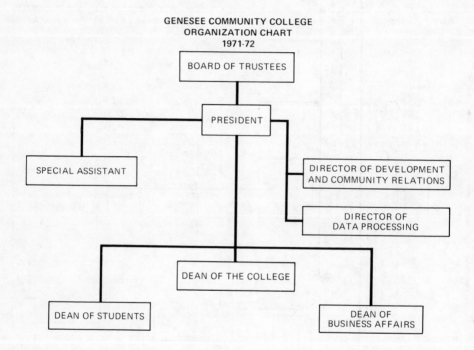

GENESEE COMMUNITY COLLEGE
ORGANIZATION CHART
1971-72

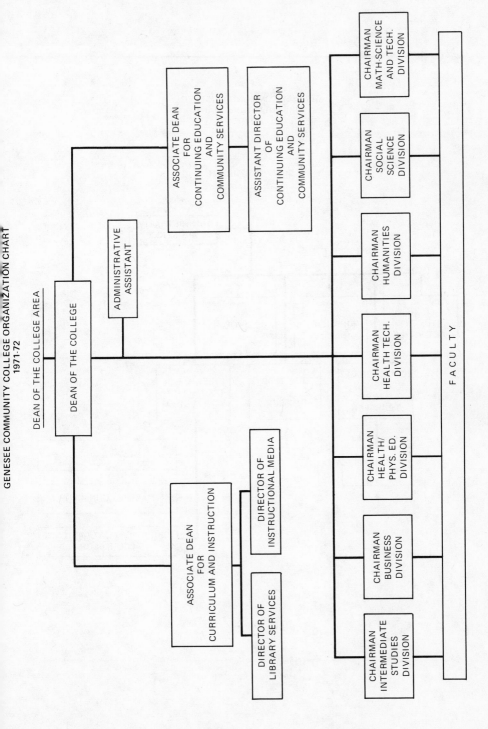

GENESEE COMMUNITY COLLEGE ORGANIZATION CHART
1971-72

DEAN OF THE COLLEGE AREA

DEAN OF THE COLLEGE

ADMINISTRATIVE ASSISTANT

ASSOCIATE DEAN FOR CONTINUING EDUCATION AND COMMUNITY SERVICES

ASSISTANT DIRECTOR OF CONTINUING EDUCATION AND COMMUNITY SERVICES

ASSOCIATE DEAN FOR CURRICULUM AND INSTRUCTION

DIRECTOR OF LIBRARY SERVICES

DIRECTOR OF INSTRUCTIONAL MEDIA

CHAIRMAN INTERMEDIATE STUDIES DIVISION

CHAIRMAN BUSINESS DIVISION

CHAIRMAN HEALTH/ PHYS. ED. DIVISION

CHAIRMAN HEALTH TECH. DIVISION

CHAIRMAN HUMANITIES DIVISION

CHAIRMAN SOCIAL SCIENCE DIVISION

CHAIRMAN MATH-SCIENCE AND TECH. DIVISION

FACULTY

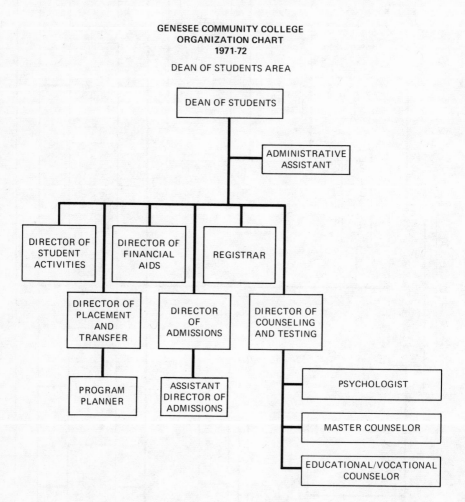

GENESEE COMMUNITY COLLEGE
ORGANIZATION CHART
1971-72

DEAN OF STUDENTS AREA

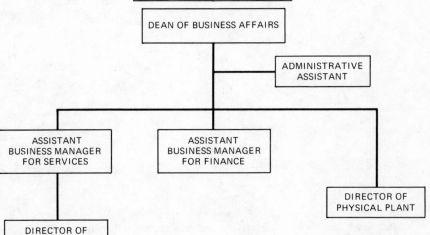

GENESEE COMMUNITY COLLEGE
ORGANIZATION CHART
1971-72
DEAN OF BUSINESS AFFAIRS AREA

DEAN OF BUSINESS AFFAIRS

ADMINISTRATIVE ASSISTANT

ASSISTANT BUSINESS MANAGER FOR SERVICES

ASSISTANT BUSINESS MANAGER FOR FINANCE

DIRECTOR OF PHYSICAL PLANT

DIRECTOR OF SECURITY SERVICES

appendix 4

I. Narrative Description:

The Dean of Administration is the Chief Fiscal and Business Officer of the College and reports to the President. He is responsible for the administration of the financial, purchasing, communications, personnel, security, college store, food services and plant operations of the College. Preparation and publication of the annual budget and maintenance of financial liaison with State and County funding authorities are under this jurisdiction.

II. Functional Responsibilities:

A. Directs through subordinate managers the following:
1. Accounting and Finance
   a. General supervision of the planning and preparation of the annual capital and operating budgets, accounting systems and practices, financial analysis and interpretation, and budgetary controls.
   b. Develops necessary financial forms and reports.
   c. Coordinates funds acquisition from authorized sources and controls disbursements and investment of funds.
   d. Coordinates automation of financial operations with computer center personnel.
   e. Develops improved and modified accounting procedures to provide appropriate controls, checks and balances.
   f. Plans comprehensive insurance program and coordinates with appropriate agencies or carriers.

    g. Establishes systems of cost and expenditure controls with all administrators to organize efficient financial operations.

2. Business and Auxiliary Operations
   a. Develops effective purchasing and materials management procedures.
   b. Develops policies and procedures for the employment of all non-instructional personnel including hours, salaries, benefits, leaves, vacations, testing, training, grievance and separation policies.
   c. Provides for internal systems of communications including mail, telephone and transportation services.
   d. Provides for auxiliary services including the college store and food services operation.

3. Plant Operations and Security
   a. Coordinates all college construction programs from award of contracts through to turnkey.
   b. Organizes and coordinates custodial and maintenance operations to provide for sanitation, cleanliness, repair and alterations of college buildings, grounds, equipment and facilities.
   c. Responsible for use, occupancy and equipping of all college facilities in cooperation with appropriate administrators.
   d. Supervises operation and maintenance of all internal college utility systems.
   e. Plans and coordinates system of college security and safety.

III. Consulting Tasks

A. Participates in development of governance planning and implementation through established structure.
B. Advises staff on financial, policy, regulatory or ethical matters related to application or interpretation of administrative functions.
C. Consults with all administrative management levels on application of personnel related policies, procedures and contracts.
D. Participates in development of operating procedures and practices to implement Board Policies.
E. Participates in consultation on new facilities planning and utilization of existing plant equipment and facilities.

IV. Required Skills:

A. Broad experience in all phases of school or college business administration or equivalent executive level experience in business or industry.
B. Specific experience in financial management, accounting, budgeting, materials management, personnel administration and plant construction, facilitation and operation.
C. Heavy experience in human relations, training management and labor negotiations.
D. Should have background in planning and developing control systems such as PERT, CPM, PPBS and management by objectives techniques.
E. Some experience, education or training in engineering, construction, utilities and/or contracting is highly desirable as well as a working knowledge of law and legal resources.
F. Should have some experience as a teacher and/or administrator in institution of higher education.

V. Educational Requirements:

A. Baccalaureate Degree in business, economics, finance or industrial engineering is a minimum requirement.
B. Advanced study or degree in educational administration, accounting, financial analysis or business administration is desirable.
C. Combinations of education and experience may be substituted where appropriate.

Salary Schedule: Administrative
Salary Grade: I

Job Description
Dean of Research, Planning, and
Information Systems

I. Narrative Description

The Dean of Research, Planning, and Information Systems reports to the President and is responsible for three major areas of institutional service: research, planning and development, and information systems. Since many departments of the College are involved in these areas emphasis should be placed on the coordination and leadership of this position.

One basic function of this position is to encourage good decision-making by insuring that accurate and timely data and meaningful analyses of the data are available to all departments of the College and specifically to the President, the President's staff, and the Board of Trustees. A major operational responsibility is the direction of the central data processing complex serving the needs of the College and of Burlington County government.

II. Functional Responsibilities

A. *Research*
1. Coordinate continuing studies in the areas of curricula, instruction, staff, buildings, facilities, and financing, working closely with departments, having operational responsibility for these areas. Assist those departments that have a research capability and conduct studies in the others or when requested by the President.
2. Coordinate the preparation of institutional reports to local, state, and federal agencies.
3. Direct studies of other areas which are considered important to the institution as approved by the President.
4. Development of programs to evaluate how well the College is progressing toward its objectives.
5. Centralize and coordinate the answering of surveys and questionnaires from outside agencies.

B. *Planning and Development*
1. Coordinate the preparation of analyses of future needs and resources, including specifically, enrollment and facilities projections.
2. Develop educational specifications for future campus development and communicate facility objectives to architects.
3. Coordinate campus design with architects, consulting engineers, other specialists, and appropriate College personnel, up to the award of the construction contracts.
4. Working closely with the Dean of Administration, coordinate budget planning for both operational and capital needs up to the point of the preparation of the annual budget.
5. Plan for the implementation of a Program, Planning, Budgeting System (PPBS) responsive to the needs of the College.

C. *Information Systems*
1. Implement and direct a College forms control program.

2. Coordinate the development of systems and procedures (manual and automated) of an inter- and intra-departmental nature, including responsibility for the control and distribution of the official Policy and Procedures Manual.

3. Direct the systems development activities of the Programmer/Analyst staff of the Computer Center for both the College and Burlington County government.

4. Direct the operation of the College/County Computer Center.

5. Prepare specifications, evaluate, select and implement new hardware which will provide needed informational and computational resources.

III. Consulting Task

1. Participates in the discussion, formulation, and administration of College policies as a member of the President's staff.

2. Participates in the development and construction of the College budget.

3. Is involved and consulted in the administration of construction contracts for new facilities.

4. Is consulted before any changes are made in procedures or methods involving any data processing application.

5. Participates in the formulation of staff personnel policies and procedures.

6. Is consulted before any significant research studies are conducted.

7. Participates in the development of the curriculum Master Plan.

8. Is involved and consulted in the building of the College calendar.

9. Is consulted in the building of each term's Master Schedule.

IV. Required Skills

Administrative experience in higher education which must have included substantial experience in educational data processing is required. Either direct experience in research and planning in higher education or the equivalent in academic course work.

V. Required Educational Background

A doctorate or substantial work toward the doctorate is desirable, with a major in higher education or educational administration.

Salary Schedule: Administrative
Salary Grade: Level I

Job Description
Dean of Student Development

I. Narrative Description:

The Dean of Student Development is responsible for the development of policies and programs in all student personnel services. He works cooperatively with the other members of the President's Staff and reports directly to the President. Since many phases of student personnel services have a direct bearing on the instructional program, there is a particularly close working relationship between the Dean of Student Development and the Dean of the College and Dean of Instruction.

He is responsible for the Student Development program at Burlington County College, which consists of a series of related functions designed to support the instructional program, to respond to student needs, and to foster institutional development. His responsibility requires that the program be well conceived and implemented and that the functions require services of a qualified staff in sufficient numbers to provide: (a) *orientation* to college and career opportunities and requirements, (b) *appraisal* of individual potentialities and limitations, (c) *consultation* with students about their plans, progress and problems, (d) *participation* of students in activities that supplement classroom experiences, (e) *regulation* to provide an optimal climate for social and academic development, (g) *services* that facilitate college attendance through a program of financial assistance, and facilitate transition to further education or employment, and (g) *organization* that provides for continuing articulation, evaluation, and improvement of the total student personnel program.

II. Functional Responsibilities (directly and/or through subordinate managers the following):

1. To communicate an accurate image of the college as a means of informing oncoming students about opportunities at the college.

2. To acquire information about the student which is necessary for determining his eligibility for programs offered by the college.

3. To obtain relevant test information by which student potential and progress may be measured and by which the students and the college objectively make educational decisions.

4. To establish and maintain records of each student's achievements from which an accurate assessment of his performance can be made easily.

5. To officially enroll students and open their records with both more efficiency and validity.

6. To establish and maintain desirable levels and standards of student performance in order that both the students and the college strive for educational excellence.

7. To assist students in meeting the costs of college attendance in gaining scholarship recognition, and in obtaining part-time or full-time jobs related to their college preparation.

8. To provide appropriate controls of social behavior, experiences in decision making through self-government, and activities outside the classroom which have an educative value.

9. To assist students in selecting study programs which will lead them successfully toward desirable educational goals.

10. To provide essential information and guidance economically to student groups.

11. To provide individualized help to students on problems of choice in order to develop maximum self-understanding.

12. To help students make appropriate vocational plans.

13. To foster college-wide concern for the general welfare of students.

14. To organize opportunities by which student personnel services staff can keep professionally informed in order that their counsel will have current validity.

15. To conduct research which continuously evaluates the effectiveness of student personnel services.

16. To provide a plan of organization that will facilitate effective services.

III. Related Tasks for Functional Responsibilities Listed Above:

1. Conferring with high school groups; preparing and distributing material; handling inquiries about college attendance.

2. Evaluating transcripts of previous course work; serving on admissions committee; synthesizing available personnel data.

3. Selecting appropriate testing instruments; administering tests to incoming students; developing normative and predictive data.

4. Developing an integrated records system; maintaining policies regarding record acessibility; conducting research on student characteristics.

5. Designing forms and procedures; processing class changes, withdrawals, etc.; projecting future enrollments.

6. Implementing academic policies; evaluating graduation eligibility; interpreting requirements to students.

7. Administering student loans; handling part-time employment; seeking funds for grant-in-aids; analyzing financial needs of students; maintaining liaison with employment agencies; consulting with prospective employers; arranging placement interview; conducting follow-up studies.

8. Advising student government; conducting leadership programs; supervising student elections; analyzing needs for activities and facilities; developing informal programs in student center; supervising activities budget; implementing social policies; maintaining social calendar; handling cases of social misconduct; training student guides; interpreting student services and regulations; introducing students to college activities.

9. Interpreting test results to applicants; interpreting curricular requirements; assisting students in selecting courses; scheduling advisees in classes; interpreting senior college requirements; interpreting study skills to individual advisees.

10. Conducting orientation classes; interpreting occupational information; teaching effective study skills.

11. Making use of diagnostic tests; conducting counseling interviews; interpreting occupational information.

12. Identifying sources of occupational information; studying manpower needs

within the community and region; developing effective methods for disseminating career information.

13. Arranging for staff to serve on faculty committees; arranging joint meetings of staff with high school counselors; arranging visits of staff to senior colleges.

14. Providing counselor supervision; arranging for faculty advisor training; arranging for staff participation in professional meetings.

15. Interpreting studies of student characteristics and needs; arranging for follow-up studies of former students; developing experimental projects.

16. Identifying and interpreting staffing needs; preparing program budgetary requests; preparing job descriptions and organizational patterns.

IV. Consulting Tasks

1. Participates in consultation on new facilities planning, utilization of existing plant and facilities and development of educational specifications.

2. Participates in development of Administrative procedures and practices to implement Board policies.

3. Participates in development of, evaluation and implementation of, the college community governance structure.

4. Participates in consultation on development of college insurance policy and procedures.

5. Participates in consultation on development of negotiated contracts with instructional personnel, including evaluation procedures.

6. Participates in development of the College Catalogue and Supplement as well as with articulation of course and programs and liaison with appropriate units.

7. Participates in consultation on development of Master Calendar and Master Schedule.

V. Required Skills:

1. Specific experience in supervision and administration of student personnel services including the areas of counseling, guidance, admissions and registration, testing, orientation, activities, student conduct, placement, financial aids, student government, special student programs, and health services.

2. Knowledge of basic financial management, budgeting, and supervision of budgetary matters.

3. Experienced in human relations and ability to relate well with students and faculty.

4. Outstanding leadership qualities and knowledge of the principles and practices of democratic administration.

5. An obviously warm and outgoing personality.

6. Teaching and administrative experience at the college level, preferably in a 2 year public college.

VI. Education Requirements:

1. Masters Degree in Student Personnel Administration or related area is the minimum requirement.

2. A doctorate or advanced study toward a doctorate is desirable, with a major in student personnel administration or in the administration of higher education.

3. A minimum of four years or 2 year public college experience in administrative or related student personnel areas is required, although combinations of experience and education may be substituted where appropriate.

Salary Schedule: Administrative
Salary Grade: I

Job Description
Division Chairman

The Division Chairman serves as the link between the faculty and the administration. The job is a difficult one because the chairman is both a teaching faculty member and an administrator. He teaches classes, he is given rank and his salary is determined by his education and experience as a faculty member, yet his responsibilities are chiefly administrative.

Division chairmen are appointed on a year-to-year basis by the Board of Trustees, upon the recommendation of the Dean of the College to the President. The appointment is an assigned one and a chairman may resign his administrative assignment as chairman without embarrassment and without prejudice to his future role as a full-time teaching faculty member. In the event he does so, during the contract year, he continues to receive the salary he received as chairman less the supplement assigned to the chairman's position.

Division chairmen are responsible to the Dean of the College and perform those functions assigned by him. These can be grouped under the two major headings of administration and co-ordination. Specific responsibilities include:

Administration

1. Working closely with faculty members in the formulation, justification, development and revision of courses and curricula including:
   a. The development of course outlines and learning packets.
   b. Selection of modes of instruction.
   c. Selection of texts and other instructional materials.
   d. The conduct of feasibility studies and the establishment and use of career program advisory committees.
2. Providing status reports on activities within the Division, such as instructional assignments, class size, and preparing an annual report for the Dean of the College reflecting Division accomplishments during the year, plans for the following year, recommendations and suggestions.
3. Assuming a major role in the recruitment, selection, direction and evaluation of all full and part-time instructional and non-instructional staff within the Division including:
   a. Developing personnel requirements and position descriptions.
   b. Participating in the development of recruitment plans.
   c. Interviewing of candidates.
   d. Recommending or approving all recommendations for appointment within the Division.
   e. Serving as the primary source of faculty evaluations for the purpose of determining re-appointment, promotion, tenure, and dismissal.
4. Development of a means for evaluating results of instruction including follow-up studies.
5. Responsibility for maintaining a file of all course outlines and learning packets developed with the Division.
6. Responsibility for the inventory, maintenance and security of facilities and equipment charged to the Division.
7. Scheduling regular meetings of the Division as required.
8. Co-ordinating and consolidating a preliminary budget for the Division and responsibility for regulating expenditures within the approved Division budget by:

    a. Reviewing and making recommendations concerning all purchase requisitions, travel requests and other expenditures emanating from faculty in his Division.

    b. Adjustment of funds (with approval of the Dean of the College) within the Division.

9. Interpreting policies of the College to members of the Division.

10. When advisable, arranging for substitutes in case of absence by the regular faculty.

11. Providing leadership to Division faculty in the study and review of literature dealing with new developments, practices and knowledge of Higher Education with special emphasis on community colleges.

12. Acting as a resource person and aid to all faculty in finding answers to instructional or curricular problems.

13. Assuming a major role in the supervision of the instructional process.

Co-ordination

1. Co-ordinating articulation of the divisional instruction program with that of county high schools and nearby senior colleges and universities.

2. Co-ordinating the efforts of faculty members who are working with career program advisory committees.

3. Working closely with the Student Personnel Services Staff to insure communication regarding matters related to curriculum and student advisement and placement.

4. Reviewing the recommendations for book and non-book media needed to facilitate the Divisional instructional program and insuring that necessary arrangements are made for the ordering of these materials.

5. Co-ordinating the full-time and part-time credit educational programs offered by the Divisions, including the service and general educational courses for students whose major lies in another Division.

6. Formulating the master schedule each term in conjunction with the Dean of the College, the Registrar and the Director of the Computer Center.

7. Developing faculty instructional schedules within parameters established by the Dean of the College.

8. Co-ordinating the planning and equipping for those parts of new buildings directly related to his Division

9. Representing the Division on the Dean's Advisory Council and providing liaison between the faculty of his Division and the Dean of the College.

10. Working with the Dean of the College to develop an in-service program for full and part-time faculty to include an initial orientation program and continuous in-service training.

11. Advising the Dean of the College with regard to policy formulation particularly in the areas of faculty, curriculum and instruction.

12. Co-ordinating and reviewing the preparation of the College Bulletin and other printed materials relating to the Division.

13. Establishing and maintaining relationships with his counterparts at other two-year colleges.

Salary Schedule: Instructional
Salary Grade: Open

Job Description
Chairman, Division of Learning Resources (Director)

The Chairman of the Division of Learning Resources is the principal administrative and planning officer for the Division. He is responsible for the successful management of all departments designated part of the Division of Learning Resources, and for the implementation of procedures that provide for maximum use of resources proprietary to each department. The Chairman has the specific duty of establishing policies that coordinate the service functions of the Division of Learning Resources with the requirements of the entire instructional program, and in that capacity he is required to take a position of leadership in the design and production of program development in all curriculum areas. The Chairman reports to the Dean of the College. He is the Dean's chief advisor on resource and production capabilities, budgetary requirements, services evaluation, and future goals for the division.

The following duties and responsibilities are performed or supervised by the Division Chairman for Learning Resources:

1. Authorizes all requests for the design and implementation of programs for instructional development and curriculum revision which are of a comprehensive and permanent nature, and which require the systematic use of personnel and materials germane to the Division of Learning Resources.

2. Prepares operating and capital budget requests and administers expenditure of the Division's annual budget, insuring that expenditures remain within approved budgetary amounts. The Chairman approves all purchase requisitions, and all purchase orders for library books, microfilm, serials, film rentals, and non-book media, that originate within the Division.

3. Plans the recruitment and evaluation of all Divisional employees. The Chairman makes annual recommendations to the Dean of the College regarding promotions and dismissals of all Divisional personnel. The Chairman is responsible for all personnel records.

4. Assigns projects and duties to all Divisional personnel as they are warranted.

5. Prepares reports, including an annual report, which effectively gauge the success of services performed by the Division of Learning Resources.

6. Maintains a procedures manual consisting of all forms and routines currently used by departments designated Learning Resources. Annually issues a revised edition of the *LR Handbook*.

7. Develops criteria and specifications for new equipment; regularly discusses the equipment needs of the Learning Resources Division with sales people and arranges for the display and testing of the latest developments in the media fields.

8. Edits the LR Newsletter as a means of informing the faculty and administration about new materials, techniques and resources in the Division. The Chairman is also responsible for using other means of informing the faculty about Learning Resources Division developments, such as in-service training seminars.

9. Confers with the faculty and administration on the development and application of appropriate learning resources.

10. Keeps abreast of current development in both the library and audio-visual fields.

11. Serves on campus-wide committees as requested; the Chairman shall also serve on county, regional, or state committees and agencies if requested.

12. Advises Division Chairmen and the Dean of the College with regard to the need for policy formulation in areas of interest to the Division of Learning Resources.

13. Serves in a leadership role for other employees of the Division. The Chairman is responsible in many ways for the professional growth of his employees and must undertake systematic means of assuring this condition.

14. Oversees the facilities growth of the Division. The Chairman has the specific responsibility of maintaining a balanced program of facilities development that will complement an expanding curriculum.

15. Writes preliminary studies of instructional programs that might be taught as an integral function of the Division of Learning Resources.

16. Interprets the role of the Division to the general college community.

17. Cooperates in the sharing of learning resources on a county-wide basis. Establishes and maintains rapport with counterparts at other institutions.

Qualifications for the Position of
Chairman, Division of Learning Resources

A Master's Degree in an area of educational communications, such as library science or audio-visual technology, and six years experience in at least one area of learning resources. The Chairman of the Division of Learning Resources must have the administrative skills and imagination to give impetus and direction to a program of utility services that will provide optimum support for instructional plans.

The Chairman must understand the instructional methodology of the college; it is vital that the Chairman himself possess a working knowledge of equipment and techniques required to implement the instructional methods used by this institution. The Chairman should have mature judgment and the ability to work successfully with peer and subordinate groups.

Salary Schedule: Instructional
Salary Scale: Open

Job Description
Educational Development Officer (Assistant Dean)

The Educational Development Officer is responsible for assisting in the planning and implementation of systematically developed courses of study. He works closely with the Division Chairmen, the Chairman of the Learning Resources Center and his staff, and individual faculty members in their instructional development efforts. One of the primary functions of this individual is to suggest alternate learning strategies for instructional projects. He must be completely aware of institutional philosophy and capabilities and be ready to articulate them to all faculty and staff at any time. In the Administrative Organization of the college, the Educational Development Officer reports directly to the Dean of the College.

Specifically, the Educational Development Officer is responsible for:

1. Working in advisory capacity with instructional Division Chairmen in establishing the curriculum priorities for their divisions.
2. Working with individual faculty members of faculty teams planning new courses which incorporate various learning strategies.
3. Assisting faculty members and teams in revising present courses.
4. Assisting faculty in the preparation of instructional development proposals for internal and external funding.
5. Maintaining a complete file of present and proposed course materials.
6. Planning and conducting in-service and pre-service faculty orientation for full- and part-time faculty.
7. Maintaining professional relations with other educational institutions in the area of instructional development.
8. Assisting Chairmen in supervising the development and utilization of various instructional strategies used to achieve specified learning objectives.
9. Handling of correspondence related to the instructional approach of the college.
10. Assisting visitors who come to observe the instructional program.
11. Making an annual report to the Dean on the state of instructional development at the college.
12. Working with the Educational Research Officer to insure that instructional activities are organized in such a way that it is possible to evaluate their effectiveness.

Qualifications for the Position of
Educational Development Officer

Teaching and academic administrative experience at the college level, preferably in the two-year college field is required. A master's degree in an academic area, plus considerable training and experience in educational system design, media utilization, and alternate strategies is required.

This position requires a person whose experience and training give him the flexibility and vision needed to work closely with all kinds of people in all academic disciplines. Since one of the primary functions of this position is to generate and sustain experimental learning experiences for our students, often using teams of faculty members, the person who fills this position must have considerable leadership ability and sensitivity for others working with him.

Job Description

Director of Continuing Education and Academic Scheduling

The Director of Continuing Education and Academic Scheduling is in conjunction with the appropriate Division Chairman responsible for the administration of activities related to Part-Time Studies, both credit and non-credit, including submission of appropriate financial information to the Dean of Administrative Services and for the development, supervision, and evaluation of all procedures related to the academic master schedule. In addition, he serves as liaison between the Academic Dean's staff and the computer center and will assist in development and implementation procedures for the validation of both full and part-time instructional programs. Specifically, he is responsible for:

1. Continuing Education functions:

1.1 Works co-operatively with Division Chairmen in the selection, supervision, and evaluation of part-time instructors who teach credit courses and is solely responsible for the selection, supervision, and evaluation of non credit course instructors with the exception of the program offered specifically by the Division of Community Affairs.

1.2 The development of the capital and operating budget request for all part-time credit and non-credit programs under his jurisdiction and, as fiscal officer of these accounts, for insuring that expenditures do not exceed budgeted amounts. This does not include salaries for part-time instructors who teach credit courses—a responsibility assigned to the appropriate Division Chairman.

1.3 Shares functional responsibility with Division Chairman in long range schedule planning to facilitate degree completion by part-time students and in investigating, developing, and instituting new programs of study designed specifically for the part-time student.

1.4 Co-ordination at off-campus locations regarding scheduling of classes and arrangements incidental to this such as leasing, custodial services, parking, etc.

1.5 Acting as liaison between the college and the evening program of the high schools and other colleges operating within the county.

1.6 Preparation of all brochures relating to Continuing Education course offerings and for furnishing the Assistant-to-the-President with information necessary for publicizing these.

1.7 Dissemination of information regarding course offerings and registration for both credit and non-credit Continuing Education students.

1.8 In conjunction with the Academic Dean and the Division Chairmen for those parts of the College Bulletin related to curriculum, courses, registration, and general academic information.

2. Academic Scheduling Functions:

2.1 In conjunction with the Division Chairmen for the development of the tentative and final master course schedule for all credit courses and is solely responsible for the preparation of all instructional space assignments and the scheduling of all non-credit courses.

2.2 In conjunction with the Director of Admissions and Registration, the development of registration procedures for all on and off-campus students and controlling registration of classes to insure that pre-determined goals are achieved.

2.3 Acting as liaison between Academic Dean's staff and the Dean of Student Development's staff in developing procedures for adds and drops, late registration, mid-term and final grade reporting, preparation and distribution of the Dean's List and probation list, final grade reports including subsequent grade changes, and evening counseling. In these areas he will have a required advisory role.

2.4 Developing the first draft of the College Calendar.

3. Other Functions:

3.1 Serving as liaison between the Academic Dean's staff and the Computer Center.

3.2 Assist in developing and implementing procedures for the validation of both full-time and part-time instructional programs.

3.3 Co-operate in developing and conducting of an on-going program of research in the instructional area.

3.4 Compilation of required data for areas under his control for local, state, federal, and other authorized reports.

3.5 Establishing relationships with colleagues in other New Jersey Institutions.

3.6 Preparing and submitting an annual report.

3.7 Performing other duties as requested by the Dean of the College.

Qualifications for the position of Director of Continuing Education and Academic Scheduling:

Experience in registration procedures and supervision of Part-Time Studies at the college level, preferably in the two-year community college field is essential. Experience in the supervision of evening or part-time programs is desired. A Master's Degree is required, preferably in Student Personnel Services.

Because of the strong emphasis of the College in institutional research, the Director must have a firm belief in the value of research and must possess necessary statistical skills for conducting research in the instructional area.

Due to the nature of the position and the team approach envisioned throughout the entire college structure, the Director should be skilled in human relations and be able to relate well to students and faculty.

He should have sufficient familiarity with computers and data processing to be able to work effectively in developing necessary computer systems.

Job Description
Instructional Assistant

General Qualifications: B.A. degree or equivalent in course work; at least 5 years experience in assigned field.

An Instructional Assistant will provide personal, qualified tutorial assistance to students working in the independent study areas and laboratories. His primary responsibility will be to assist in implementing instructional programs designed by faculty members responsible for making the final evaluation of a student's progress. Although the Instructional Assistant may perform some assigned instructional development tasks, and interim student evaluations, he will not be responsible for extensive instructional development or for final evaluation of any student.

Specific duties include:

1. On call tutorial assistance in assigned independent study area or laboratory.
2. Conducting oral quiz sections and tutorial sessions for assigned students.
3. Administering and evaluating pre-tests.
4. Administering post-test and evaluating portions of the post-tests specified by the instructor responsible for the student being examined.
5. Supervising student assistants assigned to the independent study area or laboratory where he is assigned.
6. Being responsible for maintaining those records requested by the faculty whose students are assigned to the instructional assistant area of responsibility.
7. Supervise and maintain learning materials and equipment within the independent study area or laboratory (in cooperation with Division of Learning Resources personnel).
8. Be responsible for: (using student assistants when appropriate)
   a. Maintaining inventories of specialized equipment and supplies in assigned area.
   b. Filing or shelving materials.
   c. Distributing appropriate materials to students.
   d. Collecting and refiling materials after use.
9. Complete specific instructional development projects as assigned by division chairman.
10. Perform assigned data gathering functions to assist in validating instructional procedures.

An Instructional Assistant will observe the same calendar as faculty employed on a ten month faculty contract. He will be expected to work at least 37 1/2 hours per week.

An Instructional Assistant will be evaluated by the full-time instructors whose students are assigned to the area where he works. Where more than one faculty member is involved, the evaluation will be coordinated by the division chairman. Student evaluation forms may be used if the faculty desire.

Job Description
Director of Admissions and Registration

The Director of Admissions and Registration is responsible for the entire area of Admissions and Registration, excluding development of the Master Schedule. He works cooperatively with the Dean of Student Development and other members of the administrative staff in the initial formulation of policies and procedures covering these areas. In the administrative organization of the college, the Director of Admissions and Registration reports directly to the Dean of Student Development, who in turn reports to the President of the College.

The Director of Admissions and Registration works cooperatively with the Director of Continuing Education and Academic Scheduling to assure an effective operation of the office.

Specifically, the Director of Admissions and Registration:

1. Establishes an admissions system to include development of all forms and procedures.
2. Prepares and distributes information on the College to prospective students, counselors, parents and others desiring such information.
3. Conducts pre-admission counseling and general admissions interviews.
4. Maintains a close liaison with high school counselors who advise college bound students.
5. Coordinates and disseminates information to day and evening credit students regarding course offerings and registration.
6. Cooperates in the preparation of numerous college publications when requested.
7. Provides students, faculty, and counselors with course information, except non-credit courses, needed for pre-enrollment interviews and early advisement.
8. Maintains the responsibility for coordinating all aspects of the registration process, including:
   a. Development of registration procedures for all on and off campus students.
   b. Cooperation with the Director of Continuing Education and Academic Scheduling in order to control the registration of classes to insure that pre-determined goals are achieved.
   c. Organizing and supervising the actual registration process.
   d. Adds and drops, late registration, mid-term and final grade report and distribution.
   e. Maintenance of accurate class rolls for proper functioning of College attendance policies.
   f. All transcript requests and all processing of grade changes.
9. Works cooperatively with his counterparts in other higher educational institutions.
10. Supervises the Chargeback policies and procedures.
11. Prepares input for reports for local, state, and federal agencies as needed.
12. Prepares budget requests for his area.
13. Cooperates closely with the Director of Continuing Education and Academic Scheduling in areas of mutual and complementary responsibilities.
14. Evaluate all transfer student records and veterans experience as applicable toward transfer credit.
15. Establishes a microfilm record system with retrieval capabilities and continuously updates entire student record.

16. Develops an integrated records system.
17. Maintains policies regarding record accessibility as they apply to student confidentiality of records.
18. Implements academic policies as they pertain to Admissions and Registration.
19. Handles initial input of student data (previous, academic and personal information).
20. Initiates data bank information and processes any changes in this data, e.g. change of name, address, phone number.
21. Evaluates graduation eligibility and provides students with information on their records at the College, and on requirements for certificates and degrees.
22. Cooperates in institutional research programs for his areas of responsibility as requested.
23. Assists the Director of Continuing Education and Academic Scheduling in development of Master Schedule, as requested.

Qualifications for the Position of
Director of Admissions and Registration

Admissions experience at the college level, preferably in the two-year community college field, is required. A master's degree is required and should be in some area of student personnel services, preferably including a counseling practicum.

Because of the strong emphasis of the college in institutional research, the Director of Admissions and Registration should possess necessary statistical skills for conducting research in his area.

Due to the nature of the position and the team approach envisioned throughout the entire college structure, the Director of Admissions and Registration should have a warm, outgoing personality. He should be skilled in human relations and be able to relate well to students and faculty.

He should have sufficient familiarity with computers and data processing to be able to work cooperatively with the Director of Research, Planning and Information in developing necessary systems.

Job Description
Director of Counseling and Guidance

Director of Counseling and Guidance

The Director of Counseling and Guidance is responsible for the coordination and supervision of the College Counselors. In addition, he will coordinate and be responsible for in-service training of the Faculty Advisors. In cooperation with the Dean of Student Personnel Services, he will coordinate, supervise, and evaluate instruction of the COG 100 program. In the administrative organization of the College the Director of Counseling and Guidance reports directly to the Dean of Student Personnel Services, who in turn reports to the President of the College.

Specifically, the Director of Counseling and Guidance:

1. Directs the College Counseling program which includes:
   a. Counseling and advisement.
   b. Group orienting.
   c. Applicant consulting.
   d. Career information.
   e. In-service training programs for staff.
   f. Liaison and articulation contacts with assigned high schools.
   g. Initiating and assisting in student characteristic research studies.
   h. Working cooperatively with all instructional and administrative staff to insure maximum educational opportunity for each student.
2. Coordinates the college's Faculty Advisor system which includes:
   a. Supervising co-assignment of students to Faculty Advisors.
   b. Determining quality and quantity of information to be used by Faculty Advisors.
   c. Evaluating the effectiveness of the Faculty Advisor system.
   d. In-service training for Faculty Advisors.
3. Coordinates the COG 100 program.
4. Directs the college testing programs and the interpretation of tests to students.
5. Coordinates the placement of students in appropriate courses and curricula through additional testing and assessment where necessary.
6. Evaluates the college counseling, Faculty Advisor, COG 100 and testing programs and makes recommendations for their improvement.
7. Presents educational-occupational information to the college community and keeps them apprised of changes in the educational-occupational world.
8. Supervises the initiation, coordination, and up-dating of a comprehensive educational-occupational library.
9. Counsels students part-time as directed by the Dean of Student Personnel Services.
10. Directs the College Health Counselor and health services.
11. Assigns high schools to College Counselors.
12. Prepares budget request for his areas of responsibility.

Qualifications for the Position of
Director of Counseling and Guidance

Counseling and guidance experience at the college level, preferably in the two-year community college field, is required. A master's degree is a minimum requirement and should be in some area of student personnel services. A college counseling practicum, or equivalent, is required.

The Director of Counseling and Guidance should have an inquiring mind, and intense belief in the maximum importance of every student, and an understanding of the inherent values of relevant research. He must show evidence of leadership qualities and abilities and will work closely in cooperation with the Dean of Student Personnel Services.

Due to the nature of the position and the team approach envisioned throughout the entire college structure, the Director of Counseling and Guidance should have a warm, outgoing personality. He should be skilled in human relations and be able to relate well to students and faculty.

Salary Schedule: Instructional
Salary Grade: Open

appendix 5

Opportunity for You at
Burlington County College

If you are interested in a challenging career in higher education, Burlington County College has staff openings which can offer exciting opportunities. We believe that the next few years will produce many changes in education which will require new and dynamic approaches to instruction. The college is committed to meeting these challenges.

This folder is designed to describe how Burlington County College proposes to meet the challenges of education. If you are willing to commit yourself to helping implement this program, we invite your inquiry.

The College and Its Purpose

Burlington County College opened in September, 1969. It is a two-year, open door, comprehensive community college created to provide an opportunity for higher education within the geographical and financial reach of the citizens of the county. To achieve this goal the college offers programs in five areas.

Career. Two year programs which prepare an individual for immediate employment upon graduation.

College Transfer. Programs of study which provide the first two years of study leading to a baccalaureate degree.

Community Services. Programs directed toward the cultural and educational needs of the community at large.

Developmental. Programs which provide students with an opportunity to obtain the basic knowledge, skills and attitudes necessary to enter an associate degree curriculum.

General Education. The non-vocational, non-specialized portion of each student's program that prepares him for the responsibilities he shares in common with all members of a free society.

During its third year, the college expects an enrollment of 1600 full-time and 1000 part-time students. As a growth indicator, this can be contrasted with our opening 1969 enrollment of 740 full-time and 300 part-time students.

A Systems Approach to Learning

The purpose of education is to insure learning. Convinced that the traditional teacher-centered, group-oriented lecture-recitation method of instruction is neither effective nor efficient in achieving this purpose, Burlington County College has designed an instructional system which has as its stated purpose assuring student learning. This system is built on the assumption that teaching is causing learning. Components of the system are students, teachers, instructional materials, facilities, and other persons who go to make up the college community.

If one assumes that teaching means causing learning then it follows that one can determine if teaching has occurred only when it is known what specific learning is to occur. Therefore for each sequence of topics or units in a course, a set of learning objectives must be provided. These tell the student what he is expected to be able to do, how well he is expected to do it and under what circumstances he is expected to perform. For each of these objectives tests are then developed to measure the attainment of the objectives. Next teaching-learning activities are prescribed which, if followed, should enable the learner to achieve the desired learning outcomes. After working through the teaching-learning activities, students are tested to determine attainment of the objectives. Students who succeed move on to new objectives while students who failed to satisfactorily reach specified performance criteria are provided the opportunity for further instruction. They are then permitted to try again. In every case, the results of student achievement are fed back into the system and revisions in teaching-learning activities are made until the desired level of achievement is consistently attained by the learners.

The teaching-learning activities used in achieving objectives vary widely but include large group instruction, classroom and laboratory experiences, programmed independent study, open audio-tutorial laboratories and small group seminars. In each mode a variety of media are normally utilized. The actual intermix of media and activity is determined by the particular objective of each sequence. This approach to teaching and learning is quite different from traditional methods. Its succes is largely dependent upon teachers, or managers of student learning who are responsible for determining course objectives, developing and revising instructional strategies, diagnosing difficulties and inspiring and motivating students.

Successful implementation also requires facilities which "facilitate," the provision of necessary book and non-book learning resources, adequate secretarial and printing backup, and an administration which, by its actions, demonstrates that it supports the faculty in their efforts.

The most important element, however, is *commitment.* Commitment to this approach to learning is expected of each professional staff member at the college. *Only persons willing to make such a commitment should apply.*

Pre-Service and In-Service Training

The College offers a unique program of Pre-Service and In-Service opportunities for professional growth to both its new and established faculty. Training in the instructional approach fostered by the College is offered to new faculty under the auspices of an Educational Professional Development Act grant from the U.S. Office of Education. This is a two week program prior to the fall term in which all new faculty are required to participate. In addition, all faculty are expected to participate in in-service programs for credit toward professional growth and to increase their knowledge of educational systems.

Student Personnel Services

Counseling and guidance are the focal points in a comprehensive program of Student Personnel Services. College counselors are complemented by faculty advisors in program planning. Educational and occupational information and planning, as well as orientation to self-understanding, are emphasized, in group guidance courses. Other features are a "headstart to college" summer program and personal counseling. In addition, the college emphasizes the gestalt of dynamic interrelationships among teaching, guidance and student learning as an integral part of its educational commitment.

Facilities

The permanent campus is located on a partially wooded 225-acre site bordered by a lovely, tree lined stream. Although maximum enrollment is projected at 5000 full-time students, the first phase of construction was designed for 2000 and includes two major facilities, the College Learning Center and Physical Education Center. The Learning Center houses learning resources facilities, faculty and administrative offices, computer center, laboratories, large group instruction areas, classrooms, seminar rooms, independent study carrels, the library, theater, student center, college store, dining and other facilities. The Physical Education Center includes offices, classrooms, a multi-purpose gymnasium, swimming pool and a general purpose room. Outdoor sports areas are located within close proximity to the center.

In addition the college will continue to use part of the temporary East Campus. This campus was erected on the eastern portion of the permanent site and was used to house the college during the 1970-71 school year. It includes six buildings with a total of 32,000 square feet of fully carpeted, air conditioned space. These are connected by a series of asphalt walks to the permanent buildings of the main campus.

The County

Burlington County, the largest in New Jersey, is located slightly northeast of Philadelphia and stretches from the Delaware River to the Atlantic Ocean. With a population of 325,000, it is the second fastest growing county in the state.

The total pre-college school enrollment (including free kindergartens) in 1970 was over 75,000. This reflects the fact that the county has the youngest median age (25.1) of any in the state. Each year more than 50 percent of the 4500 students who graduate from the county's public and private high schools elect to continue their formal education.

Burlington County is a mixture of suburban areas, rural farmland, and a largely undeveloped tract known as the "Pine Barrens." The county's largest municipality, Willingboro, has a population of approximately 50,000 people. One-third of the county is devoted to farming and from early May through October, the highways are lined with dozens of roadside fruit and vegetable stands.

Within easy commuting distance are a wide variety of cultural, recreational and educational facilities, including Philadelphia (30 minutes), New York (90 minutes), and Atlantic City (60 minutes). Within the county itself are located Batsto State Park, Wharton Tract State Forest, and Lebanon State Forest.

Surrounding the County's forty municipalities are scattered lake-front communities, new housing areas, and modern apartment and town house complexes. Shopping areas vary from large ultramodern completely enclosed malls to small out-of-the-way shops.

Transportation within the county is provided by a network of highways, including easy access to the New Jersey Turnpike and the newly-completed Interstate # 295. For travel outside the county there are inter-urban bus lines and rail service. Philadelphia International Airport is only 35 minutes away.

Tempered by the Atlantic Ocean, the county has a climate that is almost calendar perfect in its four seasons. Temperatures average 34 degrees in January and 84 degrees in July. Snow fall is normally limited to the period from mid-December to late February.

Community Colleges in New Jersey

A relative newcomer with respect to establishing community colleges, New Jersey is beginning to behave like the ideal late-bloomer. In 1962, the County College Act was passed. By the Fall of 1971 fourteen colleges will be in operation, with three others to follow. New Jersey should soon become one of the top ten states in community college enrollment.

Calendar

The college operates under a unique year-round calendar in which the schedule for one year consists of two 15-week semesters and two 6-week short terms. While some students elect to attend only the two 15-week semesters, most students enroll for at least one of the two short terms. The calendar allows students to graduate early, reduce the number of hours carried during the long terms, or make up time used to take developmental courses.

The ten-month faculty contract includes two 15-week semesters and one of the short terms. Depending upon enrollment during each short term a number of options are possible for faculty members pursuing advanced degree work.

PRE-SERVICE '71

MONDAY, 9	TUESDAY, 10	WEDNESDAY, 11	THURSDAY, 12	FRIDAY, 13
9 AM Welcome: President N. Dean Evans, CB-117 Introduction to Workshop: Dr. James O. Hammons Dean of the College CB-117	9 - 9:45 AM Discussion of "Instructional Systems: for Student Learning The Burlington County College Approach" Division Chairmen Science/Mth, Mr. Baker CA-136 Social Sci., Mr. Lewis CA-229 Business, Mr. Vail CA-160 Humanities, Mr. Welsh CA-227 10 AM General Discussion of Paper: Dr. H. Pierce, Act. Dean of Instruction CA-254 11 AM Print shop discussion and tour. Mr. Thomas, Chairman, Div. Of Learning Resources CA-254	9 AM Independent Study Time (Materials in CA-244)	9 AM Division of Learning Resources: Mr. Thomas CB-102	9 AM Division of Learning Resources: Mr. Thomas CA-272
12 NOON — Lunch D-108 (entire group)	12 NOON — Lunch D-108 (your arrangements)	12 NOON — Lunch D-108 (your arrangements)	12 NOON — Lunch D-108 (your arrangements)	12 NOON—Lunch D-108 (your arrangements)
1 PM Introduction Activities: Mr. Campo, College Counselor Mrs. Newman, Asst. Professor, speech 3 PM Division Meetings D-108	1 - 2 PM Introduction to Independent Study Sequences: Mr. Douglas, Educational Development Officer B-102 Independent Study Time (Materials in CA-244)	1 PM Writing Objectives General discussion: Mr. Douglas, CA-254 2 PM Seminars: Sci/Mth - CA-136 Soc. Sci. CA-229 Hum.& F.A. CA-227 Business CA-160	1 PM The Learning Packet Mr. Douglas, CB-102 a. Packets b. Self-Instructional packages	Independent Study Time (Materials in CA-244) 3 - 4 PM Seminar: Learning Packets Science/Mth CA-136 Soc.Sci. CA-229 Hum. & F. A. CA-227 Business CA-160

MONDAY, 16	TUESDAY, 17	WEDNESDAY, 18	THURSDAY, 19	FRIDAY, 20
9 AM Evaluation: Dr. Pierce CA-254 10:30 AM Computer Support: Mr. Lott, Coordinator of Instructional Computer Services B-107 1. Services 2. CMI 3. Validation	9 AM Seminar: The Community College: Dr. Hammons, CA-279	9 AM Seminar: The Student in the Comm. College Here and Elsewhere: Dr. Hammons and Mr. Beatty, Dean of Student Development CA-279 11 AM Introduction of Div. of Student Development and a discussion of their functions: Mr. Beatty CA-279	9 AM Division of Learning Resources: Mr. Belluscio LB-108	9 AM Pre-service Evaluation Session: Dr. Hammons 10:30 AM Division Meetings: Sci/Mth CA-136 Soc. Sci. CA-229 Hum. & F.A. CA-227 Business CA-160
12 Noon Lunch D-108 (your arrangements)	12 Noon Lunch D-108 (your arrangements)	12 Noon Lunch D-108 (your arrangements)	12 Noon Lunch D-108 (your arrangements)	12 Noon Lunch D-108 (your arrangements)
Independent Study Time (Materials available in CA-244) 3 - 4 PM Seminar: Evaluation, Dr. Pierce CA-254	Independent Study Time (Materials available in CA-244) 3 - 4 PM Seminar: PPIT Sci/Mth CA-136 Soc.Sci. CA-229 Hum.& F.A. CA-227 Business CA-160	Independent Study Time (Materials available in CA-244) 3 - 4 PM Seminar: Instructional Development Sci/Mth CA-136 Soc.Sci. CA-229 Hum. & F.A. CA-227 Business CA-160	Independent Study Time (Materials available in CA-244) 3 - 4 PM Seminar: System Approach: Sci/Mth CA-136 Soc.Sci. CA-229 Hum. F.A. CA-227 Business CA-160	FREE

appendix 7

Seward County Community Junior College
Liberal, Kansas
Philosophy and Goals

The concept of the community junior college is a major innovation in American education which promises to be as revolutionary as the establishment of land grant colleges a hundred years ago. Its lineage is that of the junior college, but it has been designed to possess new qualities and to function in new roles. It is not a stalagmite of the high school nor a stalactite of the university. A community college is a distinctive institution and is developing in response to major forces in American society:

The *population explosion* demands more facilities for advanced education. There are not only greater numbers of youth but also an ever-increasing proportion of them going beyond the high school.

The *knowledge explosion* demands greater educational efficiency, longer preparation and more frequent refresher and continuing education courses.

The new concept includes not only such broad social considerations, but also necessary local adaptations. The goal of the Seward County Community Junior College is a high-quality, comprehensive, flexible program available to a variety of students in a rapidly growing urban-rural community.

Educational Program

The educational program must embrace a broad range of curricula and serve a variety of objectives:

1. Academic courses, equivalent to the first two years of college or university work, transferable to a four-year institution, and applicable to a baccalaureate or professional degree.
2. Occupational programs, designed to provide the technical knowledge, manipulative skills, and general background necessary to successful achievement in technical and semi-professional employment.
3. General education appropriate for those who will terminate their post high school education in two years or less.
4. Developmental, special training, and general education programs for the high school nongraduate.
5. Continuing education. The knowledge explosion, developing technology and a rapidly changing world all give new emphasis to the importance of continuing education. It will be closely related to vocational needs and emphasize the maintenance and upgrading of technical competence. It also is likely to be related to public service activities arising out of special training needs associated with community, state, national, or world developments and to individual avocational needs. In general, continuing education programs for adults—noncredit courses, seminars, in-service and retraining courses—will make important contributions to vocational, community-service and personal needs.

Inter-related Curriculum

The terms "academic" and "vocational" should not be antagonistic concepts. Current demands for technically trained and semi-professional personnel offer a growing number of opportunities. However, over-specialized training may mean that within a few years the student finds that he has an obsolete skill and little general educational background for learning a new one. On the other hand, a student who limits himself to general or academic education may be without a ready means of earning livelihood.

The curriculum demands a "both and" rather than "either or" approach. By stressing commonalities and interrelationships, the College will provide an educational opportunity for the personal, intellectual, and occupational development of the individual. The various programs can be not only compatible with each other but also mutually reinforcing.

Counseling and Guidance

The State Plan for Kansas Community Junior Colleges specifies that the college shall "be available to all students who want, need, and can benefit from such programs." While an "open door" policy generally is a part of community college philosophy, it does not mean that every door is equally appropriate for every student. Some course offerings, in both academic and occupational areas, are highly selective. The College needs to recognize the importance of providing a variety of programs for a heterogeneous student population. Therefore, an adequate program of counseling and guidance is essential in order to help the student assess his capabilities and interests and plan accordingly. Each individual should have opportunity to explore many possibilities, even a shift in program if necessary, in order to achieve a fulfilling, productive life.

Opportunity for Innovation

The Seward County Community Junior College is part of the most dynamic phase of American education today and it is being established without a local predecessor. This newness provides a rare opportunity for innovations! This should not be interpreted to mean that all new ideas will be worked into the fabric of the College. Among the educational innovations which should be considered are: large and small group instructions, computerized learning programs, modular scheduling, flexible architecture, learning laboratories, independent study, a comprehensive library that includes electronic aides. Rather than introducing innovations in an unrelated way, it may be better to use a systems approach in which they are combined in a logical and consistent pattern.

Community Service

The major purposes of the College are reflected in the commitment to comprehensive educational programs, including education for transfer, education for employment, general education, and continuing education for adults. Yet, the emphasis on adult education may legitimately be viewed as only part of a broader relationship in which the College becomes an integral part of the community. It is anticipated that the College will eventually utilize the resources, talents, and opportunities of the community to the greatest possible extent and, in turn, offer to the community its facilities, faculty, and stimulus. The program will encompass academic, social, cultural and recreational activities.

Coordination with Other Institutions

In addition to its relationship with the community at large, the College also will emphasize its specific relationships with other educational institutions of the area. Vertically, the College will develop its programs in conjunction with the high schools, with higher-educational institutions and with vocational-technical career opportunities. Horizontally, the College will seek to cooperate with neighboring post-high school programs in order to avoid gaps and duplications. One important effort would encompass joint study of vocational needs and opportunities.

Educational Atmosphere

The newness of the College provides the opportunity—indeed, more appropriately, the requirement—for setting a general tone or educational atmosphere for the institution. Major emphasis is to be given to student initiative. Learning sought and discovered with maximum student participation is generally the most useful, the best understood, and the most likely to expand into new and greater achievement. Emphasis must be on skills in critical and obective thinking. Free and active inquiry with respect for academic disciplines and the rights of others is an essential of a free society.

Developing Unity

Unity on a commuter campus requires special consideration. Extracurricular activities, such as student government, cultural and social events should be planned to help the student establish an identity with the College. This will require special facilities.

Personnel Policy

The comprehensive College conceived here requires a superior faculty allowed the freedom to function responsibly with flexibility, security, and creativity. The faculty and the administration are expected to assume a major responsibility for the further development of philosophy and objectives and for implementing the curriculum. The Board of Trustees desires to adopt a personnel policy which will attract and hold top-level staff and that will assure professional growth. Time, encouragement, and resources must be available to the staff for the continuous progress of the program. The president is expected to be the chief executive officer, educational leader, and advisor to the Board.

The Commitment

The Seward County Community Junior College Board of Trustees is committed to the development of a truly different and distinctive institution, definitely attuned to the needs of this community. Carefully identifying and implementing goals, stressing the many community relationships, emphasizing quality in every program, taking advantage of innovations and new technology, developing an enlightened personnel policy—all are aimed at creating a College distinguished by its ability to serve post-high school educational needs in this community.

A First Choice Institution

As a matter of priority, the first concern in developing the College will be establishment of academic and vocational programs for recent high school graduates. *Geographical convenience* and *economy* are obvious advantages of the community college, but not the only ones. As universities become larger and shift more of their emphasis to upper level work and research, there is increased need to emphasize the first two years of college work in the community college. Occupational programs will also be increasingly popular because of the growing demands for technical and semi-professional manpower. Accordingly, with the implementation of a high quality program in an attractive setting, it is anticipated that the College will become a first choice institution for a growing proportion of high school graduates of this area of southwest Kansas.

Dundalk Community College
Baltimore County, Maryland
Philosophy

Dundalk Community College belongs to the people whom it serves and who support it. The college is responsive to individual and collective needs of the community. The basic purpose of Dundalk Community College is to offer comprehensive programs that will help meet the educational needs of the people by preparing them for a fuller participation and involvement in their society. Dundalk Community College will serve as a stimulus for raising the levels of aspiration and accomplishment of the people in the community. The college is a source of service for the various activities and needs of the community, and provides enrichment for the community by serving as a cultural center.

Within this area of responsibility Dundalk Community College is dedicated to the policy of providing educational opportunities that will permit the youth and adults of the area to enrich their lives and advance their careers to the limit of their desires and capabilities.

The college is concerned with the development of the individual for a useful and productive life. This position implies a deep and abiding faith in the worth and dignity of the individual student as the most important component of the college.

To implement this philosophy, Dundalk Community College operates with an "open door" policy. Any individual may enroll. The college will strive to provide for all students, meeting as fully as possible the needs of all, with disadvantage to none. A variety of programs are planned to meet the diversity of needs presented by the students. A responsibility of the college is to find appropriate, effective educational techniques to help each student determine realistic goals, discover his abilities and interests, and develop them to the fullest extent. Traditionally effective college instruction will be supplemented with new media and new methods—individualized instruction, programmed learning, credit by examinations, work-study program, fieldwork, internships—and future improvements not yet envisioned.

Dundalk Community College believes that opportunities for college education should be available to persons throughout their lifetime and not just immediately after high school. Opportunity for older students, women with children, workers, and so forth must be provided. Furthermore, we believe work and study should be mixed throughout a lifetime. Therefore, Dundalk Community College will develop curriculums which combine academic and "on-the-job" experiences.

Moreover, the college also recognizes the need and accepts the responsibility for its commitment to the community's needs. This orientation toward the community will be expressed in its development as an educational, recreational, civic, and cultural center available to the entire community.

Objectives

Recognizing that its philosophy encourages the enrollment of people with differing abilities and objectives, Dundalk Community College will offer a wide variety of curriculums and courses.

The objectives of the institution are to provide:

A. Equal Higher Educational Opportunities

A primary objective of Dundalk Community College is to provide equal opportunity for all people to attend college. This objective will be achieved through the college's "open door" admissions policy, individualized instruction, competent and dedicated faculty and staff, flexible schedule offering year-round instruction both day and evening, comprehensive course offering, developmental courses and services for students with limited academic backgrounds, low tuition, and proximity to the student's home.

B. Educational Programs

1. *General and Arts and Sciences Education*—Courses designed to meet the needs of those students planning to transfer to four-year colleges as well as those students who wish to upgrade their academic achievement in order for more satisfactory participation in society.

2. *Occupational Education*—Occupational education includes curriculums that are intended to prepare students for employment in a wide array of job opportunities ranging from the semi-skilled to the professions. Programs will be designed for persons preparing to enter an occupation, as well as courses designed for retraining or occupational advancement for persons already employed. Dundalk Community College programs will vary in length from a few weeks to two years. In some instances, such as the professions, additional work leading to the baccalaureate or more advanced degrees must be pursued at four-year colleges. Emphasis is given to those occupations of the technical and semi-professional level for which approximately two years of college work are considered appropriate. Estimates of labor experts suggest that this occupational level will expand rapidly, percentage-wise at a considerably greater rate than other occupational levels. Associate degrees or certificates are offered at the successful completion of all occupational programs.

3. *Developmental Education*—Courses and programs designed to upgrade the basic academic achievement of students in order to prepare them for full and satisfactory participation in college-level courses.

C. Counseling Services

The college regards the counseling programs as one of its major responsibilities to the student. The counseling function is viewed as one of vital importance in helping students assess their aptitudes, determine their future vocational and educational goals, select their curricula, plan their courses, acquire productive study habits, and develop satisfactory personality traits.

D. Community Services

The community-services program makes available the resources of the college to the local community for the purpose of assisting the community in the solution of community problems through educational processes. Community service programs include special courses and programs to meet cultural and educational needs of the community. Programs are offered through credit and noncredit courses, seminars, institutes, workshops, conferences and other educational media. These approaches are designed to provide assistance in planning programs of community development and leisure time activities.

Increased participation in civic affairs through greater awareness of public issues, community achievements, problems, and local, state, and national government will be developed through community-service programs. The college will also provide cultural enrichment for the community in such areas as art, literature, music, and drama.

Burlington County College
Pemberton, New Jersey
Philosophy of the College

Burlington County College is dedicated to those moral and spiritual values which are inherent in the noblest ideals of the American democratic state. As an integral part of a nation under God, the college will always strive to teach the principles of individual freedom, personal responsibility, and brotherhood among men. Each student is recognized as a human being in search of his own destiny, and all the resources of the college are available to assist him in this quest.

Created because of a community desire to provide an opportunity for higher education within geographic and financial reach of the citizens of the county, its chief purpose is to determine present and future post-high school educational needs of the region it serves, and to provide educational opportunities to meet those needs to the extent of its legal, physical, and financial abilities.

As a comprehensive two-year public community college, Burlington County College is part of one of the most dynamic movements in American higher education. The college, as an open-door institution, is dedicated to extending the privilege of higher education to all who can benefit from the experience. The educational programs of the college will always be creative, flexible, and dynamic—designed to better serve the people, business, industry, labor, and the professions. The pursuit of excellence in teaching and learning is an integral part of the philosophy of Burlington County College.

As an investment in the human and economic resources of the county, the college constantly seeks to serve the various facets of community life. Most important of all, Burlington County College is dedicated to help each citizen develop his talents and human potential to the maximum degree.

Institutional Objectives and the Means of Accomplishment

1. To provide a variety of educational offerings to meet the various post-high school needs and abilities of the citizens of the county.

Means. Associate degree curriculums in the liberal arts and sciences parallel the lower division offerings of four-year colleges and universities, and are designed to enable students to transfer to a four-year institution upon successful completion of the required learning sequences.

Various career programs leading to the associate degree are designed to prepare students for employment in the rapidly expanding and changing technical, semi-professional, and public service fields.

Developmental and remedial programs enable students to upgrade basic skills before embarking on regular college level work.

Various continuing-education courses, both credit and noncredit, will meet the diverse needs of many adult citizens. Opportunities are provided to train for employment in new fields, to upgrade present skills, to enhance family life, to provide cultural enrichment, and to contribute to greater civic responsibility.

2. To provide the best possible teaching-learning experience.

Means. Curriculum development has a high priority. Each educational program and course of study is carefully developed from values and objectives that are clearly stated and constantly evaluated. For each instructional sequence, obectives are specified in behavioral or performance terms. Teachers describe the patterns of behavior or learning outcomes expected from the student by the end of the course. Appropriate subject matter content, teaching-learning methods, instructional media, and evaluation procedures are then programmed.

Four major modes of instruction are employed: large group, laboratory or classroom, independent study, and seminar, with the intermix determined by specific objectives and the most effective means to achieve them.

Students assume considerable responsibility for their own learning in the independent study mode, and the seminar discussions are the catalytic agents in the entire learning process. Discovery, inquiry, observation, reflection, problem solving, and experimentation are stressed. Students are encouraged to form their own generalizations, concepts, conclusions, and insights.

3. To encourage innovation and experimentation.

Means. The administrative staff and faculty continually strive to improve the college—its goals and resulting instructional processes. Evaluation is constant, and new research findings are applied in an attempt to make the institution responsive to the society it serves. The spirit of innovation and experimentation is always encouraged.

4. To provide necessary guidance, counseling, and career services for students.

Means. Constant student-faculty interaction is sought. The teaching staff is vitally involved in the guidance function. A reasonable ratio of counselors and students is maintained for specialized counseling. Each student is assisted in finding an educational program best suited to his aptitudes, interests, abilities, and his developing career plans.

5. To enhance the physical, emotional, and social growth of all students.

Means. Emphasis is on the development of a variety of carry-over type sports skills, student activities, and other individual and social pursuits designed to involve all students.

6. To offer a broad program of community services.

Means. Through activities such as plays, concerts, film festivals, and lectures, the college seeks to enhance the cultural life of the county. The Little Theatre, Learning Resources Center, and the Physical Education Center are available for community use.

The college resources and facilities are available for such programs as educational workshops, seminars, and public affairs forums.

7. To involve faculty and students in the total program and life of the college.

Means. Through such organizations as a Faculty Senate and Student Government Association, all members of the college community participate in goal determination, program planning, and evaluation.

Administration-faculty-student interaction is stressed throughout all college activities.

appendix 8

Board Policy

Title: Instructional Personnel, Appointment

Date:

Supercedes:

1. Initial Assignment of Salary and Academic Rank:

a. In the employment of new instructional staff members, the President will recommend the starting salary and the academic rank to be assigned, based on the Criteria for Academic Rank and the best judgment of the administrative staff. In determining initial placement, the administration will award credit for previous experience and course work according to the relevancy of such activity to the person's position with the College.

b. Librarians and student personnel services personnel shall be placed on academic rank on the same basis as regular instructional personnel.

c. Persons on the administrative salary schedule may be assigned faculty rank as determined by the President.

2. Physical Examinations:

a. The following personnel must present as a prerequisite of employment, a currently dated health certificate from a physician and negative report of a chest x-ray or a negative Tine or Mantoux Test; and as a prerequisite of reappointment, a negative report of a chest x-ray or a negative Tine or Mantoux Test:

336

(1) Instructional personnel (including both credit and non-credit, part-time and full-time instructional personnel)

(2) Administrative personnel (same as above plus positive results on an annual physical)

3. Members of Same Family—Employment of:

a. The President of the College may recommend for employment members of the same family.

4. Criteria for Academic Rank:

a. The following is a guide for *initial* placement on the schedule:

(1) *Instructor* — Master's Degree in subject field, *or* Bachelor's Degree[3] plus at least three years experience in technical field.

(2) *Assistant Professor* — Master's Degree in subject field, and 15 semester hours of relevant graduate work beyond the Master's plus three years *college teaching*[1] experience, *or* Bachelor's Degree[3] plus at least three years experience in technical field and three years *college teaching* experience.

(3) *Associate Professor* — Master's Degree in subject field and 30 semester hours of relevant graduate work beyond the Master's plus six years *college teaching*[1] experience, *or* Bachelor's Degree plus three years experience in technical field plus six years *college teaching* experience.

(4) *Professor* — Master's Degree in subject field and all course work completed for doctorate except dissertation plus nine years *college teaching*[3] experience, or Doctorate in subject field plus nine years *college teaching*[1] experience, *or* Bachelor's Degree[3] plus three years experience in technical field plus nine years *college teaching*[1] experience.

Notes:

1. For librarians and student personnel services personnel, relevant experience in college library and college student personnel work is equated to college teaching experience.

2. The minimum educational requirement for student personnel services personnel, librarians and faculty teaching in college transfer courses is the Master's Degree (or five year Bachelor's Degree in library science).

3. Normally, the minimum requirement for faculty teaching in highly technical career program areas will be the Bachelor's Degree and suitable professional experience.

4. Technical experience may be equated for teaching experience; however, no individual *should* initially be placed beyond the Assistant Professor level without at least one year of acceptable college teaching experience.

Administrative Procedure
Title: Guidelines for Initial Placement
on the Instructional Salary Schedule

Date:

Supercedes:

1. General Statement

a. At initial employment, the salary rate established need not provide for credit for all previous experience in business, government, industry or teaching. In all cases, experience should be evaluated in terms of the relevancy of such experience to the person's anticipated position with the College.

2. Initial Employment Guidelines

a. For purposes of initial placement on the salary schedule, past experience and education for full-time faculty members, student personnel services personnel, and learning resources personnel will be evaluated according to the following guidelines:

   (1) One year experience for: each three years relevant experience in elementary and junior high, grades one through eight. A maximum of five years equated experience may be given.

   (2) One year experience for: each two years relevant experience in senior high schools, grades nine through twelve. A maximum of five years equated experience may be given.

   (3) One year experience for: each year of relevant full-time college experience.

   (4) With approval of the President, exceptions to the above may be granted.

b. Credit may be granted on a one-to-one basis for each year's experience in government, business, industry, or military service which is directly relevant to the individual's position with the college subject to the following restrictions:

   (1) For individuals with only a high school diploma, first subtract seven years.

   (2) For individual's with only a Bachelor's Degree, first subtract three years.

c. In some cases, educational achievement may be substituted for experience requirements. When this is done, the following guidelines should be observed:

   (1) Determine the rank and salary placement the individual will be eligible for by virtue of his education and experience.

   (2) Award one credit for each 15 semester hours the individual possesses in excess of the minimum educational requirement specified for that rank (to a maximum of three).

(3) Individuals with the doctorate will not normally be employed below the Assistant Professor level.

d. On occasion, it may be desired to initially place personnel at a higher rank than their education qualifies them for. In general, this should be discouraged since it obviates the requirement for a person to continue his education. However, when circumstances indicate that additional education is either not available in that particular field or is not needed by the individual concerned, an adjustment of one rank may be made. When this is done, placement on the salary schedule will be determined in conjunction with the President.

e. In awarding credit for part-time or graduate teaching experience, the evaluation should be made in terms of what percentage of a full-time position the part-time work constitutes. For example, a person who has five years of part-time teaching at the rate of one course per term, for two terms a year, would have taught ten courses. This would be roughly equivalent to one year of full-time teaching. Credit for graduate teaching may be awarded only when the applicant had full responsibility for the course.

f. No individual should *initially* be placed beyond the Assistant Professor level without at least one year of relevant college experience.

g. In evaluating experience, a maximum of one year's credit may be awarded for each calendar year of the person's employment.

h. Initial salary determination is a matter between a prospective employee and the College.

Board Policy

Title: Supervision of the Instructional Program

Date:

Supercedes:

Since one of the main institutional objectives of Burlington County College is "to provide the best possibile teaching-learning experiences," it is imperative that a comprehensive supervisory program be organized and administered, involving all persons concerned with the learning process. Modern supervision is positive, democratic action aimed at the improvement of instruction through the continual growth of the student, the faculty member, and the supervising administrator.

The President is authorized to develop and administer procedures for supervision of the instructional program that will include the following:

1. Professional assistance to the faculty in curriculum development, including the writing of objectives, the identification of content, the provision of adequate learning resources, and the construction of necessary tests and measurements.
2. Aid in mastering the various modes of instruction used at the college.
3. Regular visitation of laboratories, classrooms, seminars, independent study areas, and large group lectures by supervisory personnel.
4. Conferences with faculty to evaluate progress in teaching.
5. Attendance at appropriate professional conferences.
6. Encouragement of wide reading in one's discipline.
7. In-service programs and workshops for new and experienced faculty members.
8. Encouragement of instructional and institutional research, experimentation and innovation.
9. Assistance in developing a cooperative approach to teaching.

Administrative Procedure

Title: Supervision of the Instructional Program

Date:

Supercedes:

The following personnel will assume major responsibility for the effective supervision of instruction: the President, the Dean of the College, and the Division Chairmen.

1. During the periods assigned under the faculty load formula for curriculum development, professional and clerical resources and supervisory assistance will be provided faculty members. The facilities of the Learning Resources Center are always available. Division Chairmen will supervise the process of curriculum design and evaluation.

2. The Dean of Division Chairmen will supervise the selection and use of various modes of instruction and appropriate learning resources to attain the objectives of the curriculum. The Director of Learning Resources will be a vital staff assistant to this process, working with the Chairmen and individual faculty members.

3. The President, Dean of the College, and Division Chairmen will set up schedules for the regular formal and informal visitation of all teaching-learning activities, including laboratories, classrooms, seminars, independent study, and large group lectures. Follow-up conferences should be held with faculty members to jointly assess student progress toward the objectives, and the instructor's growth in teaching skill. A brief written summary of each formal visit (one complete teaching session or more) should be placed in the instructor's folder, with a copy to him.

4. The Dean and Division Chairmen will plan for regular involvement of faculty members in:

   a. Attendance at professional conferences.

   b. Visitation to other community colleges.

   c. Attendance at special seminars and workshops in the field.

5. Professional collections, research materials in teaching and learning, and curriculum development resources will be maintained, and wide reading in each field will be encouraged.

6. As appropriate, in-service programs and workshops for administrators and faculty members will be held.

7. Faculty will be encouraged to suggest projects in instructional research and innovation. A spirit of free inquiry and experimentation will always be maintained, and the necessary resources for implementation of research provided.

8. Each Division Chairman will work closely with the faculty members in his division to develop a cooperative approach to instruction. The strengths of each person should be sought and utilized. For example, in the instructional team, one person may write objectives; another present large-group lectures; others conduct classes, laboratories or seminars; and another construct and analyze test items.

9. In courses labeled counseling and guidance, the Dean of the College will work cooperatively with the Dean of Student Personnel Services in developing the course content, learning resources, and methods of instruction.

Board Policy
Title: Learning Resources Selection Policy

Date:

Supercedes:

1. Objectives

a. The primary objective of resource selection shall be to collect or produce materials necessary or useful for the instructional program and the intellectual growth of the college community. All selections will be made solely on the merits of the resource in relation to the building of the collection and to serving the interests of the users. The Learning Resources Center must preserve a judicious sense of need for the present and the future when adding or producing resources that not only support instruction, but maintain the growth and balance of the collection.

2. Definitions

a. *Learning Resources*
Learning Resources, as used in this document refers collectively to both book and non-book material, such as tapes, films, slides, computer-assisted programs, information storage and retrieval systems, photographs, video transmissions, textbooks and similar materials. The term resources is given the widest possible meaning and it is implicit in this policy that all forms of teaching and learning resources, whether of permanent or temporary value, must be included.

b. *The General Collection*
The general collection of learning resources provides material for the intellectual enrichment of all college personnel and the public at large without regard for use of this material in a specified instructional program.

c. *The Instructional Collection*
The instructional collection of learning resources provides direct support material for specific instructional objectives, and is limited in use to students and faculty.

d. The public at large is defined as all persons not presently affiliated with Burlington County College in the capacity of student, faculty or staff.

3. Statement of Intellectual Freedom

a. As a responsibility of the Learning Resources Center all resources will be chosen for values of interest, information, and enlightenment of students, the faculty, and citizens of the community at large. In no case will learning resources be excluded because of the race or nationality or the social, political, and religious views of the authors or producers.

b. The Learning Resources Center will provide resources presenting all points of view concerning the problems and issues of our times; no learning resources will be proscribed or removed from the premises of the Learning Resources Center because of partisan or doctrinal disapproval.

c. Censorship will be challenged by the Learning-Resources Center in the maintenance of its responsibility to provide public information and enlightenment.

d. The Learning Resources Center will cooperate with all persons and groups concerned with resisting abridgment of free expression and free access to ideas.

e. The rights of an individual to the use of learning resources and materials will not be denied or abridged because of his race, religion, national origins or social or political views.

4. Acquisitions Policy

a. *The General Collection*
All college personnel have the privilege of requesting the Learning Resources Center to buy or produce any resource they consider necessary or helpful to the academic program. No restriction will be placed on the number of requests that may be submitted by any person or division provided they are within budgetary limitation, and within the *Procedures for Resources Selection and Removal.*

It is recognized that the Director of the Learning Resources Center has the authority to supervise and coordinate the systematic development of the collection and to assign priorities to all requests.

b. *The Instructional Collection*
The Learning Resources Center provides the faculty and student body with materials and services in direct support of the instructional program. All requests for resources in this collection must be made within the *Procedures for Resources Selection and Removal,* established jointly by the Learning Resources Center, the faculty, staff and students.

c. *Gifts*
The Learning Resources Center accepts gifts provided their content meets a recognized need within the criteria applied to purchased or produced materials, and if any conditions imposed by the Donor are not in conflict with the impartial sense of this policy document. Where necessary, the Center's staff will solicit the opinion of faculty members knowledgeable in the various disciplines.

5. Removal Policy

a. Removal of resources already in the collection for reasons other than physical deterioration and routine changes in course work requirements is viewed as potential infringement of intellectual liberty. Any person or organization requesting the removal of resources already in the collection must follow explicitly the methods outlined in the *Procedures for Resource Selection and Removal.*

6. Use of the Learning Resources Center by the Public at Large

a. The public has the privilege of using the Learning Resources Center's general collection and reference services, but at this time they may not remove resources from the physical confines of the Learning Resources

Center. However, this policy can be rescinded or modified by the Director of Learning Resources if demands made by the public constitute an impediment to the function of the academic program. The instructional collection is restricted to the exclusive use of students and faculty.

b. Should a question arise regarding service to any segment of the public at large, preference will be given to the citizens of the county.

7. Purchasing Policy

a. In accordance with Chapter 402 of the New Jersey Statutes, the Board of Trustees shall, within the limits of funds appropriated or otherwise made available to the Board, purchase the following without advertising for bids therefor:

(1) Library materials including books, periodicals, newspapers, documents, pamphlets, photographs, reproductions, microforms, pictorial or graphic works, musical scores, maps, charts, globes, sound recordings, slides, films, filmstrips, video and magnetic tapes, other printed or published matter, and audiovisual and other materials of a similar nature;

(2) Necessary binding or rebinding of library materials; and,

(3) Specialized library services.

b. The acquisition of all items to be purchased by the Learning Resources Center will be initiated by the Director of Learning Resources in compliance with policies and procedures as established by the Director of Administrative Services.

Board Policy
Title: Budget Preparation and Adoption

Date:

Supercedes:

1. Fiscal Responsibility

a. The Board of Trustees has inherent responsibility for the establishment of the financial framework within which the college must operate.

b. This framework or budget will identify the sources of income and application of expenditures necessary to meet the college objectives.

2. Preparation and Approval of Budget

a. The Board shall delegate to the president, the authority to prepare the detail and summary budget for all areas of the college for a specific fiscal year.

b. The president shall present the initial draft of the budget at the regular meeting of the Board of Trustees in December of each year. This budget shall reflect the financial requirements of the college for the fiscal year beginning July 1st of the year following and ending on June 30th one further year hence and the anticipated sources of income to support such expenditures.

c. The Board shall approve and adopt said budget after incorporation of any changes considered necessary. Such approval and adoption shall take place no later than the regular January meeting of the Board.

d. By approval of the budget, the Board authorizes the expenditure of funds itemized therein for the purposes identified, restricted only by dollar or procedural limits prescribed in other Board Policy. The president shall have the authority to redirect the allocation of funds only within the framework of each fund account and limited by the total budget amounts.

e. Permanent transfer of funds between or among fund accounts must first be approved by the Board. Temporary transfers, not exceeding 30 days, shall not require Board Approval.

f. Disposition of surplus or deficit balances in each fund account will be made at the recommendation of the president and approved by the Board. Such transfers will normally not be made until after the annual audit.

3. Distribution of Budget

a. The approved budget shall be prepared in the forms prescribed and submitted to the State Department of Higher Education by February 23rd.

b. The budget shall also be submitted to the Board of School Estimate by February 1st of each year.

c. Copies of the budget shall be distributed to staff administrators having budgetary responsibility.

Board Policy
Title: Sponsored Research and Grant Programs

Date:

Supercedes:

The college recognizes the value of engaging in sponsored research and grant programs, when they are consistent with institutional goals and philosophy. The college encourages all members of the staff to consider participating in such programs as they relate to their own curriculum areas. Ideas for sponsored research and grant programs may originate at any level, however, the President's Office will have the responsibility for coordinating and approving all sponsored programs and will take the leadership in seeking federal, state and private funds to finance these programs.

Administrative Procedure
Title: Sponsored Research and Grant Programs

Date:

Supercedes:

1. Responsibility—Responsibility for coordinating and approving sponsored programs rests with the President's Office. The President had designated the Director of Community Services and Public Information as coordinating agent for all sponsored programs.

2. Initiation of Proposals—Proposals may be initiated at any level. Each division (Instruction, SPS, Community Services, Computer Center) will determine their internal procedures for processing proposals. All proposals must have the approval of the dean or director of that division in order to proceed with an initial draft of the proposal.

3. Coordination and Budget—The originator of the proposal will consult with the Director of Community Services and Public Information in order to construct the budget and to receive guidance in the areas of proposal design and construction.

4. Submission—After the final draft has received approval from the appropriate dean or director it will be sent to the President's office for signature and for submission to the appropriate agency. Copies of the proposal will be kept on file at that office as well as with the initiator and his dean or director.

5. Resources—The Director of Community Services and Public Information will maintain current information regarding the availability of federal and private funds for research and other grant programs. The Director of Community Services and Public Information will from time to time hold in-service workshops for faculty members in order to acquaint them with such items such as the availability of funds, program priorities and changing regulations.

6. Proposal Writing—The Director of Community Services and Public Information will be available to consult with staff members concerning ideas that may be generated with regard to proposals. The actual writing of proposals may be an individual or a joint effort depending upon the technical nature of the proposal and the requirements involved.

7. Grants Management—The Director of Community Services and Public Information will maintain a central file of all active grant programs. He will coordinate efforts in order to assure adherence to current practices and procedures in regard to filing reports and other related administrative matters. The Director of Community Services and Public Information will work closely with the Director of Administrative Services in maintaining fiscal control of all grant programs. A joint effort will be maintained in order to adhere to all required fiscal practices with regard to disbursements and reporting.

appendix 9

Administrative Procedure
Title: Interim Plan for Involvement in the
Governance of the College

Date:

Supersedes:

To implement board policy No. 903, "Responsible Involvement of Persons in the Decision-Making Process of the College," this revised plan for involvement in governance is issued.

To assure maximum participation in decision making, three major councils are included in the plan: president's council, instructional affairs council, and student personnel services council. Meetings of all councils are open meetings. The faculty senate and the student senate complete the organizational pattern.

The accompanying organization chart and procedural statements for the three councils explain the operational implementation of the plan at the council level.

As necessary committees of the councils will be appointed by the president or by the councils with the approval of the president. Examples of such committees are the exceptions and appeals committee and the student conduct committee.

President's Council

Purpose: This council, as the chief advisory body to the president, is involved with communication, long-range planning, institutional purposes and goals, budget approvals and change, institutional systems and procedures, and inter-institutional cooperation. Recommendations are made to the president for his action.

349

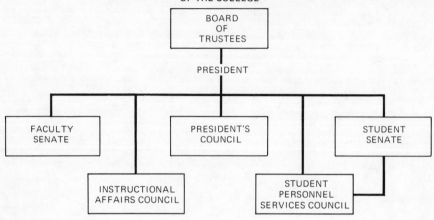

INTERIM PLAN FOR INVOLVEMENT IN THE GOVERNANCE
OF THE COLLEGE

Membership:	President of the college.
	Dean of the college.
	Dean of student personnel services.
	One representative of the president's staff, appointed by the president.
	One division chairman (elected by the division chairmen).
	Four instructional staff members (three elected at large; one elected to represent LRC and SPS).
	Four 14,noninstructional staff members (two nonsupervisory personnel and two supervisors) to be elected by the noninstructional staff.
	Four students, elected by the student senate.
	One secretary (nonvoting).

Meetings: As called by the chairman, or upon petition of five or more voting members of the council.

Chairman: President of the college (voting only in case of a tie).

Minutes: Distributed to members of the council, and a copy filed in the LRC. Abstract to be published in staff *Newsletter*.

Agenda of   Tentative agenda to be published with abstract of minutes.
next meeting:

Continuity: Members to be elected annually in May and to begin serving at the June meeting of the council. Approximately one-third of each constituency's membership is to be elected each year. The method of election is the responsibility of the constitutency; the method of staggering is the responsibility of the council.

Alternates: Each constituency should elect an alternate for each regular member.

Instructional Affairs Council

Purposes: Review and recommend to the president of the college for his action all matters related to:

a. Addition of new courses, development of new curricula, deletion of courses, changes in title, or numbering of catalog descriptions, course prerequisites, and course transfer problems.

    NOTE: It is intended that all suggestions for curriculum additions, deletions, or revisions originate at the division level. Following general divisional review, they are then referred to the instructional-affairs council.

b. Faculty curriculum advising.

c. Academic standards, grading practices, degree requirements, and other special considerations dealing with academic problems.

d. Learning resources—selection and utilization.

Membership: Dean of the college or his appointed representative.

Four instructional staff members, one elected from each instructional division.

One student personnel services staff member, elected at large by SPS.

One LRC instructional staff member, elected at large by LRC.

Four students, elected by the student senate.

One division chairman, elected by the division chairmen.

One noninstructional staff member, elected at large by the noninstructional staff.

Meetings: As called by the chairman or upon petition of three or more voting members of the council.

Chairman: Elected by the council at the first regular meeting of the new council.

Minutes: Distributed to members of the council, and a copy filed in the LRC. Abstract to be published in staff *Newsletter.*

Agenda of
next meeting: Tentative agenda to be published with abstract of minutes.

Continuity: Members to be elected annually in May and to begin serving at the June meeting of the council. Approximately one-third of each constituency's membership is to be elected each year. The method of election is the responsibility of the constituency; the method of staggering is the responsibility of the council.

Alternates: Each constituency should elect an alternate for each regular member.

Student Personnel Services Council

Purposes: Review and recommend to the president of the college all matters related to students.

Membership'   Associate dean of student personnel services or his appointed representative.

Four instructional staff members, one elected from each instructional division.

Four students, elected by the student senate.

One LRC instructional staff member, elected at large by LRC.

One student personnel services staff member, elected at large by SPS.

One noninstructional staff member, elected at large by the noninstructional staff.

One secretary: director of counseling (nonvoting).

Meetings: As called by the chairman or upon petition of three or more voting members of the council.

Chairman: Elected by the council at the first regular meeting of the new council.

Minutes: Distributed to members of the council, and a copy filed in the LRC. Abstract to be published in staff *Newsletter* and the college newspaper.

Agenda of
next meeting: Tentative agenda to be published with abstract of minutes.

Continuity: Members to be elected annually in May and to begin serving at the June meeting of the council. Approximately one-third of each constituency's membership is to be elected each year. The method of election is the responsibility of the constituency; the method of staggering is the responsibility of the council.

Alternates: Each constituency should elect an alternate for each regular member.

appendix 10

Emphasis
Innovation on the Campus

With this issue, the *Journal* offers a firsthand look at representative innovative programs and ideas which thirteen junior college districts (comprising the League for Innovation in the Community College) are adopting in order to improve their total learning environments. The following index will serve the reader as a quick summary of what is to come.

Chicago City College

Accounting–A Practical Application of E.D.P.
American Indian History Handbook
Black Studies Directory
Black Thought and Culture Course
Child Development Curriculum
Compensatory Education
English Composition
English–Pattern Drills
English–Remedial
Ethnic Minorities Course
Federal Budget–An Analysis
General Education
Learning Resources Center
Programmed Material
Science–A First Course
Social Dialect Remediation Game
Visual Arts in the Community
Miscellaneous Programs

Cuyahoga Community College District

Academic Credit in Escrow
Afro-American Studies
Audiotutorial Learning
Cleveland State University–Cuyahoga Liaison
College Skills Program
Community Services
Computer-Assisted Instruction
Computer Center Services
Court and Conference Reporting
Educational Media Center
English–Remedial Composition
Grading by Audio Devices
Integrated Humanities Courses
Libraries–Automation
Media Applications
Paraprofessional in Dentistry
Professional Assistants
Released Time for Faculty
Special Media Projects
Speech Compression
Student Tutoring
Taping Service for the Blind
Use of Student-Made Audiovisuals
World Affairs Briefing Center

Dallas County Junior College District

Audio Systems
Biology–Audiotutorial
Campus Organization
Career Advancement Now (CAN)
"Core Program" Approach to Occupational Curriculums
Data Processing and Telephone Service
Fine Arts Facilities
Group Dynamics-Communications
Guided Studies Programs
Honors Program
Humanities 101 Course
Library Cataloging–Micromation
"Long" Courses
Mini-College
Physical Fitness Laboratory
Student-Faculty Communications

Delta College

Computerized Evaluation and Analysis
Developmental Reading Program
Expansion of Independent Study
Geography–Team Teaching
Integrated Basic Science
Interdisciplinary Travel Seminars
Nursing–Audiotutorial
President's Credit Seminar
Reading Development Programs
Sociology–Open-Circuit Television

Foothill Junior College District

Automotive Technology
Biochemistry–Lower Division
Biology–Audiotutorial
Biology–General Education
Consultant–Multicultural
Coordinator–Multicultural
Data Processing Wireless System
"Disadvantaged" Analysis
Draft Counseling
English Composition Seminar
English–Remedial Small Groups
English–Team Teaching
Experimental Student College
Geology Field Study
History of California Project
Individual Study Courses
Interdisciplinary Minorities Course
Law Enforcement Program
Library-Use Films
Management
Marketing–Video Tapes
Mathematics-Physics Study Center
Mathematics Tutoring Tapes
Minority Scholarships
Mock Legislature
Music Dictation Films
Physics–Cooperative Project
Project–Black, Brown, White Students
Psychology Laboratory
Psychology Tutoring
Reading Handicap Correction
Recruiting Minority Students
Sensitivity Sessions
Speeches–Videotaped
Student-Faculty-Administration-Board Conference
Student-Faculty Retreats
Study Skills Center
Television–Closed-Circuit
Tutoring Course
Typing–Multimedia Approach

The Junior College District of St. Louis

Accounting–Dialog Tapes
Accounting–Team Teaching
Biology–Audiotutorial
Biology–Introductory
Biology Laboratory–Audiotutorial
Book Catalogs of Library Materials
Business Classes–Computer Game
Business Education–Audiotaped
Business Education Laboratory
Chemistry–Audiotutorial
Commercial Art
Computer Terminal

Counseling–Decentralized
Dial-Access Systems
Dialog Audio System
Economics–Dialog Tapes
Educational Objectives
English–Audio Recorders
English–Audio Tapes
English Laboratory
General Curriculum Program
Human Anatomy
Human Anatomy and Physiology
Humanities–Audiovisual Booth
Humanities Course–Team Teaching
Humanities Course: "The Impact of Science on Man"
Instructional Television–Dental Auxiliary Department
Instructional Television–Video Tape Request
Instructional Television–Self-Evaluation
Instructional Television–Student Assistants Learn Production
Market Research
Marketing: Consumer Survey
Mathematics
Multistudent Response System
Physics Course–Audiotutorial
Psychology Laboratory–Programmed
Spanish
Speech and Drama
Trigonometry
Video Tape Recorders

Kern Junior College District

Administrative and Instructional Data Processing Applications
Architectural Drafting Program
Community Involvement
Contemporary Concerns Seminar
Dial-Retrieval System
Economics Courses
English–Large-Class Sections
Ethnic Studies Curriculum
Faculty Advising as a Means of Implementing Counseling
Forums
Graphic Arts Laboratory
Instructional Television
Journalism Internship
Library Technician Program
Management Program
Nonpenalty Grading
Nursery School Teacher-Assistant Training
Police Science
Programmed Instruction
Program "O" Reorientation
Recording Booths
Recording Facility
Social Welfare Aides
Spelling Improvement Program
Teacher-Aide Program
Team Teaching
Tutoring

Los Angeles Community College District

American History Course—Audiotutorial
Developmental Studies
English Composition (Freshman)
Humanities—Interdisciplinary Seminar
Humanities—Nontransfer Course "One Semester" Vocational Curriculums
"One-Woman Tutorial Center"
Project New Careers
Roving Position for Curriculum Study
Student Counseling Assistants
Student Tutors
Study Skills Center

Los Rios Junior College District

Audiovisual Workshop
Biology Laboratory—Audiotutorial
Business Division Laboratory—Wireless Stenography
Chemistry Laboratory—Audiotutorial
College Awareness Program
Counseling Department Projects
Credit/Noncredit Grading
English—Educational Television
English—*Effective Listening*
Essay Examination Evaluation
Film-Making Project
History Course
Instructional Resources Committee
Newspaper—*Evening Collegian*
Nursing Education—Multisensory Approaches
Physical Education—Skill Development Project
Political Science Program
Psychology—College Discovery Program
Psychology—Video Tape Library
Psychology—Video Tape Use
Reading—Development Laboratory
Shorthand—Restructured Approach
Social Science Division—Instructional Enrichment Project
Social Science Division—Instructional Evaluation Project
Sociology Project—National
Speech Program—Video Tape
Studies—Independent and Directed
Theatre Arts Project—Video Tape
Trades and Industries Division—Single-Concept Loop System
Tutoring Project—Experimental

Orange Coast Junior College District

Agricultural Laboratory—Audiotutorial
Air Transportation
Allied Health—The Core Concept
Arithmetic—Applied
Arithmetic—Remedial
Business—Video Tape
Computer-Assisted Learning (CAL)
English—Basic Review

English Composition (Freshman)
Faculty Fellowship Program
Film on the Computer in Instruction
Fine Arts—Painting
Forum
History and Political Science Project
Music—History and Appreciation
Political Science Project
Problems of Man's Environment

Peralta Junior College District

Afro-American Studies
Basic Encounter Groups
"Body Shoppe" Class
Experimental College
Experimental Education Program
Inner-City Project
Institute of Environmental Studies
Intergroup Services
Learning Resources Center
Sensitivity Training
Sensorium
Special-Help Laboratories
Student Enterprises
Upgrade Project

Santa Fe Junior College

Educational Objectives
Success Grading System
The Self-Concept Course
Basic Courses
Multiple-Role Instructor
Faculty Orientation
Unit Organization
Curricular Patterns
Air Pollution Technology
Demonstration Factory
Early Childhood Center
Educational Aide
Hospital Housekeeping
Midmanagement Retail Program
Practical Nursing
Registered Nursing
Vocational Rehabilitation

Seattle Community College

Adult Education
Anthropology and Archaelogy Course—"Dig-In"
Associate of Applied Science
Chemistry Laboratory
Civil Service Program
Curriculum Development
English as a Second Language

Family Life Education Department–Preschool Laboratory
Hospitality and Food-Service Programs
Instructional Television Course
Marine Programs
Operation Understanding
Parent Cooperative
Precollege Development
Programmed Learning
Project New Careers
Regional Training Center for the Deaf and Hard of Hearing
Rehabilitation Training
Sociology–"On the Street"
Storefront, Noon-Hour, and After-Hour Classes
Vocational Instruction

appendix 11

Board Policy

Title: Purchasing, General Policy

Date:

Supersedes:

1. The general purchasing policy of this college shall conform, insofar as possible, with the code of ethics of the National Association of Purchasing Agents as interpreted by the National Association of Educational Buyers.
2. Principal responsibility for effective administration of the purchasing function shall rest with the president of the college. Authority to perform these functions may be delegated by the president in order to meet organizational objectives.
3. By approval of the annual budget, the board of trustees authorizes the responsible officials to spend up to the amounts budgeted. All purchases in excess of $5,000 must receive board approval.
4. Within the limitations stated, purchase orders shall be appropriately reviewed to assure availability of budget appropriation and for completion as to specification, quantity, price, discounts, etc.
5. All purchases, when required by regulations and statutes of the state and/or the Department of Higher Education, shall be subject to bid procedures as outlined therein. In general, such bids shall be advertised in local news media and award will be based on lowest bid price consistent with quality, delivery, performance, and specification compliance.

6. Insofar as possible, tie bids and quotations will be awarded on following preferential selection:

   a. County bidders.

   b. State bidders.

7. Exceptions to these procedures will be made where a specific item having unique characteristics of purpose or performance is available from a single source.

8. As permitted by state law, library materials are excluded from the bidding procedures in # 5 above and the limit for single purchases is extended in this instance to $10,000.

Administrative Procedure
Title: Purchasing, Operating Practices

Date:

Supersedes:

1. General Guidelines

a. The general purchasing practices shall conform to the guidelines of the operations policy and the code of ethics made a part thereof.

b. Responsibility for the administration of the purchasing function is delegated to the director of administrative services who shall make further assignments for effective purchasing practices.

c. All purchasing shall be performed through this channel and no purchase order will be issued by any other department except by special arrangement with administrative services.

d. Requisitions in proper form may be made for items which have been included in the fiscal budget. If items not originally budgeted are requisitioned, they will be subject to replacement negotiations.

e. Negotiations for placement of approved requisitions may be initiated and placed subject to budgetary appropriation and in accordance with the following limitations:

   (1) Placement of purchase orders of less than $500 shall be at the discretion of the purchasing staff.

   (2) Purchases of more than $500, but less than $1,000, shall be made only on the basis of no less than two (2) written or verbal quotations. When the latter is received, an internal written record shall be made and filed by the person receiving the quotation.

   (3) Purchases exceeding $1,000, but less than $2,500, shall be made only on the basis of no less than two (2) written quotations.

f. Purchases exceeding $2,500 must be by written bid received in response to bid invitations or public advertising in local news media. Award will be made based on lowest bid consistent with quality, delivery, performance, and specification compliance. Bids not responsive to requirements or not delivered within specified time limits will be declared void. Insofar as possible, tie bids will be awarded, first, to county vendors and, second, to state vendors when all other requirements are likewise met. All such bids must be approved by the board of trustees before purchase is confirmed by purchase order or contract.

2. Procedures

a. Requisitions for materials, equipment, or services must be prepared in triplicate on prenumbered form provided, with the copy retained by the originator and the original and duplicate forwarded to the originator's supervisor for approval and subsequent transmittal to the purchasing function.

b. The purchasing department shall determine whether the requisition is to be filled from existing inventories or by purchase from an outside vendor.

c. All requisitions must be priced, classified for accounting purposes, then routed to budgetary control before placement. The anticipated purchase order number must accompany the requisition to be used as a budget encumbrance control.

d. The purchase order will be prepared in seven copies and distributed as follows:

(1) Original to vendor.

(2) Acknowledgement to vendor for dating and return.

(3) Accounting (with duplicate requisition) to accounting department with invoices after receipt of goods or services.

(4) Receiving copy to central receiving.

(5) Purchasing (with original requisition) to open purchase-order file.

(6) Data processing to computer center.

(7) Requisitioner's copy returned to requisition originator.

e. When materials or equipment are received, receiving copy will be completed and signed by receiver and entered on receiving log. Together with any packing slips, freight receipts, bills of lading, etc., these papers will be sent to the purchasing department as substantiation for the vendor's invoice.

f. No invoice will be processed for payment without supporting documentation or other proof of delivery unless approved by the director of administrative services or purchasing agent.

3. Restrictions

a. Formal bids, as required in section 1-f, must be opened in the presence of at least two of the following officials:

(1) Chairman, board of trustees

(2) Treasurer, board of trustees

(3) President of the college

(4) Dean of the college

(5) Director of administrative services

(6) Purchasing agent

All or any bidders may also be present at the bid opening and upon request will be provided with a bid summary.

b. Once bids have been opened and lowest bidder determined, the bid shall be reviewed with the request originator to assure that item(s) bid are responsive to specifications and that all technical requirements of the proposal have been met or indicated to be met.

c. Bid provisions shall not apply to the following classes of purchases:

(1) Purchase of patented or manufactured products offered for sale in a non-competitive market or solely by a manufacturer's authorized dealer.

(2) Purchases for resale.

(3) Purchases of insurance policies, surety bonds, public utility services, or services of the state, the federal government, or any agency of the state, county, or municipal governments.

(4) Replacement parts for existing equipment or capital assets.

(5) Highly technical equipment having unique characteristics and limited or exclusive sources.

(6) Personal services based on singular skills or professional expertise.

d. No member of the board of trustees or any officer or employee thereof shall either directly or indirectly be a party to or be in any manner interested in any contract or agreement with the college for any matter, cause or thing whatsoever, by reason whereof any liability or indebtedness shall in any way be created against the college. Any violation of these regulations shall cause such agreement to be null and void and no action shall be taken thereon against the college.

Index

LB
2328
.E9
1973